THE ELEMENT OF LAVISHNESS

The Portrait of a Tortoise: Extracted from the Letters and Journals
of Gilbert White of Selborne 1946

I'll Stand by You: Selected Letters of Sylvia Townsend Warner
and Valentine Ackland *edited by Susanna Pinney* 1999
Sylvia and David: The Townsend Warner / Garnett Letters
edited by Richard Garnett 1994
Diaries *edited by Claire Harman* 1994
Letters *edited by William Maxwell* 1982

ALSO BY WILLIAM MAXWELL

All the Days and Nights: Collected Stories 1994
Billie Dyer and Other Stories 1992
The Outermost Dream: Essays and Reviews 1989
So Long, See You Tomorrow 1980
Over by the River and Other Stories 1977
Ancestors: A Family History 1971
The Old Man at the Railroad Crossing and Other Tales 1966
The Château 1961
Stories (*with Jean Stafford, John Cheever, and Daniel Fuchs*) 1956
Time Will Darken It 1948
The Folded Leaf 1945
They Came Like Swallows 1937
Bright Center of Heaven 1934

For Children
Mrs. Donald's Dog Bun and His Home Away from Home 1995
The Heavenly Tenants 1946

ALSO BY MICHAEL STEINMAN

The Happiness of Getting It Down Right:
Letters of Frank O'Connor and William Maxwell 1996
A Frank O'Connor Reader 1994
Frank O'Connor at Work 1990
Yeats's Heroic Figures: Wilde, Parnell, Swift, Casement 1983

THE ELEMENT OF LAVISHNESS

Letters of
Sylvia Townsend Warner
and William Maxwell

1938–1978

Edited by

Michael Steinman

COUNTERPOINT

WASHINGTON, D.C.

"What You Can't Hang Onto" first appeared in *Story* magazine.
Eighty-five of Sylvia Townsend Warner's letters to William Maxwell first
appeared, many of them in different form, in Mr. Maxwell's edition of *Letters:
Sylvia Townsend Warner* (London: Chatto & Windus, 1982; New York:
The Viking Press, 1983).

Library of Congress Cataloging-in-Publication Data
Warner, Sylvia Townsend, 1893–1978
The element of lavishness : letters of Sylvia Townsend Warner and
William Maxwell, 1938–1978 / edited by Michael Steinman.— 1st ed.
p. cm.
Includes index.
ISBN 1-58243-118-3 (alk. paper)
1. Warner, Sylvia Townsend, 1893 — Correspondence.
2. Authors, English — 20th century — Correspondence. 3. Maxwell,
William, 1908 — Correspondence. 4. Periodical editors — United
States — Correspondence. I. Maxwell, William, 1908-. II. Steinman,
Michael (Michael A.) III. Title.
PR6045.A812 Z494 2001   828'.91209—dc21
00-064459
FIRST EDITION

Book design by Mark McGarry
Set in Dante

Printed in the United States of America on acid-free paper that meets the
American National Standard Institute z39–48 Standard.

Counterpoint
P.O. Box 65793
Washington, D.C. 20035–5793

Counterpoint is a member of the Perseus Books Group.

In memory

Sylvia Townsend Warner
1893–1978

Valentine Ackland
1906–1969

William Maxwell
1908–2000

Emily Maxwell
1921–2000

The personal correspondence of writers feeds on left-over energy. There is also the element of lavishness, of enjoying the fact that they are throwing away one of their better efforts, for the chances of any given letter's surviving is fifty-fifty, at most. And there is the element of confidence—of the relaxed backhand stroke that can place the ball anywhere that it pleases the writer to have it go.

MAXWELL ON WARNER, 1982

Never mislay a pleasure. I might die in the night, so I will write to William now.

WARNER TO MAXWELL, 1973

If you had not loved to please, you would never, I think, have evolved that prose style that has given me an unbroken line of pleasure extending back for thirty years. When I was looking for the first time through *The Osaka Woodcuts*, Kate's godfather said, "How did you get your love of Oriental art?" and I said rapturously, "I got it second hand," without thinking, but surely that is how all pleasure is got—from the rubbing off of somebody else's pleasure in something. From eye to eye and skin to skin. A cousin of love-making.

MAXWELL TO WARNER, 1961

CONTENTS

ILLUSTRATIONS

Sylvia Townsend Warner in 1954
(*Photograph by F. Carlos Pickering*)

Valentine Ackland and Sylvia in the mirror at Frankfort Manor, "that lovely house so much too large for us but never too large for our love"
(*Sylvia Townsend Warner–Valentine Ackland Archives, Dorset County Museum*)

Frome Vauchurch, in Maiden Newton, Dorset, as seen from the river
(*Sylvia Townsend Warner–Valentine Ackland Archives, Dorset County Museum*)

"As you see, I cannot work unless I have perfect order around me":
Maxwell to Warner, February 24, 1970
(*Courtesy William Maxwell*)

Brookie and Kate
(*Courtesy William Maxwell*)

Emily and William Maxwell at Yorktown Heights in the mid-1950s
(*Photograph by Consuelo Kanaga*)

INTRODUCTION

by Michael Steinman

Between 1938 and 1978, the inimitable writers Sylvia Townsend Warner and William Maxwell exchanged more than thirteen hundred affectionate and witty letters. Their at first formal relationship—he was Mr. Maxwell, the *New Yorker* fiction editor; she was Miss Warner, the distinguished contributor from Dorset—soon deepened into "a real, unshakable love." Twenty years after Warner's death Maxwell told me, "I still remember the pleasure of walking into the apartment and finding a letter from her on the hall table." *The Element of Lavishness* celebrates that pleasure, part of the larger pleasure both writers shared equally—the pleasure of writing well for a friend, one whose every reply was a gift in turn.

A forty-year friendship seems a monument to constancy, but it is easy to imagine an alternate universe in which Warner and Maxwell admire each other's work but never meet. In 1970, she said as much to him: "Suppose I had been in the hands of some eminently worthy and painstaking person called Halibut? What we both would have missed." When Maxwell was a graduate student at the University of Illinois, his close friend and mentor Garetta Busey gave him a copy of Warner's narrative poem *Opus 7*; he went on to *Mr. Fortune's Maggot* and *The True Heart*. In 1935, when he had written his first novel but as yet had no connection to *The New Yorker*,

Warner submitted a story to the magazine in a bet against herself: "We had
an American friend staying with us [the poet Jean Starr Untermeyer] and I
was telling her of some absurd thing which had happened in the village
and she said, 'You really ought to write that for *The New Yorker.*' I said, 'Ba
Pooh! I can't write for *The New Yorker.* People who write for *The New Yorker*
are a special race—they are like nothing else. *I couldn't write for The New
Yorker!*' And she said, 'Oh write it; I think they'd take it.' I said, 'Bet you
they wouldn't!' She said, 'Well, try it!' I said, 'I bet you £5 they won't take
it.' And they did, so I had to forfeit the £5. But on the whole, it was a good
bargain." Her first letter to the editor, Harold W. Ross, was a masterpiece
of sweet audacity: "I have been reading *The New Yorker* for years, with such
veneration that it has never occurred to me that I could write for it. Now
that blasphemous thought has lodged in my head." Warner's "good bargain" was just that; her first editor, Katharine S. White, ended an early letter with the words "You can't send us too many stories," and *The New
Yorker* published one hundred fifty-three between 1936 and 1977.

In 1936, Maxwell got a job as Mrs. White's assistant; part of his work was
to write letters to authors to convey his superiors' decisions. He could
approach Warner only as an apprentice copyeditor, along such lines as
these, scribbled in the margins of her October 1937 letter about "Stanley
Sherwood": "Maxwell— Seems OK except that I can't interpret all of her
marks. Just do what we want on punct., I guess taking her suggestion
wherever possible." Mrs. White left the magazine the next year to live in
Maine; she told Warner that she could correspond with Maxwell or his fellow editor Gustave S. Lobrano, but did not tell her Maxwell's first name.
When Warner wrote to him, she apologized for her "discourteous envelope," and they began exchanging friendly letters. Encouraging her to submit poems, he told her that he admired *Opus 7.* Sending American reviews
of *After the Death of Don Juan* that she might not have seen, he added,
"In general, I'm afraid, they are far from conveying how good it really is."
Informing her of a rejection, he mitigated it by praising a detail that had
charmed him: "For my part I like anything which has 'hark' in it because
I know a woman who always used to say to me 'Hark, child' whenever
she wanted me to stop what I was doing and go upstairs and get her
sewing basket." Sixty years later, he told me that "reading the Sylvia / *New
Yorker* correspondence of the 1930's is like seeing again the part of the

movie where you came in. I am surprised at how long we remained on formal terms."

In 1939, he learned that Warner would be coming to New York to deliver
a paper on "The Historical Novel" at the Third Congress of the League of
American Writers (along with Dashiell Hammett, Thomas Mann, Lang-
ston Hughes, and Dorothy Parker). He invited her to lunch, officially to
"talk about possible pieces for *The New Yorker*," less officially, I am sure, to
meet her. When they met late in June, he was enthralled: "She was dressed
in black. Her voice had a slightly husky, intimate quality. Her conversation
was so enchanting it made my head swim. I did not want to let her out of
my sight. Ever. I urged her to stay in the United States, where bombs were
less likely to fall on her, and she said she thought she would go home and
raise vegetables." Her note of thanks to Maxwell was brief, but their letters
became more playful and informal.

Maxwell left *The New Yorker* in 1940 to work on his novel *The Folded Leaf*,
and, although he returned to the magazine after, Lobrano became
Warner's editor. She continued to submit stories and poems, but was burdened by her war work with the Women's Volunteer Service. The house
she shared with the poet Valentine Ackland, her partner from 1930 until
Ackland's death some forty years later, "was full of strange beasts at the
time, evacuees and billetees and what not." Maxwell wanted to sustain
their friendship even if he was not her editor, and sent copies of his novels
They Came Like Swallows, *The Folded Leaf*, and *Time Will Darken It*. Warner
wrote admiring letters for each one, reciprocated with *The Museum of
Cheats*, and invited the Maxwells to visit her in Dorset. (He had married
Emily Noyes in 1945; Warner and he exchanged letters about their domestic lives for nearly a quarter-century.)

Writing paper and envelopes were scarce in Britain during and after the
war, so Maxwell had *The New Yorker* send them and asked Warner what
else she needed. She told him that reports of food shortages were untrue,
but he chose to believe otherwise. He refused to take credit for the magazine's generosity, but many of Warner's letters into the nineteen fifties
begin with thanks from her and Valentine for canned meats, butter, or
other provisions. He later said that "their gratitude for the food made their
relationship to *The New Yorker* much more personal than it would have
been otherwise." He closed a letter of August 1945 with "Now that the war

is over, we expect a visit from you," which did not happen. By 1947, Maxwell was now her editor for good: "Lobrano admired Sylvia Townsend Warner's stories very much indeed, but on the theory that a thing belongs to the person who cares the most about it, he gave her back to me."

He could now write Warner that the point of a letter was "to tell you that I love you dearly." However, they still addressed each other as Miss Warner and Mr. Maxwell. He first began a letter with the words "Dear Sylvia" when writing to her of Harold Ross's death; later he apologized for his impulsive act. This endearing breach of decorum became a landmark in their shared history: twenty years later, Warner asked him to retell it, and I have included both versions. She started addressing the Maxwells as "dear William, dear Emmy" after the two couples met on a 1953 visit to Dorset. Unfortunately, the visit was marred by a maid's theft of his wife's antique pin. Maxwell later remembered that, although Warner and Valentine "were tireless in driving us around to see the important ruins, a Tudor house, etc., I was uncomfortable with her for the first time, and when I got back to New York found it a little harder to write to her as easily as I had before. This she noted, I think in her journals. Nothing escaped her. With time we fell back into our easy habit of corresponding, there being always something to correspond about, and I was never uncomfortable with her again. Liking and disliking are perhaps, as Maeve Brennan would say, all a dream." Warner did not share his doubts and wrote in her diary, "They are perfect people to take about, they see everything, & *smell* everything. The only flaw in the day, that they must go tomorrow evening."

Maxwell described the joyous freedom of their correspondence in his introduction to a selection from Warner's letters: "The personal correspondence of writers feeds on left-over energy. There is also the element of lavishness, of enjoying the fact that they are throwing away one of their better efforts, for the chances of any given letter's surviving are fifty-fifty, at most. And there is the element of confidence—of the relaxed backhand stroke that can place the ball anywhere in the court that it pleases the writer to have it go. No critic is looking over his shoulder; the writer's reputation is not at stake..." Yet a willful modesty underlies this, for he says nothing of *their* forty-year correspondence. Warner, he said to me, "needed to write for an audience, a specific person, in order to bring out her pleasure in enchanting," and the correspondence shows how he and she were ideally matched.

In 1997 he said, "I suspect that of all the writers I edited I was most influenced by Sylvia Townsend Warner, though I have never looked into the matter." Asked to elaborate, he said, "I think what you are infinitely charmed by you can't help unconsciously imitating." When *The New Yorker* published Warner's first story, she was fully formed, yet Maxwell was an invaluable collaborator on over a hundred more: I think those he edited are her finest work, and her letters show how much his discerning comments shaped her writing. He was also her ally even when writing ruefully that a new story had been turned down by Harold Ross or William Shawn. The closing sentence of his first rejection letter, from June 1938, is wonderfully gentle: "We are very sorry to have to send back anything from you but we hope you will be forgiving and will send us something else right away to take the place of this."

During the four decades of this correspondence, Maxwell and Warner wrote more than twenty books. Creative labor was an abiding subject, and each was the other's most trusted sounding board. Maxwell told her that he feared *The Château* was a travel diary, not a novel, talked of historical improvisations in *Ancestors*, described his troubles with the farmers of *So Long, See You Tomorrow*. She reported her battle with the Scott Moncrieff family over a new translation of Proust, commented on T. H. White's sexual obsessions, tantalized Maxwell with glimpses of the latest story-in-progress.

In his fiction, Maxwell gave familiar scenes intense emotional energy without calling attention to doing it: the losses of *They Came Like Swallows* and *The Folded Leaf*, a family visit that unlocked passions in *Time Will Darken It*. He used deceptively unadorned language to write to Warner about his domestic life and marriage, but conveyed deep feeling by quietly refusing to treat the apparently ordinary as if it were so. (And she never missed the point; he said, "Sylvia was *terribly* perceptive. She could see through a vault.") In *Mr. Fortune's Maggot* and *Kingdoms of Elfin*, Warner presented the remarkable, the otherworldly, as if it were everyday. She and Valentine, a devoted lesbian couple in a conservative landscape, may have lived at a greater distance from their surroundings, yet she depicted their life without self-dramatization. Trusting that the Maxwells would read her words and understand her experience with great sensitivity, she wrote of her marriage as equivalent to theirs, so that she and Valentine seem to double-date by mail with William and Emmy.

Letters written to send someone the news run the risk of becoming for-mulaic, but Maxwell and Warner seized upon what they saw, what amused, perplexed, or moved them. No subject was unworthy; what Maxwell called "delight at the way everything is" made scenes and people immediate and tangible. Warner entertained herself and Maxwell by fold-ing juxtapositions into her single blue air-mail page, defying the postal regulation "AN AIR LETTER SHOULD NOT CONTAIN ANY ENCLOSURE." Unusual behavior pleased her always, even when the subjects were her friends. Here is one couple, the husband an organist, the wife with abso-lute pitch: "He has only to say, Ruth. B flat, and she obliges. So he doesn't need his tuning-fork. If one were to include one-tenth of the remarkable people one knows, in one's fiction, no one would accept it. Real life remains one's private menagerie." She described the intellectual nurse who boasted of having bathed T. S. Eliot, considered the astrological impact of television antennas, re-created an all-tartan Scottish bedroom. Maxwell was less a satirist, more an impressionistic painter who considered the shadings of natural light and darkness, the Turner landscape in early-morning Manhattan. Warner said that she and Maxwell were "made out of much the same clay—quiet characters, with a simple savage delight in cata-clysms," and his descriptions of a hurricane and the 1965 Great New York City Blackout are matchless short stories.

Warner was "that odd thing, a musicologist," an authority on Tudor church music; she and Maxwell loved opera, paintings, drawings, so they wrote happily about music and art, moving freely among genres. A moment in *The Magic Flute* was the best way to describe the roses; Chardin summed up the essence of a short story. They sent each other new books and wrote lyrically of the ones they knew by heart. Prized books were not by definition antiquarian: see her 1968 letter about Hubert Selby Jr.'s *Last Exit to Brooklyn*! Reading for joy, they illuminated Samuel Butler, Hardy, Byron, Shelley, Goethe, the Woolfs, James, Balzac, Proust, Rilke, Yeats, Eli-nor Wylie, Francis Kilvert's diaries, the Goncourt journals. However, read-ers trolling for gossip about their artistic contemporaries, the lively malice found in Dawn Powell's diaries, must look elsewhere: here, the inside sto-ries are about Lady Ottoline Morrell and Madame de Sévigné, not about J. D. Salinger. They satirize few people, although an American professor who had presumed to write a book about Warner and the neighbor whose negligence made Maxwell get poison ivy are given what they deserve. Typically, the political events of the day provoked Warner and Maxwell; they were terrified by the Cuban missile crisis, appalled by Eisenhower, Nixon, the Vietnam War.

Both of them were prone to respiratory illnesses, so many letters were written to console and commiserate; Warner began one with *"J'ai mal de ma poitrine."* Perhaps because she was so often the victim of "influenza," she gave unsolicited medical advice generously, including home remedies (goose-grease, raspberry-leaf tea, a restorative diet of ham and fresh pasta). In a 1972 letter, after offering remedies both homeopathic and conventional for hives, nervousness, and kidney stones, she concluded, "You know I am the Maxwell Family Prescriber." Reciprocally, Maxwell worried that Warner's house was dangerously cold and begged her to let him pay for a modern heating system. He tried to make her wealthy in the only way he could, urging her to write more and earn the bonuses *The New Yorker* gave prolific writers, even suggesting ruses to forestall taxes. Happily, this shared advice was unusually effective: Maxwell celebrated his ninety-first birthday in 1999; Warner had few financial worries.

A fiercely enthusiastic writer, Warner sometimes sent Maxwell three letters while waiting for his reply to her first, explaining "I might die in the night, so I will write to William now." Often she wrote to him twice a day, and to Emily and to Kate, his elder daughter, as well. Astonishingly, she corresponded with two dozen other friends, kept a daily diary, wrote novels, stories, a biography, poetry, translated Huguenin and Proust. When a new story was the occasion, Maxwell would write her several times in succession, but during the four decades of their correspondence he also worked and corresponded with John Cheever, Harold Brodkey, Eudora Welty, John Updike, J. D. Salinger, Maeve Brennan, Frank O'Connor, Shirley Hazzard, John O'Hara, Mary Lavin, Kay Boyle, Mavis Gallant, Irwin Shaw, Ludwig Bemelmans, Mary McCarthy, Tennessee Williams, Peter Taylor, Nancy Hale, James Thurber, and Vladimir Nabokov. He could not reply to each letter from Warner as it arrived, but would write to her as a pleasure deferred. At first, reading the complete correspondence, I thought that Warner dominated it by the number of letters she had written, but Maxwell edited it by his responses much as he edited her stories.

In Warner's last decade, the pace of her correspondence seldom slackened, even when her subject was the somber details of Valentine Ackland's final illness. When Valentine, a dozen years younger than Warner, died of breast cancer in November 1969, Warner was devastated. Eight days after her death, Warner began to reread their love letters and found herself compelled to arrange them, annotate them, and write narrative passages linking them. It was a private literary endeavor; she did not consider publication until her friends urged her to do so. She had the letters typed, then sent them to Maxwell, installment after installment. Years later, he called them "the most beautiful and moving love letters I have ever read." (Excerpts have been published as *I'll Stand by You*.) Valentine had had a decade-long affair with an American woman, Elizabeth Wade White, which Warner had hinted about to Maxwell at the time, but which she now wrote about—as she wrote about all their life together—with tenderness, candor, and insight. When she had sent Maxwell the final envelope, she left the post office "feeling that I had posted my guts and that you would look after them," which he did.

Nearly eighty, curiously invigorated, she began a series of improvisations about elfin kingdoms: "I suddenly looked round on my career and thought, 'Good God, I've been understanding the human heart for all these decades.' Bother the human heart, I'm tired of the human heart. I want to write about something entirely different." Maxwell, enchanted, was ever her finest advocate. In 1998 he said, "It is likely that *The New Yorker* would not have published the elfin stories except for me. Many readers and members of the staff protested. I was wild about them. I have always loved fairy stories and these struck me as electrifying. I felt they were written out of firsthand knowledge." She completed twenty, stopping only when William Shawn inexplicably wearied of the series.

As obliged to by company policy, Maxwell stepped down from *The New Yorker* on January 1, 1976, when he was sixty-seven. Warner wrote, "I wish you a happy departure, a blissful retirement—another book? But woe to Sylvia!" He tried to reassure her, because he had trained her new editor, the writer Daniel Menaker, and wrote, "I am certainly not departing from you, only from 25 W. 43rd Street." After retiring, Maxwell read her stories with even greater pleasure and his letters of 1976–78 are expansively leisurely, surely because he never again had to write that a story had been rejected. Their final collaboration was a volume of her letters, a book she wanted him to edit, published four years after her death. When Maxwell, now her devoted researcher, asked her whom she had written to "most often and most intimately," he learned that he was that person and the knowledge pleased him greatly. Warner did not suggest publishing their joint correspondence, but she thought Maxwell's letters outshone Henry James's; he said that hers made Virginia Woolf's letters seem "very poor reading." Editing the book over his shoulder, she insisted: "Do not let my letters to you be elbowed out by letters to other people: modesty can impel one to fatal acts. Damn the other people." Maxwell envisioned at least two volumes, but the published book contained only a fraction of what she had written.

As she grew older, Warner's failing health concerned Maxwell greatly, and his letters grew more tenderly anxious. The Maxwells planned to visit England in 1978 "for no other reason but to see her," and her last letter to them, written on March 5, ends "But meet we will." They arrived in London on April 30 but never met; she died on the morning of May 1. Maxwell recalls her funeral in a postscript, and *The Element of Lavishness* ends with his fable "What You Can't Hang Onto," previously unpublished in book form. Evoking Warner and her house by the River Frome, he "exaggerated her possessions and invented the correspondence with Thomas Hardy" in an affectionate, deeply felt memorial.

In October 1995, when I had finished editing the letters of Maxwell and Frank O'Connor, a few details had to be settled before publication. O'Connor's widow, Harriet Sheehy, a close friend of the Maxwells, arranged for me to visit them in Manhattan, where I spent a day I do not expect to equal, attending to particulars, trading anecdotes, and laughing. I would gladly have asked the Maxwells to adopt me had I not thought that the suggestion would embarrass them. When it was time to leave, I stood in the doorway and said, "You *will* let me know if you have any other projects for me, won't you?" He smiled and said that he would. When *The Happiness of Getting It Down Right* was published, I asked his permission to begin a book about his fiction. He liked the idea and wrote: "I have a certain quantity of my own letters that have come back to me—the correspondence with Warner, for example—and if you ever want to see them just let me know. I doubt it there is much in them about my own work but I haven't reread them." She had returned his letters to him a year before her death.

I agreed instantly: any letters from Maxwell would be a pleasure, as I knew from those he had written me. Like his fiction, they are brief, plainspoken, yet warm and evocative. Envelopes full of them came a few days later. The yellow, beige, white, and blue pages were typed and handwritten, well-folded and well-read, annotated in an unfamiliar handwriting. Most were undated or labeled only "Tuesday," "March 11," and so on. All were delightful; even brief notes about editorial business (choosing "vender" or "vendor") were loving and witty. The "mountains" of letters Warner preserved speak of her love for him; she had told Robert Henderson, another *New Yorker* editor, that her house was "so small that nothing gets kept in it, reliably, except cobwebs." Maxwell, luckily for us, was an even more conscientious archivist.

Reading these pages for the insights they offered on his fiction was rewarding, but the letters themselves cast a deeper spell. Soon I was trying to fit Maxwell's letters to the excerpts from Warner's that he had published, looking for evidence in details of publications, events, occasions. Wherever I turned, I was listening to two dear friends, casually memorable about any subject, be it Proust or the locksmith who came when Maxwell forgot the house keys. The result was an immediately gratifying contrapuntal conversation, echoing the Maxwell–O'Connor letters only in the deep feeling on both sides.

But much of the conversation was missing. After her death, Maxwell had given all of his Warner and Ackland papers to the Dorset County Museum, which maintains collections of their work. With his help, I requested copies of Warner's letters from Richard de Peyer, the museum's curator, who graciously sent them to me through 1997. When each bulky envelope arrived, I would begin to read a new sheaf of letters and disappear into another world until summoned back to this one. I had thought Warner and Maxwell had written to each other often, but "often" turned out to be an understatement. After months of research, I arranged the letters in sequence, admiring their writers more whenever I could fit a part of their conversation into its proper place. I bless Warner for beginning every letter with the date and place she was writing from, even when this routine so bored her that she invented new addresses, such as "Cequatia" when it was raining. When she thanked Maxwell for a "beautiful fourteen word letter," it was a triumph to know which undated page it was, when he had written it, what story they were discussing.

Not every letter survived; Maxwell said, "Some may have disappeared during the Second World War when the building superintendent took it upon himself to donate *The New Yorker*'s correspondence files, then stored in the basement of 25 W. 43rd, to a scrap paper drive in Larchmont." Between 1941 and 1944, Warner wrote to Gus Lobrano at *The New Yorker*, not Maxwell, and no letters from 1949 exist. What survived, however, amounted to more than half a million words, which made a collected edition impossible. When Warner and Maxwell were discussing a book of her letters, her response to her own prolific nature was quick and direct: "You must either cut or select. It is not as if I were Fitzgerald." Neither choice was easy, and reprinting a smaller number of letters in their entirety would have narrowed the conversation considerably. Their informal writing was so consistently remarkable I was reluctant to abandon any of it, even a two-sentence observation. Both Maxwell and Warner had wide-ranging interests, and few letters were restricted to one topic. Thus, in addition to complete letters, this book includes excerpts and substantial passages from more than five hundred others. I have not included every passage from Warner's letters that Maxwell chose for his 1982 book, but have restored much that he deleted due to modesty. Editing was necessary because Warner did not keep copies and could retell anecdotes. She also repeated herself for emphasis but knew full well when she was doing that; I cherish her admonitions about flu shots in four summer 1976 letters. Gratitude and love are on every page; purely for reasons of space I have cut many such heartfelt lines, believing that readers can easily imagine deep, shared feelings.

　　Their correspondence was simultaneously personal and professional, but their working letters were always animated. Maxwell was quick to praise a new story, often in a cablegram of ten ecstatic words or less. But some letters were necessarily devoted to details of style, grammar, and usage. Maxwell said, "Often questions raised by the editor of the magazine, or by the proofreaders, intruded upon the flow of our remarks and had to be dealt with." Though *The New Yorker*'s quest for textual perfection can approach the sublime, the step-by-step record of the editorial journey makes tedious reading; consequently, I have omitted most such passages. Within a letter, a break between passages of text indicates that a sentence or more has been omitted. If the first line of a passage is also the opening of a paragraph, it is indented; if it is an excerpt, it is not. I have avoided the ubiquitous ellipses because their presence makes readers think that something offensive has been removed, which is not the case in this correspondence, remarkably free of malice. I have, however, included a few pointed exceptions to the general goodness of spirit. In a few cases, since an unflattering reference might cause someone pain, I have substituted arbitrary initials (A. B., C. D.) for the name of a private person. Famous personages abused in these pages have received far worse in the press.

Perhaps because he spent much of his working life untangling knots other writers made, Maxwell wrote first-draft letters that were easy to follow and to read. Except when on vacation or recovering from an illness, he always typed his letters. (He once told Warner, "The thought of dictating a letter to you, or even sending you one from somebody else's typewriter, fills me with horror.") Warner's letters resemble the Christmas packages she sent the Maxwells, boxes filled with beautiful, apparently unrelated things. He told me that the "great charm" of her conversation was that "you never could anticipate what she was going to say, or even the direction the conversation would take." Perhaps because paper had once been scarce or because her small house became cluttered quickly, she filled the blank half-pages of Maxwell's letters with notes, shopping lists, menus, drafts and revisions. Because she kept his letters at hand, their pages were ornamented by rings from her coffee cup, the bites and paw-marks of the nearest cat. Although she typed many stories and letters until late in life, writing to Maxwell was a pleasure, never business, so she sent many handwritten pages. Even when she wrote carefully, her script, "elegant as a vine," she said, was occasionally puzzling. Maxwell gallantly said it was his "pride and pleasure to decipher it," but now and then had to ask her what she had meant. She invented new uses for common words, improvised on familiar expressions, preferred "'tother" to "t'other," used "&" and "and" in the same sentence. I have preserved these habits as well as Maxwell's American and Warner's British spellings, but I have corrected errors and regularized the titles of works. In a handful of instances, a brief, crucial word ("is" or "you") was left out; I have put it back when its absence would have been perceptible. Some explanatory notes seemed necessary, for every reader might not immediately recognize Stockmar, *A World of Love*, or "Mr. Smith, I believe?" However, I have not peppered the text with annotations, for many references that initially seem puzzling unfold themselves a few lines later.

Offering thanks to those people without whose help a book would not exist is the national anthem of acknowledgements, but I have good reason to stand up with my hand over my heart. I believe that readers will be glad to have so much of Warner, unfolding herself with abandon on so many subjects. Readers will be grateful that William Maxwell invited her to lunch, nurtured her work, wrote to her, saved her letters. I owe him even more, for the easy kindness evident in these letters was extended to me. As I began my research, he urged me to ask him about whatever I found obscure, and I did that, off and on, for three years. Sometimes, I confess, I asked about something I half-understood for the pleasure of his explanation. He easily recalled the past, identified people referred to only by their initials, explained the Defenestration of Prague, and never said, "Have you ever thought of consulting an encyclopedia?" I am also grateful to Emily Maxwell for her graciousness and to Katharine Maxwell for allowing me to read letters Warner wrote to her.

I am indebted to Susanna Pinney—first Warner's typist and friend, now the executor of her estate—for her support of this book. Richard de Peyer, curator of the Dorset County Museum, kindly made Warner's letters available to me; in the process, I enjoyed Mary Bennett's efficiency and Philip Toogood's accuracy. Ray Russell, founder of the Sylvia Townsend Warner Society, offered wise advice, as did Claire Harman, Warner's biographer. Melissa de Meo of the *New Yorker* library annotated Warner's stories and poems; Jenny Naipaul of *The Spectator* did the same for Warner's book reviews. Kathleen Kienholz, archivist of the American Academy of Arts and Letters, documented Warner's honorary membership. I am grateful to my colleagues at Nassau Community College for friendly expertise, among them Marilyn Rosenthal, who hunted down out-of-the-way texts, and Robert Blake and Charline Sacks, who repaired my Latin and French. Warner had a wise, modest editor; I have had the good fortune to work with Christopher Carduff, this book's Maxwell. Closer to home, I am saddened that my mother did not live to see this book. Norma and Dan Levenstein have been extremely supportive once again. My wife, Carol, has been my Number One Cheerleader, as always.

THE ELEMENT OF LAVISHNESS

LETTERS, 1938-1978

Maxwell to Warner, July 18, 1938:

A long time ago I read a narrative poem of yours about a woman who had a green thumb [Rebecca Random of *Opus 7*]. I was suddenly reminded of it today when Miss Louise Bogan, who, as perhaps you know, is a poet who does critical articles about poetry for *The New Yorker*, sent me your poem about the man walking through the apple tree ["The Man in the Tree"]. Miss Bogan thinks it's a fine poem, and so do I. And what I want to know is, would there be any chance of *The New Yorker*'s getting some verse from you?

Warner to Maxwell, February 4, 1939:

I hope very much that I shall be coming to New York for the Writers' Congress in May. I look forward to meeting *The New Yorker* if I do.

Maxwell to Warner, June 13, 1939:

I should like very much to have lunch with you and talk about possible pieces for *The New Yorker*.

Warner to Maxwell, June 27, 1939:

Here is the piece about my mother, and the poem about the wolves. Thank you very much for sending on your letter and the ms which I forgot to take.

I promise to leave my hat next time.

Maxwell to Warner, July 14, 1939:

I'm sorry you're leaving New York for various reasons. Your mere proximity was a pleasure. In any case, we hope to have poetry, casuals, sculpture and Gregorian chants turning up in our mail.

Warner to Maxwell, August 30, 1939:

I have been in a hundred minds about whether or no to go back to Europe. Now it looks as though Mr Chamberlain were having some more fun with nettles, so I feel less inclined to hurry back. This means that if you like to leave the matter of the auctioneer poem for a couple of weeks I could then come and work it out in the office. I would rather do this myself.

Warner to Maxwell, September 2, 1939:

My address, so I am told by my host, will be Celo, North Carolina. But I can't believe this is enough, so please ring up the Viking Press for it. I am sending them the exact address tomorrow, when I can get it from my host. I shall be there for a fortnight. After that I make no plans—though I would rather stay in U.S. if my soul will let me.

Maxwell to Warner, September 5, 1939:

If your soul shows signs of becoming self-sacrificial or even patriotic, catch the first train to New York and I'll drop everything to argue you out of it.

Maxwell to Warner, September 29, 1939:

It was as I suspected: Mr. Ross thinks the revisions are fine, and a check is enclosed. Two checks do not make a flood, I suppose, but they certainly indicate rising waters, so please give up worrying about plumbing and other matters in that house in England.

Warner to Maxwell, September 30, 1939:

I really must tell you what a delightful day I had yesterday. In the morning I got a cheque for 285 dollars from *The New Yorker*. In the evening I dined at Giovanni's, saw Katharine Cornell act and met her afterwards; and when I came home I found a cheque for 54 dollars from *The New Yorker*. I feel that this is one of my best lyrics.

After this no type is sufficiently small and cringing, no ribbon faded enough, to add that I am sailing for England on the *Manhattan*, Oct. 4th. It seems that in the depths of my being I am an unappeasable idiot. I have the profoundest doubts about this war. I don't feel that it is being fought against Nazidom, and while Chamberlain is around I doubt it will be. And I can't suppose that going back will better it or me. But for all that I feel that my responsibilities are there, not here, and an unacted responsibility is worse than nettlerash.

But even if you think me an idiot, please don't think me ungrateful. I am extremely grateful for the kindness of *The New Yorker*, and for your kindness. And I hope I shall go on sending you contributions, to do that would be a real mitigation of the sort of regrets I shall undoubtedly feel when I'm back.

Warner to Maxwell, October 24, 1939:

And exactly as I expected, my evacuees welcomed me with cries of Thank God you're safe at last! So far, they are perfectly right and justified. I could not be safer in the Metropolitan Museum. Everything here looks unreally green and peaceful. It is rather like being in that section of hell where Dante met Moses and Plato and Lucan, and all that lot.

Warner to Maxwell, October 29, 1939:

You see I keep my promises, and here is a possible story for *The New Yorker* ["A Viking Strain"]. As it has its eye on Christmas, if you do decide to do it, will you please deal with any questions and revisions in proof for me? I know I shall always be at ease with any alterations you make.

The *luminous dogs* are true.

I'm sorry to send the typescript without a shirt-front, but one is thrifty with paper.

Maxwell to Warner, December 8, 1939:

I have a kind of an egg-shell (snow-white) that I put over my head and that makes it possible for me to dictate rejection letters without getting too low in my mind, but this time it didn't work. There may be a crack in it, but I have looked at "A Viking Strain" (which we have all read and like and would have thought perfectly usable had it come in late in September) steadily for two weeks trying to get up enough gimp to send it back to you. Because it's so charming, and because I don't quite know how to explain to you what you must never have noticed, probably, and that is, you are the founder of a school of fiction. The stories about your mother began it, I think, and now there are a number of English writers who approach contemporary problems through the eyes of the tiny English village that you brought to life. It's become the established way of writing about England's problems, and (strangely) even creeps into the London Letter, now that Miss Flanner is on this side of the water. It's still a good way of dealing with England's problems, of course, but while you were turning around three times before settling down in Dorset with your evacuees and your New Zealand (not New England) spinach, we've been flooded by stories like "A Viking Strain," the only difference being that they were not half so well done.

If it were a substantial and at least partially rounded narrative, it would have done, no doubt, but the interest of course lies chiefly in the country point of view toward the war, and the country perpetrator, both of which are familiar to us (we are so dreadfully informed, as you know, and can tell at least three days ahead of the actual moment of invasion when any European nation is going to be invaded) now.

I'm sending the ms. back by boat and trust that it won't be damp when it reaches you. And I hope and trust that I've not permanently confused you by my remarks on the state of contemporary English letters. The thing is if you do a rounded story, you're safe from the journalistic boys and girls, who seize upon things like the luminous dogs, and with that and very little else make a just possible story for *The New Yorker*. When you

really square off (as with "Plutarco Roo") nobody can touch you or anticipate so much as a word, or a semicolon.

P.S. Shirt-fronts aren't in the least necessary, and I hope you are parsimonious with paper from inclination and not from necessity. But if paper is
scarce over there, for one war reason or another, it certainly isn't here, and
we'd be enchanted to send you a box. Just say the word.

Maxwell to Warner, December 29, 1939:

After the first of March you will probably be hearing from Mr. [Gustave
S.] Lobrano instead of me. Before I came to work here three years ago I
used to do a little writing and I'm going now and do some more. One of
the utter pleasures of working on *The New Yorker* has been writing and seeing and talking to you. Though shyness prevented my saying so while you
were here, as long as I can remember I've loved your books, especially *The
True Heart*, and so many things out of them have become part and parcel of
my life. For example, only the other night the angelic mother of one of my
friends was fiercely defending the Standard Oil Company, and inevitably
and for the hundredth time I thought of your little girl who realized that
nobody ever felt sorry for wolves.

When you come again to Carthage, will you drop me a note, care of
The New Yorker? I shall more than likely be in New York and it would be
such a pleasure to see you.

Warner to Maxwell, January 31, 1940:

I am extremely sorry to hear that you are not staying with *The New
Yorker*. If it were not that I so much sympathise with your reason for going
I should find myself looking on your departure as a personal tragedy and
nothing else. First I lose Mrs White, then you. I shall feel that *The New
Yorker* is staffed with gazelles. I suppose that when I have learned to love Mr
Lobrano—perhaps it would be more befitting to say when I have taught Mr
Lobrano to love me—he too will be snatched away. Or—a thought equally
gloomy—Mr Lobrano and I may not transcend the ordinary relations of
editor and contributor.

But subduing my baser nature—just as I did about that farm in Maine that Mrs White went off to—I do very sincerely hope that you will have a lovely time writing. If it goes well there's no pleasure on earth to compare with it, and even when it doesn't it is an enthralling dissatisfaction; and I think you are doing just right.

It is very pleasant to have you saying such nice things about my writing, when you have been a writer as long as I have you will know how very reviving it is to hear such things. It is not merely one's pride and vanity that is eased, but a queer sort of sense of responsibility, like finding that some tree one planted and cared for and quitted is getting its proper pruning from a new owner. Being a writer makes one a ghost before one's time— the kind of ghost that likes a libation. War—or rather a state of things that antedates war—makes one feel more ghostly still; and so your words were doubly welcome.

I hope I shall come again to Carthage, I certainly intend to. Be sure I will let you know if and when I do, for I should like another meeting very much. If you ever feel inclined to write letters I should like to know where you are, and what the view from your window is, and how you are doing. And please let me know when you have a book out.

Maxwell to Warner, March 15, 1940:

I have all but one foot out of the office, but continue to work a little each day on manuscripts, and will for another month and a half, with the mornings free to work out my own salvation. Your last letter couldn't have pleased me more if it had been printed on Joseph Smith's golden plates instead of grey stationery. But you must not grow anxious about *The New Yorker.* I've been eating out of Mr. Lobrano's hand for years, and always with pleasure. I'm sure you have nothing to worry about.

The view you asked about, the view from my window, consists of tree-tops, ailanthus tree-tops, a courtyard, and a six-story box factory with fire escapes that descend in alternating musical scales, and with windows that I know the way I know my own face. There is also a drain that all the alley cats in the neighborhood pass in and out of, sooner or later. My apartment is cheerful and bright as a birdcage, and seems a good enough place to write in, with no dogs, no friends, no relations, no refugees. Only a straggling pot of ivy to worry over.

I wrote slowly and it may be years before there's a new book to send you and so I'm shipping under separate cover an old one [*They Came Like*

Swallows]. It was published in England but for some strange reason they put the first line of every chapter in caps, big ones, so that chapters begin: "THE GRASS UNDER THEIR FEET WAS trampled..." I'm sending you the American edition. If you find it hard going don't chew on it. Life is too short to read books you don't like.

Warner to Maxwell, April 3, 1940:

How very kind of you to send me your book. Sometimes book-sending is a miscarrying kindness, for it is very painful to receive the gift of some one's spiritual child and then to be forced to say one doesn't think much of it; but your present is an unqualified kindness, for I like the book very much indeed.

I do admire you so much for being able to write as a grown-up person about children. Too many people jump that problem by writing about children childishly; sometimes it's not too bad but it's never satisfying, one smells the expedient all the time like an oniony knife. At first I thought: Well, this Bunny is the achievement; but Robert is even better, especially Robert on the roof. And the slightly abrupt perspective of the grown-up characters, seen as one used to see grown-ups, is admirable.

Indeed I congratulate you; both on this book and on the others you will write. As for the Spanish influenza, you have added (and really I did not think it was possible) another cubit to the stature of my horror of pestilence. You must have had fun with that, the first creaking ominous orchestration of that theme.

Warner to Maxwell, November 4, 1946:

It was extremely kind of you to have Faber send me your book [*The Folded Leaf*], thank you very much for it.

It has impressed me a great deal. I think it is beautifully done and more than that I think it is seriously and formidably done. Certainly when I saw a number of well-established gentlemen of all sizes and demeanours all with their shirts hanging down over their trousers appearing as confidently as the stars in the foyer of the Yale theatre I sensed—after my first wild rush to the assumption that they would come on somehow in the second act— that there was more to it than, for instance, to Eton's Pop; but your book has made me understand the well-established gentlemen have every reason to look confident—if lineage is a reason for confidence as well as for fear.

It is always dangerous to tell authors that one book is better than another; but I will take the risk, and say that I think that this is a great advance on the *Swallows*. I am glad it has been so well appreciated in your country, and I hope it will do as well with readers here.

Maxwell to Warner, May 26, 1947:

You never complain about shortages that must make your life difficult, and I sometimes wonder if there is something like bath soap or canned tomatoes that we could send you to brighten the corner where you are. If there is, will you tell me?

P.S. Also, there is something that you ought to know about the gentleman named A. B. [a literary agent] which I am not professionally free to tell you until July first, at which time I will be very happy to. On that date I am leaving *The New Yorker* once more (presumably for good although the last time the cat came back) in order to retire into the country and finish another novel. So, much as I'd enjoy having you under my wing, emotionally and actually, I won't be able to. But let us not depend on publishers' announcements for news of one another.

Warner to Maxwell, May 30, 1947:

If you had heard the cry of distress that broke from me when I read that you are leaving *The New Yorker* on July 1 you would have begun to know what a good editor you are. If it were not that you were going to finish another novel I don't think I could be magnanimous enough to send you my best wishes for a happy retirement. As it is I ache in every limb with the strain of being so selfless. Indeed and seriously, I am sorrier than I can say.

Maxwell to Warner, June 13, 1947:

And now, lest you forget that the relationship between editor and writer can be as wearing as anything in the Old Testament, I have to tell you that the decision is against "The Finches of Abracadabra." As you know, Mr. Ross loves the Finch stories, but this one seemed a little too allusive for the readers of this magazine, many of whom, I'm afraid, are under the impression that English literature began with Scott Fitzgerald and reached its peak with Thomas Wolfe.

I'm glad you think I am a good editor even though a still small voice tells me that there is no such thing for writers of quality and that they should be left strictly to their own devices. I'm glad also that life in England is not as Spartan as the papers would lead us to believe. I would have been perfectly miserable in Sparta, and I can't help suspecting that the Spartans were also. Otherwise they would have left the Athenians alone.

Maxwell to Warner, May 16, 1948:

Anyone who was weaned, as I was, on your stories will not be surprised to have the police suddenly break in and arrest a nice young man ["Under New Management"].

Staying at home the last eight months I've finished another novel [*Time Will Darken It*] which I suspect to be far from crystal clear and I suppose that is one of the charms of the form, that one can be vague as to one's intentions and collect royalties from all the people one has left floundering. Before I die I hope to convince Mr. Ross that the way to handle all such matters in *The New Yorker* is to print the stories as they are written and simply run footnotes disposing of all knotty questions.

Warner to Maxwell, May 16, 1948:

Last May, I think, it was Mr Lobrano's break-down which fetched you back. This year, it is Mrs. White's operation. I am sure I wish her a comfortable unhurried recovery—it is always a mistake to scamper through a convalescence: sooner or later one won't have a convalescence, and then how one will regret having slighted those one did have—but if I had the evil eye it would be very wrong of you to give me such provocation to swivel it round to West 43rd Street whenever I chanced to yearn for a little variety and a breath of old times.

Do you like having finished a novel? It would be a very philanthropic state of mind on your part, since you write good ones; but I shall not congratulate you on your condition until I have your word for it that you would not prefer my condolences.

For my part, you can send me as many black-edged wreaths as you like. I finished one months ago [*The Corner That Held Them*], and can't quite forgive myself for having been such a damned improvident maniac. Nobody really wanted it but me, and now I've gone and parted with it.

Warner to Maxwell, December 3, 1948:

Your book [*Time Will Darken It*] came, and I certainly did not think of it as a boomerang. I began to read it, and soon saw that it was the kind of a book I like (how grateful I was to you for that calm opening—there is nothing I dislike more than opening pages that give me the feeling I have arrived, late and alone, at a party where everybody is rather drunk); but by the time I'd finished it I had the admiring sensation that something had hit me—a very well contained and well delivered blow.

I hope you realise what an extremely powerful book it is. It will be a long time before I get Oedipus Austin King out of my mind; and by that time I shall want to re-read it. It is full of admirable things: Nora Potter is exquisitely right, especially her mashed departure, which is a stroke of genius; and Randolph's major domo demeanour in calamity, and Ab, who is really supernaturally true, and the shift of colour and smell from the King's house to the Danforths' house; and the many small polished cat-clawings, such as old Mr. Ellis knowing a surprising amount about the boll weevil; and that hallowed passage on visits that last over four days; but the thing I really praise you for is the management of form and pace, and the decorum with which you conduct these people into their torments. A sheepdog could not have done it better!

I do indeed praise and admire you for this book. Instead of remarking that I wish more people wrote like this I shall be candid enough to say I'm thankful they don't. I would hate to smudge the smallest parcel of my pleasure in your writing.

Warner to Maxwell, April 29, 1950:

At the moment I am feeling quite reconciled to the rest of the human race (with the usual exceptions, of course) and I shall look forward to hearing from Miss Busey. Even if I were in a state of the blackest misanthropy I should like to meet the person who first introduced you to my books, since that was a preliminary oil to being introduced to you myself—by myself, as I remember; and then I have never yet met anyone called Garetta, and yet further I have never to my knowledge met a Bahai. I used to see them in the past, going rather barefootedly towards a meeting-hall in Kensington that bore a placard saying

Bahai Breathings 5.30 Wednesdays and Saturdays.

I frequently wondered just how one breathed in that way, but I never had the enterprise, or the intrepidity, to walk in and find out for myself. Now that you have told me that they are sweet-tempered and Persian and religious I think that the lady in the green chemise who was also tending towards the Breathings must have been a priestess of the sect. It was in the middle of the season, at a season when green chemises are even more striking than they would be in mid-winter, when one wears anything that comes handy. It was semi-transparent, came halfway down her shins, and was accompanied by sandals and a string bag, and beneath—no, inside it, was the lady. She was strolling along very tranquilly and no one was paying her the slightest attention. All that was in the twenties, when London really was a metropolis, and just about the date when my wine-merchant remarked to me that if anyone liked to build a high wall round Bayswater (the quarter where the wine-merchant and I were living) he would have the finest lunatic asylum in Europe.

I have an earlier letter of yours on my desk—a very kind one—that has waited a long time to be answered. I meant to answer it from Paris, where you read the reviews of *Time Will Darken It* and realised that nobody had understood your beautiful book—*in Paris, of all places*. But no reviewers ever understand one's books; and if they praise them, they understand them even less. Praising reviewers are like those shopwomen who thrust a hat on one's head, a hat that is like the opening of the Judgement scroll in which all one's sins are briefly and dispassionately entered, and then stand back and say that it is exactly the hat that Modom needs to bring out her face. I have never yet had a praising review that did not send me slinking and howling under my breath to kneel in some dark corner and pray that the Horn would sound for me and the Worms come for me, that very same night. The horn doesn't and the worms don't, and somehow one recovers one's natural powers of oblivion, and goes on writing.

Maxwell to Warner, August 5, 1950:

I find, on consulting the inner oracle, that I am always sorry to send you an author's proof, because it is only a step from there to page proof and the magazine and, miser that I am, I would keep your stories for myself alone.

Warner to Maxwell, November 3, 1950:

I would like to live here [Great Eye Folly, Norfolk] for ever—the owners come back at Easter—but that no one could do, for in five years' time the sea will have eaten it. The young man who came out from Holt yesterday to bring another cylinder of gas for the cooking-stove said to me, talking of the rate at which the sea is advancing, that his father could remember loads of corn being drawn inland over the bridge. What bridge?— said I. *I* can remember the bridge, said he. It was there. And he pointed to where our track runs out on the shingle, and the high water mark ribbon of sea-weed is.

At the other end of the track is the coast road, and the village of Salt-house, where every one is most humanely solicitous to make our flesh creep. It was unaccountably delightful to be told that I need not worry at all until I saw the cattle being taken off the marsh (there has been nothing on the marsh but geese for the last two days), and to be told by the grocer about underground passages between the pillbox on the beach, which the sea has already undermined, and the pillbox that is fastened to the side of the house, and how, if I go and listen at high tide—but I have, and not an underground gurgle did I hear, so I'm afraid it is the usual monkish underground passage story, but brought a little up to date.

Another reminder of when this was a fortified coastal point is a tight little brick hut, with a door lettered: Bomb Disposal. Private. I like the English moderation of this. The door is fastened, but the cat goes in by a crack in the threshold—and knowing how bombs get left about and over-looked I was rather nervous at first. He is the happiest cat in the British Isles—three pillboxes and a whole system of trenches to play in, and the spindrift to chase and the sea-tangle to explore.

I think I had better not go on. You will think that real estate has come between us. But in fact, one reason why I like this place so very much is that I believe I shall do quite a lot of writing here.

Maxwell to Warner, February 1951:

"Matthew, Mark, Luke and John" is adorable and scheduled tentatively for Easter Sunday. While I was adoring it, the first time through, I was also lost in the absolute command of technique, the white heat of technique, in the writing. That you, fortunately, hadn't recopied it after your revisions added a still further pleasure, of being, so to speak, at your elbow. Though I'm glad you are not, I think you could have been a mathematician.

Now for the hurricane. During the night whenever in November (the fourteenth?) that it started, we were both wakened and Emmy particularly irritated by the wind banging the shutter. For some reason women do not like wind. In the morning after breakfast I went outside and found the shutter had blown loose from its mooring hook, and the hook had disappeared into the iris bed. The trees were rocking, it was raining hard, and it was obviously no day to be driving to town with a car full of lampshades, cooking utensils, chairs, clothes and books; but on the other hand, Belva White, the colored cleaning woman who worked for me for a spell in 1945, had been told to come to our apartment at eleven, her telephone number was in my desk here, and I didn't want her to have a long trip down from Harlem in the rain, to wait for an hour in the foyer of a building on 38th Street where we weren't going to be. So we finished loading the car and started out about nine-thirty. Going up the hill by the Kitchawan filling station, an approaching car honked as only cars driven by old friends do, and before I could identify the friend, we saw the reason for the honking—a fifty-foot pine tree directly across the parkway with its topmost branches resting on the highest pump. So we drove under the porte cochere, and on down the parkway. The windshield wiper is tired, and the vision of our 1936 Ford touring car poor, but we drove twenty-five miles an hour and so did everybody else, and occasionally swam into small ponds of water that splashed up over the windshield and obliterated all vision for the next thirty feet. I got stiff as a board from the tension of being ready for any form catastrophe chose to take, and it chose to take no form at all. The sidecurtains stayed on while we passed over the Hendrick Hudson Bridge during a temporary lull, and once in the canyons of the Upper West Side, it was like any rainy day, but then we came to the park and people seemed to be having trouble boarding the bus. I thought we might have to swim when we got to the tunnel in the park, but it had excellent drains, and we arrived on East 38th Street

on the dot of eleven. No Belva. At twelve, having unpacked and put away
the car and the lampshades, et al, we went out for lunch. The radio was
telling people to keep off the streets, but we had no radio and besides you
can't keep New Yorkers off the streets. At 3rd Avenue and 42nd, we went
into an Automat, paid our nickels and carried our trays to a corner table,
adjacent to acres of plate glass. And after lunch went shopping along Forty-
second Street, which was rather strewn with soggy papers and garbage, and
having accumulated several sacks, were turning back when we heard a high
shrill EEEEEEE and looked just in time to see a large, middle aged woman
passing us horizontally about two feet above the sidewalk. She fell on her
face and did not get up. Before I could overcome surprise and early training
with packages, and shock at seeing her pink girdle, three men came running, picked her up and carried her into a store. And then off went Emmy,
into the arms of a man three stores away, who had stretched them out to
catch her. She thanked him nicely and we withdrew into a sheltered place in
front of a creamery and the storekeeper came running out and said "For
God's sake don't lean against the plate glass!" The plate glass was cracked
and taped, like our sidecurtains. If we had stayed a little longer we would
have seen the traffic policeman, an impressive example of his profession and
doubtless a credit to his Irish ancestors, blown away like a dandelion seed.
But instead we bought doughnuts, and this and that, and were suddenly
stopped by a trompe l'oeil—the A and P without any glass in the plate glass
windows. It is a very agreeable sensation walking through plate glass,
though I dare say you have done it often enough so that it no longer presents any novelty. But dreamlike, I found it. The signs were hanging up by
one hinge, there was garbage everywhere, and people were immensely
pleased and cheerful. And it continued to rain. Just about dark that night I
went out with a supplementary list, and this time the plate glass was continuous, many stores were closed and dark, and to get into others you had
to enter through inside doors, in office buildings. It was also odd to see
some stores covered with boards and others wide open, like a nice United
Cigar store, with cigarettes to last a lifetime and nobody looting. I didn't,
unfortunately, have a perambulator, and I had all I could manage with the
paper sacks, which melted like spun sugar, leaving the remnants to be
juggled. Along about this time of the evening, *The New Yorker*'s building
dropped a good many tons of brick and concrete cornice on West 44th
Street, injuring twenty-five cars and five people. There was a picture of it in
the Sunday *Times*, and I didn't recognize what it was. Do you sometimes

find yourself confronted with a manuscript that you *might* have written twenty years before but have no idea whether it is yours or not? I have never really understood Ulysses's dog. Anyway, it calmed down by eight o'clock and we went off, in a cab, to the theater. A friend had had a play open on Monday, to appalling notices, and it was closing that night and we were papering the house. It wasn't as bad a play as they said; in fact it was rather interesting, if you hadn't paid for your tickets, and there were eighteen people in the audience. The cast said afterwards that it was their best performance. Here the scene changes to the seacoast of Bohemia.

Several times we wondered about our house in the country—by that time the news had reached us that it was a sort of by fits and starts hurricane. I told Emmy that if the roof was blown away somebody would surely call us, because that's all Elise Guiterman has to do is watch our house and tell Mary Rocheford who came to dinner last night, and she had our number. Nobody called, until Monday morning, when I came down and was mildly annoyed that the desk was covered with grit, and nobody had thought to give it a once over with a feather duster. Then I looked out the window and saw the remains of the cornice and the origin of the grit. After a while a neighbor called and said that our apple orchard, roughly a hundred years old and very ornamental, was gone. Everybody's trees were gone, he said, but he is the happiest of alarmists and has prophesied famine, the end of the world, and I don't know what all. But it *was* interesting, he said. About five o'clock, the ground began moving in waves, like a wheatfield, only the grass was short, and it was the lawn that was moving in waves, and then one after another, as the last extremities of the roots gave way, the trees went over. One of them fell on the Dansereau's grey Chevrolet, with Poilu, their French poodle, in it, and he chewed up all the upholstery, as he often does. He suffers from *Angst*, and that's his way of disposing of it, sometimes on a bright calm day in front of the Grand Union. The car was ruined, said the alarmist. Well it wasn't, of course. They're still driving around in it, with a rakish cavity in the roof, and shreds of upholstery dangling. But what happened was that Mrs. Dansereau was in town and she called up Mr. D Friday night to tell him to call the Berches and tell them that the D's couldn't come to the B's for dinner Saturday night. The B's were expecting the D's a week from that Friday but no matter. So Mr. D waited in the house all day, with the telephones working, until just before five, when they stopped working, and then when he couldn't reach the B's by telephone, he got into the car, drove up the road, parked in front of a huge pine tree, beside another that had just fallen, and went into the house and when he realized what had happened to the car, gave up and stayed for dinner. The 4 tires were flat with the air still in them.

For several days there was no electricity, and therefore no heat, sometimes nothing to cook on, and all that, and the roads everywhere were blocked, and the landscape materially altered, but our orchard not gone, just changed. Where it had been before a double allee of enormous, carefully spaced apple trees, it was now a random, casual and not unpretty (if you ignored the casualties) orchard. Nothing happened to the house, and since we had been worried because there wasn't as much sunlight as there used to be, we couldn't feel irresponsible or totally sad about the damage to the orchard. As somebody remarked in the *Telegram*, the trees are really ours only on loan, so to speak. The man who was supposed to come with an electric saw and saw the uprooted ones up has, I am confident, not done so, but in March there will not only be him to call, but the carpenter who promised to put the folding ladder to the attic in and hasn't, and the plumber, the electrician, the garageman, etc. And perhaps they will all come at once and we can offer them beer.

So you see, it was a rather nice hurricane. I don't like to appear greedy, but if you *should* happen to think of another story, there is no limit, you know, to *The New Yorker*'s spongelike capacity to accept its chosen authors. One a week would be about right, so far as the readers and editors are concerned.

Warner to Maxwell, February 9, 1951:

I should have written before to thank you for that deeply satisfactory story of the hurricane: I enjoyed every moment of it, you could not have enjoyed it more yourself: I fancy we must be made out of much the same clay—quiet characters, with a simple savage delight in cataclysms. When the orchard began to writhe, I was in ecstasies; that was something I should not have thought of myself: and the art by which the astonishment of the orchard was followed by the tranquilising behaviour of the poodle (tranquilising, I mean, because it bore out one's *Pudelanschaung*) was delightful. But I am sorry about the appletrees because I like formal plantations of fruit trees best. They accumulate a stronger scent that way, and are processional for bees. On the other hand, your scattered trees will be far lovelier in win-

ter, when their patterns will be more distinct. I can't remember the cornice,
so I don't know whether to be glad or sorry; but if it was a valued cornice,
no doubt Mr Ross will replace it, and have a lot of fun making sure that the
blue-prints work out properly. Alternatively, you could have some gigantic
statues, like St John Lateran. Minerva is never out of place.

I should have written before—as I have already begun to say—and
thanked you for liking M, M, L & J, and saying such very pleasant things
about it, and even finding something to enjoy in the outrageous state of
that typescript, like those who going through the vale of misery use it for a
well, only for the last ten days or so we have been tossing about among
houseagents. Valentine's mother's doctor has given a bad account of her
heart, and combined with it an absolute demand that she should not be
told how shaky it is (all doctors are under this illusion that their patients are
terrified of death, whereas in half the cases at least, it is the doctors that the
patients are afraid of); and so we are dancing among the incompatibles of
not doing anything that might seem in the least bit out of the usual and
doing a great many things we don't ordinarily do, such as hanging about in
the vicinity of the Mothers' Union meetings, like peris. Meanwhile Ruth, I
am on the whole glad to say, continues along her ordinary course, addressing the united mothers, leaping on and off moving buses and giving herself
a little cold meat at midnight. As for having anyone living in her house, she
would prefer cobras. There are no more houses in Norfolk than in any
other part of England; but we have looked at a number of derelict palaces.
They all have Aga cookers. Apparently when people have spent a hundred
pounds putting in an Aga cooker, they die insolvent from the shock and
strain. You can see that in this state of things the two cheques which came
this morning are exceedingly soothing and comfortable. If I do not appear
to cash them immediately it will be because of the differential calculus.
When I was young I had a young friend who was extremely sensitive to the
cold. He was at Haileybury, rather a bleak and bracing public school; and
then in this sixteenth year his place in class got him next to a radiator. From
that moment until his schooling ended two years later, he gave his whole
mind to remaining by the radiator. He told me it required the exactest calculation and foresight to remain at just that level of scholarship. It did not
do, he soon discovered, to be just inertly stupid. That angered his form
master, who marked him down. He had, so to speak, to row, and yet
remain by the same tuft of reeds. And in summer, when the radiator was
apt to slip his mind he had to be as alert as a mosquito not to give way to

emulation and the line of least resistance. He stayed by the radiator, however, and left with a scholarship, much to every one's annoyance and surprise. In much the same way, if I am to make the most of my earnings I cannot afford to earn too much in any financial year, because of the graded income-tax. And this year I have been rather extravagant in my earnings. I suppose this is the differential calculus. Arthur said it was the best guide to the radiator. It was a mathematical scholarship he left with.

I have just come back from Norwich. There is always something to be brought away from there, as well as what one buys in market that goes on round Sir Thomas Browne. Today I noticed a brass trade-plate in a side street saying that the tradesman was a Fellmonger; and after lunch I got into conversation with an old lady, a conversation that by some hook or crook got round to judges in their robes, and how very rare it is to find a judge whose train is held up properly. 'Have you noticed,' said she, 'that whenever men want to be impressive they get into women's clothes?'

Warner to Maxwell, February 16, 1951:

Here are the four Evangelists, with not much to say about them ["Matthew, Mark, Luke, and John"]. On galley seven I have substituted *clattered* for *flounced* for the noise that Rosalind made with the bucket. If you have a bucket handy, and some nice echoing floor, and snatch the bucket up and put it down again rather violently in much the same place that you took it up from, that will be what I chose to call flouncing with a bucket; and any one who has taken part in church decoration, especially at Easter when tempers are at their worse, will recognise the action; but I daresay some of the *New Yorker* readers only go to quiet things like baseball matches; and so perhaps *clattered* would be better. I leave it to you. It does not matter more than half one pin. But she remained in church, that is firm. She is the kind of woman who would stay to the last primrose, if only to be a martyr. On galley nine I do not know whether bo-peep would be better with a capital B. and P. But it must have a hyphen, or it will look like something that rouses sluggish livers—though I don't know why. To be honest, I know very little about the English language, I spend my life as a writer in astonishment and speculation about it; and naturally, ignorance makes me as obstinate as a mule, once I have got an idea into my head.

Warner to Maxwell, March 17, 1951:

A magnificent ham arrived, and I should have written before to say how wonderful it looked against a background of grey sea; but I hoped to combine the letter with another story, and have been hanging on to that hope. It is all done except for one sleeve, like the nettle-shirt in Hans Christian— but then a lot of noisy things began happening, and now we are packing to go home, so I shall have to put it off until I am unpacked and in my right mind again.

One of the things that happened was that we nearly became an island. There was a wonderful concatenation of new moon and northeasterly gale and telephone conversations with the coastguards at Cley; and I felt just like that small boy in *The New Yorker* who I last saw defying the police from a washing-line, when the coastguards asked me, 'What's it like down your way,' and I was proudly enabled to reply, 'About two hour ahead of its usual tide-mark, and coming in very full now.' All this was very much as I liked it, and the sea was lovely to see, I have never seen anything enjoying itself more. But this car is all the car we shall ever have, and it became obvious that we could not keep it dry-foot much longer unless the wind shifted, and when the coastguard finally and rather obscurely remarked, 'Well, I should say that prevention is better than cure,' we made a hasty dusky getaway, with the dog, the cat, and a carcass of chicken—for I was determined not to waste the goodness in its bones; and as the wind bowled us along the causeway we saw the spray jumping over the shingle ridge like hounds, and the water just beginning to lap across.

We went inland to friends, and I made chicken soup that night. (The ham? It was in my bedroom. I knew the sea wouldn't get at it there); and when we came back two days later, some morose waves were mumbling away at a completely reshaped beach, with a lot of gaunt remains of tank traps unburied, and looking like some sort of mineral nettles. You could tell that man had been there.

We leave on Monday; and today I have been going round tearing myself away from fishmongers and greengrocers and bakers, and Mr Morris the saddler. It is very painful for me to leave them because they like me so much. I am much more of a social success in East Anglia than in Wessex, and I don't look forward to being just that peculiar Miss Warner again, after being loved and laurelled all the way down Holt High Street, and knowing the Christian names of every one's cat. Wessex is a dog locality, but Norfolk has very large cats and worships them.

Warner to Maxwell, April 11, 1951:

Meanwhile, we are home. Valentine has re-arranged all her books because I imported an inheritance of Horace Walpole in nine snuffy volumes, and decided where to plant another flowering currant (this is the time of year when one feels there cannot be too many of them about), and I have cleaned the herb-bed and moved all the furniture around. If it were possible to keep books on the ceiling, this house would be unexceptionable. If one never wanted to read them, it would be quite possible, penning them behind glass and wire doors (or floors); but I have never been able to work out a satisfactory way of getting down the book one wants without having to combat a good deal too much of the force of gravity. The other day I said to a clergyman I met that though I always read in my bath, as all sensible people do, I disliked the moment when one has to decide whether to wash one's hands or go on reading and respecting the binding. He said that if I were to content myself with the burial and baptismal service, this problem would be overcome, as both of them are issued by some Church of England publishing house with waterproof bindings. Did you know this?

Warner to Maxwell, April 19, 1951:

By my own pedigree there was every reason for me to be a clergyman. Canon Townsend was so much a clergyman that he went with his wife to Rome to convert the Pope (Piu Nono). They got their audience, and I believe their arguments were most convincing, but unfortunately, they both (Townsend and Mrs T.) addressed His Holiness in Latin, and they spoke with the English pronunciation and Piu could not understand whet they said. When I was in Rome I was on the whole very glad they did not succeed. Though it might have given me Rome as a birthplace (for I think Mrs T. would have stayed there to keep an eye on things), Rome would not have been the same Rome, and those noble bare walls round the Vatican would perhaps have had roses climbing over them, and rock-gardens at the foot instead of sleeping policemen.

Warner to Maxwell, June 5, 1951:

I am so glad that you and Emmy have got an electric lawn-mower, and you will love it all the more for the anguish of its arrival. Electricity is so serene, until it goes wrong; and when that happens, there is no half-hearted doubt about it, either, no cossetting or tinkering. One wipes the blue flash from one's eyes and waits like Luther for the Proper Man. It was a far better choice than those motor mowers. England has never been herself since motor mowers came to us. Lawns, that used to be all peace and eating white raspberries on seats painted green, are now disorderly scenes of strife, with mowers, the human part of the mechanism, jolting round the corners or falling off into the rhododendrons, or—worse—galloping along after the horrible thing with their mouths choked with daisies. We have a nice old-fashioned one, and a little boy called Colin [House] is all the motor it has, and afterwards he goes fishing in our reach of the river.

Warner to Maxwell, June 12, 1951:

I am thankful that Emmy is back. In her absence you do not spell as well as at other times. Does she know this? It is a delightful tribute, she should wear it in a brooch.

Warner to Maxwell, September 11, 1951:

When I was a small child my father, poking about in the boxroom where I spent a great deal of my time, found a piece of paper on which I had written on ruled lines, 'It was a long tale, my masters, a long and a sad tale.'

That was all there was of that one. Now, here's another.

Maxwell to Warner, September 26, 1951:

The picture of you I have chosen for hanging in my study is at the age of nine, leaving the large chair and the dark corner and Tacitus to go and inquire if it is true that the phoenix appears from time to time in Egypt.

Maxwell to Warner, November 1951:

When I wanted to write you and couldn't because I felt so bad about "Ullinthorpe" [a rejected story], I read *Summer Will Show*, for the first time. In a trance. Where in God's name did you get your knowledge of Paris? Did you live there for years, or simply throw yourself into the state of mind of one living in Paris? In forty-three years I have been granted six weeks of living in Paris, just enough to know that that novel really takes place there. Did you feel very poor for a long time after you finished it? The effect of richness, or squandering, of pockets and desk drawers and jewel cases emptied, and mattresses ripped open, in an attempt to drown the reader in a cascade of ideas and emotions and images is what it seemed like, to me in my trance. Surely it is the least cautious and most prodigal of your novels? At times I felt as I were at a street fair and at other times as if there had been a death in the family. Perhaps the third time I will read it instead of feel it, visually. I hope meanwhile that you are sufficiently fond of it.

I notice you are slyly noncommittal about what got you into a fever of writing, and that surely is a good sign. October was excessively fine here, too. I hesitate to tell you what gardening excesses it drove us to. We even moved a tree, with our bare hands, so to speak. And speaking of the historical novel, do you know about the woman—Mme. de Brinvilliers, could her name be?— who tried out her poisoned pigeon pies on the poor, a contemporary of Mme. de Sévigné, she was, and operating under a wealth of mixed motives that seemed to me, at the time I came across her in the *Britannica*, to make her an ideal heroine. I don't have and never will have if I continue to be a reader of manuscripts, the erudition to do her properly. Has she been done?

I don't suppose you read the lecture on the historical novel, so there is probably no copy extant of your remarks? I have any number of theories on the subject, such that it is—the love of history is glandular, and that on one's fortieth birthday or thereabouts one simply finds oneself with a book of memoirs or Gibbon or what not in one's hand, instead of the familiar novel. Another is that anybody who is at all curious about life is ultimately driven in that direction by the paucity of information in every other, literary and actual. I am now in an intermediary state, of writing a novel and reading history. The next step is obvious.

Warner to Maxwell, November 8, 1951:

It is Paris's familiarity with me, rather than my familiarity with Paris that accounts for that confident tra-la-la in *Summer Will Show*. I never got there until I was in my thirties, and then as the taxi drew out of the Gare S Lazare I not only recognised the names of the street as I came to them, but knew what street would come next. No wonder, really, with almost all the novelists telling one beforehand, and telling one so well. As for the book, it had been accumulating for years, beginning with the name Sophia Willoughby, and Minna's voice in the first sentence of her narrative, and it was only when I was finally force-of-gravitied into beginning it that I realised I had better study some of the facts. So I collected all the contemporary accounts I could get from the London Library, and when I had discovered that none of them agreed about anything I felt I might know as much about as they did, and went back for another look at Ste Clothilde—and on that visit saw the wineshop cat. It is a book I feel great affection for, though I am apt to be abashed, when I re-read it, at such a quantity of flukes coming off better than I deserve. As you say, 'the least cautious' of my novels.

Warner to Maxwell, December 6, 1951:

Yes, it was caution that kept me so non-committal about the book in hand [*The Flint Anchor*], and also astonishment, incredulity, and lack of breath. I got out of my bath and began writing it about the middle of October, and have gone on at a canter ever since. While I was in my bath I had been speculating about my great-great-grandfather, who stayed in a pious East Anglian family just long enough to beget my great-grandfather, and was swept off to die on a voyage to the West Indies, while the pious family constructed a sort of inscrutable grotto round his memory, alleging that he was a *mauvais sujet* and never supplying any evidence for it. But except for the date, any resemblance to the facts stayed in the bath.

It seems to be a steady north-easter of a book—north-wester to you, I suppose: that wind that dries one's skin and paints the landscape with a gaunt gaiety. But I have been so much in it that the other day I found myself thinking very sadly by what a narrow interval of time I missed the chance of knowing Keats.

I have never written at anything like this rate before—but I shall be able to spend my usual years and years on revising, I daresay.

Maxwell to Warner, December 7, 1951:

Dear Sylvia:

By the time this reaches you, you will undoubtedly have heard or read about Mr. Ross's death, after a lung operation in Boston, yesterday. I don't think there will be much if any change in the magazine. His various editors had won all the battles and he had won the war, some time ago. The staff, including me, was not only devoted to him personally but I suspect deified him, never of course admitting this to themselves or to one another. For the last two months, though his illness was not considered serious, or at least not that serious, there has been a sense of Change, of the Drastic, hanging over the office. Something is going to happen, people said leaning in doorways and at the water cooler. The poetry editor had intimations that he was going to be fired. He isn't, of course. We were, of course, simply facing the possibility of change. So much is made journalistically of his eccentricity and irascibility, and what you never read anywhere is that he was an imaginative and intuitive man. Intuitive with people, and imaginative in his acts of kindness. Without my ever having mentioned the fact that I was writing a novel to him, he suddenly asked me one day if I would like to take the rest of the year, four or five months, off, with pay, so I could finish my book. I did. It was *The Folded Leaf*, which he never read but preserved, with the *Times* review, which mentioned him, so that his daughter would someday know—she was then a child—that he was an encourager of talent. Or so he told me. He said, of course, many wonderful things— opposite the scribble "Shelley who he?" must be put "Talent doesn't care where it resides." It is characteristic of this place and an indication of how much he still means that this morning nobody has been near me and I have not left my chair, there is no gathering in the halls, it is very much—it is *much too much* like any Friday morning.

Affectionately,
William

Warner to Maxwell, January 18, 1952:

And you can address me just as you feel inclined. I daresay it will take me a little while to come out of Mr Maxwell, it is endeared by use and so much else. But I shall come to William in time.

Warner to Maxwell, February 12, 1952:

Poor Niou [their Siamese cat] has just had his first affair of the heart, and of course it was a tragedy. As a rule he flies from strange men, cursing under his breath, and keeping very low to the ground. Yesterday an electrician came; a grave mackintoshed man, but to Niou all that was romantic and lovely. He gazed at him, he rubbed against him, he lay in an ecstasy on the tool-bag. The electrician felt much the same, and gave him little washers to play with. He said he would have to come again today to finish off properly. Niou who understands everything awaited him in a dreamy transport and practising his best and most amorous squint. The electrician came, Niou was waiting for him on the window-sill. A paroxysm of stage-fright came over him, and he rushed into the garden and disappeared.

He'll get over it in time; but just now he's dreadfully downcast.

Warner to Maxwell, March 24, 1952:

Your letter arrived this morning, and made me very happy—but who is Mr Shawn? If you had been writing me a novel I would have known that any one introduced to that particular tune would turn out to be the immensely important character later on; but in a correspondence he may just as well never recur, and yet you have riveted my attention. Is he a new President of the USA? Or does he sometimes appear in the shape of a shaggy black water dog with a long thin tail that has brushed through the banshee and been cold ever since? [William Shawn became the editor of *The New Yorker* after Harold Ross's death.]

Warner to Maxwell, April 9, 1952:

It cost me a struggle to be pleased that you had found a copy of *After the Death of Don Juan*, you should have asked me for one and I would have been pleased and proud to send it. Only Mozart can write like Mozart, but I have never regretted trying to, like falling out of a tree it was wonderfully exhilarating while it lasted. As for the present one, it shaped itself within my arms a lump of cold tapioca pudding and not a man; but then I put it in a box and left it to repent while we went away, and there it can stay until it's in a better frame of mind. I shall write some sonnets instead. That'll learn it, learn it, learn it, as the Badger so wisely said. Don't you find, too, that there is a stage when one's book turns round and *hates* one? Or yawns in one's face?

Maxwell to Warner, April 14, 1952:

Telling myself all the while that it was a mistake, that I must go slower, look around me and pay special attention to the flowers on the roadside, I raced through the last half of *After the Death of Don Juan.* The siege of the castle seems like something I must have dreamed. It has over it that paradoxical light by which, in your dreams, you see perfectly well in the dark. Terribly well, in fact. And it *is* written like Mozart. I speak as one who has seen the house where he was born, and therefore knows. It is a perfect novel.

I am tempted to suggest that we exchange lumps of cold tapioca and go on from there, but I think I won't. It is too much the sort of thing that would appeal to you, and when one's own book hates one, it is possible to say that it is all in the family.

Maxwell to Warner, April 25, 1952:

How misguided of you to get sick in the springtime, and how fortunate that there is an ocean between us and I can't drive you to distraction with sympathetic attentions. I don't even know which is more hateful of your two afflictions [shingles and chicken-pox]. I've had them both but not simultaneously. My older brother used to bring home a light case of this or that, and then there would be a quarantine sign on the door, and two weeks later to the day I would start in having the same thing but with a certain flair. His chicken pox was worse than mine because he SCRATCHED. As I watch Little Gray and Floribunda [their cats] and their varied behavior according to whether we have remembered to slip them a pill, I wonder more and more if virtue (at least in children) isn't simply a vitamin deficiency.

About Coke of Norfolk—on the day you took sick you wrote me that I was to tell you as soon as possible how Coke of Norfolk set me off. An historian at Yale, name of Notestein, wrote, along about the year 1932 or three, to the Bahai I tried to send to you, in whose house I was living, and grading freshman themes, in exchange for room and board and the freedom to write novels. (It was an ideal arrangement which I do not hope to repeat short of heaven.) Dear me, how untrustworthy memory is. Part of that is right and part is quite wrong. I hadn't even thought of writing novels. That arrangement came later, after I had spent the money I was supposed to be getting a Harvard Ph.D. with, floating serenely and homesickly from one West Indian island to another. But earlier, when I was a graduate student, and teaching my own ungrammatical freshmen, but living in that wonderful Victorian house, he did—Wallace Notestein did ask Miss Busey if she would like to do a forty page condensation of the two volume life of Coke of Norfolk, from which he would later do a section of a book on various English characters. Without telling him that she had dragged in a ringer, she accepted the offer, and then divided Coke in half, giving me (with a generosity that I was too young and grasping to fully appreciate) Lady Mary and her divorce and her obsession about the Empress Maria Theresa's taking her servants away from her, and the pea-green and silver and the gold fish fishing, and the last dreadful picturesque disorder of mind and belongings, and a wonderful ball at Holkham, and all the dramatic and descriptive opportunities, including that shooting accident. And *she* took the agricultural parts. As a matter of fact, they interested her. And together we sent off the forty page life of Coke of Norfolk, and I'm not sure but I suspect that it later had all to be done over again by some other ghost, because I remember taking the book off a library shelf in a house in New Haven and looking in vain not merely for a sentence I had written but for any of the set pieces that had given me such pleasure to do. And having started, I could not stop.

Warner to Maxwell, April 26, 1952:

I had shingles, they are bad enough. I also had doctors, and they are much harder to recover from and far more dangerous. After tentatively dabbing at me with chicken-pox they tried to give me smallpox, and for a while it seemed they might whirl me off to the isolation hospital as a suspect,

where, however inoffensively I went in I should not have come again without really catching it, and probably scarlet fever and diphtheria too. Fortunately, by the morning the three spots they had been building their fairy
castle on had gone away and the injections that worked on shingles had
worked, so they had to go away saying how much relieved they were and
looking signally flat.

Every word that Molière says about doctors is true. And owing to the
workings of the National Health Act, they now appear in swarms, and
invite each other to parties all over one. But today the last dreg of them is
gone and the house seems wonderfully fresh and sweet and calm and
wholesome, and Niou has left off walking with his hackle half up and
growling under his breath, and Valentine is resting with her feet up.

So all I have got to do is leave off brooding on my wrongs, and turn my
mind to the tapioca. Your suggestion that we should exchange is very
tempting—I noticed, however, that you had no sooner made it than you
began to back-pedal. One does cling to one's own half-licked cups of tapioca, when all's said and done.

Maxwell to Warner, May 1952:

I do not associate you, ordinarily, with nerves, I suppose because you don't
complain, and the two do seem to go together. Speaking of tapioca, since I
first read "...the lady patronesses and the female orphans, who sat
grouped around him, the lady patronesses in the shade and the female
orphans in the sun,"* I have left behind me I don't dare think how many
tastes and pleasures, lost a good deal of hair off the top of my head, had a
year or two of insomnia, married, been to Europe, paid off a mortgage,
and resigned from *The New Yorker* three times, but that sentence I read, two
days ago, with exactly the same rapture as I did the first time. Like so many
of your sentences, it is cast in bronze and could last even longer.

* From the first paragraph of Warner's *The True Heart*.

Warner to Maxwell, June 8, 1952:

That noble parcel of butter—was it to launch me? The only time I have
seen a ship launched I behaved like every other woman, and burst into tears.

It is the shock of seeing anything so very large and stately, tottering like a baby, I suppose. It was unjust to insinuate that I wept for the champagne.

After a slight setback of entertaining Inescapables, I am so much better that at any moment I may begin to write again, so the butter will not be misapplied. I could perfectly well have begun earlier, if I had not decided to polish a bureau. Having polished it so beautifully, I was rash enough to turn my admiring proud gaze round on the rest of the house, and then of course it was my grandmother and the biscuits all over again. Brought up sternly in Charlotte Square, Edinburgh, my grandmother was allowed down from the nursery to see the dining room arrayed for one of those dinners after which it was quite customary for some of the gentlemen guests not to come up to the drawing room at all, but the word would be given by my great-grandfather, and my great-grandmother would give a tactful low whisper to one of the ladies, and she would presently rise unobtrusively and go downstairs to where her respected lord had been propped up to wait for the moment when he could be guided to his carriage. Well, there was the sideboard with the dessert set out on it, and among the dessert was a dish of sweet biscuits. My grandmother took a light nibble from one of them. Replacing it, she saw that the nibble was only too plain. She nibbled all round the biscuit, with a hope that it would appear to be no more than a decorative edging. This only emphasised the undecorativeness of the remaining biscuits. Mad with terror, frantic as a rabbit biting its leg off to get out of a gin, the child nibbled round every damned biscuit on the dish.

Fortunately, my great-grandfather was a very intelligent humane man, and though he could not do much to restrain my great-grandmother's sense of duty—and certainly not about the dark room that followed the biscuits—he saved her from complete slavishness, and she grew up a very intelligent and enjoying woman. I say this, in case you lie awake all night, wishing you could get at my great-grandmother. For myself, I have come to the conclusion that these wishes, however laudable, are vain; and that children experience terror however they are brought up; in some generations it is better and in others worse, but it always has to be gone through, and when it is put off in childhood it is only to pounce down on adolescence. Oddly enough, I can't feel that this is any reason not to want to get at my great-grandmother. If one's impulses did not perpetually war with one's conclusions, I daresay one would be senile in a week.

At this moment, *Enter the Cat, singing and dancing*. I must go and cook his mackerel.

Warner to Maxwell, June 19, 1952:

Valentine's mother is so anniversary minded that one never knows when she won't say in the middle of lunch, This is Celia Jackman's day. And she has very neatly insinuated a custom that on the main death-days of her year she has to be given a little present. I doubt if there is another woman in the Christian world to be so nearly an adumbration of Kali-Durga. Human sacrifices gayly consummated. Valentine has a box in which she keeps china rabbits, small trinkets, travelling clothes-brushes and so on, all ready in case a Celia Jackman creeps up unbeknown, and known as The Death Box.

If things like this could somehow be given to future anthropologists, it would make them happy and busy for weeks.

Warner to Maxwell, July 23, 1952:

I have no story just now for *The New Yorker*, but a piece of information that I send on, as I think *The New Yorker* still takes a morbid interest in television. I was talking to an astrological friend the other day, and he was very happy in his observation that the television antennae (the thing on roofs) is the sign of the planet Uranus. Uranus is the disruptive planet, breaks up homes and so forth; and he felt pretty sure that people who fix that sign on their roofs will get more Uranus than they wot of. Another person in the conversation, recently back from your country, said that the antennae on US roofs is, by our reckoning, fixed sideways (our is an upright H shape). The astrologer said that this would make no difference to Uranus. He would know his own, whichever way up his devotees fixed the dedication.

I am glad to know an astrologer just now, because of my sensations on being turned out of the house of Sagittarius because of the effect of time on the procession of the zodiac. Instead of moving on to the He-Goat, so familiar and reliable, I belong to that unfortunate group of Sagittarians who are being shoved into the house of a zodiacal jump-up called The Serpent Bearer. This has unsettled me, and I am too old to move house, but my astrologer is looking up that Serpent Bearer for me, and soon I hope to know what sort of character I can expect to have, and which of my bones will be likeliest to break, and so forth. But meanwhile, I am not easy. It strikes me as only too probable that those born under a serpent bearer will be designed for a career of public philanthropy and good works, So far, I have not felt it; but if and when I know, shall I not be let loose into my true destiny? And won't that be very disagreeable both for me and every one I come into contact with?

Maxwell to Warner, July 29, 1952:

How nice to be welcomed home by you. We arrived on our front doorstep at one thirty last night, and the cats received us quietly and politely, but today it is different. Floribunda is communicative, you know— whenever something has happened to her, like being put out in the street by old Mrs. Delano or shut up over Decoration Day Weekend by God knows who, she has told Emmy about it for a solid day, coming incessantly to be held while she unburdens herself of all that happened and how she felt at the time, how she never expected to get home, and so forth, and today, Emmy said over the phone a few minutes ago, it has been like that only much more so even than usual and finally she realized what was behind it: Floribunda thinks that Emmy was shut up for a month and that somebody just came yesterday and let her out. And on that subject she had even more to say than about being shut up or put out in the street herself.

Maxwell to Warner, August 4, 1952:

Did you know that since you were last in America there has been a schism and you can have either custard ice cream cones, which are soft but do not run, or the standard hard kind that does? 24 flavors in Oregon. Emmy's little niece recites them, and it makes a very good litany.

Warner to Maxwell, August 4, 1952:

There is an astronomer called Hickey—a New Englander by birth—and a book of his has recently been published over here under the title *Introducing the Universe*. He has a piece about it, explaining how and why it is happening. You had better look it up for yourself; my reports of astronomical explanations are like the paths traced by the moon on the sea, wide and radiant, but you can't safely walk on them. He is one of those Jeans astronomers, with a passion to show one round in interstellar space; no doubt that is why he allowed his book to have that terrible title.* Every one blows on such people, and as you see, I do too; but if there were not astronomers of works as well as astronomers of grace, I suppose we should still, the rest of us, believe that the sun went round the earth. Perhaps the best thing to do would be to write to him. In the mid-twenties, when we were all dining out on astrophysics, I had a briefly seen but striking theory about the quantum proceeding discontinuously, and wrote off to Jeans about it; and he wrote back most affably, saying that there were various things against it, but that one never knew, and he would bear it in mind. And Mr Hickey would feel nothing but the purest pleasure, I am sure, to get a letter that did not ask him about rockets and the moon. What a bore all that is. Fortunately, it is only a small affair, a few planets.

We make a wonderful variety [of ice cream] with blackcurrant jelly, it is a deep vicious mauve, the exact shade I used to see on highclass fallen women when I was young. I notice the recognising and awed start of recognition in any one of my generation to whom we offer our blackcurrant ice.

Shop ones here have air pumped into them, and are like ectoplasmic cream, and very nasty.

* The English physicist James Hopwood Jeans (1887–1946) was the Carl Sagan of his day, the author of such popular works on astronomy as *The Universe Around Us* and *The Mysterious Universe.*

Warner to Maxwell, August 19, 1952:

We have Niou's younger brother staying with us, on approbation— Niou's approbation. The first day was dreadful. Niou stayed out till midnight, sitting under a willow tree in the rain, fetched in by Valentine he threw himself down on my lap and roared like Othello. He developed a whole new tessitura to do it in, an octave lower than his usual voices. And instead of sleeping on me, as he usually does, he slept on my petticoat. If it had been possible to return the kitten the next day, we would have done so; but we were pledged to keep him over the week-end. Now they ramp through the garden in wildness and amity, but the kitten is frowned on when he comes indoors. But I begin to hope it may do. The kitten retrieves, is a natural born retriever. Throw an apple, he races after it, turns it over till he can bite the stalk, and canters back to have it thrown again. But only very small apples, he has not got the muscles for full-sized ones, though he tries them, for honour's sake.

And the other thing that has happened this week is that Valentine has burst into business, and has opened, not a shop but the room of indeterminined purpose that houses the piano and the sewing machine and the geraniums, for the sale of Victoriana and antiques. For her talent for finding sleeping beauties in mixed lots at local auctions has made the house so overcrowded that we must either unload or move into the toolshed. And today the most Transparent of our neighbours, so Transparent that she is the Queen's (to the best of my belief) second cousin twice removed, visited her and went away clasping six plated dinner forks, which she said would make a great difference to her happiness, besides several small objects which we shall later have a chance to buy back if we want to from her stall in aid of Poor Ladies. And pausing on the way out she admired Niou and the kitten, and asked how many other kittens she had had—but I do not think Niou heard this, and if he did, he seems none the worse.

Warner to Maxwell, September 27, 1952:

Did Emmy's Lachaise fire properly? I can't think of a more agonising constraint for the artist. It is bad enough to put one's dear cake in the oven. I suppose dramatists suffer next worse. But at least, the dramatist can get into the oven during rehearsals. I remember a dress rehearsal of *Heartbreak House* when Shaw bounded on the stage and became a young girl. He was infinitely better at it than the actress; even when she had studied him, he far out-girled her. He had a tirra-lirra twirl of the waist that I went home and practised by the hour. I couldn't do it, either.

Warner to Maxwell, October 12, 1952:

You will be pleased to know that I finished my book [*The Flint Anchor*] on Friday, on the stroke of midnight. Five cats were present at the obsequies.

Now I am in that state when I can't remember a word of it—even the words I have suspicions of: I am going home this afternoon, and on October

30th I am going off with Valentine for a fortnight's perambulation in Shropshire. Charles 1st said that the view of the Severn from Bridgnorth was the loveliest in his dominions—and I want to see it again before I die (I do not propose to do this immediately).

Maxwell to Warner, October 16, 1952:

How lovely. And how kind of you to write and tell me. On the stroke of midnight, in the presence of five cats. I might as well have been there, it's all so present to me. Your not remembering a word of it is a very good sign, as are, of course, the others. It was like that with operas with me when I was young and loved operas. The corpses came out between the curtains and bowed and retired and bowed some more and it would be several days before I could hum a note of it.

The only news I have to match it is that we have booked passage on the *Liberté,* sailing April 10th. I have not yet told Mr. Lobrano, because it would present itself to him as a problem, which of course it is, but a problem that cannot be solved until next spring, at which time there will be no bookings. So here I sit, having taken the bull by the horns.

And the election is killing me. It is very strange—everybody whose brains or talent or principles I admire is for Stevenson, and everybody whose money I admire is for Eisenhower. Which outnumbers which is the thing. It is a pity you are denied the maddening pleasure of the Nixon television broadcasts. You might almost have made him up, so neatly does he fit every possible kind of irony. But he is, I'm afraid, a monster, which your characters never are.

It is not enough that you do not propose to die immediately. You must promise me never even to entertain the thought of dying.

Warner to Maxwell, October 21, 1952:

Liberté, Liberté chérie! Bless the boat...My mind will remain fixed on April 10th until you tell me the next date, the date when you come to this country—I imagine you will land in France. I hope you will, because of the smell. Arriving in Calais in 1949, seeing the ruins and the paper hangars, I

was saying to myself, O my love, my love, what have they done to you?—
and a minute later an off-shore breeze puffed me exactly the same smell.

I am in a fidget about the election, too. I would be easier in my mind
about Stevenson's chances, if there were some little scandal or dash of
blackguard about him. People with votes develop that odd mixture of
patronage and quixotism that swings them towards handicapped candidates, provided the handicap is louche or ludicrous. If Mr Truman had
been of godlike form and intellect, he would not have got in last time. Personally, I cannot endure Eisenhower; the man is perpetually in tears; even
for a military man, he cries too easily. Whichever way the election goes, I
suppose he will cry on Stevenson's bosom, and that must be a disagreeable
thought for Stevenson. I think I am giving way to national prejudice,
though. Public characters in this country are not supposed to weep in public, except about cricket.

Maxwell to Warner, October 29, 1952:

The governor has come and gone, and I find life much too quotidian.
On Monday night I drove our car in a torchlight procession in Harlem, and
Tuesday noon was all but trampled to death in a weaving mass of a quarter
of a million people in the garment workers' district, and that night failed to
get into Madison Square Garden, because it only holds 22,000 and a
hundred and seventy-five thousand Democrats came. While I was in the
garment workers' district, Emmy was at a Volunteers-for-Stevenson luncheon, and came home with stars in her eyes. He's adorable, was all I could
get out of her. Simply adorable. But Eudora Welty, who was at a table in an
overflow room, said that he passed through her room, on his way into the
big one—this is the Commodore Hotel—stopped, and said "I understand
that you are overflow. I'm very sorry you can't get into the big room," and
thereupon he got up on a chair (he's a short man, is that handicap enough?
Much shorter than Mrs. Roosevelt) so they could see him, and gave *them* a
speech. When he had passed into the next room, a woman sitting at Miss
Welty's table turned to her and said "I will remember him as long as I live."
New York City has fallen in love. Nobody does anything but talk about the
election. They tell each other, as if it were news, that Stevenson only has
to carry California, Illinois, or Massachusetts, figuring that he already has

New York and Massachusetts. No one really knows what he has, except the hearts of those who can read. I come upon politics late in life, as I came upon Europe, and with the same demonic intensity. I could not endure it if he does not get in next Tuesday. Planting roses, and covering old plants for the winter, I am going to get through the day somehow. I think, I really do think he is going to get in. But I wish you could have been in the car with us—Emmy and her brother, in the front seat, and in the back seat, Brian Urquhart, who is in the U.N., and his wife, who is American. We were standing in a doorway by the station at 125th Street when his train drew in, and a wonderful carnival crowd (made up in equal parts of terribly hand-some Society Members, terribly high-minded young people, and the usual inhabitants of Harlem, but fused, happy, friendly, their faces lighted by red flares) was chanting We Want Adlai; and Brian looked up and said there he is—Not where the chanters were looking, but on the back observation car of the train, looking down quietly, and smiling. The smile seemed affec-tion, rather than satisfaction, but I warn you I am not a trustworthy reporter. He passed through the rickety, filthy old station, got into an open car, with a police escort, in the midst of an ovation, and then the ovaters with one wild last cheer ran for their cars, which were parked for blocks under the elevated railway, and covered with signs and posters, and I found ours but despaired of the others coming in time, and there they were, falling in, and off we went, three cars abreast, with a river of people, black and white, carrying placards ("Cleaners and Dyers for Stevenson") all around, going, everybody going the same way, and the cars honking, and the band playing, and singing, and smiling, and Emmy's brother lit a flare in the front seat, and so we had a smell of brimstone and burnt wool (which for me will always be the true smell of politics) with us all the way to the Hotel Teresa. The speech, candor compels me to admit, was not up to the occasion. He kept talking about General Eisenhower—a subject of no interest to that audience. But when he finished, I thought surely he isn't going to stop, and all around me voices said quietly, and then louder, shout-ing, MORE. Last night's speech in the Garden was all jokes and gaiety, and wonderful, and it was even wonderful to be turned away. I heard some-body ask a policeman how many people were there trying to get in, and he said "I don't know. I never *saw* so many people!" And Emmy was lifted off her feet and hung on a No Parking sign, and people thought they were being routed into the Garden by way of a cafeteria, and we were a group of twelve; otherwise, between the horses and the policemen's legs somehow, by hook or crook, I would have got myself and Emmy IN. And twelve people, burdened down with fried chicken and bottles of wine, are no good in a crowd, so far as mobility is concerned. I must remember that if I am ever at the barricades, a sandwich in the pocket, and let somebody else provide the wine. And one of the twelve had a wooden leg. But to be there, to be alive, in the mild drizzle, was so lovely. New York is not the United States, and much depends on the farmers, who are not as susceptible to charm, or good speechwriting, or even, it sometimes appears, self-interest, as other segments of the population; but love is, God knows, never static—it must be going out in waves from this enlightened city. If Nemesis will only settle for small things, like the fact that the public address system didn't work for Stevenson's largest crowd, in the garment district, because the wires were trampled to pieces under the feet of the crowd. Do you think that Nemesis, generally speaking, is well-disposed toward a person who continually drops very good jokes, is small, neat, serene, bald, discriminating, dedicated, and fast becoming a great man? And brave? Brave as a lion. And not guilty of talking to Negroes in Harlem or to garment workers on 7th Avenue, or ladies in the Hotel Commodore? No matter what the audience, it's always the same man talking. I feel you know more about Nemesis than any other living person. I have bought two more $5 coupons, campaign contributions, just because things do seem to be going well—one for each crossed finger.

We are coming to England first, and I don't expect that there is anything the Maxwells don't like; barns, swans, cathedrals, avenues, Lord Curzon's bath, the Chesil beach . . . it is impossible not to be happy travelling. We will have two weeks. No time at all, all time's delight. Not a tour of the British Isles, though; just a sort of pretend poking around, sociable, scavenging—you know. As if we lived there, and could go see Anne Hathaway's cottage some other time.

Maxwell to Warner, November 5, 1952:

As it turned out the General was not in tears: With my own eyes and ears I saw and heard (over television) him say to the assemblage in the Hotel Commodore ballroom "I think you're sumpin!" I think we are in for four years of the human touch, and when I woke up this morning I thought

I couldn't bear it. Really. It was like a traumatic shock. But hatred has been helpful. I got very drunk last night and used abusive language to a number of Republican ladies and one or two gentlemen. The waste of four years in the life of a great man is insupportable, and probably will have to be supported. I am not alarmed lest the General, on his much advertised trip to Korea, be killed by a passing shell, blessing us with Senator Nixon, because I think the General is an ignorant hypocritical bastard, and sufficiently worthy, in his own right, of loathing. But it was not accidental, or the fault of the press, or unknowing, or any easily pointed at thing, though the number of guilty elements is large, and includes accident, the press, the Irish Catholics, Korea, the mothers of soldiers. The grasping, the ignorant, the simple minded are all complacent today. On the way to the station I had to make the car swerve so as not to run over a dead cat lying on the pavement, and thought I ought to go back and then thought of the train, and then, after a mile, turned the car around and did go back. The road to the station is littered with animals—now and then a fox, often a skunk or a woodchuck or a chicken or a squirrel—but seldom with cats. It was still there when I stopped, and I had to wait while four more cars passed over it, before I could move it to the side of the road where the person who was probably at the moment calling it would perhaps find it. Left in the road it would soon become two dimensional and unrecognizable. It was disemboweled, and soft and I think not very long dead. And it felt, in my hands, much calmer and at peace than I did. Emmy said I slept like a baby. I woke up with the daylight and the tears started running down my cheeks. The office is very quiet, and people avoid each other, the way they did when Mr. Ross died. I still cannot bear it.

Warner to Maxwell, November 13, 1952:

It is damnable. Nothing that I can say could make it worse. As I don't doubt our newspapers have misrepresented us as usual over your politics, I will say that so far I have not met any one who was pleased with the result and most of them were furious. The fury was non-political—just natural basic good sense; for he [Eisenhower] made himself very unpopular here, long before the election. He was considered to have no manners.

Our caretaking friend has done a great deal of useful work in the garden, including building a compost heap five foot high on top of the snow-drops. But she has built it so carefully and architecturally that I don't suppose it will be hard to remove. She has left a hairnet behind, and that I find harder to forgive. It is one of those morbid hairnets made of hair. Somewhere in the Bible there is an injunction about seething the kid in its mother's milk, and I think there should be something of the same kind against putting up live hair in dead. But she has had a beneficial effect on the cats. They did not like her as much as they liked us, indeed, I gather that they combined together to make her life vexation; and so as a result they are on the most amicable terms, as affable as two Abels—or two Cains—and Niou at last seems able to love his little brother even after sundown. Till now, he has become disagreeable every evening, and full of injurious remarks about kittens not being allowed to sit up to late dinner.

Maxwell to Warner, January 5, 1953:

I have learned that it is not the better part of kindness to tell writers what I think of a story submitted to this magazine before the editors have arrived at a decision, but I must say you put a heavy cross of temptation on me with "Uncle Blair." I could not and cannot believe that you wrote it for any other reason than to make me wildly happy. Possibly the editors take a less personal view of the matter, but they are not, in their own way, a bit less enthusiastic. Is Jeanie for adoption, do you know? Would she like a good home—two in fact? I have need of her.

Warner to the Maxwells, April 23, 1953:

Dear William, dear Emmy—and how pleasant it is, to know and endear you as a consort—when we got back yesterday the cats looked about for you, and said how foolish of us to mislay you so soon; just when we had got acquaintances, they remarked, that they could completely sanction and approve of. We felt much the same. It was shocking to be without you. We began to talk about how you will come back, and find that little house, or that apartment in a stately stone mansion, and be here long enough to be showing me things that *you* have found: rare orchises, and the most completely amiable toll-house. I see perfectly how it can be managed. My genius for interfering is already got to work, and all that is needed is for

William to become *The New Yorker's* Letter from England. It might be going too far to despatch Mollie Panter-Downes, so shall I arrange for her to have a baby?

Warner to the Maxwells, May 16, 1953:

A retired seaman with a grudge has made almost life-sized effigies of his daughter and the doctor, and hung them upside down in a tree. I wish to God you could see them, they are made of stuffed sacking, with short sausage-link arms and legs, and the faces are passionately painted in house-paints. There they dangle in the wind, with placards on their breasts, passionately scrawled in black house-paint. The daughter's inscription is a failure, he tried to be funny and obscene, and this was beyond him, but the doctor's is so fine that I got it by heart. *Pills is a defaulter to the Hipocratic Code. As he cannot heal the sick he torments the poor and needy.* What really happened is that the daughter, a middle-aged woman and the village schoolmistress, suddenly quarreled with her father, and refused to lie with him any longer. Pills was invoked, got into a moral altercation, and knocked the father down. The daughter has somehow managed to go to America, and the father, having tried to bring an action for assault and battery, and being told by the local lawyer that in the circumstances he'd better not, has fallen back on art. The daughter's effigy's face is almost as good as a Rouault, and to come on these creatures in their tree at the side of a lonely road over Toller Down, is to be shot headlong into the seventeenth century. It is one of these simple village communities, and apparently no one has complained, for the effigies have been there for the last ten days. It may be that they are saved by this being such a very law-abiding country, the tree is on the father's ground, and for all I know the police cannot interfere with what he hangs in his own tree.

Maxwell to Warner, after May 22, 1953:

I am so pleased that they took the story you read to us ["Shadwell"]. I felt constrained at the time about expressing my enthusiasm because I would not be here to influence the decision or share in the blame if it was an unhappy one, and I couldn't bear for you think, even for a second, that Mr.

Lobrano felt one way and I another. We do, once in a blue moon, disagree about a manuscript, but never about yours. How much energy is wasted in these elaborate structures of delicacy, but never mind, they bought the story. What my ears remember my eyes now read.

Warner to Maxwell, July 16, 1953:

I am so very glad to hear that the French novel [*The Château*] is lively and arching its back under your hand. I felt it was going to be crucial, that visit to France, a matter of life or death, and that you were at once right and reckless to go. I am thankful it was life. As for me, for the last two months I have been grovelling about in my novel, not merely pruning, but root-pruning, you never saw such a mess in your life. I wrote it under the impression that I was writing a narrative, good God, it is nothing but a Treatise on the Passions, most of it by Eliza Cook.

Maxwell to Warner, July 29, 1953:

And do you keep carbons of your stories? The corrections make me suspect that you don't, and if not, I implore you to change your ways. Manuscripts do disappear in the mails. When Carl Van Doren was editor of the *Century*, Elinor Wylie started sending installments of *The Venetian Glass Nephew*, and he started printing it before she finished writing it, and there was never anything but the one draft, since she wrote it in her head before she committed it to paper, and during those days that he knew an installment was in the mails, he was beside himself. No part of it was ever lost, but when I knew him, he was terribly grey-haired, and not much good for anything either. I blame it all on Elinor Wylie, who did have that streak of perverseness in her, apparently. Her ghost hangs around the MacDowell Colony. An unhappy composer [David Diamond], who felt he was being discriminated against socially, because of his silk scarves and sandals (and actually wasn't), saw her plainly, and in the middle of the afternoon. He was using her study, and afterward the help admitted that she was seen from time to time, red hair and all. But what a long digression. And is there a name in rhetoric for the device of proving your point by stating the opposite example?

Warner to Maxwell, July 31, 1953:

For the last thirty years I have been saving up the de Goncourt *Journal* for my old age. I have now broken into the larder, and find it perfectly entrancing. I follow Valentine about the house, telling her the latest gossip of 1874. What deaths, and what horrors! The vultures after the battle of Isly, who fed delicately on the eyeballs of the dead, and fell inebriated from the heavens. I feel as if I had fallen asleep in the cemetery of Montparnasse and were dreaming it.

Warner to Maxwell, October 4, 1953:

My old friend, Jane Ann, died the week before, all in a flash, and though death cannot close an inn when there is not another within sixteen miles of it, I rang up her brother thinking I would put off, and only changed my mind when he said, She had everything planned for you. So not to go there would have been an impiety. Life has never seemed such a fleeting thing as it did in that house, the same chairs, the same cut glass dishes, the stuffed fox and the prize curling-stone in their old place, the same brand of matches in the bedroom candlesticks, the same voices in the tap-room, the same smell in the early morning of the hills and the river outside and porridge cooking inside. Everything was so familiar, I might have been dead myself.

Warner to Maxwell, November 28, 1953:

I called my novel *The Flint Anchor* and finished it last week. I only hope it is not too finished. It goes very fast, and I am still feeling as if I had been put suddenly down on my feet after being driven all day at speed.

We have just come back from Theodore Powys's funeral. He died sooner, and with less misery than any of us dared expect, probably because he had made up his whole mind to it. I do not mean that he was resigned; but he was resolved. There was a great deal about the funeral that he would have approved of. To begin with, because of the lay-out of his front door, the coffin came out upright, as though it were walking out on its own volition, or rather, as though he were walking it out to its burial. It was a mild grey-skied day, the doors of the village church were open during the service, and while the parson was reading the lesson from St Paul a flock of starlings descended on the churchyard and brabbled with their watery voices, almost drowning the solitary cawing rook inside the building. The parson, an old man, and a friend of Theodore's, must have believed every word he said, and after the blessing he stood for some time at the foot of the grave in an oddly conversational attitude, as though, for this once, he had got the better of an argument.

Another parson, who was just one of the congregation, for some reason left his broad brimmed black parsonical hat on the threshold of the house, and a young black cat who presumably had never seen a funeral before— for he was a taking a deep interest in all that was going on, saw the hat, and very cautiously stalked it, approached near enough to give it one sniff, and then darted away with an I-don't-think-much-of-that-after-all expression.

Warner to Maxwell, December 3, 1953:

I expect you are already reading Virginia Woolf's diary. If not, do. It is probably all the better because so many of her vitriolic comments on other people had to be cut out. The other people would be in the way of what is the entrancing thing of the book—its picture of a writer experiencing writing. When you read how she craved for flattery and commendation you will understand how gratefully I lick up yours.

Warner to Maxwell, December 13, 1953:

I am sorry and ashamed that I do not also enclose a short story. The truth is, that not only is *The Flint Anchor* finished, I was to all intents and purposes finished along with it. I have never felt so tired, so emptied, so swept and garnished—and not the smallest little devilkin coming in to enjoy the void after any previous book. But I shall recover. Yesterday I even felt a sort of twitch in the machinery.

Maxwell to Warner, January 7, 1954:

I feel that we are less the owners of that exquisite book of *Scènes* [*Scènes de la Vie Populaire à Paris*] than the custodians, and how shall we ever thank you sufficiently? For that matter, I don't understand how you could ever bring yourself to part with it. No form of color reproduction yet devised could, of course, have duplicated the colors—especially the women's clothes. Even the brush strokes, which show when you tip the page—are French. I spend as much time thinking—following in my mind—the life of the woman (because I feel it was a woman) who colored the plates as about the plates themselves. She lives in a large room, an attic of an older and higher building than the immediately surrounding ones, with many children, and not all the furniture has legs. There is a particularly good sofa, Louis XIV, which sits directly on the floor. The swallows swoop under the window. The water she mixes her paints with has to be carried up five flights, and often, so that the colors will remain clean. Her back sometimes aches, from sitting too long, but while she is painting she is in the scene she is painting, she is elsewhere—on shipboard, *au cirque, au théâtre, dans la rue.* Her coloring is the best, and so she receives a small extra amount for each plate she colors. Her love is concentrated on the scarves. She has a friend who is a milliner.

What with one thing and another, including our conversation in the back seat of the car, whisking through the Dorset and Somerset landscape, I am at work on the French novel again, and intend to finish it—or finish what it is, because it is something, though it may not be exactly a novel.

Warner to Maxwell, January 15, 1954:

I have so many things to be grateful to *The New Yorker* for, and now another: that they brought out 'Uncle Blair' on the day they did, just in time to please Leonard Bacon.* His daughter wrote to tell me of his death, and said I was to know that 'Uncle Blair' and a letter had helped to make his last day a happy one. This I can believe, since he was so plainly a man with a cultivated talent for being pleased. I have never set eyes on him, but that does not make me feel less bereft. Ever since he sent me a copy of his translation of the *Lusiads* we have been writing to each other with perfect freedom and carelessness—very much, as he said, in the manner of a couple conversing at a masked ball. I feel that I am on less intimate terms with myself since I can no longer write to him. I suppose the word for him was Humanist: he was so packed with personal erudition, things he'd learned from tramps, old women, and stall-keepers in markets. Whatever knob one pressed, out shot a secret drawer with odd specimens of information in it, all in perfect condition, moose, Casanova, what you will.

* Poet who won the Pulitzer Prize in 1941 and published verse in *The New Yorker* as "Autolycus."

Maxwell to Warner, January 1954:

I don't know what I would have done—yes, I do know—if I had known that you and Leonard Bacon were in the habit of conversing through the mails. I met him, for the first time to talk to, last fall, at the Century Club, where it was my task to tell him that one of his oldest and best friends [the literary journalist Rodman Gilder], who was also a friend of mine, had sat back with his arm behind his head, to think about something and never finished the thought. He broke down, and then, in a manner extraordinarily like Cyrano de Bergerac, composed a wholly unsuitable obituary notice, though it would have served nicely for a bronze plaque, and then the two of us went off in a taxi to comfort the widow, who, so tangled is the plot, was courted long ago by Emmy's father, and when I left he left with me, and went to the Yale Club, and from the Yale Club he went, surely, to Heaven. But it would have comforted him—it would have taken his mind off his grief—because he was the most easily distracted man I ever met—to have been able to talk about you.

Warner to Maxwell, February 2, 1954:

Now I must turn my mind to something highly absurd. Paul Nordoff, the composer, did a cycle out of some poems of mine, for mezzo-soprano, the sentiments being of that sex. Now a tenor is longing to sing it, and thinks it will do just as well for him except for one line, which is,

the needle in the patch, the dedication in the song;

will I please supply an alternative to the needle? The needle is the expression, you see, of wifely devotion. Now, having thought of *the money in the bank* as the tenor's equivalent, I really can think of nothing else so close-fitting. But did you ever?

Warner to Maxwell, February 19, 1954:

I have been reading a book that enthralled me and I think it would enthrall you. It is a Larousse, of 1952, the *Guide des bons usages*. Everything is in it, how to conduct a wedding or a funeral or a bottle party, how to pick up meat and vegetables on your fork if you are eating in England, how to be well received in a Swiss house (Don't kiss hands. Give a day's warning. Wipe your feet thoroughly on the doormat. Take flowers—), how to tip Mother Superiors of boarding convents (in kind), how to—everything, in short. And among all the conventions that should be known and observed, some pieces of much humane good sense; after a winter funeral in the country, serve a very hot soup.

After I had finished it, it seemed to me that it mattered very little whether or no France had a government—it hadn't just then. I looked over the edge of the book and saw them getting on beautifully, never showing any sign of recognising people who happen to be looking out of their windows, not eating juicy fruits in railway carriages and serving those very hot soups.

Maxwell to Warner, March 1, 1954:

Do you know what has happened in the country? Some neighbors, city people, have bought the old house across the way and are afraid of the dark and have searchlighted not only their yard but ours, right up to our front door; to see the stars I suppose we will have to climb over the Lewissohns' hill. And as for trying to sleep on the porch! Modern life gets less and less worth living, is my solemn conclusion. Wherever you go there are always people.

Warner to Maxwell, March 1954:

How awful about those iridescent neighbours! I can't imagine a more exasperating calamity, coming back every night like a nettlerash. Do they know that lights attract Vampire Bats? Can anything be done by getting to know them, and trying to work on their humanity—or would this be worse than mutely enduring and loathing. Isn't it curious that science never invents antidotes? There is no means of spreading darkness, or of spreading silence.

Warner to Maxwell, April 2, 1954:

Yes, it is spring. Today Old Friday came to the door. Here is your water cress, he said, as if he had been bringing it every Friday. Where he hibernates during the winter is not known, and I have never got it out of him, but it is strongly suspected that soon after the autumnal equinox he commits some well-adjusted crime, and spends the hard part of the year in jail. He is a man of great enterprise and industry, he gets up very early and steals the best water cress from the beds in the Sydling Valley, and walks for miles to his faithful customers. He has a wonderful pair of leather gaiters, shiny as apples, and is the only person I have heard say Ma'am with the long A and sound natural.

Maxwell to Warner, May 1954:

Missing you, I realized that my collection was not complete after all, and I went up and down 4th Avenue one afternoon and came home with all the volumes of poetry except *Time Importuned*, which hasn't yet turned up, but will. *Opus 7* enchanted us both; I had read it in my youth, when I was too young to have a taste for the rhymed couplet, and Emmy never had. The earliest volume is of course a door opening upon what has always been a mystery to me—the origins of your prose style. It shows who you loved in your youth, and therefore, in part, who made you. Or so I imagine. Since I loved you in my youth, and therefore you, in part, made me, it has considerable familial interest.

Warner to Maxwell, May 24, 1954:

I have in the house my mother's copy of *Time Importuned*—fine condition, practically unread—and I am sending it off today. It has the most of the not-many poems I can feel decently satisfied with. By then I had escaped from the influence of the Carnegie U.K. Trust and had not turned the impetus of my mind to prose. Perhaps I should explain the influence. They gave us, the Tudor Church Music Committee, a machine for rotagraphing, and there were always a few redundant plates, spoils or photographers' duplicates, and I walked off with a handful of these and found their versoes most agreeable to write on, and exactly the size to be filled with a short lyric. So being as clever then as a waggonload of monkeys, I began to fill them, and wandered into one or two poems where I was more interested than clever. With £150 a year from the U.K. Trust and no acquaintances, I led an ideal life, with all London to walk in and at the end of the street a neglected branch, a neglected cul de sac, of the Paddington Public Library, with a repertory of invaluably dull and stuffy books, all smelling alike of some public disinfectant. For some one with a fair amount of ingenuity and no ambition, it was a paradise. Oh, those long stuffy summer evenings, full of melancholy and the sound of washing-up in the basements of cheap hotels!

Warner to Maxwell, June 3, 1954:

A package of the most delicious and gluttonous beef arrived yesterday, and could not have been more timely, as I began the day by inattentively cascading down the stairs on my back. I was bruised, Valentine suffered shock, the beef was exactly what we needed (no, I wasn't so bruised I had to apply it raw), and I dined in bed with the beef and FitzGerald's Dictionary of Madame de Sévigné, nothing could have been more harmonious and restorative. I won't say that he goes too far in disliking Madame de Grignan, why shouldn't he, if he wants to?—but I do think it a mistake to use the evidence of a Mignard portrait against the poor wretch, for have you ever seen a Mignard portrait that made the person look amiable? The beef was so delicious, you see, that I was prepared to think more tolerantly than I usually do about Madame de G. My own theory is that she inherited a considerable dash of her great-grandmother—a most estimable saint, but not comfortable in a family life.

Warner to Maxwell, July 5, 1954:

Raspberry leaf tea, if East Anglia is to be believed, will give Emmy an easy delivery. It is not official, but it is recognised in books on herbal medicine. It is slightly astringent and a stimulant, and according to Mrs Grieve, an authoritative Bible, 'should be drunk freely during parturition—warm.' I don't suppose Emmy will be allowed her little kettle, modern methods being so sternly exclusive; but as an evening drink during the autumn— unless it is excessively nasty—it might be worth trying. I share your con-

cern over Emmy, for the most natural reason in the world, because she is
such a darling; but not only do quantities and quantities of babies get born
every year, but a considerable percentage of them must be given birth to
by darlings; so, replenished with philosophy, we will continue to feel concern, and be very glad, on the whole, that Emmy's doctor is taking such
care of them.

I gather you didn't see the poor eclipse. We were feeling just the same,
the morning was cloudy, and anyhow the eclipse was being blown on
because it wasn't a total one. Valentine had to go to a junkshop at Stur-
minster Newton, the only place where Mr and Mrs Thomas Hardy were
happy together and therefore, as they didn't stay there long, rather a sad
one; and after that we drove our car into a field gateway and ate cold
sausages and cherries, and when I got out to shake off the crumbs it
occurred to me that I might as well look up to see how the eclipse was getting on. The cloud was just the ideal thickness, and we had a very good
view of it. The sun was silver, like a moon, and very much smaller than
usual, because of having its disk defined. And while I was watching, I had a
rush of astronomy to the head, and realised that the round shadow on the
sun was not a shadow, but the moon. There was the sun, here was me, and
that was the moon between us. For a few seconds I felt myself an inhabi-
tant of the solar system—a delightful and enlarging sensation. I daresay
Thoreau felt like that all the time.

I daresay you know that *The Times* demurely listed the eclipse under
Arrangements for Today.

Yes, I knew the remark about the wolves [from *The True Heart*]; indeed, I
am very seldom either astonished or disbelieving before quotations from
my books. They fly back into my heart like the scattered bones reuniting in
Donne's grand passages about the resurrection. I write so hard, you see. I
write with such intensity. You know *The True Heart* very well, was it the
first S.T.W. you read? How silly, how exasperating, I was in New York that
winter, guest-critic for the *Herald Tribune*, we could have met and had the
pleasure of each other's acquaintance that many years earlier. You know it
very well, but did you recognise the sub-structure?—it is *Cupid and Psyche*,
from [Apuleius's] *The Golden Ass*. I wanted to do some serious technical
study—to develop my wrist for narrative. So I thought I would write a
canto fermo, as one does in learning counterpoint. *The True Heart* is on a

canto fermo, and so is *Elinor Barley*, for which I chose a folk-song, by the sortes Virgilianae, from a collected volume; but *E.B.* was a slighter exercise, as the canto fermo was a much sketchier and undemanding affair. I was very happy when I identified Queen Victoria with the Winter Persephone. I stuck clues all over *The True Heart*—Rew and Grieve in the rectory kitchen, being ferried over to the island by Zeph, Mrs Oxey's peacock; but not a single reviewer noticed them. My mother was on it at once.

Maxwell to Warner, after July 13, 1954:

I rush home with your letters, so Emmy can read them, and then when I want to answer them they are not here. I did not guess that *The True Heart* was a charade, but then I never would. In me the quality of gullibility is not strained. It seems most remarkable, though, and on two counts. One, that the charade owes nothing in vitality to the original story, but moves always as though you had dreamed it and put it down, intact, on waking. Two, as a revelation of the wider than supposed (by me) sources of literary energy, I almost feel I shouldn't tell anyone about it, so as not to endanger the advantage you have over all other writers.

When we succeeded in getting to the country, at the end of the first week in June, I said sternly to myself that the French novel, which I have been working at on and off (though never uninterruptedly) for six years was a will-o'-the-wisp, a novelist trap, and should be abandoned. So it went to the attic, filling a rather large cardboard carton. All boiled down, it amounted to a hundred and twenty pages, and then fragments of things to come farther on, and then the ending, which was a series of codas, in the manner of, I'm afraid, Liszt. Well anyway, it went to the attic, and then I had a week off, and spent two days recovering from jury duty and excessive gardening, and then sat down in order to find myself happily in a more fruitful novel, or at least a story of sorts. This led to an intensive sorting of the books in the attic. When they were all grouped according to subject matter, in cardboard cartons, with the sides trimmed down, and the books spine upwards, so that, kneeling in the half light, one could read the titles, and the boxes stowed away in under the eaves, I brought the carton containing the French novel downstairs, pulled out the beginning, and rapturously fell to rewriting page after page. The joy of having a Folly, a true Folly to work on and improve, by complication upon complication, details

that can only be read upside down or in a mirror. How could I ever have
been anything but grateful for a project so after my own heart! so unlikely
ever to reach consummation! I expect the next six years to pass in the same
dream. Twelve years is all too little to spend on a Fragment.

Emmy is fine, but we have a woodchuck. He first ate his way right down
thirty feet of Emmy's bush beans, and rounding the corner, topped a few
beets. There was no hole, and I suspected him of undoing the catch on the
garden gate, but decided that there might just be room for him to squeeze
under the fence, in two or three places, so I put stones, big stones, in strategic places. And for several days there was no further damage, though he
was seen eating apples in the back yard. Then I thought but couldn't be
sure that more beets had been topped than I originally remembered, and
while I was brooding about this in private Emmy had an encounter with
the depredator inside the garden fence. A girl who lives on our road once
got so angry at a woodchuck who had ruined her entire summer's work in
one night that when she saw him she raised a very large stone and in righteous fury killed the animal dead. Very gentle girl she is, too. With this as a
guide and with several large stones handy, Emmy nevertheless couldn't. If
I'd had a gun, she said, I could have shot it, but not with a stone. Not an animal . . . So she said instead "Woodchuck, show me how you got into the garden." And he did. He simply passed right through, not under the fence.
Floribunda has often passed through the eye of a needle, while we watched
her, so this only mildly surprised Emmy. It surprises me, though. Who
would have thought that woodchucks were only fur, when they look so fat
and heavy. If there is anything still growing in the garden tomorrow afternoon, I will set to and line the fence with chicken wire, but one further
depredation that I forgot to mention. In France, in 1948, we ate ripe gooseberries with sugar on them, and it became one of our favorite desserts. We
have had it once this summer, and were about to have it again, but the
woodchuck ate them instead, spitting out the skins neatly. I could get a gun
but I don't know that guns and the excitable temperament go well together.

Maxwell to Warner, August 1954:

Fourteen pages from the end of *The Flint Anchor*, which came by special
arrangement of Providence, just in time to take to the seashore. All the
pleasure I promised myself all those months it has given me, and more. I

am, in fact, rather stunned by it. What it is like is going up to the attic of an old house and finding there, in the bleak light, not only discarded pieces of furniture but people—with cobwebs trailing from their foreheads to the nearest rafter, and not all their ways of thinking and feeling discarded by any means. Some—especially the feelings—appallingly familiar. Since you have made it all, you would, I feel sure, have been strong enough to have endured the Victorian Age somehow. I would have exercised the orphan's talent for getting out of uncomfortable situations by the side door—*Also William, son of William and Eva Blossom Maxwell, Born August 16, 1818. Died Jan. 27, 1819.* . . . What I also feel is that I have been reading George Eliot and Thackeray rewritten. The two ages, ours and theirs, so woven together that neither can deny the facts or the connection. But I do not wonder that you were exhausted when you finished it.

While John Barnard was considering his guilt, I reflected on ours, in coming to Maiden Newton at a time when you were so deep in a book, obliging you to turn your back on Anchor House for four days during which—but it seems to have survived. And looking back I realize that you were full of it, and that it reflected in your manner and conversation. Making me wonder what our visit would have been like if we had come during the writing of *The Corner That Held Them* or *After the Death of Don Juan.* The ending is so beautiful—and it was such a pleasure to read that bravura passage on the sound of the waves while looking at and listening to them. Another of the effects that I admired extravagantly was the reassembling of Julia's dressing room in the attic. And Thomas's defense of his honor by the statement "You believed me then," and his refusal to be innocent one more time. And all the Barnards are as real to me as my cousin Peg, who is capable of being quite like them, for the simple reason that she reasons like them. But also those extremely minor characters—Crusoe, for example— are so haunting—one never gets enough of them—and the minor minor one, who makes one unforgettable appearance, like Crusoe's wife and Minnie Cheyney's brother Roger, and even those who don't quite make any appearance at all, like Mr. Eustace. All so alive, so interesting. There is only one step further to go—Those terribly real people that exist only in Gogol's figures of speech, in "The Overcoat," or as offstage relatives in *The Inspector General.*

I have just been discoursing to Emmy on *The Flint Anchor* and the sea. What the book means to me is a morality play, with John Barnard as Everyman. The waves (his love) break on the shore (experience) and recede (in disillusionment) foaming. And in the period of disillusionment, the quality of life is in the ascendancy; things get better. Then a new wave arises, bringing with it the full force of the will that things should be different from the way they are, and immediately things get worse, for him and everyone else. Do you love him? Emmy asks, and I say no, but he has stature. You don't love Everyman. But you die with him. That is what I meant about the beautiful ending. No, it is just beautiful, quite apart from any authorial identification. Moving and beautiful.

Warner to Maxwell, August 29, 1954:

You wrote me a most gratifying letter about *The Flint Anchor*, and I ought to have thanked you for it earlier, and would have done so if I had not mislaid it in the bathroom. Now it has fallen out of *The Care of the Cat*, and I have read it again and like it even better. I think the first blast of praise is rather defeating, it whirls away one's susceptibilities.

But don't say, and never think, that your visit here was anything like an interruption. My danger is quite other, is to become undistractable; my preoccupation turns into a black and stagnant pool, on which my invention goes round and round, slower and slower, like a drowning fly. I am ready to believe it is physical, an auto-intoxication; and I know that if something distractingly agreeable did not come in time to break the spell, I should long ago have become incapable of writing anything. If I am caught like that with my next book, there will probably be a cable to you and Emmy and the new Maxwell, imploring you to come at once.

Maxwell to Warner, September 22, 1954:

Do you know I always believe implicitly in the places you describe as not only existing but being part of your life? Once read about, they remain intact in my mind, and I could move right into any house or piece of property you have ever written about. It occurred to me, on the train this morning, that perhaps you ought to have me insured.

Last night I took the dust jacket off *The Flint Anchor*, put the flap with your picture between the leaves, and threw the rest away. When I was a little boy, I used to notice the way women took their hats off when they decided —when they changed their minds suddenly and decided to stay. It was then and still is my firmest intention to keep them near me, and this was a form of ritual—I induced you to take your hat off, in short.

Warner to Maxwell, September 25, 1954:

I take it that the fourth room in the country house will be the nursery. I should like to contribute towards its furnishing, and I shall send you three small china prophets. My father had them when he was a boy, and was much attached to them, and I expect it was his fierce nurse, Tabby (who said of the very Caravaggio picture of Judith and Holophernes that she didn't rightly know who she was, but the one on the bed was Our Lord), who broke off the top of Confucius's hat. The other two are Mahomet and Zoroaster. They went to Cambridge with him, and at Harrow they were in his dressing room, along with an attar of roses flask and a small magnet. It pleases me very much to think of them setting out for a new nursery—or rather, your new nursery. Such a set of three rogues you never set eyes on, and I expect your son or daughter will learn a wide and Gibbonian outlook on comparative religion from them.

Warner to Maxwell, November 22, 1954:

I came back from London in a dazzle, having been asked to translate [Proust's] *Contre Sainte-Beuve*. Chatto has the option from Gallimard, but when it is a question of Gallimard that doesn't mean much. (Ignace Legrand had his novel sent back by them because he was heartless enough to write a letter asking when they would get on with it, and the letter arrived the same day as Gide died.) It looks perfectly entrancing; very little about Sainte-Beuve, and a great deal about the Guermantes, and sleep, and Paris, and Combray, and lilac trees. I feel as if I were just about to begin life in a series of magical caves, a Proustian Lascaux. There never was a clearer sense of perfect love casting out fear, for I accepted without even considering whether I could encompass it.

Warner to Maxwell, December 16, 1954:

I am having a wonderful amour with Proust. I feel like Persephone when frighted she let fall those flowers. Dear William, we poor authors don't know what comfort is. Just think—one can be interrupted, one can answer a telephone, cook a dinner, extinguish a fire, go into the garden to cut a cabbage leaf; and when one gets back, the thought is still there; one has only to find the place and go on. If you want to prepare a happy serene life for the new Maxwell, encourage it into a foreign language and let it become a translator.

Warner to Maxwell, January 1955:

The Suffolk *Oracle* told me nothing about colics; but old Dr Lander for whom I dispensed during a war-year, and who was renowned for his knack with babies, swore by dill—of much the same vintage as raspberry leaf. (How tranquil and distant those days must now seem when you sat drinking raspberry leaf tea!) Being a little oracular myself, I will go on to ask if Katharine spends enough of her time face-downward. However queenly, she is still a quadruped, and quite recently was a fish; and it is a great mistake to keep babies always on their backs. If you have her on your knee when you are telling her about Elaine the lily maid of Astolat

And that good man, the clergyman,

she will be able to wag her arms and legs with much less effort to herself than if she were lifting them upwards all the time, and most likely she will wag the wind out of herself and no more trouble with colic (but before she feeds, not just after, or she'll puke). You should sit on a straightback chair without arms, so that she won't knock herself, and your knees should be higher than your seat to cradle, so have a footstool. My mother being an ayah's baby spent most of her infancy face downwards, and till her dying day she never knew what indigestion was; and she practised the same method on me, and with the same carefree results. She used to feel very cross with the great masters of Christian Art because none of them knew how a baby should be held, and attributed every case of dyspepsia to some ass of a young mother wanting to look like the Blessed Virgin.

Warner to Maxwell, January 29, 1955:

See what lovely onion-skin you have sent me—and I am very grateful, and I will *prove* my gratitude before long, I swear it. Though I doubt if my next short story will be recognisable as mine, because yesterday I was sent (by its author) an article from the *Gazzettino* of Venice about me, in which I am referred to as La Townsend Warner. As a result, I have developed a compass of over two octaves, flawless throughout, the agility of a rhesus monkey, the legato of a swan, and a commanding stage presence.

Warner to Maxwell, April 1955:

Now that I have read it ["My Father, My Mother, the Bentleys, the Poodle, Lord Kitchener, and the Mouse"] in type I like this piece with its long coda in the relative minor. There is something very refreshing in such an odd construction—rather like those rooms where there is a window with a view above the fireplace, flames running upwards and birds flying past. I see, too, that my amour with M. Proust has taught me a much firmer footing in the long sentence, soon I shall be able to stop halfway across and put up an umbrella. Chatto and Windus do all that can't be done with Gallimard, I have nothing to do but enjoy myself. In spite of the French editor's claim that Proust could have made as good a critic as he was a novelist, he is really quite weak and superficial *except when his feelings are engaged*. There is a long section on Balzac in which after heaping up a great mass of lively clutter he begins to write about Balzac like Balzac describing a character in the *Human Comedy*. This is glorious—I think quite unintentional: a case of possession.

Maxwell to Warner, April 1955:

Do you know you have the most astonishing gift for bringing imaginary houses to life? You left me standing in that one where there is a window above the fireplace, flames running upwards and birds flying past. Has anyone ever written a novel about just a house, with no people ever in it? I regret the failure of that book with Kate's namesake in it, but at the same time am comforted that other writers' eggs—that your egg, really, because I do not care the same way about other writers, doesn't always hatch. It makes the failure of that French novel to go on and be a novel more acceptable. It dies of too many interruptions, but it was never a novel, in any case. For those I seem to have to go back to the Middle West, a place that, in its present phase, I cannot bear. And don't.

Dear friend, your advice is not advice in any ordinary sense—it is stories you tell us, that we in turn act out. There was a woman, you say, who was expecting a baby and drank raspberry tisane, and Emmy drops the letter half finished and rushes out to the garden. Our lives are enormously the richer for your suggestions, and also the three thousand miles that separate Emmy from her parents makes it difficult for them to fulfill this aspect of the relationship. They are a model to mankind, so far as not interfering goes, but one also likes suggestions, if they consist, as yours in essence always do, of going to the attic and rummaging around the boxes and trunks for empty bird cages, masks, and disguises. It is, in short, *releasing* advice, not the binding kind, and I only hope you have someone who gives it to you.

Oh yes, would you by any chance happen to know the name of the young Frenchwoman, of I rather think the late seventeenth century, who said to a bishop who was speaking of St. Denis's picking up his head and walking 9 kilometers, *"Monsieur, dans une telle situation, c'est le premier pas qui coûte"*? If you do know, I will reward you, by telling you, if you don't know already, about the death of Philip IV of Spain. But then you do know about P IV, I'm sure. Never mind, I'll make something up.

Warner to Maxwell, April 30, 1955:

Kate with her Shakespearian name is making a good beginning. I don't believe one can begin him too early. I can't even remember where or when I was first cognizant of him, but I remember falling into *Macbeth* with a wallop when I was about six, and how on Sunday evenings when my nurse went out to some sour little chapel and my parents went to church because their position expected it of them I used to go down to the kitchen where our kind Emily with time on her hands as Sunday supper was in the oven, the roast potato part of it, and the cold beef and salad in the larder, used to prance round the table with me, a mute witch, except for bubble-bubble.

I was so very slow in learning to read and then in a flash could read and did read everything that I think someone must have taught me the cauldron verses. I love them with as much appetite now as I did then. See that Kate learns them early. They are invaluable, and not only a private pleasure, but in social intercourse. A baboon's blood sets one at a great advantage among one's contemporaries—as Flora knew when she told her little brother that Nero was an angler in the lake of darkness. I hope you recognise *Ravenshoe* [Henry Kingsley's 1862 novel]. A most misbegotten genius, and never did anything right; but after Fielding he is the only, the ONLY English novelist with pace.

Warner to Maxwell, October 12, 1955:

Yesterday I did what I have dreamed of doing for years, and went to the Villa d'Este. We went in splendour, hiring our car and driver through the American Express, and got there so early in the morning that we had it all to ourselves, painted rooms, and cypresses and fountains, and gardeners snipping at box-hedges. I realised that such fountains come out of the same vein of Italian genius as the immense crystal chandeliers that fly like swans in the roofs of baroque churches and hang in a ladder all the way up the transepts of St Peter's. The water that falls in a fringed curtain from the goblet fountain is not so much water-works as water-sculpture.

Everything falls in our laps like ripe plums. We arranged to arrive at San Lorenzo fuori il mura at the same moment as a funeral—with such a hearse, gold angels all over its roof, and sitting on either side of the coachman in a glistening black cocked hat and black cloak. And a fat priest in his vestments came out of the first coach like an overgrown dahlia, and roared his way through the service with a speed only to be matched by the speed of the organist, who kept tripping him over with the first chord of the response, like a Rugby tackle. After that a sexton, equally brisk and efficient, tossed us and two stout travellers from Southern Italy into the confessio and left us to contemplate de Gasperi's coffin. After this rivetting introduction we all went for an affable walk in the Campo Verano, where the simpler southern gentleman was absolutely spellbound by the verisimilitude of a marble mattress (with a dead lady on it), and kept on poking his finger into its dimples with sighs of admiration. I thought the lady very fine, too, especially the lace on her nightgown; but he had eyes only for the mattress.

Twice over we have seen a double rainbow planted in the Forum, which should be a signally good omen. And the Tempietto is even lovelier than I expected it to be; and we live in taxis, and drink innumerable small black coffees, and visit several affectionate colonies of cats with mortadella. I am happy to tell you that the status of cats has gone up a great deal since we were here last. They have a great many patrons, and one of them, a dignified matron in the Marius colony, took a large slice of mortadella from the packet Valentine was holding, called up her special cat a mother too— and formally introduced us. They sprinkle the grass as brightly as if they were in a mosaic.

Warner to Maxwell, October 19, 1955:

We came home yesterday, to find that the well-intentioned woman to whom we had lent the house for her change of air had slaughtered my dearest geranium by leaving it out all night in a hard frost (she had thought the beautiful midday sun would do it good, and forgot the kindly action as soon as it was performed), had not liked to use the frig in case she damaged it, but inadvertently turned off the switch, so that when I came to open it the inside was like that hell of Dante's, I can't remember which storey it was on, that was a cold puddle and stank, had unearthed the caddy in which I keep our best tarry Souchong, and used it for making the gardener's tea, only she had to use more that twice as much because it was so pale otherwise, and hidden all the letters that came for us with such care in case it had really been a burglar she thought she heard going upstairs that it was some hours before she could be quite sure where they all were; so, dear William, by the time I came to your letter, the bitterness of death was past, and I learned that you, collective you, were not taking 'The Snow Guest' as calmly as a water-lily, the uppermost thought in my mind being that *The New Yorker* would never have forgotten my geranium, etc., nor made a milk jelly on purpose for our supper, either.

This is rather a protracted sentence, but not more so than I felt at the time.

Maxwell to Warner, March 1956:

The last month I have been too upset to feel anything, and only yesterday and today have begun to miss Mr. L.* It seemed simply intolerable that

I couldn't take your story to him in my hand, and I have done so many times before with stories of yours, and toss it on his desk and say, "This one's for you to enjoy." The other editors all concurred with my opinion, which I conveyed to you without waiting to find out what they thought, knowing in advance that they had no choice but to concur; but he shared with me a special love for your work, and it may please you to know that the only book he ever borrowed from me and failed to return was one of yours. I had to go out and buy another copy, smiling to myself at human frailty, and the indirect ways admiration expresses itself.

* Gustave S. Lobrano had died of cancer on March 1.

Warner to Maxwell, September 20, 1956:

If you order the October number of a paper called *Mademoiselle*, you will find a long section of my Proust translation. The Gallimard USA agent (who like everything to do with that august firm moves in a mysterious way) put it there, where it looks rather odd and somewhat of a pelican (I have just seen the foundry proofs) among young ladies exchanging brassieres and tearing out their eyebrows; but I cannot hold anything against him, since it is coming out next month, nicely in time for you to read it aloud to Emmy (Take deep breaths). And when you have read it, when it has sunk into you, you will begin to understand why I have been so bleakly silent and unproductive for so long; for with this amazing cauldron to stir, scum, and as my French cookery books says, adjust the flavourings of, I have had my hands and heart full—apart from the exasperating fact that as I worked on it it seemed to me that I was getting better and better at it, so I was continually going back on my tracks to revise, recast, and titivate.

Warner to Maxwell, November 6, 1956:

Styles and signatures are a queer business. 'Here's William,' I said to myself, about halfway down the first column—and for the life of me I can't say what touched off the recognition—nothing verbal; more like the way one recognises a painter's work, a depth and play of textures, a warmth and stillness, as if you were hatching it in the same way that Chardin's pictures are *couvés*. It ["The French Scarecrow"] is a lovely story, especially in the way that nothing is propelled. It all sits on the narrative like the narrative's feathers.

Maxwell to Warner, February 20, 1957:

As you will see from the attached form, the quantity bonus begins at four. If you were really to set to and write stories for a while, there is no telling what glorious, extensive, and stately checks I might not be sending you. It is one of the few regrets of my life that I haven't so far managed to make you rich.

Warner to Maxwell, April 23, 1957:

Using the toilet seat is the first step towards literature. I learned to read off the Bromo carton—'succeeded after long experiment in combining the curative properties of Bromo-chloratum'—when you've cleared that fence, the world is before you.

Maxwell to Warner, July 25, 1957 [cable]:

I PERSONALLY THINK YOU HAVE HAD THE MOST BEAUTIFUL LIFE ANYBODY EVER HAD

WILLIAM

[His reaction to "Wild Wales"; Warner told Emily Maxwell that the cable "delighted the telephone operator almost as much as it did me."]

Warner to Maxwell, September 24, 1957:

Today began with a friend of Valentine's saying: 'I can't stop. I've got to pick apples, and the hurricane is coming at twelve'—as though it were an aunt, Valentine remarked. I think you may like this example of how the English, though they have no pound, and no future, and no nothing, are prepared to deal with any hurricane that comes along.

However, it did not; but yesterday, even before we had been told what to expect, was a very queer & alarming day: classically still and brooding, and both our cats with staring coats, and slinking about at my heels in the most woe-begone way. They have a wonderful talent for being Cassandras, only unfortunately they cannot prophesy with any explicit detail, so we never know whether to expect floods, lightning, or visitors.

Maxwell to Warner, January 8, 1958:

The twelve-month quantity bonus period expires on January 21, which doesn't mean that we wouldn't take a relaxed attitude about a story that appeared a day or two later, but I also had another idea, rather immoral, and it is this: If the story is there, like one of Michelangelo's half-carved angels, and you haven't quite recovered the momentum to deal with it, you could send me the manuscript of the rough draft, which I think does exist, doesn't it, with instructions not to read it (or to read it if that would be in any way helpful to you) and I will fire it back to you but then be able to say truthfully that it is a revise we asked for of a manuscript that came in before the deadline. Of course I could simply lie, without any paper being committed to the mails, but that would involve you also in the performance, and spoil the aesthetic line. All this comes of my being so grasping for you.

Kate said yesterday morning as I was dressing her, apropos Brookie's being my delight (Kate is officially her mother's delight) and she, Kate, my treasure, "Will I be your treasure when I am old and tired and dead and gone?" and I said, after a moment's reflection devoted mostly to who was going to be old and tired and dead and gone before whom, "Yes, I think you will be," and it seemed to me, by the way her face cleared, after a moment's reflection devoted to she didn't say what, that she was reassured by this statement.* Probably she knows better, but had heard what she wanted to hear. And of course it is true, or would be, if it were possible. Do I remind you of Act I of *Rosenkavalier?*

* Brookie is the Maxwells' younger daughter, born in 1956.

Warner to Maxwell, January 24, 1958:

Talking of defying prejudice and fashion, a friend of mine in Glasgow has just moved into a new flat and I asked her to tell me what she saw from her front room window. She gave me a detailed list, and one of the objects in view is a Gas-Ometer. She can also see a railway line, a signal box, part of the main road to Edinburgh (the signal box has some lovely fires burning in it), a football field, a steel works, the two chimneys of a new power station, and a railway cleaning shed. 'And at night when the lights go on in the windows and works and roads and railways, I put our lights out and look out of the window and think it is like fairy land.' In short, at last she has a room with a view. You can see just from this what a heavenborn letter-writer she is.

Warner to Maxwell, January 26, 1958:

But why do I *invent* stories? It must be pure self-indulgence. For today I was at one of the Dorset Music Society concerts, and behind me were three ladies who at every break in the programme went on with their discussion as to the best method of drying flowers and foliage for winter decoration. Two of them were traditionalists, and used glycerine, but the third had a way of her own, far more satisfactory, and costing nothing. All she did was to put boughs and seed-heads of delphiniums and bracken—at this point Louis Kentner coughed, and began the *Bénédiction de Dieu dans la Solitude*—'Well, where *do* you put them?' the two glyceriners inquired. 'Just under the carpet, and *tread* on them for two or three weeks.' 'Really! I must try that. What do you think that last thing was. It didn't quite sound like a scherzo. And is that all you do?'

Warner to Maxwell, January 28, 1958:

Writing a libretto, I have discovered, is very much like supplying the electrical underpinning for a car.* It is not a chassis or an engine but it is part of the works. One would think that as one so seldom hears the words in a properly sung opera, it would do just as well to write Bah and Bo. But the words must be right to make the singer sing as the music needs him to sing, while at the same time they mustn't distract him with technical troubles, he mustn't be asked to sing *eee* on a high note or *Goethe* on a low one. It is great fun to do, and soothing, because one knows from the start that it can't be perfectly right. There are no perfect libretti, I fancy. You would think that a Mass would sneak by, wrapped up in its hoary venerability, in fact it is most unsatisfactory, and Henrician composers like Taverner, who wrote really splendid flamboyant masses, used to leave out great chunks of it, just as Paul does with me. And if one considers Bach in B mi. it is really a great foaming spouting prancing dolphin ending in a very small tail. Bach would have appeared to have thought so himself, since he throws his hand in with that *dona nobis pacem*. Beethoven facing the same weakness in his libretto, got out of it in a noble scramble into drama; but his scramble galloped him right off the course of liturgy. I myself thank God for it. *Il me faut une fin splendide pour Félicité*, in fact.

Upstairs sits poor Valentine, while an Earnest Soul is Pouring Out its Troubles to her (I can hear them wallowing on, like greasy water going down a half-choked sink) and here sit I, delightfully pouring out my opinions to you. But it has been going on too long. I cannot any longer rejoice in this disparity, I must go upstairs and cheerfully proffer the Soul some tea. At the mere sight of me she will loosen her hold, with any luck she won't even want tea.

* Paul Nordoff had written the music, Warner the libretto, for an opera based on her
Mr. Fortune's Maggot.

Maxwell to Warner, February 1958:

It will not surprise you to hear that when I was a little boy I preferred the company of women to that of men, and so I knew before I had turned the page of your letter how she dried those flowers. Emmy's aunt by marriage had extraordinary winter bouquets of dried flowers by that technique, but she also seemed to have access to extraordinary weeds and grasses. We had a lump under our bedroom carpet all through November and December and in mid-January Emmy produced a two-dimensional bouquet of autumn leaves. Rather pretty, they are, but it is capable of a good deal more refinement, the method.

Warner to Maxwell, February 22, 1958:

It is painful to me to disagree with Mme de Sévigné; but I cannot like her daughter. I saw her once, at an exhibition of French portraits—done up in cherry-coloured bows, and far too many of them. I saw her across the room, and took an instant dislike to her, and it bruised me to discover who she was. There are times when I see that story as part of a dreadful pattern, on the lines of the Harper's Song; *denn alle Schuld rächt sich auf Erden* ["For here all guilt brings expiation," Goethe]. Mme de Chantal, the grand-mother, entering her convent across her son's body when he threw himself down across the threshold to prevent her (which is counted heroic virtue in her sanctification, but seems like hell-bound egotism to me) and Mme de Grignan made into a sort of instrument of vengeance on the mother who was loving and innocent; and too often compelled into being tiresome, too, because her love got such an inadequate response.

I sometimes toy with the idea of doing a small study of Mme de G.'s constitution; how chocolate got into her blood and enraged it. But it wasn't only at that date that people had remarkable constitutions. The other day I heard of an old lady who for years has been subject, off an on, to her blood running the wrong way. She could perfectly register when it was doing so, and went to bed, the only expedient, till it reversed. Not an old cottage woman, either, but a most respectable well-brought up old party, who painted holy-water-colours.

Maxwell to Warner, February 1958:

And I do hope you are serious about doing a study of Mme. de Grignan. She was of course like her grandmother. (I was in my middle forties before it occurred to me to wonder if I was like my father's father, who died just before my elder brother was born, and I asked my father, who happened to be visiting, and he said "Of course," quite crossly, though how he thought I should have known I can't imagine, since he had never pointed this out, and I am rather a freak in the family, so it would have been helpful to know.) I cannot bear to think about that poor young man's feelings as he got up off the floor, dusted himself off, and realized how little he mattered to his mother. I suppose he was never young again.

Warner to Maxwell, March 9, 1958:

I am glad I provoked you into re-reading Hardy's poems; the pessimism is his own, and so, I suppose, is that 'abounding in things petrified' acquisi-tiveness for odd words; but there is a ghostly tinkle of Tom Moore's guitar, which he must have heard in his youth, preserved in the lyrics of Thomas Haynes Bailey: 'When other lips', and 'Scenes that are brightest', and 'She wore a wreath of roses', trilled through by Emma Lavinia, and bellowed out by the crack singer in the village public-house; and when he was old, it came back to him, and he made ravishing use of it. His poems *set* very well. Do you know Ben Britten's group of them?

Maxwell to Warner, April 9, 1958:

I have often thought that we were meant for each other—you to write to me and I to read you—and this naturally carries with it what a loving parent bestows on a child—the color and shape of his eyes, the texture of his hair, the stamp of his characteristic expressions. I never consciously sat down and said to myself "How would Sylvia do this?" because I would have to see you plainer than a child sees a parent to do that. But every sentence I have ever read of yours gave me immediate intense pleasure—at the world as you saw it, and at how you said what you were saying—the intense pleasure of appreciating a personal style. The influence has long since gone into my bones. And to have you feel that I am a credit to you is enough to bring tears to my eyes.

Warner to Maxwell, April 19, 1958:

I don't understand how you and Emmy ever tore yourselves away from Provence; I don't know we shall, either.

For instance, at Gordes there is a *crêche animée*. You drop 20 fcs into an angelic collecting box, the angel bows his simpering face, the lights go on, a musical box plays, and a procession of *santons* begins to file round the Holy Family. Everyone in the village is there, the miller, the truffle-hunter, the shepherdess knitting her stocking, the waiter from the inn, the chasseur with his long gun and hopefully enormous game-bag, the lady who has just bought a fine large chicken, the farmer with a duck under either arm—they all have the right faces, are perfectly dressed to their parts, and are about 18 inches high. They go slowly round, even making a little turn inwards towards the Holy Family, who pay no attention, being entirely taken up with admiring the baby & entertaining The Magi. You must bring your daughters to admire them, it is all the charms of a circus, and all the consolations of a pastoral.

I am sure it is as you say, & that our ingredients were cast into some slow-simmering alembic to work out into this harmonious arrangement of the Aunt of my Nephew, the Nephew of your Aunt. Nothing could be more agreeable, could it?

Warner to Maxwell, August 11, 1958:

Here is a story ["A Question of Disposal"] about some detestable charac-ters. It should also be a moral to parents not to provoke their children to detestability. Or it could be construed a study of heredity. The queer thing is that, like God, I have a sneaking affection for them. *For he knoweth they are but dust,* is how Holy Writ accounts for this phenomenon.

Warner to Maxwell, August 26, 1958:

Yes, please, may I have a financial statement from Mr. Mason? I wish to gloat over it. And when there is a gigantic cheque added up for the Kirbys ["A Question of Disposal"], I would like it; but there is no hurry at all, any time between now and October. Is it very inconvenient for *The New Yorker* to carry this hoard of mine? I like to have it to repose my mind on, partly because Valentine's abject family are behaving with what seems to me the utmost stupidity over a family property which consists almost entirely of mortgages—the kind they pay, not are paid. They are now raising another loan to pay the interest which secures the income they get from the prop-erty itself. It seems to me that in a couple of years they will be bankrupt; and it is then that I look forward to flashing out like a wicked fairy, and brandishing my dollars in their faces with remarks on the lines of Yah!

I really don't know why I should bore you with all this, except that it is best that you should know the full baseness of my character, and the vipers I coddle in my bosom.

I broke off there to get lunch, and turned on the one o'clock News, and heard that Ralph Vaughan Williams was dead. A fortnight ago he was here, talking of the continuo he was making for the *John Passion,* of the *Wedgwood*

Ode, of how, after Brahms's death, the executors found a little notebook headed, Good Second Subjects. And, the conversation turning to what one choose to do given another life, he said in the manner of a man who knows what he's talking about, I shan't be doing music. I shall be being it. He was partway to that, anyhow. Ursula, his wife, said, Ralph always dreams music; but the other morning, a most amazing thing, he said to me, I have been dreaming of a large yellow cake with sultanas in it. And that afternoon they went out to tea and there was a large yellow cake with sultanas in it. There they sat, he so glorious and she so happy.

Maxwell to Warner, September 1958:

The peach tree has its first crop, of white peaches that taste like nectarines. The roses are about to bloom once more, and they'd better hurry. The cloud compositions are the best in years. And both children have had their hair cut, which always has the effect of putting them in quotation marks for a few days.

Maxwell to Warner, October 1958:

There should be a symbol on the typewriter for a sigh and another for a deep sigh, from the heart, and one for the wringing of hands. What I need now is the third—because it lies so well within the province of possibility for you to turn this ["Part of the Story of Timmy Yates"] into a story that *The New Yorker* would want, and I remember all those other times when I tried to act as a go-between, not greatly to your advantage. Suppose I just tell you what we think, and let you decide what you feel like doing then.

Maxwell to Warner, after November 17, 1958:

That cold went, and my chest is as happy and free as a seashell, at the moment, so I cannot believe I shall ever have another. But if it shows signs of becoming habitual, I will ask you to procure some anti-Bi-san and a doctor to administer the injection (I don't suppose they fumigate doctors as they do bulbs at the customs, and there is so much more reason to, I would think) since American doctors are so perverse, about suggestions from patients. I have never yet succeeded in finding one, not even one eighty years old, who would enthusiastically assist me in the matter of doctoring myself, or even repeat their own past successes, when you remind them of them. "Oh?" they say. "What was that, do you suppose? And it worked, did it? Well, I have no idea what it was..." and start writing out a prescription that they won't remember about the next time.

The first week we were married, Emily filled a bushel basket with my prescriptions and emptied them into the garbage can. I was too horrified to protest. And said to myself, well, in time, I will get them all refilled and replaced. But never had occasion to, or even to try to, since it turned out that they were one and all specifics against the lonely celibate life.

Maxwell to Warner, December 30, 1958:

Someone gave me a copy of a paper-backed one-volume edition of the journals of the brothers Goncourt, and I am beside myself with pleasure over it. Every night I get through one page, and then sit and hold it, all of it, in my mind, with rapture. At such times, knowing, alas, that it isn't true, I say to myself that all I ask of life is the privilege of being able to read.

Warner to Maxwell, January 6, 1959:

Yes, the de Goncourt *Journals*... what rapture; and you and I have both been well-starred, coming to them rather late, so that one knows many of the people, has thought them over, formed surmises and conclusions; and then one meets them in the journals, contemporarily, they come out of the great picture à clef where they have been heads and numbers, 1 V. Hugo, 19 P. [Puvis] de Chavannes, they come out as they were, complete in every everyday detail, smelling of tobacco, smelling of sausage. And as well as this, counterpointing this, is the unintentional portrait of the Goncourt brothers. I am especially devoted to the pages where the servant Rose is discovered to be the fiend in human form that one might expect to inhabit that horrible little den on the top-floor. It is the best story Maupassant ever wrote.

How scantily we would exist if it were not for 19th century France. I realised this all over again the other evening when a local boy came to consult me about becoming an artist (I hope he may. He had got some promising faults). He is the son of the local builder and decorator, he has never been outside Dorset, barely outside Maiden Newton, he has seen nothing except reproductions and the pictures in the Dorchester art shop which he took a firm breath and assured me he didn't think much of. He talked about Cézanne and van Gogh and Degas and Picasso as if they appeared familiarly to him in visions every night.

Warner to Maxwell, February 4, 1959:

We have had another flood. It roared all around us, but just didn't get in, only some watery pawmarks under the back door. It happened about midnight, and was mostly gone by the next day. The old lady who lives on the hill above us told me today how she looked out, and saw the moonlight shining on the water, and the village all lit up with the lighted windows of those who were afraid to go to bed. She said it looked quite like a Carnival.

Maxwell to Warner, February 12, 1959:

I have every hope that Mr. Shawn will think as highly of your immoral story ["On Living for Others"] as I did. I divided my pleasure between watching how serenely you threaded your way through all that esoteric musical terminology and observing the niceness with which you had superimposed an essay on a story.

This morning while I was typing with concentration, Brookie suddenly touched one of the releases, the carriage shot out from under me, I roared at her, and she went and knelt like an Arab under the dining room table, with her face against the floor, and would not accept the apologies that I, also kneeling like an Arab, with my face next to hers, sincerely offered. It is the first time I realized that the typewriter is a sacred object.

Warner to Maxwell, March 3, 1959:

You must think of something else for me to bring you back from France, for you will get my RSA [Royal Society of Arts] lecture anyhow. They bring out a Journal with all the season's lectures in it, and that is what I propose to send to you, for it is always profitable to have a lucky dip, and the RSA, preserving its 18th cent. views on Art, goes in for the useful variety as well as the artful; so you will be able to learn a great deal that is extraneous and unforeseen, Habits of crocodiles, Improvement of turnips, and Rheology, or the science of the plastic flow. I asked the secretary what rigid flow may be, but as the lecture hadn't yet been given, he was imprecise.

Maxwell to Warner, April 10, 1959:

Think of me, on the day that is dedicated to the muguet, having a hunk of calcium cut out of my right shoulder, at Harkness. It is not serious. Two days in the hospital. But when I gardened I couldn't sleep afterward, and I have to garden. We are all fine again. Emmy is going from school to school, to see about entering Kate in some kindergarten next year, which means that we may be living in a city apartment during the week and the three winter months, and using the little house in the country weekends and in the summer. The school problem has caught up with us, or is about to. How I rejoice that I will never go to school again. Middle age is the only time one ever has things the exact way one wants them, and a hunk of calcium in one's shoulder is a small price to pay for it.

Warner to Maxwell, April 13, 1959:

I am sorry that Kate is leaving Eden. I went to a Kindergarten myself, for a year, after which I was expelled as a bad influence. And I can still remember the rapture of the first day—making rows of blue blobs with a fat brush and readymixed Pr. Blue in a little gallipot. But this palled—quite soon—and nothing replaced it. It did not even replace itself, which it came round again a week later. That was the end of my formal education, after that I went to classes from time to time, and had a governess who taught me masses & masses & masses of Wordsworth. But in those calm days the state did not require female children to be educated, we grew up like flowers of the field, playing duets & speaking a very little French, and occasionally hounded through the Church Catechism for the Confirmation Stakes.

It is my belief that no one really & rationally enjoys school. The unanimity, the rhythmical tum ti tum of mass action & mass endurance, may beguile the young into thinking they are engaged in something they like; & then there is the thought of every day bringing one nearer the end of term; but I doubt if it goes further than that. It is a conscript experience. No one would naturally go to school. (Perhaps a few Sadists might, for the joys of baiting their teachers & torturing their juniors.) At Harrow there were those awful school songs, about what a splendid rollick it all was, or else about how regretfully you'd look back on those days afterwards. Balder & Dash, those old Saxon deities. There was also an invigorating moral one, about early rising, with parables from nature, how

> *delicate things on feet and wings*
> *Are busy finding work to do.*

Warner to Maxwell, May 5, 1959:

I think you wanted to hear nightingales. This [Brittany] is where you should come for them. They sing all night, not in ones & two, but in bands of nightingales as far as ear can reach. Our hotel is on the outskirts of the very small town, beside the River Dronne, & the nightingales live in alleys of poplar & aspen along the river bank and in all the surrounding woods, no doubt, that stretch for miles and miles between us and the view from Montaigne's tower. Which we did not inspect, as it is preserved in the fearful château built by the 19th Cent. descendants. I cannot stomach preservations. Things should survive, or fall away, but not be preserved. Instead, we smelled his air, delicious, & looked at his views, and came on here.

Maxwell to Warner, May 1959:

Now I know where to go to hear nightingales, and it is more comfort to me than you can possibly imagine. I am all recovered from the operation, can make splendid figure of eights in the air with my right arm, and have been at work for a week. We have also found an apartment in town, so our worst worry and deepest uncertainty is behind us. It is at No. 1 Gracie Square, but we probably won't be living there before some time in September. It overlooks a little park, named after Carl Schurz, who, Webster says, was a German-American statesman and orator. All I know about him is that he had a talent for getting parks and high schools named after him. Beyond the park is the East River, and the Triborough Bridge, all of which we can see since we are on the eighth floor. Kate's kindergarten is three blocks away, and Gracie Square is a dead-end street one block long, run-

ning between East End Avenue and the river, at Eighty-fourth Street. Do
you think you could find your way to it, with these directions?

I hadn't been in a hospital since I was in college, and am glad I had a trifling little operation like this one now because I will know later if surgery
is waved in front of my nose enough to say no thank you. It is not natural
to be operated on. They cut things that aren't supposed to be cut and it
hurts. The whole thing is a mistake. I will go to Saratoga Springs instead,
and take the baths and massage. But it was only mildly uncomfortable, I
was home in three days, and am fine. It hardly kept me from the office, and
it didn't keep me from gardening. I gardened with my left hand, impossible
though, as you quite rightly pointed out, this is. The only thing that is
more impossible is not to garden at all. For some reason the purple lilac has
ten times as many blossoms on it as it ever had before, and we lost a big
apple tree. It just got tired, and, loaded with its own white blossoms, split
down its whole length and hanged itself on its own cabling.

Since I don't know where you are, and don't want you to be worrying
about you, I will write you at home, and see what happens. Maybe you will
see this letter when you walk in, and read it standing, with your hat on
your head, while Valentine goes for the puppy and the cats. If so, welcome
home, and in any case, my love.

Warner to Maxwell, May 19, 1959:

We got back yesterday evening, but I couldn't read you in my hat as I
would undoubtedly would have done, because you were still accumulating
at the post-office. You arrived this morning, with a great flump as the postman cast down the mailbag in which he had brought the accumulation. So
instead I read you wearing a breakfast tray.

I am thankful you have escaped from hospital, and can swing your right
arm, though what a pity you could not pay the first fruits of this fine resort
by whacking the surgeon.

I am so glad you have found a flat, with amenities by Carl Schurz. I
could find my way there; though I think when I was last in New York it was
mostly palisades, rattlesnakes, & catalpas. New York grows so quickly. I
wonder how long it will be before you are doing a little furtive pruning in
that park.

Warner to Maxwell, June 17, 1959:

THERE I broke off, and went to a performance of *Murder in the Cathedral* in the Greek theatre at Bryanston School. The theatre is in a wooded dell. Every summer they give a play, acted with all the brio of English boys, supposedly so stiff and tongue-tied (and last night Becket's sermon was breath-taking, and the four knights bitingly modelled on local conservative speakers), and every summer I am forced to the conclusion that Greek audiences must have been midge-proof. There was a young woman yesterday displaying her lovely brown young shoulders, who cried out after the first act that she would give a penny for every dead midge delivered to her.

Maxwell to Warner, September 1959:

I cannot think how I didn't tell you about my stomach except that I must have expected you to know without being told.

But about my stomach—since March 14th I have been at war with it, until I more and more feel at war with myself. From expensive experience I saw how excellent all your advice was, or most of it; the part that I hadn't yet tried I am trying. One of your curries I am sure would be salutary. And when I was vacationing at Martha's Vineyard I ate two smallish broiled lobsters without hearing one word about it from my stomach afterward. But then when I came home and started shaving and dressing and rushing for the eight-fourteen, I went to dinner at Alfred Knopf's and spent a week of torment afterward. As I say, it should be your curry. I suppose the reason I didn't tell you is that it coincided with your departure for France and I thought it was a mere indisposition, instead of what I now realize it must be—anarchy in the soul. Of course if I had gone to Brittany with you and Valentine . . . but I didn't. After floating through a series of doctors, I found one who was not a stomach doctor and stayed with him. He is a cancer specialist, and such a nice man, and he keeps telling me what I care most about hearing, which is that it isn't cancer, and encouraging me from his own experience with the tiresome state, and prescribing a drug called probanthine, and cancium, and this and that. For about ten days, I think I am really getting well, and then I stumble. But it is really three things, a nervous stomach, diverticulitis, and colitis, and the easiest cure for one is not the best cure for the others. In those pills is a tiny amount of pheno-barbital, which I begin to think is irreparably changing my nature. Instead of over-reacting to emotional or in fact all situations, I don't react at all. The children fall and scream and I listen for the sound of Emmy's foot-steps, instead of leaping. I could walk through blood without thinking whose blood is this? It is not natural. And of course, during this time, Emmy has had to furnish an apartment, get the children off to the beach and back again, and us moved into town. I don't know how she has man-aged it. I don't think she does either.

Your raising your eyebrows at two bathrooms makes me realize how long you have been out of the country. The bathroom is no longer the dividing criterion; the last statistics I saw showed that there was a bathroom for every man, woman and child in America. In order to be luxurious, you would have to have two—one for morning and one for evening, or perhaps one for Sunday and one for every day. Cars aren't the dividing criterion any more either. Too many cheapskates are driving around in Cadillacs. Motor boats are. The Hudson River, Long Island Sound, the Connecticut coast, the Jersey coast—the waters have blossomed. Unless you have a good-sized one, you aren't really holding your own in the matter of conspicuous waste.

Warner to Maxwell, September 16, 1959:

What an unholy trinity to house. I am sorry for you, and sorry for Emmy too. She will be thankful to see you in your new flat, away from commuting, and protected by those nice solid silencing walls. When Valen-tine has had colitis, the nerves from her ears plunge straight into her stom-ach. Did you know that cold ham is sovereign for colitis? So is pasta, only it should be fresh, that lovely floppy pasta that one can buy where Italians buy it. It was old Thomas Horder who put Valentine on to ham and pasta. I expect he calmed many royal stomachs with it. Oysters might apply. They are almost as digestible as water, and extremely nourishing. I have twice saved cats with oysters, and your affinities put you among the cats. But I am sure mood is as important as food, perhaps more so. *When I came home and started shaving*, you say. Why not grow a beard, and rid yourself of one responsibility? One can sometimes find the answer on one's periphery, some fret that gets lodged there. Have you had your eyes tested? Are your shoes too heavy—most men's are; could you work standing at a lectern instead of sitting down? Dabbling one's feet in water, salted or pined, anything that stings, is very good for the nerves; so is massage at the base of the scalp. Both redistribute one's vitality and call it off from preying on one's centre. If you could bring yourself to believe your doctor, prosaically and not just thankfully, when he tells you you have not got cancer, then, when after a spell of being better you stumble, you wouldn't think you were stumbling into the pit. But what's the use of prescribing belief? All I know of it is that it doesn't come with prayer and fasting. Perhaps the likeliest climate for it is inattention, a little wholesome neglect. One thing, though, weighs on my mind. William, have you a Doctor Fell? My father's nervous stomach was brought about by a Doctor Fell, a new-come headmaster at Harrow, a dank, pious, fidgeting man, whom he had to see a great deal of and couldn't stomach. Phenobarb is no answer to Doctor Fell, though ratsbane might be, *if you could give it to him.*

I'm afraid I assault you with a great deal of advice, but it would be worse if I were Elizabeth Segar. Elizabeth Segar came into my life about three weeks ago. In the last decade of the 17th century she wrote down a quantity of cookery and medicinal recipes in a stout parchment-bound book—oh, such rag-paper! cuttle-fish coloured—and after two glances I bought it. She spells hash, harsh, and vermicelli, balmajelly, and calls for two civil oranges, and a recipe for dolce de leche is headed Spanish Pap. And the proceedings for A Soope take up a quarto page and end by throwing in two fowls, for lagniappe. One of the medicinal recipes remarks, Take 600 woodlice. What industry—and what exactitude!

Maxwell to Warner, September 29, 1959:

Your letter arrived safely at Gracie Square, giving us both immense pleasure, and spurring me on to a rather drastic action. I stopped taking any medicine. I am no worse for it and possibly a little better. Emmy was terribly taken with the idea that a beard would solve everything. Unfortunately I don't really have the makings of a good beard. Only of a rather wispy Van Dyke. I think if I were to finish something it would amount to the same thing in the end.

The summer is lingering on, and when I stick my head out of the window of a morning, and see the river swathed in its mists, the lights pale, and the smoky sunrise, I think not even when we were staying in the Palais Royale Hotel Beaujolais have I had such a scene to awaken to. There is some sort of hospital far up river that has the outlines of the Castle of St. Angelo, and there are the bridges, and the river itself, and in the early morning, Brooklyn looks like London seen from the top of St. Paul's. I keep thinking we must have a party, with 5–7 A.M. on the invitation.

Maxwell to Warner, October 1959:

We are in a kind of island ourselves now, only it is air that flows around us. It is still warm, still summer in New York, with the windows open and the nights sometimes breathless, and occasionally a wind comes up, forcing us to close the windows and warning us of storms that are coming down the East River this winter. Emmy has discovered that from eight stories up you can tell exactly how much money people have, the people who walk down East End Avenue. It's quite true. You can't see whether they are happy or unhappy, kind or selfish, stupid or clever, but you can see their financial status. It is simply a matter of getting far enough away from them, apparently. In a dozen different ways, it shines out. On the other hand, you can tell if the dogs are happy or unhappy, kind or selfish, stupid or clever. The poodles are way ahead, on all counts.

Maxwell to Warner, October 22, 1959:

That rash throwing aside of all medicine paid off. I am so much better I can stand to look at myself in the mirror when I shave in the morning, and Emmy said yesterday, mournfully, "Your face is back. I never thought I'd see it again." Ghastly pale, puffy, cadaverous, awful. Well, I am three quarters well, I should think. I eat with a certain amount of care, and show no interest in an occasional flicker of stomach-clutching, which, if one is not interested, proves to be uninteresting, and unimportant. Also, since we have moved to town, life has become so much easier in every way. And I have the noble river to take my mind off myself, and fill my mind with pictures. The other day I was sitting with my back to it, reading, and seagulls flew across my glasses, reminding me of that story of yours which has a mirror over the mantelpiece that reflects the outdoors and the sky—do you remember?

In a book I had as a child there was a picture of a girl on a stairway, rather grand the stairway, and she was in costume, and the title under it was "Josephine's Twelfth Night Ball." It was an illustration for a story that had been torn out of the volume, and so, ever since, Twelfth Night has had a dreamlike frustration about it for me. Like getting on a train, as I did last night, with large heavy clothes hanging from coathangers, one in each hand, which I had to hold high while boarding the train, and which made finding a seat more difficult, and the discovery that the train was going in the wrong direction all the more maddening. I spend I cannot tell you how much of my sleeping life on trains, missing trains, trying to get off or on trains, and if I am fortunate it is a boat train.

Warner to Maxwell, October 27, 1959:

I am once again semi-married to Proust. But this time with a substantial bolster between us. Chatto and Windus want to perpetuate the Scott Moncrieff translation before copyright runs out, but they also want to emend it and bring it into correspondence with the new NRF text. And, thank heaven, to retranslate the last volume entirely. They have got a young man called Andreas Mayor who for years has been noting Sco. Mo's slips, and he will do most of the work and I shall titivate and throw in any corrections I have also spotted. He is translating the last volume, and I, like Lady Gregory, am to put the style on it. However, this has not started yet, as he has gone to Pakistan in a bus—which is, of course, a highly fashionable thing to do. I presume the buses charge up and down the Khyber Pass. So if you have got any emendations or captious critiques, from now on is the time to mention them.

Maxwell to Warner, November 1959:

And I am delighted that you are to do something about Proust. I have been needing something to make me able to read it all straight through. Since I was twenty I have been reading at it, in one language or the other, but never once have I gone the whole course. Looking for the work of your hand is just the thing. If you had a hundred lives, one of them I would ask to be spent in redoing the whole damn thing, since, as you know, I am not an admirer of Sco. Mo's. Long winded people weary me more every year. Since you have only one, this arrangement seems admirable. It will leave time for stories and novels and letters to me.

Warner to Maxwell, November 2, 1959:

Here—*ex ore leonis*, between one visitor and the next—is a story.

I would feel very lank & uncorroborated after writing something if I did not know that you would soon be reading it. I love this boy ["Youth and the Lady"] as a cat loves her tom kitten.

Maxwell to Warner, November 9, 1959 [cable]:

WE ALL LOVE YOUR BOY TOO

WILLIAM

Warner to Maxwell, November 22, 1959:

While you are getting a stereoscope, we are playing with a tape-recorder, a small Grundig, equally of course a period piece. Valentine manages it as M. de Guermantes managed the stereoscope—a slightly solemn domestic diversion. When I heard myself played back, a casual remark about ears for music and eyes for measurements, I was instantly persuaded *that I was dead*. To be there on record, preserved like a fossil, made me feel completely posthumous; and I am in two minds about my existence still. Later, when we have grown cleverer at the distance-intensity ratio, we hope to get some very fine recordings of our cats singing for their supper. Valentine meanwhile has recorded the *Gloria in excelsis deo*, in order to examine her Latin accent.

Your cable about the Young Naturalist ["Youth and the Lady"] was extraordinarily nice to have. No one has explained why it is that certain creatures of one's imagination should call out these parental loves & solicitudes. I am sure it is not a moral reason, and I don't suppose it is a rational reason either. Something obscure and fortuitous like genes and chromosomes, I daresay; as if some of the things one composed were heirs and inheritors, and others just foundlings left on one's doorstep that one has given a name to and done one's best for. How embarrassing it would be to bring up such a foundling and see it, week by week, developing a stronger resemblance to one's grocer, say, or one's bank-manager. This must often have occurred in the past, when people lived out their lives in the same little town, and had no cheap means of transport.

Maxwell to Warner, November 27, 1959:

It is one of the pleasures of my life, that your stories come directly from you to me. So close does it bring us that I feel as if I could reach out and take the pages as you add the last correction, bunch them together, and decide that it is safe to let go of them. Since I know the room where all this happens, it seems really that it does happen. And of course once, in effect, it did happen, with "Shadwell." If we could literally do that, and if we could exchange perennials, at the time of digging them up and separating them— no, even that wouldn't be necessary, if I had a ring out of the Arabian Nights, because I wouldn't, after all, want to be a pest, and as a neighbor I might be. Though I think even that is unlikely because it takes time to be a pest, and I have as little free time as I have hair on my head. The thinness of the thatching seems to amuse Brookie, who loves to point out to me how little there is. If it were anyone else I would be cut to the quick, but not with her, not with those big brown eyes and starfish hands and passion for talking. "Would you like to trade me for a Daddy with more hair?" I asked, while I was dressing this morning. "Yes," she said, teaching me a lesson.

Warner to Maxwell, December 12, 1959:

I waited to answer your letter & to thank you for the boy & his cheque because I hoped to have the glad news—glad for me, I mean—that I had another story coming. But it miscarried; looked me in the face one morning & said, 'I'm dead, you know.' So now I write both late and empty-handed.

Indeed, I wish you were a neighbour. You would never be a pest, I assure you, and there would be so many things we could exchange besides perennials. Slighter things, annuals, no, diurnals. Today, for instance, I was sent a post preliminary which said: 'This essay rings with truth and plausibility.' I would run across the meadow with things like that. And a week ago I would have rung you up about midnight to say 'William, look at Sirius.' You wouldn't have minded getting out of bed, Sirius was so extraordinarily brilliant just then. It was one of those occasions when one sees a star *in* space instead of just *on* it.

We could also share the mellow pleasure of joint valetudinarians — what a word, I thought I'd never come to the end of it—you are losing your hair, poor William, and your daughter would trade you for an Esau.

I hope Brookie isn't lacking in normal sexual instincts of domesticity. My mother's father was bald, and it was the delight of his daughters to polish him with silk handkerchiefs. But you are not ripe for polishing yet, of course: only for mathematics, which is not a normal sexual instinct. Though I once heard an interesting semi-folk song called "Neath the Willow Dig My Tender Mother's Grave', which had a rollicking Willikins & his Dinah kind of tune, & a great many verses, one of which, as sang from memory, went

> *Oh!— (long howl) there's no friend like a Mother*
> *And you'll never feel her loss till she's gone.*
> *Every hair on her head then is missing*
> *And is mourned by a daughter or son.*

Which just shows what Folk-Art can do. Never at a loss.

Warner to Maxwell, December 17, 1959:

One of the pleasures of London was meeting Laurie Lee. His book, *Cider with Rosie*, is doing uncommonly well; it is his first success, & he is so unaffectedly cockahoop that he is like a rather small tom kitten that has just killed its first rat. It is lovely to see anyone so spontaneously, ebulliently, modestly enjoying success—for there is real modesty in openly admitting the enjoyment. If he comes to New York, as he may, may I give him an introduction to you? He is a most heart-warming tom kitten, & sensitive to the whisker-ends.

Warner to Maxwell, February 16, 1960:

You are always right, even when you praise me. I remember that when you wrote to me about *By Way of Sainte-Beuve* you said that I used one word when Scott Moncrieff used two. Since Christmas, I have been putting this to the test, for Chatto & Windus are considering a revised edition of *Remembrance of Things Past*, and want me to have a hand in it, if it hatches. So I have been enjoying myself very much, toothcombing *Combray*. All the raptures of the chase without having to stir foot. Grown up in piety towards S.M., I am now much taken aback to find how he doodles and twaddles, and how unabashedly he interpolates. He is a sailing vessel with the wind in his sails, he is brilliantly supple and spanking, but when the wind fails, he flaps, oh how he flaps and staggers.

Maxwell to Warner, February 1960:

One snowy night as I was walking East from Madison Avenue I came on the bookshop, and the double defenestration was still in the window so I went in and tried to buy it.* The man who runs the shop said that he couldn't get to it till he changed the books in the window and would I mind waiting till next Thursday. So I paid for it (very cheap it was) so nobody else would get it and went home and came down with a cold and two weeks later as I was walking East from Madison Avenue I remembered about it, but didn't pass the store, so I started looking earlier the next night, and to my horror came to a dusty pane of glass with the sign stuck to it: This store for rent. This filled me with doubts about the future and the past, for about a week, and then one night as I was walking East from Madison Avenue, one snowy night, I came to the bookstore (as unstable as Aladdin's palace it is) and went in and got the picture, which perhaps from staying too long in the window was brittle, or perhaps from being old; anyway, as the man started to roll—no, I started to roll it, because it was a windy evening, and he said no, let me do it and so he was the one that tore it, not me. But I brought it to the office, where it stayed several days because my father tried and tried and could not cure me of procrastination, and Frank O'Connor viewed it with interest as we were going over some galleys, and said he knew about the incident it portrayed, and I begged him to tell me but all he would tell me, with the gentlest of smiles, was "I think they were Protestants." After that, Miss Rachel MacKenzie, whom, if I am ever run over by a truck, you must ask to have as your editor, remarked that she did not see how I could stand to have such a thing around, and to spare her feelings I called for an office boy at last and it was dispatched to you. You will note, as I did finally, that it is really a triple, not a double, defenestration. And please do not treat it as anything more durable or keep it around longer than you would something I picked up on the beach and sent to you. It is not a nice picture. But if I had seen it as a child, it would have figured in my autobiog raphy if I weren't an autobiographical novelist and so had deprived myself of the delights of writing my autobiography. Speaking of which, I am reading or was reading the most deadly book about Yeats, by an American professor named Richard Ellmann. No conversations, no anecdotes, no descriptions of what he wore or had to eat. He could just as well have been a certified public accountant. *No astonishment.*

My head was turned by what you said in re the S.M. translation of Proust. Could it just possibly be true that I am always right, I ask myself, and then in the person of the person who is always right I have to tell myself No, alas, it is not true.

I appear to the only person in New York City who was moved by Camus' *Caligula.* The little girl who said Nobody ever feels sorry for wolves [from *The True Heart*] was a distant cousin of mine, and I felt very sorry for Caligula, and was entranced by the beautiful play that Camus had written about him. The production left something to be desired—that is, there were stairs and steel struts, and I felt sure that in Paris it would all have been done with cheesecloth and some of those acute-vanishing-point backdrops that I once saw at a school children's matinee of *Phèdre*, and a packing-box or two. But there was an air of considerable moral disorder, even so, over the whole thing, largely by having the Roman soldiers' armor cover up what for practical reasons could have been left bare and leave bare what for practical purposes should have been covered. One slash and they would have been slit from navel to chin, but their cheekbones were well protected and one had the feeling that they were horrid and inhuman if one could only see what they looked like. Caligula was horrid, I suppose, but very human, in that he objected to growing old and dying, and in general I felt I understood him like a brother, even though he went to extreme lengths to dramatize his emotional distress. I don't need to, is the only difference. In itself growing old is sufficiently distressing without having to poison, strangle, or rape anybody. This is perhaps because I was delicate as a child, and had to drink iron through a glass straw, and take cod liver oil and maltine in its pure uncapsuled state. Anyway, I was interested to read, in Suetonius, when I got home, that he did die saying "I am still alive," poor man. Camus's Caligula is more sympathetic, though. And what a pity Tacitus's got lost. It would have been so interesting, I feel sure. I met Janet Flanner in the elevator and asked her what it was like in Paris and she said "Gérard Philippe was very beautiful" and went off to meet somebody at the Algonquin. "Look in the Paris letter for 1946," she called back. There was nothing about the staging, Camus's *Caligula* struck her as "a futile, Forum *Hamlet*" (I always thought Hamlet pretty futile, really, though it never kept me from caring what happened to him) and there was nothing about how beautiful Gérard Philippe was. It is possible that he got more beautiful with time, but equally possible that you never can really find out anything by poking around in old magazines. The way to find what the past was really like is to invent it. Right?

* The Defenestration of Prague, which began the Thirty Years' War. Maxwell recalled that the picture depicted "throwing the victims out of an upper story window to their death. On the left was the very large window, the three men were struggling not to be thrown out of it, but no doubt were."

Warner to Maxwell, April 3, 1960:

Whoever was throwing out who, I am impartially delighted to have it—in fact, the uncertainty improves it. Only the other day I was thinking how valuable it would be to have a compendium of Christian martyrs: not only every Christian variety, but those non-Christians whom the Christians martyred, too. Done from earliest times, and arranged as far as ascertainable in chronological order, it would be a very interesting book. Each copy could be sold along with a sturdy lectern.

Did I tell you about our garage's cat? When it was a kitten, it was such a spitfire and pest that they called it Dante's Inferno. Then it grew older, and its character improved, and they thought it wrong that its past wickedness should be perpetuated, so they changed its name to Daniel. Then it went and had kittens. 'So now it's Dante again.' Dante, in short, was an Italian girl who kept an inferno. She is black all over, a charming cat, and loves lying on flowers.

Warner to Maxwell, May 29, 1960:

Now I must tell you something quite sublime. Two nights ago I had a blazing row on the telephone with Valentine's elder sister who for years has been telling us how much better it would have been if we had done as she advised and whose blood I have for years been languishing for. Well, I quenched that thirst; and when I had landed my last blow I said—'I won't go on; or I might lose my temper. Goodnight.'

Maxwell to Warner, June 13, 1960:

I have asked the bookkeeping department twice for the report on your earnings, and it is promised for tomorrow. I think they are embroidering it in petit point, with an appropriate motto, which is fine except that they would have done well to consult you about the motto.

Maxwell to Warner, June 1960:

I am not sure—I have so many times almost written it, and so many times composed the sentence in my mind—but I think I have not mentioned the fact that I finished, last Friday, the manuscript of a novel [*The Château*]—the one we spoke about, shooting along those country lanes, or perhaps it was out in the open, with a view of Glastonbury Tor, but it was, in any case, behind Emmy's and Valentine's backs, in the month of April, in the year 1953.

Maxwell to Warner, June 22, 1960:

Here are some new galleys ["On Living for Others"]. Most of the queries are matters of style, and you mustn't feel bullied. I have conveyed the queries about musical terms out of a sense of duty. I cannot imagine you mistaken about them, though there is always the possibility of a typo. I await your comments with my usual eagerness. Once Auden returned a poem in galleys with the comment "I think you people are batty," and it was only by the merest chance that I saw the remark. Think if it had gone unread into the files.

The children have reached the stage where it is like looking at flowers. Will they ever be so beautiful again as they are this second, I think. Highly demanding works of art is what they are. And smelling like honey bees.

Warner to Maxwell, June 24, 1960:

Your letter gave me the greatest joy and reassurance. I have so often thought of that novel you spoke of, in the month of April in the year 1953, and at times felt considerably gnawed—or as Valentine says, gnawn—by the reflection that if you were writing it, I was taking away much too much of your time. I am thankful that it survived my vampire kisses.

How weak & glorified you must now be feeling. When you had finished it, physically finished it, drawn the colophon & squared the pages, did you walk out of the room backward? Seven years of one's life, squared & colophoned, is something one can justifiably regard with awe.

I remember that conversation very well, and how you grew slightly pale & how I nearly cried out, 'No! Don't tell me!'—because of *Never seek to tell thy love*; and it can be a dangerous and a chancy deed. But you did. And I have been a sleeping collaborator ever since, & now you write to tell me it is finished. The next time I am in Somerset I will mention it to a hedge, and leave the birds to disperse the news elsewhere.

Maxwell to Warner, July 7, 1960:

Your blessings arrived on the most beautiful shade of moss green, and have been sinking in slowly until today, when a suffused softness took possession of me—the softness of allowing myself to believe that it is done, that it is all right, that I wrote what I meant to write. Anybody that wanted to could take me by the hand and lead me right through the looking glass.

Warner to Maxwell, late August 1960:

I hope you took back Leonard's [Woolf's] first volume because you are going to review it. I was slipped an illicit advance copy, and I am still under its spell. As a revelation of a good character, a character consistently, electedly good, what a noble ease it maintains; no whining, no striving. If Moore [the philosopher George Edward Moore] had influenced no one but him, I should still be convinced of the excellence of Moore's method; though I fancy Moore was lucky in the material, for I suppose it would be considerably easier to teach ethics to someone who had never had a sense of sin. Dear Leonard, whom I don't know well, though I love him dearly. When I *think* of him, I feel a certain awe, but as soon as I am in his company I feel perfect freedom.

Maxwell to Warner, October 4, 1960:

Mme. de Pompadour died last night at bedtime (Miss [Nancy] Mitford's, I mean; she doesn't seem to agree with any other evocation, but persuaded me, nevertheless. And to die in the act of making a *mot* of such excellence —who could not have loved her, even if they had never seen those crossed ankles and that elegant high instep) and I am at a loss where to settle down next, in French history. You wouldn't consider doing a biography just for me? Of anybody. I am not in the least particular so long as it is you writing it. I discovered, with a sense of shock, reading Rilke's letters, that he had stayed at the Hotel Paris Dinard, and probably in the very room that we stayed in, and this led me to the obvious conclusion that the tiny hotels of Paris must have, at one time or another, held all the artists and writers who have ever lived; not a linen cupboard that shouldn't have a plaque beside the door. And all anonymous, forgotten. Like Modjeska in California, without the excuse that it is, after all, California.

Maxwell to Warner, October 12, 1960:

Laurie Lee turned up, as you prophesied, and I was enchanted with him. I felt that we had played together as children.

Warner to Maxwell, October 20, 1960:

No, Mme de Genlis was the governess to the little boy who eventually became Louis Philippe, alias M. Poire, the last King of the French. She was born of a somewhat down-at-heels flighty provincial family, she was taught to play the harp and to say her catechism, she harped her way onward and upward into court circles, and became the mistress of Philippe Égalité, Duc de Chartres and then d'Orléans. She had an insatiable talent for improving people's minds, and her own. When she wasn't practising the harp, collecting a mineralogical cabinet, writing little plays, and planning improvements in industry, she was teaching other court ladies about astronomy and spelling. Philippe É. made her governess to his daughters, then to his sons. She educated them from head to foot, from religion to gymnastics. She plunged them into cold baths and took them out in the streets of Paris to become acclimatised to the common people. She was a prig and a fidget, and her memoirs are only accidentally amusing (though they contain the hermits who lived in a forest supporting themselves by making silk stockings) but she is a fascinating picture of that immediate pre-Revolution period, riddled with incompetent good intentions. In a way, she is for that period what Chateaubriand is for the post-Revolution. She has all the common sense and intellectual enterprise he hasn't, and none of the passion and poetry.

And 'qu'avez-vous de mourir si souvent' was Mme de Sévigné, to Mme de Guitaut, who had been at death's door, and recovered, and then relapsed before her friends' congratulations were dry on their lips. (It's all right. She got well in the end.) When I have told you that if one wants to be knowing one sounds the s in Genlis, I will leave off being like Mme de Genlis. I cannot think of a more natural lap for your head to be in than Sévigné's. You must often encounter mine there. Her charm is quite inexplicable except on the hypothesis of genius. If any other woman went on talking as she did about that great lump of a daughter, she would be intolerable. Did I ever send you my poem about M. de Grignan? He too had a point of view.

A Bore is at the Dore. Alternatively, A Baw is at the Daw. I must go.

Warner to Maxwell, November 3, 1960:

Your letter came just in time to save me from cutting my throat. I had taken a great deal of pains to construct a delicious lunch for a friend of Valentine's she wished to honour. He ate it as though it were hasty pudding & said that animals had instinct which in man was replaced by faith & reason. I was washing up the remains of this defeat when you came in and revived me. I am now able to take comfort in the thought that there is a great deal of the apricot mousse left over—and that quite a lot of my instincts have avoided being replaced.

Warner to Maxwell, November 25, 1960:

I think there should be a border of acknowledging buttons round the dedication of this next book of stories. It has now moved from *that* to *this*, as I mentioned it as a possibility to Chatto & Windus, who are being rather materialistic. The thought of the dedication spurs me on. It will be such a pleasure to dedicate a book of stories to you, dearest William.

You write so beautifully about your daughters and I would like to think that you would write more than in letters. It should be recorded at the time, for when a girl child reaches puberty, she gives herself a shake and all that kitten-fluff and kitten-airs are gone, gone! Mine is a ruthless sex.

Re-reading 'The French Scarecrow' in the *Collected N.Y.* I thought, William is the only person who pleases me where Turgeniev pleases me.

Maxwell to Warner, December 6, 1960:

When I was a little boy I was sometimes stunned with pleasure, and I thought I had lost the faculty, but it seems I haven't. First the book of short stories—the very thought of one of your books being dedicated to me is enough to make my head feel that it is about to fly from my shoulders. And then you mention Turgeniev casually. I had to sit down, in order to finish the letter.

Maxwell to Warner, December 12, 1960:

In my last letter I tried to say something and had an attack of shyness. When I was young I was ambitious. Very. It is not terribly long, maybe fifteen years, since I suddenly realized, with a sense of shock, that I was never going to be president of the United States. Either since there or before, I put aside, one by one, all sorts of ambitions, including that ambition to be the editor of this magazine, the ambition to be awarded the Nobel Prize for Literature, etc. etc. and finally there was one ambition left that I found myself still entertaining in daydreams, knew that I should send after the others, and couldn't quite bring myself to. It was to open a book of yours and see my name on the dedication page. You know Maxwell's Law, don't you? *Whatever you want with your whole heart you can have.* A perfect example of it.

Warner to Maxwell, December 15, 1960:

Your letter gave me true pleasure. As I have already said, I adore to please. I feel that this time I have done it; and the glow will last. You have done so much for me—don't suppose I have been unaware of this—ever since those first days of *Dear Mr Maxwell*, and done it with such delicacy & intuition & patience, that I am now firmly persuaded that you enjoy it all as much as I do.

I was very fond of Dear Mr Maxwell from the start, I may say. I had—as one has with certain reserved short-coated cats—that fore-sense of a purr *in petto*. And then, almost immediately, it was cats we were writing to each other about. Do you know, I still often remember Little Grey, & grieve as freshly as ever.

I feel very worried about your weather. The *Times* and the wireless are dumbfounded by it—in other words, they are extremely and horribly eloquent about it; and I have horrid visions of William shovelling snow, William pushing a stalled car, William crossing the East River like Eliza in order to rescue some poor strayed dog. My cousin Cecily & I used to secrete ourselves in my grandfather's church (the church of the Four Evangelists) in order to play at Eliza. This consisted of putting hassocks at wide intervals along the aisle, and leaping from hassock to hassock. As the aisle was tiled, & highly polished, the hassocks had a most life-like instability, and the hassock one had just taken off from as Eliza would rebound on Eliza's pursuer with disconcerting impetus. She was a very rewarding cousin. Once a needle went into her knee, and came out months later at her elbow.

Maxwell to Warner, January 1961:

If you had not loved to please, you would never, I think, have evolved that prose style that has given me an unbroken line of pleasure extending back for thirty years. When I was looking for the first time through *The Osaka Woodcuts*, Kate's godfather said, "How did you get your love of Oriental art?" and I said rapturously, "I got it second hand," without thinking, but surely that is how all pleasure is got—from the rubbing off of somebody else's pleasure in something. From eye to eye and skin to skin. A cousin of love-making. When I was in my early twenties I went to the Chicago Art Institute with a Russian painter, the husband of a friend of mine, and to my surprise he headed for the basement instead of the rooms of paintings, and what he was nosing out was a room full of Sharakus, the Buckingham collection. "Do you see?" he said excitedly, pacing from picture to picture. I saw. I still, thank God, see. And what I see or seem to see in the faces of the Osaka woodcut actors is a certain characteristic and pessimistic dubiety. Sometimes this is delicately modulated by disbelief as at the sight of a new kind of butterfly or a remark that transcends all expectation. But what stripes, what use of squares and circles, what sympathetic blues and grief-stricken greens. What prolonged premeditated and still unaccomplished murdering. What snowstorms and rainstorms. What *theater*!

Christmas was indescribable—that is to say, I could describe it but won't. The high point dramatically was the Accident. The Christmas tree fell or rather was knocked over, with all its ornaments on, the morning of the day before Christmas. Kate and Brookie were playing house back behind it before breakfast, and Brookie forgot how much she has grown in the last few months and stood up. Over it went. Kate's tears, sounding like Phèdre weeping for her lost innocence. She can't bear breakage and there was a great deal of it, so thorough-going that you couldn't deduce from the glass shards what had perished. Only one of any importance—the drummer-soldier, and his gun was broken off when he was brand new, showing that his destiny was short and tragic in any case. But when the tree had been stood up and tidied up, we saw to our great pleasure, that it was now right, for the first time. It had had too much on it. There is a moral of course, and like all morals it is better not pursued.

This morning the living room is full of half-played with toys. You remember the look of something half-played with? Brookie wants me to read her the opening chapter of *The Wind in the Willows*. Do you remember how it begins? "The Mole had been working very hard all the morning..." For the nine thousandth time, I wish we lived near one another, for the propagation and sharing of pleasures, in this life.

Warner to Maxwell, January 7, 1961:

Oh poor Kate! I see it all; that sombre strong edifice with its glitter, heeling away from her, the sigh and swish of the boughs, the outcry of broken glass. I would have wept with her. 'Woe, woe! Thou has destroyed it, that beautiful world —' The thought enters me like a dart that one day or other,

Kate will have to see a living tree felled. She must read a great deal of sorrowful poetry, laments for summer, ballads where young lovers die and roses start up from their graves, the Dirge in *Cymbeline*. It is the only armor for such as she. My father's study was rather unorthodox, since it contained, as well as a carpenter's bench, a very large rocking horse. He used to mount the rocking horse, holding me on before him, and rock, and read poetry aloud. I still remember 'The Swan's Nest among the Reeds' to the accompaniment of a wet summer afternoon and the bump of the rocking horse, I still remember my whole hearted dive into tragedy and acceptance of *sunt lacrimae rerum*.

Even if you haven't a rocking horse...

Maxwell to Warner, January 25, 1961:

I wish I had read the Victorian novelists when I was of an age to read anything, because then I could read them now in moments when I am driven back on crackers and milk, instead. There was only Dickens and Balzac and Wilkie Collins, all in microscopic print, and since none of my elders ever spoke of them with pleasure I didn't know they were pleasant, and went on reading *Tom Swift and his Dirigible* and *Tom Swift and his Electric Elephant Gun*, etc. Now, I cannot read them because I haven't read them in the past. The pace irritates me, and I see everything coming for miles and miles. I think you and Mrs. Woolf between you gave me such a taste for surprises that the whole Victorian age was thereby cut off from me. Not that it isn't full of them, of the most awful sort. But the approach requires a patience of steel. Would you, to please me, do a *New Yorker* piece around the rocking horse?

Warner to Maxwell, January 28, 1961:

I wonder if I shall come to the end of this letter, there is such a frightful gale blowing, a north-wester. I might enjoy it, I am rather prone to storms, but up on the hill about two miles away there are two gipsy caravans and in one of them there is a sick baby. We were driving along the ridge two evenings ago when we were stopped and asked to take a message to the doctor. The caravans were halted at the side of the road, the ponies were grazing about, and there was a fire and dark shapes sitting round it in a dip of ground, their faces like metal in the light of the flames. And I thought then, how unstable a caravan looks perched on its high wheels. One of the girls was down here this morning, we have a good name with gipsies, and after hearing that the doctor went, and that the baby is better but not well, I said they had chosen a windy site this year—as a rule they camp in the lee of the hill; and she said that it was because the ground was so sodden after these months of rain, and that if you camp on a summit your feet don't get so cold. But I'm afraid they must be regretting it now, I don't see how those caravans could stay upright. And the gale has swooped so suddenly that even with their look-out on the weather I doubt if they could have hitched up and moved off the ridge in time.

They appear like strange flowers at this season, having spent the earlier part of the winter in the New Forrest, and moving on into Somerset in early spring. The old women take a deep interest in Valentine's health, and prescribe for her. At this moment she is taking honey and vinegar against rheumatism. It works. I think we get more out of the bargain than ever they do, they prescribe, and pour their black honey voices into our ears, and sit on the doorstep like wild empresses.

I think you will come to Balzac yet. When one has disproved all one's theories, outgrown all of one's standards, discarded all one's criterions, and left off minding about one's appearance, one comes to Balzac. And there he is, waiting outside his canvas tent—with such a circus going on inside.

Maxwell to Warner, February 1, 1961:

In the south of France, in 1953, after we left you—at Aigues-Mortes, as a matter of fact, I encountered some gypsies, several caravans of them, and found myself surrounded with a circle of the fiercest, the most dangerous looking small children I have ever set eyes on. Imagine eight or ten of the little boy in "Truth and Fiction." They were not at all satisfied with the coins I had taken from my pocket and hastily I cleaned myself out. Nothing further happened. But I felt I had been momentarily exposed to a world out of the most remote past, where niceness had not yet been thought of. There used to be caravans in Illinois when I was a child. They were popularly believed to kidnap children (my older brother addressing himself in this fashion: "Mr. Gipsy, what's that you've got in your bag?"—a true story —always featured at large family dinners) and no doubt did kidnap chickens, but one of my earliest memories is of struggling to get not only my tricycle but my cousin Peg's, abandoned by her in her flight, up onto the safety of my grandparents' porch, as a caravan ambled slowly past, and my heart beat wildly. Most of the best things about gypsies published in America have been written by Joseph Mitchell and published in *The New Yorker*. Roosevelt, calling in the gold, caused them to settle down in the city slums. Why is modern history always impoverishing, never the other way round? I hope the baby is all right.

And will you tell me where, with Balzac, one should begin? I have read, in school, *Eugénie Grandet* and *Père Goriot*, as what schoolboy hasn't. But the rest is all unknown. For three nights in a row I have made a frontal attack on Trollope's *Dr. Thorne* and been thrown back each time, in disorder. I keep telling myself that further on, once the book is well started, it will be amusing. But meanwhile I so detest the quality of his language that I cannot really believe he is capable of pleasing me. If only I had read him when I could read anything. Say about the age of nineteen or twenty. My regret is, even so, only skin deep. At nineteen or twenty I was reading *Don Quixote* and you.

Warner to Maxwell, February 6, 1961:

    About Balzac. My father would have said, Begin with *La Cousine Bette*. But I myself say, Begin with *Les Illusions Perdues* and be damned to it. Skip all the treatises on paper manufacture, etc, and cling to Lucien. But I think you should leave all this till the summer vacation. Balzac's material is Clay, human and otherwise. If one can only read him from time to time, the clay sets, and it is difficult to begin again. I have an idea, anyway, that one should aim to read at the tempo at which the author wrote. Balzac wrote fast and recklessly, and read that way he emerges very much himself. I shan't grieve for your inability to read *Dr. Thorne*. I would have to be very hard put to it either to remember anything about it or to wish to refresh my memory.

Maxwell to Warner, February 9, 1961 [cable]:

OH, OH, OH   .   .   .

                         WILLIAM

[His response to "A Spirit Rises," about the rocking horse.]

Warner to Maxwell, February 11, 1961:

The following conversation took place yesterday morning.

I have a cable here for a Mrs Sylvia Townsend Warner, addressed to Frome Vauchurch, Maiden Newton, Dorset. Can you take it?

Yes, it's me.

It's from New York.

Yes.

There are only two words in it, really.

Well, what are they?

Quite an obvious pause; then, in a tone of utter nakedness

It says, oh (O.H.), Oh, Oh, William.

Oh!

I'm afraid he may think that I have broken your heart and that this is your outcry. Or he may think we are exchanging secrets about battleships. The latter, I hope. I would hate anyone to think I had broken your heart when you have so eloquently intimated that I have pleased it. I am very glad to have pleased it, dear William. The cable made me gay throughout the day.

Did you hear the news from Cambridge that the universe is expanding and will eventually expand till it is no more a universe? This was announced on the wireless, along with the deaths from influenza, the newspaper row, the queen's cold, etc. *De l'univers je suis la fervente*, I hang on news of it. Hoyle's theory (but now he has discarded it) that our sun is the survivor of a twin star, a widowed sun, a sort of Queen Victoria surrounded by the progeny of a lost Albert, seemed to me one of the most beautiful conceptions conceivable. One astronomer quoted yesterday, while agreeing that the universe is expanding, added that when the galaxies had expanded to their limit they might begin to contract. A fine thought, too, but suppositious only, and perhaps a trifle anthropomorphic.

Maxwell to Warner, February 1961:

Kate was in bed with a slight temperature yesterday, and I played a card game called "Go Fish" with her for a while, and then read both Brookie and her a children's book called *The Heavenly Tenants* that I wrote before we had any children. With some trepidation, and of course apologies, and explanations that if it was too old or too boring they were just to say so. They liked it, and Kate said, with surprise, "I didn't think you'd write a book that would be so interesting." (Four syllables, the interesting.) There is no doubt that, on a rocking-horse twelve hands high, I would cut an altogether different, and more in-ter-est-ing figure.

Maxwell to Warner, February 20, 1961:

I cannot read the rocking-horse story without my eyes filling with tears.

Warner to Maxwell, February 27, 1961:

I am glad you have been rebuked by a Jesuit [a reader annoyed by Maxwell's review of E. M. Forster's *Guidebook to Alexandria*]. It is a further bond between us. There is another piece of false reasoning in his little letter. If you enjoy complete ignorance of the nature of theology you cannot be expected to know the finesses required to do the right thing by theologians. I'm afraid he is a triple-gendered ass. But it is broadminded of him to acknowledge that your state is enjoyable. Thank you very much for sending him to me. I love any chance for glib and superficial mockery. My talents have been dreadfully be-napkined since Valentine became an R.C. She used to be so very skilled at it herself, and this gives me the sort of feelings that a very chivalrous terrier might be expected to feel when a rat started up before it and its fellow terrier was chained to a kennel and couldn't join in. Loyalty chains her. I will not believe she doesn't notice the rats.

I should like to hear *The Heavenly Tenants* myself. If I go to bed with a slight temperature, Valentine will send you a cable and you will fly over one afternoon and read it to me.

Maxwell to Warner, March 1, 1961:

On the way to you at this moment, crossing the ocean, is a copy of my novel [*The Château*], which contains a trick thunderstorm that I put in just for you, in emulation of your designing *The True Heart* so that it exactly overlay the story of Cupid and Psyche. No one else will know what in the world I am talking about, and I couldn't care less. I have decided to enjoy this book, the way married couples enjoy their final child. I am not going to read any reviews, I am not even going to ask Emmy to read them for me. I had a perfectly wonderful time writing it. The pleasure lasted me through twelve and a half whole years and I never once wanted to be writing anything else, though I often wished I understood a little more clearly what I was up to. If I had spent twelve and a half years in France I couldn't have enjoyed them a bit more, though a voice behind my chair points out that I would have learned to speak French. Well, in my next life I will *be* French, so why add one unnecessary regret to this one?

Warner to Maxwell, March 4, 1961:

You have written a novel, you have finished a novel, it is on its way towards me at this instant moment. I am thrilled and delighted and proud beyond words (quite why I should be proud, I cannot exactly analyse, but undeniably I do feel proud).

How sly you have been about it—and how wise! Twelve and a half years lovemaking with a novel, and never word or sign of it. But I remember how you were ill for so long & so mysteriously, two years ago. That must have been a dreadful interregnum. But I don't suppose there is a trace of it, not a stain, not a hair-crack wrinkle, on the book itself. It was in France, keeping an eye on the vineyards, and knew nothing about it.

I am most grateful to you for not telling me until after my copy had started on its journey. I would have died of impatience if I had had longer to wait. I am almost dying of impatience as it is. I am so intensely curious to learn what you have to say. Your mind is so congenial to me, so in-ter-est-ing, and there have been things in your letters which I have carried in my bosom for days and days. And I am to have twelve & a half years of William's mind enjoying itself at peace and leisure.

I have never been given a thunderstorm before.

Maxwell to Warner, March 7, 1961:

It has taken me roughly six months to do a review of Kilvert's diaries, and I feel as if I had just put him on the train and waved goodby.*

* *Kilvert's Diary*, edited by William Plomer, a selection from the Reverend Francis Kilvert's diaries of 1870–79.

Warner to Maxwell, March 10, 1961:

Thank you for the 'Spirit Rises' cheque; and for the prospect of reading you on Kilvert. I am forever in his debt, because it was his accounts of the Black Mountain country that made me want to see it. It is as lovely as ever he said and still almost as innocent and remote; and next week I hope to be looking at it again. The people have very beautifully pitched speaking voices—not that arrant Welsh singsong of farther West, but *poised* voices, and clear diction. It is a country of small farms, and one sees Noah's Ark fields with a couple of cows, a horse grazing, twelve sheep, some pigs, a dozen geese, a goat perhaps; all dwelling in unity and looking as contented as the primroses on the banks. The valleys are so narrow there is no room for anything more ambitious.

Warner to Maxwell, March 23, 1961:

I am completely under the spell of *The Château*. It is a heavenly story, and one of the compartments of its heaven is its length. Eugene has just said *Une catastrophe*, thank God I still have a long way to go. William, it is masterly, it is not like any other book in the world, it is like the cobweb you have spun over France, tough, pliable, artful, giving with every puff of wind and never letting go. I am so happy about it, I can't express my delight; but I share yours, your creative delight in making it, your twelve and a half years love affair, and that rapturous, that truly creative state of mind of not—as you said in your letter—positively understanding what you were up to. Your faith in the power of statement, your refusal to account for why the wind, just at that moment, blew cold, why a burst of sunlight suddenly rested on one particular roof and nowhere else, is totally convincing. I had almost forgotten that the quality of conviction was still available, not shut up in the classics. Now I find it circulating through *The Château* like the circulation of the blood. Think of my pleasure, my doubled pleasure: that a book should be so wholly good, that the book should be by you. I hope you are one half as happy as I am.

And you have given me a thunderstorm—as much a tour de force as any of God's, and much better than most, and glorious in its irrational appearance. I read it with such absorption and complicity that only after it was over did I come to my senses and say, But that was my thunderstorm. So I immediately read it over again, preening and glittering like a peacock. Do you know one of the marks of real literature, one of the tests?—that when the reader recognises something known or experienced, he feels, not a hark-back to his own life but a participation in the book. Valognes, I thought. I've been to this Valognes. So you see, the spell was cast from the very beginning.

I wish this were not one of those mornings when everything interrupts and Valentine's poodle barks incessantly. It is so unfair that she can express herself by yelling when I can't—or don't. Where was I? At Valognes. In your next life you will *be* French, you say. Meanwhile, I don't think we need worry about that. In this book you *are* France. That ferry! That semi-circle of conversational chairs, and that truly evangelical quality of the left hand being quite unaffected by the doings of the right hand, that consistent schizophrenia that is so maddening and so uplifting. By an amazing stroke of kind fortune, the sort of thing one supposes might happen to other people, we are being given a week in Paris, next week in Paris. I shall set out as if it were the most natural thing in the world to be returning to Paris after spending so much of this week there.

Maxwell to Warner, April 5, 1961:

You have a way of putting praises that makes it hard for me to walk afterward. My feet have a tendency not to touch the ground. Listing a little to the right or left, I levitate, in danger of cracking with happiness. When one has been pleased one's whole life as profoundly as I have been pleased by your work, one does terribly want to do a little pleasing in return. I mean I love you.

We are sitting in the back seat of the car, Emmy and Valentine are in the front, talking about I don't remember what, Glastonbury Tor is off to the right, on a gloomy hill, and I say very guardedly that I am thinking of writing a novel about France. (I am actually five years along in it, but doubtful) and you say, generously, "A novel about France—are you going to do it in the French manner? What a pleasure to do," and I don't say anything because I know in my heart I cannot manage the tone and method of Mme. de Lafayette, and that you could, with one hand tied behind you. And there you go, in the encouraging vein of the grey-eyed daughter of Zeus, breathing purpose and resolution into me, and by the grace of God we are not killed by a van at the crossroads.

I don't know whether I was more delighted for you or for myself that you were tooting off to Paris for a week. It has been bothering me that there was no mention of a little tour in your letters. Now I have this to look forward to. And I find, happily, that I cannot imagine with any certainty what you will do in Paris, where you will be staying, what shops will draw you. So you must tell me. Or not, as you feel like. It can be a bore to describe things that you have enjoyed so fully at the time that you don't need to describe them any more. Any more, I mean, than a good meal eaten and digested and forgotten about.

When you spoke, two or three letters back, of the congeniality of our two minds, the thought that went through my head was *The only person I really see a great deal of, among all my friends, is Sylvia*. And it is true.

Warner to Maxwell, April 13, 1961:

I remember very clearly that conversation in the back of the car, and the *immense* self-control I exercised in order not to trample your book to death by asking questions about it. You said that it would be about France; yes; and later on you said, adding a little more of the colour of the cat to show through the basket, that you thought it would have a good deal about attics in it, attics & their furniture. Do you remember that, too? Indeed, I am very glad we were not wiped out by a van at the cross-roads.

Paris was rapture. The trees along the Seine were just newly in leaf, springing up like green fountains. Little boys on roller skates were darting about like swallows. I watched two having a formal fight. They rushed forward, they met, and immediately their roller skates swept them apart again. The same principle as jousting, but improved by being speeded up. What shops drew me? I bought a bag of garlic, seeds of chervil, Belleville sorrel, the little saucer-shaped marrons, and of volubilis and Belles-de-Jour on the Mégisserie quay; and found it very hard not to buy a dozen or so of little cordon apple-trees, two foot high, & *such* standard rosetrees—while Valentine was yearning over tortoises & water-snakes. The recommendation on the back of the packet says: *la transplantation fatiguant beaucoup les Belle-de-Jour*, they must be sown where they are to come up. I understand this so well.

And the petticoat shop was Guerlain's on the corner of the Place Vendome: a lofty square room, done in pale biscuit-coloured panelling; and eight young women, very pretty & demure, sitting in pairs, coupled like doves, a pair to each wall. Of course, they are sometimes selling, & on their feet. But we happened to strike an unoccupied moment, & there they were, being doves. The notice beside the Odéon box-office says *"Tenure négligée."* No other language can manage just that. They were doing *Occupe-toi d'Amélie*, & it was very unselfish of me not to fasten on that. But Franklin [Paul Nordoff's friend] had not seen *La Dolce Vita*, Valentine wanted to see it again. And my virtue was rewarded, for the only place left showing it was in the domestic wilds of Montmartre; and I shouldn't think a touch of alteration had fallen on it since the days of early Westerns & *Broken Blossoms*. Mulberry-coloured, with gold fleurs-de-lis, and two gigantic *art nouveau* candelabra extended like *art nouveau* vultures over the very small auditorium.

I am glad to think you love me. I love you. It is part of the congeniality of our minds, dear Mr Maxwell.

Warner to Maxwell, April 16, 1961:

I can almost promise you that I will never stop going to France. I am slightly in France at this moment, for I am translating *La Côte Sauvage*, a short novel by a new writer called [Jean-René] Huguenin—a distillation of a theme of incest.* If I had gone to Sears-Roebuck, I could not have found a sharper antithesis to *Contre Sainte-Beuve* and I am enjoying myself.

* *A Place of Shipwreck* was published in 1963.

Maxwell to Warner, May 9, 1961:

It is a matter of passionate importance to me that you shall have money. This is only partly out of concern for your comfort and peace of mind; it is also from aesthetic reasons. I like to see what you do with it. No one that I know knows better what to do with money.

As a result of not reading reviews, I can remember, for the first time, things that people I cherish—you, for instance—have said about a book after it is published. Suddenly, as I am walking along the street, a phrase from your letters rises to the surface and a sort of transubstantiation occurs. I mean I feel like sweet butter.

Do you know, the walk from Maiden Newton to Toller Fratrum has been transposed as neatly as a piece of music; it is now not something I did but something I dreamed. It is all dream country, including the barking dog, and the farmer who spoke in the Dorset dialect, and the cuckoo. But I like to think that you are in such close proximity to one of my pleasantest dreams.

Warner to Maxwell, May 11, 1961:

Have you ever slept between pink flannelette sheets? For that matter, have you ever slept in a tartan bedroom? We spent two nights, on the recommendation of a friend, in a hotel in Teesdale where both these experiences were lavished on us. You never, never saw such a bedroom. The tartan was one of those exceedingly red tartans, and all the upholstery was tartanic. There were little sporrans dangling everywhere where there were not sprigs of dead heather bristling. The only non-tartans were the flannelette sheets and a picture of the Good Shepherd—a spirited attempt, I suppose, to show Jesus in his most Doric aspect, & indeed it was only on our second day that I realised he was not Burns in a rather florid negligée. I was glad to move on, though it meant leaving the noise of a moving stream, and a view of limestone hills from a window eight foot high; but it is embarrassing to be perpetually in a state of incredulous mockery of objects which their owner is sincerely pleased with.

Warner to Maxwell, May 12, 1961:

What about Proust, indeed! I did not tell you at the time, it was all too odious to write about. The copyright of the Scott Moncrieff translation (it is also too odious to type about) belongs to his nephew. And he had at first appeared to be perfectly reconciled to uncle being put into line with the new Pleiade text, and some of his gaffes removed or amended; and then he suddenly began to have doubts about the whole thing. And last October he and his sister and Ian Parsons and Norah Smallwood and I, and George Painter called in as a consultant, met for dinner at the Garrick, and a nastier evening I have never sat through. Not only would they not consent; they wouldn't produce any reason for why they wouldn't. And when finally reminded by George Painter that if the copyright of the uncle's translation were not re-secured by a revised edition it would fall into the common domain and very likely be superseded by God only know what, they said with one voice that they wouldn't mind in the least.

And there it still rests. Several other people have tried to make George S. M. either listen to reason or explain why he won't. Nothing has come of their attempts either. I have a theory that I am the obstacle, for G. S. M. is a rigid and ring-tailed Papist, and to such I might very well be anathema. I have urged Chatto and Windus to try along these lines by intimating that I am ready and willing to drop out, if that will secure his uncle's work; and Andreas Mayor, my partner in the job, is heroically prepared to go on single-handed. But Ian won't hear of it, and won't consider the chance that I may be right. It is all very tiresome, and painful and disgraceful—and private, by the way. So if you have any comments to make, you must keep them for me. Though a few prayers that George and Joanna S. M. may drop dead would not come amiss.

Maxwell to Warner, May 16, 1961:

And how shall I thank you for the lovely present that I found waiting for me when I got home yesterday—the tartan bedroom. Just what I wanted. You always know.

Warner to Maxwell, May 30, 1961:

It is not a review [of Kilvert's diaries]. It is a work of art, a Silver Swan. I had been impatient for it, a growing impatience, I began reading it with that sense of *I've got you now*. But before the end of the first paragraph you had mastered me, I read at your pace, as one floats at a river's pace; and here and there I recognised a dragonfly, or a clump of meadow-sweet, a leaning willow, the reflection of a house or a mountain. That's Kilvert, I said to myself, William is carrying me on through the landscape of Kilvert, finding his way as a river does. The management of time, of Thursdays and Februaries, is done with such art, such sureness, that I sighed for pleasure. My dear William, what an uncommonly good writer you have become by writing *The Château*. How well you navigate, how well you start, and hold on your course and come to an end without a waver or a flurry.

Did you know, when you were dealing so humanely with Kilvert's half-baked sadisms—yet rightly sternly, for indeed they are shocking—that Kilvert père was probably the genuine article? At one time he kept a boys' school, and Augustus Hare was a pupil there, another misery in that martyred childhood; and his report makes it fairly plain what manner of father-figure he was. Inherited, or implanted, I don't know; but I imagine that our Kilvert must at some time have been terrified of Kilvert père. There is a feeling of truancy, a vividness in his adventures, in his acceptances, that is like someone who has escaped and can scarcely credit it. But this is really a silly, beside the point question. It doesn't matter in the slightest whether you knew or didn't know. You read the diaries and the diarist's heart, and you have written the most sensitive and comprehending and perfect summary, and Kilvert's ghost can rest in peace.

And never a titter. Bless you for that.

When we fetched our cats away from that very luxurious boarding establishment where they go when we are away (a little chalet and garden to themselves, a wide cushioned window-sill, infra-red lights over their bed on cold nights) Niou was so entranced to be home that he rushed into the garden, chose a patch of dug ground, laid himself down on his back, and rolled like a horse. A feudal rolling. *My* garden. *My* earth.

Maxwell to Warner, June 1961:

I lay down and rolled in your praise of the Kilvert review. I have a feeling that that is what catnip does to cats—makes them feel so thoroughly praised that they cannot tell whether they are going to sneeze or burst. I did know—there is a hint of it in Plomer's introduction to one of the volumes—about Kilvert's father's affection for caning little boys; but since there was nothing whatever about it in the diaries, I stuck to the text. And isn't it curious, isn't it interesting how completely Kilvert's wife has covered up her tracks? She could have ruined the diaries and instead all she did was remove herself. You have never been tempted to write a novel about her? No one else could do it.

Warner to Maxwell, June 23, 1961:

Valentine's mother died early this month. She was in her eighty-fifth year, she had been failing for some time, it wasn't a shock. Yet it was. When people are as old as that, you accept that they will decline but you don't accept that they will go out. Valentine was the last person she recognised, the last thing that gave her pleasure, and she died like the fall of a feather.

Warner to Maxwell, July 3, 1961:

Dear William.

That is really all I have to say. Here is that piano-tuner piece ["In the Absence of Mrs. Bullen"].

Maxwell to Warner, August 1961:

You won't believe it of me, but I have just finished reading *The Way of All Flesh* for the first time. In a way, of course, it is a pure stroke of luck. The book has been a handy weapon in the hands of the young, I'm sure, but only a thoroughly middle-aged person is in a position to appreciate the beauty of that reverie of the dying Christina, wherein she spends Ernest's inheritance on her husband and the *other* children. The vista it opens is long and shadowy and like the aisle of, say, Wells Cathedral. And the terrible suffering that the innocent must undergo in order to reach the point where they can raise a hand in their own defense—the vision of that. But there is no end to its marvels and we are all indebted to and descended from Butler. There is no other way into the Twentieth Century but through him, that I can see.

Warner to Maxwell, September 13, 1961:

It [*The Way of All Flesh*] was my father's favourite novel, and I probably came to it too young. One knows a great deal at thirteen, but what one doesn't know is appreciation. And I rioted through it for the fun and the story. I don't know how often I have re-read it since, and I love it better each time, and admire it more. But still, I think yours was the more excellent way, and I am glad you had it so. He wished to be remembered—you know that sonnet?—on the lips of men. How fulfilled, delighted, and in agreement he would have been with your remark that there is no other way into the 20th century but through him.

Maxwell to Warner, September 20, 1961:

I got them to send me a confirmation, as it is called, of your cable, because somebody's voice is not anything like as good as a piece of paper, for feeling communicated with. By rights we should cable each other the first thing every morning. At length. About the kind of morning it is, and how we slept, and how we feel. And what the children said and what we have been reading, and any particularly vivid dreams. I don't suppose Mr. Truax would mind, really.* Except in principle.

I shall miss Valentine's mother. From time to time I was tempted to be funny about her, and restrained myself, remembering that I did not after all know her, and that she was undoubtedly not funny to Valentine. But she was larger than life size, and in the round, and beautifully in character always, and in a manner of speaking, I loved her. That is, I loved reading about her. Do you think she would make a satisfactory ghost?

---

* R. Hawley Truax, vice president of The New Yorker Magazine, Inc., authorized the editors' business expenses.

Warner to Maxwell, November 3, 1961:

When I was young, a friend and I invented a repertory of Informative Lies about London: By paying half-a-crown you can drive under the Marble Arch. On March 25th (the Vernal Equinox) the Serpentine is ceremonially opened for bathing, at dawn, by the Mayor of Kensington. It is customary for newly-appointed Deans of St Paul's to drink tea with the Canons in the vestry, using a silver teapot bequeathed by Dr Sacheverell; and so on. Afterwards we found that several of our lies were in fact truths. We also found, which was more to the purpose, that one can pass off any lie if one trims it with something circumstantial, like the silver teapot. Holy Church knows this too, and demands evidence of miracles in a process of sanctification.

Maxwell to Warner, November 13, 1961:

Your deciding that Mr. Thurber must have been a good person reminded me of my favorite scene in *The True Heart. On mort comme on est né,* as Reynaldo Hahn used to say. He was a very complicated person, and sometimes very generous, is as near as I can come to agreeing with you. And of course a marvelous writer. Do you remember the woman with the short leg—Mrs. Albright?—who doctored people with herbs? It is in the book about people from Columbus, written fairly late, in the fifties, I think. And so solid.

Maxwell to Warner, November 29, 1961:

I picked up the *Times* this morning and saw that the thing I had been dreading had happened: Brian Urquhart, who is an old friend of ours, had been dragged out of a house in Elizabethville and beaten by Katanganese soldiers. He grew up in Dorset—in Dorchester, I believe, and remembers seeing Private Shaw on his motorcycle. I think it is likely that he passed under your eyes at some time or other, because he knows the country around you by heart, and it was he who urged me to walk to Toller Fratrum, as we were coming down to stay with you. He was in a parachute division and his parachute failed to open and he fell two thousand feet and landed in a plowed field, breaking every bone in his body. The division went on to North Africa and every man of officer's rank was killed, so it would appear that he has a charmed though not sheltered life. By this noon I had heard that they had had a telegram at the U.N. saying that his nose was broken and he had had to have several stitches in his head, etc., but "that he was in very good form." His own words, obviously. I cannot tell you how many times in the last thirteen years he has looked in to my face and asked, "Dear Bill, are you in good form?" I am not, very. I am too heartsick. I keep hearing that British voice saying "Oh, steady, steady!" as the rifle butts started descending. Also, my nose hurts.

Warner to Maxwell, December 3, 1961:

When I was studying musical composition, on one occasion I took in an unfinished exercise in which I had left a gap of several blank bars; and the man who was teaching me remarked 'Those are the most promising bars you have done so far, Sylvia. They show that you have developed a sense of form.' I looked at him most carefully, but he meant what he said; and if I hadn't developed a sense of form before, I did then.

Yesterday we learned that this house is threatened. A by-pass road will be carried through our meadow, & possibly right up against us. Not yet, but within a few years. We have yet to see the plan, but I'm afraid we're dished. Incessant noise & stink, lights all night (it will carry a great deal of the Midlands to Plymouth traffic), trees felled, and the house shaking to pieces. It's curious. When we came here, over twenty years ago, we never meant to stay: we looked on it as a convenient little pis-aller; and now, when we have grown into it, grown very fond of it, and had every inten-tion of dying in it, we discover that we were never meant to stay. It is the trees and the garden that I grieve over most, because I feel a hopeless responsibility towards them: Valentine's red willows, the aspen with its rainy voice, the balsam poplar, trees we have planted and nursed up; and the yew trees that were here before us. But we must look for something else, & hope to sell this to someone who likes a lively outlook. Somewhere in this neighborhood, we think, so that we can retain the practical advan-tages of being cherished as old inhabitants by tradespeople. A devoted gro-cer, a fishmonger who remembers one's taste for bass and John Dory are not lightly to be parted with.

But all this is the decisiveness of shock. My hair hasn't even lain down yet, and here I am talking of plighted grocers.

Who knows, we may find ourselves fastening on a house in Cornwall (Valentine has a passion for inspecting impossible houses, I for seeing possibilities in them). But I hope not. It would be very inconvenient, and silly too, to plant ourselves on a peninsula among Celtic Methodists who stone strangers.

Warner to Maxwell, December 13, 1961:

I'm afraid you will have to believe about that road: though you can come to it gradually, for the bulldozers will not be in our meadow (called Cornum, poor meadow, what a fate for a meadow called Cornum) for some years yet. This was discovered for us while we were in Cornwall by a sympathetic neighbour who is a county councellor, and has approaches to the department that will do it. It is a large scheme, and will be done in sections, and Maiden Newton is towards the end of it. So for the moment, we are reprieved, we shall have time to look about for something we can like, we shall not be hurled incontinently into the outskirts of Bournemouth, among the conifers and the dog-breeders. Look we must, however. As Valentine says, if we wait too long we shall be too old for such sports. Indeed, I discover that we are already a trifle sered, since we only theoretically considered a house in Cornwall, and are pusillanimously inclined to remember the advantages of remaining *en pays de connaissance*. When I think of the garden, the old roses that I have nursed back into a new lease of life (only last summer a nameless timeless old Methuselah rewarded me by displaying itself as a Camille de Rohan), when I ask myself, But who will feed the birds? I am in despair. But I have to admit that flashes of infidelity traverse my mind when I think that there are other fish in the sea. When you come to write your book on the English, dear William, and dedicate it to my memory, you will enjoy yourself in the exposition of our polygamous devotion, our quite genuine mandrake howls when uprooted, our equally genuine exploration of a change of soil. So grieve for those ruined water-meadows as I do, rather than for us, since we do not sorrow as those without hope.

Maxwell to Warner, January 4, 1962:

Hokusai—that is to say the blue wave—I encountered at the age of
twenty-one, when I went to Harvard as a graduate student and saw it on
the wall of a poet's room. The poet was Robert Fitzgerald, who has translated Homer and a good deal of Sophocles and Euripides into most excellent English verse, as well as writing it himself. Thereafter it hung, for
years, in a facsimile, that is, on the wall of my room, wherever that was.
But it is all I knew or have known until now. Each time I go through the
book, even if I have looked through it five minutes before, I see it with new
eyes. What is that little kite doing blown against the bundle of faggots on
the woman's head? A pastry shop on closer inspection turns into a print
shop. The design of a flowered kimono or the representation of a piece of
fruit stops me in my tracks. Also, I don't remember in any other Japanese
printmaker anything like so much *talking*. But what an eye for the world!
Toward the end of the introduction I found this: "In his declining years,
when in poor health, Hokusai used to say to his daughter: 'I don't want to
die yet! When I was seventy-three I understood the very substance of
nature, animals, flowers, birds, and insects. When I was painting them it
seemed to me they would fly away from my paper...If only the gods
would give me ten or at least five years more, I could become a perfect
artist.'" Well, they must have, since he lived to be eighty-nine, and died saying "Freedom, wonderful freedom...when we go to fields in summer we
leave our ephemeral bodies there." And the whole time in debt, in trouble.
I suppose I shouldn't, but I find the lives of the artists so much more edifying than the lives of the saints; so much more saintlike, if you leave God
out of it. Can we leave God out of it? That it comes from you is also an
essential part of the pleasure of looking at it. I had a mathematics teacher
in college who so loved his subject that we used to tease him openly in
class, while not dreaming of hurting his feelings by not learning everything
he wanted us to learn, with the result that before the end of the year we
were dancing around in and out of differential and integral calculus and
non-Euclidian geometry. But it was not learning, it was merely the trans-
mitting of pleasure. Everything I have learned from you has been like that.
I do not think it began with you. I suspect behind you the presence of others, your father and mother perhaps, a long line of pleasure lovers who
could not bear to keep their pleasure to themselves. Coming on Confucius,

Mohamet, and Zoroaster in a basket of toys, I stole them and put them on my desk, where they now are.

Warner to Maxwell, January 11, 1962:

Saints and artists. I go further, not only do I find lives of artists much more edifying, but in most cases I find lives of saints positively disedifying: they are such ungrateful fidgets—and as for, We thank thee for our cre ation, preservation, and all the blessings of this life, which is a sentiment that any normally construed person would really quite often express, it doesn't seem even to occur to them. I suppose the answer is joy. And there, manual artists are by far the most fortunate, they have joy down to their fingertips (executive musicians can be in the same blessed boat, and they too are often very edifying, like Lotte Lehmann, her joy living on into teaching others). Yet even if they are not so well circumstanced, saints should be able to manage a little enjoyment; and when they do, like Teresa of Avila, who certainly enjoyed herself more often than not, how out- standing they become, and how much easier to believe in. But justice obliges me to add that saints are usually very unfortunate in their biogra- phers; perhaps they are not so bilious as they are painted. And of course, with the exception of hermits, saints have had to spend a great portion of their lives in the company of pious and religious people, and we all know how disheartening that can be, and even, so to speak, disfiguring. *C'est assez sur la saintété.*

Maxwell to Warner, January 1962:

This morning, as every morning, as I walk Daisy along the esplanade, I think of you when I come to the tip of Welfare Island. The buildings come to an end, there are a few trees, now bare, an iron fence, and a narrow con- crete promontory perhaps a hundred yards long, ending in a small copy of the Pharos of Alexandria. Behind this is the other half of the river, but it looks instead like a small, square, very safe harbor. And the harbor is framed by detail-less buildings that in the early morning compose well, and are sometimes part of a Whistler and sometimes part of a Turner, depend- ing on the weather. With luck, at this time of the year, the sun is just emerging from some part of Queens that I have never and will never be able to say that I have been in. Red gold, it was, and often is. And punctually, I thought of you. I share the intense pleasure with you every morning of my life, for the simple reason that I don't know anybody else who deserves it or would appreciate it properly.

Warner to Maxwell, January 31, 1962:

The Viking Press said in a recent letter that *A Spirit Rises* will be published shortly, and I have told them that the moment they have a copy to send anywhere they are to send it to you.* But perhaps I am too hopeful, shortly can mean anything. Once, when the Warner family was travelling in Scotland, the train waited for a long time at some unscheduled stop and my mother seeing a station-master put her head out of the window and asked him when the train would start. 'Shortly,' said he, soothingly. But unsoothed, she asked again. 'Shortly? What does shortly mean?' 'In a wee while,' he answered, doing his best for the poor English body that didn't properly know its own language.

I have also engaged myself in a story ["The Beggars' Wedding"] which no doubt could be a rather good one if it were humanly possible to do it at all; but the object of it is to construct a solidity of vile behaviour out of three essentially trivial characters, build a Dark Tower on a foundation of sand. I'm afraid I shall have to do it before I find out it can't be done. I think I would discard the whole business if one of the characters hadn't started into the life the moment I called her Ottilie. One does call them up, you know. One accidentally steps into a pentagram, and calls them up.

* This is the collection of stories she dedicated to Maxwell.

Maxwell to Warner, February 1962:

   I am so delighted to be going to Orta with you and Valentine.* How did you know that it has been uppermost in my mind for some time now that one of the Italian lakes would be the place to go to. I hope you will find nothing changed since 1912. Though I have never seen any of them, I feel I had seen them all because of the canvas curtain—a scene surrounded by advertisements in square boxes—of the Majestic Vaudeville Theatre in

Bloomington, Illinois when I was a child. Those urns dripping with roses, that blue sky and crumbling stonework, those balustrades and lattices, all the unadulterated beauty.

* Maxwell said, "Since I was tied to New York City by my job, and liked travelling, we enjoyed the fiction that I travelled with them."

Maxwell to Warner, before March 14, 1962:

If it were up to me I would not, like the writer of the dust jacket material for what I most passionately think of as my book [*A Spirit Rises*], compare you to Jane Austen, Trollope, Galsworthy, David Garnett, Elinor Wylie, the Sitwells, or any others, or even to yourself, but to a summer's day. And here are all my friends come home again, Miss Rawson and Dr. Hutton, Ellie's mother, the Kirbys, poor Barnby Robinson, Mme. Turner and the red-haired man from the poppy-infested plains of Hungary, Reverend Mother, and Randolph—but who *is* Randolph? *The New Yorker* apparently wouldn't have him, but I don't remember and don't understand why. Was I away? Have I forgotten his desolate face? I don't see how I could ever have met him and not remember him. As for example I remember Hugh Whiting and that mad Mrs. Benson, and the man on the rocking horse, for whom I have a special love, because I fancy, correctly or incorrectly, that he was modelled on your schoolmaster father. If he wasn't, I don't want to know it. "The Snow Guest" I have not forgotten. Nor that frightening Mr. Herzen. My beautiful, beautiful book!

Maxwell to Warner, March 20, 1962:

This is one of the times when I fail you. But I don't totally fail you, in that I know how much you love the story ["The Beggars' Wedding"] and so feel the blow with you that I am helplessly obliged to inflict. There are times, and this seems to be one of them, when a piece of writing means something quite different to the author than it does to most readers. As if, in passing from one to the other, it had literally been bewitched. The length offered no problems, it was the story itself and if I say what it was that didn't seem right to us, you will surely say to yourself But that isn't the story I wrote.

You this afternoon, and Kate this morning. At the breakfast table she implored me to tell her—just tell her—which came first, the chicken or the egg. And when I began with single-celled animals and parthenogenesis and lizards that became birds, she was frantic. Just tell me, she begged, which came first, the chicken or the egg. So I began again with the single cell and she quite properly burst into tears. All in the world she was asking for was St. Anselm, and she got Darwin and Huxley.

I know you will forgive us because you have in the past, but that doesn't make it any less melancholy.

Warner to Maxwell, March 23, 1962:

Don't be sad. The burden is unevenly distributed. You have to say the story won't do—with nothing to mitigate the painfulness of saying it; except a good conscience, and we all know how much comfort that is. I had three weeks of rapture, selfish remorseless rapture such as I had thought I would never feel again. Of course I'm sorry that you don't take it, and I am sorry without any of course that you had to tell me so. But perhaps I feel a trifle like a Bacchante coming home from a night on the mountain and saying, 'Did I tear up Uncle Lysander? Oh dear, I'm so sorry.' I don't suppose it will reoccur.

I wish like Hell it might.

The hen came first, as in Genesis. An egg can't lay a hen, as in Dialectical Materialism. Before the hen and the egg there was a lot of wiggle-waggle. Then came the hen.

Warner to Maxwell, March 31, 1962:

Dear William, Valentine says why don't I ask you to be my literary executor. I have never had one, partly from modesty, partly from inattention. Now I have had to remake my will and it has all boiled up again, and I was saying there was no one my ghost would feel easy with, and why not burn the lot, and Valentine said, why don't you ask William Maxwell? And instantly, of course, I saw it was the perfect repose for my ghost and just what I should like. So here I am, doing it.

In fact, I don't think much execution would be involved. What I would like would be a caretaker for my written remains, and for my diaries. There are diaries of the second half of the twenties which are entertaining and might in time be interesting as a picture of how one lived and wrote in London at that date. I was looking at them the other day, hunting up references to T. F. Powys for a man who is doing a book about him, and I thought what a delightful easy society it was and what an extraordinary number of things we talked about; and that if a home could eventually be found for them in some university library, there would be good pickings for students of that date. And as I am so much more kindly esteemed in the States than here, it would only be right and grateful to acknowledge it in such a way. Besides, since we have so many conversations together, this would continue them.

So think of it, dear William. But I don't want to be a Bore or a Burden. Above all, I don't want to be an obligation. Yet if you should incline to it, I would feel very happy. And I would do some preliminary sorting, and make it as easy as I could. By the way, I am not intending to die. It was the mortality of others that made me recast my will.

Maxwell to Warner, April 7, 1962:

Yes of course I incline to it. I sometimes think that almost the only good thing I can say for myself is that about practical matters (and literary executorship is certainly that) I am practical. Since I get the same pleasure from reading a sentence of yours—any sentence—that I get from listening to Mozart and Schubert (and the rest really—including the Divine Sewing Machine, can go hang) it is a responsibility that has about it a certain aura of May Pole Dancing, if you know what I mean. As opposed to being a Bore and a Burden. (No, I forgot Papa Haydn and Gluck. Those four.) Tell me, little by little as it occurs to you, what you want done, and if I don't, like Mrs. Malaprop, precede you, it shall be done. As you say, it will give us one more thing to converse about.

Warner to Maxwell, April 27, 1962:

I am truly and profoundly grateful and immensely pleased. Now I look forward to a happy summer of tidying my remains and making myself as convenient to execute as I can. I shan't be as exemplary as Samuel Butler, but I will do my best to follow his example.*

---

* Three days later, she wrote Maxwell, asking his help in finding the right word for her translation of Huguenin, and apologized: "Poor William! I am always making you my literary executor, I really should have the decency to wait till I'm dead."

Maxwell to Warner, May 8, 1962:

This noon, I was telling Brian Urquhart, who came over to have a sandwich and a cup of tea on my sofa, that what I wanted was to be a team of identical acrobats, two to handle *The New Yorker*'s affairs, one to work at home, one to be a good husband and father—and one to—

One to be laid up for repairs, he interrupted.

One to read the galleys of the paperback edition of *Time Will Darken It* was what I was going to say. But I see six isn't enough. Seven acrobats, the seventh to do my travelling. Don't you think it is a first-class idea?

Warner to Maxwell, May 11, 1962:

Dear William, you must be eight acrobats. Travelling is not enough. You must also live near by, say at Toller Fratrum, so that we can stroll round each others' garden, and hear the first cuckoo on the same morning.

Warner to Maxwell, June 10, 1962:

It touched me very much to know that Mr Lobrano loved 'The House with the Lilacs', it enables me to think that Mr Lobrano might have loved me. Mrs Finch is my only essay at a self-portrait; her conversation and her ineffability. A limited and very laudatory self-portrait, but the resemblance is there.

I have been leading a series of double lives, rushing to bed with another assignation with another Tractarian. It began with a most astonishing change of heart towards Newman. I have always disliked Newman's Newman, the *Apologia* makes me grind my teeth. But I had the curiosity to read a new life of him, that takes him on into his career as a Roman Catholic; and his adversities were so ludicrous, and he bore them so handsomely; and the slights put on him were so outrageous; and he took them with so much dignity and ease; and he lived among third rate minds and his own mind was enlarged by it; altogether, he turned from a trumpery little silk purse into a honest respectable pig's ear. Then I read a very dull life of J. A. Froude—but *he* wasn't dull. Then I had a wallow with Faber, whom I had previously supposed had been created for the specific purpose of annoying Newman; but there was more than that to him: a pleasing habit of referring to the Virgin Mary as Mamma—which I sparingly practise on Valentine when I think the moment is propitious; and one amazing flash of poetry; and now I am sadly happy with Clough, who with better stars and some money might have worked out as well-nourished as Goethe. And Pusey lies before me, and Keble, and Ward. What bliss. When it is all over, I shall re-read the 39 articles. Never a dull moment.

It wasn't a mirror over the mantelpiece, William, where the birds flew. It was a window. The chimney went up on either side. One sat in front of the fire and saw the wind blowing and the birds flying.

Maxwell to Warner, June 13, 1962:

I hardly know how to tell you and yet I feel that tell you I must: I am taking piano lessons. I have picked up where I left off, forty-two years ago. If I am I, which is certainly open to question.

Warner to Maxwell, June 18, 1962:

It is my fortunate lot that I am continually being delighted by my friends (though partly my doing too, as I choose them out so very carefully). It delights me to hear that you are playing the piano again. You couldn't make a wiser decision. One must have music as well as words; and if one is to have music properly, one must have a hand in it; if only to show composers how much one loves them. Like making pilgrimages on foot. Besides, now you will always have something to look forward to. You will take up with Frescobaldi, or find someone to play duets with, or an oboe wandering companionless. Did I ever tell you about my great-aunt by marriage Emmie? She was a widow, and lived in Wales, and time went on and she continued to be a widow, and to live in Wales, and one day a nephew to whom she was little more than a name found himself staying in a town that was her post town and thought it would be rather kind to look poor old Emmie up. So he ascertained the way to her house and borrowed a bicycle and rode out in a summer evening. As it was in Wales, he lost his way and by the time he had found it again it was late, so late that he felt pretty sure she would have gone to bed. But having got so far, and his teeth into a good action, he persevered. On his way to the front door he passed a lighted window, uncurtained, and heard music, and looked in; because if

Emmie was having a party he wasn't dressed for it, and would slink off. She was having a party, sure enough. Wearing a low cut dress, and her diamond earrings, and looking majestically happy, and all alone in the lighted room, she was playing some Beethoven.

Warner to Maxwell, August 3, 1962:

Here, too late to lie in waiting for you, though I had designed it should, is a story ["Their Quiet Lives"]. 'By me.' *'By you?'* 'By me.' I am infected by my stupefied drudge of a heroine. I tried, you may not believe this, but I tried, to abridge it. But it is a story of development and stories of development become stories of envelopment and turn into boa constrictors before you can say, Down, Ponto! I hope that is the reason, and not that I am infected by Pusey. Four Thick Black Quartos of Pusey attend my bed, Two at the foot and two at the head, Two to preach, and two to teach, And Four to send me off to sleep. He is not what one would call exciting, or profound; but his nose turned up at the tip, and he has a gentle, irreducible impertinence which I find agreeable. He could be the son of Catherine Morland and Henry Tilney (chronologically, I think this is so), and would be his mother's pride, interspersed with giggles, and his father's entertainment, dashed with despair.

Warner to Maxwell, August 31, 1962:

I am still going to bed with Pusey. He is an old man now. Every one he loved is dead, every one he attached himself to has failed him (or disagreed with him, which amounts to the same thing); all his hopes have failed, all his plans have miscarried, he has been cruelly disillusioned in Mr Gladstone; and throughout he has remained patient, polite, sweet-tempered, honourable, he has borne no malice, he has harmed no one. And suddenly he staggers into action, and spends his last energies, his last breath, in defence of—of the Athanasian Creed, dear William. There had been an impious proposal to make it non-obligatory in the Church of England liturgy.

Have you ever read this remarkable production? My father once described it as 'Hitting freely all round the wicket'. It reconciled Pusey and Mr Gladstone, however.

Warner to Maxwell, September 16, 1962:

Thank you for those cuttings. I have never read any provincial reviews before. I am pleased to see that they lay stress on my moral tone. I sometimes think that I am alone in recognising what a moral writer I am. I don't myself, while I am writing; but when I read myself afterwards I see my moral purpose shining out like a bad fish in a dark larder. Have you ever seen this?—the bad fish, I mean. You'd never think a mere haddock could look so elfin.

What will I do when I have killed Pusey off? I shall go on to Keble.

Maxwell to Warner, September 17, 1962:

And speaking of wonderful things, Brookie has named one of her paper dolls after you. Your name comes up sufficiently often in conversation between Emmy and me, and Brookie, playing on the floor, gathered up a name and went off with it. Except that you have to allow for what happens to things that pass through a child's mind. The doll's name is Cynthia Townville, but Kate assures me that it is named after you, and she should know.

Warner to Maxwell, September 25, 1962:

Oh, I am delighted to be Cynthia Townville! She sounds like the heroine of a late 18th cent. comedy, an heiress with a muff and an enormous Duchess of Devonshire hat, who will subdue the rake & then marry him.

Maxwell to Warner, October 2, 1962:

It is wonderful that you were unaware of your moral tone. I dare say that Jane Austen was also. The thing is you are moral but not didactic; you call the shots and add up the score but never say how things ought to be, so I am not sure that you can be said to have a moral purpose at all. You have a moral *tone*. To be without it would be from the point of view of the art of story-telling at a disadvantage, and the one thing you are not is at a disadvantage.

Warner to Maxwell, October 11, 1962:

And thank you for that revealing distinction between my moral tone and a possible moral purpose. You have set my mind beautifully at rest. I would not have liked to think of myself going about with a latent moral purpose—that is so horribly contagious.

Maxwell to Warner, after October 22, 1962:

For the moment, I am not anxious [during the Cuban missile crisis] and I think by this time you are not either, though one is more than one realizes conned by the news broadcasters, who are in the anxiety business. For a day, I had the same emotions that I had in August 1939, and was horrified at identifying them. I wanted to sit down and weep. I discovered afterwards that I was not the only person who had surreptitiously been taking a last look around at—oh all sorts of things, including Brookie's face. Emmy, who is more stoical than she appears to be, was simply stoical. It does not appear, over here, that an invasion of Cuba is intended. What is not clear is whether someone won't throw a monkey wrench into the machinery, but even if that occurred the two countries are not now in a position, without a good deal of backing and squaring around, to do the things they might have done last week. In 1939 my grief was for my friends—with the coldness that writers have at their disposal I did not intend to be shot at, and knew that somewhere there was a hole in the net where a little fish could slip through. Now there is obviously no such hole, and the net covers the globe. (Still, it is the business of fish to go on swimming, as long as they are in the sea.) And my grief is still for others, for the children, who are under the misapprehension that nothing can really happen to them because Emmy and I are there to protect them. (Unless possibly they aren't, after all. Three days ago Kate asked for the front section of the *Times* and took it into her room and appeared with it an hour later and said nothing. She has never looked at it before.) I find myself envying people who believe in the Management, but that isn't of course the same thing as believing in it. One is never sufficiently sympathetic with all those Romans who had to live their lives out during the several hundred years of the Decline and Fall. I wouldn't even dare aspire to being an ancient Greek, but shall we modestly do our best to live up to the standards of the decayed Romans? In the end,

I think, remembering how you once rose from a ditch and finished your sentence—have you forgotten?—it is a matter of style and aesthetics. It is a reflection on the way we have lived to ask us to take part in a mass incineration, when we have counted on a particular end. In any case, you at least have courage, like Emmy.

Warner to Maxwell, October 27, 1962:

I think of you so often. You might turn round in the street and see my anxious ghost looking after you. But with the look of anxiety on every face, how should you recognise mine?

There could be a great deal to say, but this seems no moment to say it—though I certainly never thought I would be tongue-tied in a letter to you. What is needed is a Mauve Fairy, to cast everyone into a sleep. Meanwhile, I suppose, every day that the surface of an every day is preserved is a day's step towards sanity, and a chance for the U.N. to speak it. I was saying this last night to Valentine, and five minutes later the ten o'clock News assured us that an invasion of Cuba was all ready to go. Now I am waiting for another such sedative draught. I think I will leave off now, before the cup comes to my lips.

O my dear William—we don't deserve it.

Warner to Maxwell, October 30, 1962:

Oh, what an infinite relief to be writing nonsense as usual.* A reporter from Washington to our BBC said the USA was unmoved, and flocked to baseball matches. But I know that kind of immobility. One has it in dreams, when serpents or scarecrows pursue, and one can't get away.

---

* President Kennedy and Soviet Premier Khrushchev had reached agreement on an end to the Cuban crisis.

Warner to Maxwell, January 7, 1963:

Like everyone else in the south of England, we have been snowed up since Dec. 29th, when the first blizzard hit us. Like everyone else, we are absorbed in keeping birds alive. A topical talk on the BBC yesterday which recommended bacon-rinds was interrupted in its course by a lady who had telephoned to say that bacon-rinds must be cut in small lengths if birds are not to choke: this was duly embodied.

A friend of mine, elderly and infirm, is now belatedly experiencing the excitement and tiresomeness of adultery. She has a tame robin, who spends much of its time in her sitting room. The other day another robin also flew in. Both robins immediately fought. The air was full of feathers, wrath, and bits of Christmas tinsel. The interloper was driven out; but a few hours later it had found another open window and made its way into her kitchen. So now two tables have to be spread, two windows left open, and every door kept shut in case the rightful robin should hear Don Giovanni chirping in the kitchen.

Warner to Maxwell, February 27, 1963:

I heard something so beautiful that I long for you to have heard it too. I desperately hope you have, for I cannot see how I can manage it for you from my own resources. A Radio-Television programme from Paris of people remembering Proust: people who had known him, a little girl who had been fetched out of bed, to the fury of her English governess, dressed and sent down to the salon to meet a gentleman—with a beguiling voice— who urgently needed to meet the fledgling model for Mlle de Saint Loup; an acquaintance at Cabourg whom he questioned about all the passers by, explaining *'Je suis un peu concierge'*; a friend who had studied him so intimately that he could assume his voice and launch into one of his interminable entangling sentences; and at the end of all, Celeste Albaret recounting his last days and death. Twice she broke down and wept; and took courage and went on, always with the same impassioned dutiful accuracy—as though this were something too sacred to be falsified. I can't tell you how moving she was; with a low-pitched voice that had a ring in it. As I listened, I suddenly realised that I was listening to the hearth of French culture: that the voices that spoke Racine's new tragedies spoke like this, that what the Comédie Française remembers and perpetuates is Celeste Albaret still alive.

I long for you to have heard it. You must hear it. You must be an importunate widow to CBS or something till they relay it.

Maxwell to Warner, March 1963:

When I was a little boy, I was always coming down to breakfast to learn that the night before there had been an unusually brilliant display of the Northern Lights. It used to make me frantic with frustration. I was grown before I ever saw them. The other night, our dearest friend [Muriel Tannehill], who lives across the road and in her youth lived with the de Reszkes in Nice and was a protege of Reynaldo Hahn (at seventy her voice is still unspoiled and exactly right for Mimi and Manon, the most tender lyric soprano), looked across at our house, she said, and didn't see any lights, and was afraid to call us, but there was the most marvelous program on the television, all about Marcel Proust. I looked at Emmy and she looked at me. We both wanted to kill her. "I had an instinct that I ought to call you, that you wouldn't mind being wakened for it, and I always should follow my instinct . . ." There was no stopping her. Not even by glaring at her. The least people can do who don't follow their instincts is never tell a living soul. And in time I will forgive her, I dare say. I have a defective sense of rancor, and grudges fade away, and the first thing I know I am beaming at someone I suddenly remember I shouldn't even be speaking to, and by that time it is too late.

The rabbits are eating the crocuses, though I hope I have given them all diarrhea by sprinkling the garden with water-and-epsom-salts, out of the sprinkling can, and snow-drops it seems are not appetizing to them. Nor daffodils. We are about a month late, and though the weather was marvelous for a few days, it is now cold again. Emmy's father is coming for Easter, from Oregon, which is far advanced by comparison. And I am reminded of my father's hats. Did I ever tell you about them? On Easter morning, my brother and I got up around five and went out into the yard and looking for Easter eggs, and found them here and there and everywhere, nesting in green grass inside my father's hats. He was very particular about his clothes, and wouldn't at all have liked having his hats rained on, and colored with Easter egg dye. When were they put there? How was it managed? My mother? The Easter bunny? I cannot figure it out.

This morning, waiting for the crosstown bus, I saw a tall well-made man with grey hair, in his forties, saying goodby to a little girl of nine; he bent down and kissed her and she said "When will you be home?" and he said "Not until it's night," and then she floated off down the street and I watched him watching her, and at the corner she looked back and waved and he waved at her and then she was gone, around the corner, and he was gone, into his *Times*. But it was such a pretty love scene. I wish I could send you his smile, as he watched her. It was of the same order as apple blossoms.

Warner to Maxwell, April 16, 1963:

Ever since the cold weather Valentine has been feeling increasingly tired and unwell; and the first expedients of our doctor doing nothing for her, he went on to investigate with blood tests and x-ray views of her heart. And the upshot is that he is pretty sure she has a tubercular inflection of the pericardium. It is a very rare and recondite condition, and he wants his opinion checked by a specialist. So presently I suppose we shall go to London, and then it will be decided what is to be done: a major operation, or a quiet life under a cloud. She is not in pain; and by means of rest in bed and the consolations of philosophy she even looks and feels better. But I don't look beyond the day that is; and we both intend to take a great many opinions before assenting to the operation. It made us smile grimly when the doctor remarked that it is such a rare condition she could be sure of the utmost skill and attention in hospital.

So if I do not send any stories for the present, you will know it is not a fault of will.

I was thinking about your piano playing the other evening. Why don't you now settle in with the 48 Preludes and Fugues? Heaven and Bach between them have so arranged it that for every player there is one prelude, or fugue, that lies within his means. And after that there is a choice of 95 to mouse about in. I myself think that you might find yourself very happy with the fugue in E major in Book II—the one that Samuel Sebastian Wesley called 'Saints in Glory'. The steady slowness it requires will make you much more agile in pursuing speed when next you feel inclined. One should always study by opposites, as well as straightforwardly.

As for the ornaments, disregard them, they are dear little creatures; but their time comes later. Sooner or later, you will find that you are putting them in naturally—as Bach did. But *never* put them into a fugue subject until you can supply them in the inner voices as well as on top. I don't know why—a matter of mere morality, I daresay.

Maxwell to Warner, April 1963:

Oh I am so sorry. Do you know—and how can you not know?—Valentine isn't like anyone else I have ever met. One from time to time sees a child who is genuinely good but a grownup never. They are only nasty-nice. (Excluding saints, of which I have met two or three, and they were another kettle of fish entirely.) But though she is in no way childish, I felt about everything she said and did a kind of purity of nature that somehow was going to have to be paid for, and expansively. I will spare you my incorrigible optimism. Faith is what is called for, and that you have already. I am glad she is not in pain. I know you are. When you don't write I will know why, and when you do I will hope for news that is encouraging. If it were me, I would choose the quiet life under a cloud, because, as it happens, that is the kind of life I prefer—by which I mean it exactly describes the climate of my childhood. My parents, resurrected from the grave, would have no difficulty proving that I was brought up in uninterrupted felicity, but that is not what it seemed like.

Warner to Maxwell, May 1, 1963:

It wasn't the worst. The London man followed another clue and found out that her constricted heart was caused by a blood condition, not a TB infection. So no operation, no tubercle; but a course of treatment in the Brompton Hospital, where after three murderous days in a room with two other very noisy, very intimately harassing other patients she was moved this evening to a calm room to herself where she can hear the blackbird in the hospital gardens instead of television. The treatment is a drug; and makes her first tired and intensely melancholy. But she will begin to rest now, and to sleep, and be able to respond to what they say should cure her —though it is as delicate as a Sauce Béarnaise, for if the drug overdoes its function of liquifying her blood—it clots now, and this has probably been at the bottom of her ill-health for a long time—she will bleed, and they will have to give a braking injection and then begin all over again. The hospital is very humane, and I go in whenever I please and stay as long as I like.

I am still feeling dizzy with the shock of relief.

Warner to Maxwell, May 21, 1963:

We are home again. I needed all your optimism as well as my own to believe we would be. Fortunately, Valentine's doctors were so interested in her reaction to their ratsbane drug (it is in fact exactly the same drug that kills rats by liquifying their blood so extremely that they bleed to death) that they did not notice that her general condition was getting worse and worse. It was a very humane hospital, and allowed me to stay all day with her; but the food was uneatable, and it lies in the path of planes arriving at London Air-Port. They grazed the roof all night—all day too, but could scarcely be heard doing so because of the racket of routine shindies and a building going up nearby.

It was Dryden who got us out. During the penultimate day I read aloud the whole of 'The Hind & the Panther'. I meant it as a sedative but it worked as a tonic. And the next day, scarcely believing it, we scattered hypocritical farewells to all those kind people, and went off like cats from a hamper.

She must still go on with the ratsbane & the blood tests, but she is, slowly & fitfully, gaining strength, gets up for half the day, drives the car even. Drives it as well as ever, too, though she can't write because her hand shakes too much.

It was odd to be in London, that I know so well and love so much, under those conditions. Here one moment and gone the next—like those stabbing flashes of the Mediterranean one sees from the tunnel railway along the Ligurian coast. But Londoners as substantial as ever. This was a considerable reinforcement, because once inside the doors of the hospital, one was caught up in a sort of Nation's *désordonées*. All the lesser fry, and a number of the nurses, were foreign, and ranged from a Finn to a Filipino. The Filipino was by way of being an intellectual, and told us with emotion that she had washed T. S. Eliot.

A craggy business, I would think.

Maxwell to Warner, May 1963:

When you have an idle moment, will you please tell me where one gets the courage to face the things one has to face. Your poor knees, is all I can think of. If London is crammed, it may well be crammed with Bahais. You remember the friend I tried to bring about a meeting with [Garetta Busey]? She is there, for example. Their clock has struck (and maybe ours too) and they are meeting in London to celebrate the hour. It occurs to me that, now you have dealt with bathrooms remembered, you might take up the subject of London hotels. Having been there in this season, I have no trouble placing you in my mind's eye, against the flowers in the window boxes and the particular spring light in the sky. Speaking of blackbirds in hospital gardens, I suddenly two days ago was given back a pear tree in full bloom in a hospital garden when I was nineteen years old. What old age is going to be like I don't dare think. Like cleaning out the attic, don't you think? Give Valentine our love, and tell her I think it was immensely clever of her to escape from both the telly and the operating room.

Warner to Maxwell, July 4, 1963:

It shows what a state I was in that it was only during the last month that I began to look through an accumulation of *New Yorkers*, and found your story of March 9 ["A Final Report"]. It is beautiful. As dry and sparse as a dead leaf skeleton; and like a dead leaf skeleton, the more one looks into it, the more form and artistry one sees. I have read it several times, each time with more affection. What an immense amount of discarding it must have entailed.

Maxwell to Warner, July 15, 1963:

What I liked best about that story ["An Act of Reparation"] is the oxtail stew, naturally. And what I liked next best is Fenton. The very thought of him brings tears to my eyes and I start yearning. What a grand (in the sense that Sir Joshua Reynolds used the word) bore. I sometimes think people aren't as boring as they used to be when I was young, and you have renewed my faith in human nature.

Maxwell to Warner, September 17, 1963:

We had a quiet vacation. A nice big—almost huge—house right on the ocean, in a place that has slyly kept itself unchanged, except that eleven houses were swept into the sea by a big storm and the ocean is steadily eating away at the beach—since 1922. The cretonnes were pleasantly faded, the white wicker chairs and sofas all had a list to port or starboard, and the walls were painted white or Wedgwood blue or moss green, instead of that depressing brown varnish. Upstairs rooms opening out of rooms opening out of rooms, and the waves breaking from such a small distance away that at night I felt myself raised, softly, mattress and all, and then deposited again, just as softly. But the seashore is so full of tricks. We all dreamt wildly, night after night. Emmy got a cold, which she could not shake off, swollen glands in her neck, and conjunctivitis, and Kate had a succession of sties, my brother-in-law reached his hand up to shave and became immobilized for the following week, with bedpans and all, and I finally produced a walnut in my cheek. The doctor said a staphylococcus infection, beginning with Emmy and moving through the family. I myself lean toward a poltergeist. Though it would have to have been a disembodied one and they are always embodied in a teenage girl, aren't they? But before that, I was wildly happy, went swimming four and five times a day, bicycled the whole front of me away, and something of the backside, and spent the inbetween times leaning out of the window considering the waves, and passed my fifty-fifth birthday feeling seventeen. So I know it was a nice vacation, but can't get back past the damp washcloths that it all ended in, the penicillin shots, and the visits to the doctor. One very curious thing. We had company for Sunday lunch and were standing on the upstairs porch when to my astonishment I saw a scene out of the Old Testament: the Crossing of the Red Sea. Only they weren't crossing it but walking on the shore. A mile long string of people, walking closely together in twos and threes, as if the town of Cherry Grove had decided to move to Ocean Beach. I cannot tell you how strange it was, until Emmy perceived the explanation. Beyond the Israelites, in the water, an arm raised and disappeared, and another and another. It was a long distance swimming match, and the spectators were keeping abreast of it on foot.

And there was an embarrassment of a personal sort. We went to church, by way of protective coloration, "for the children," and I discovered to my considerable uneasiness, that when my mind decided once and for all that there wasn't a word of truth in it my heart was not consulted. That is to say, I love singing hymns, I am elevated by the language of the ritual, I was even interested in the sensation of being preached to. I *like* going to church. And I don't, I still don't believe a word of it. Perhaps if I am quiet it will all pass off, like the walnut in my cheek.

Warner to Maxwell, September 22, 1963:

I don't think I should go to that house again—in spite of the rooms opening out of each other and the waves rocking you on your mattress. It sounds to me as if that house felt lonely, having lost eleven neighbours, and has decided to keep some tenants. Most old houses have staphylococci at their disposal. This one decided to use them.

Perhaps the company of the sea through so many long winters makes houses go a little mad. Great Eye Folly showed the same playful possessiveness. Did I tell you of the Christmas morning during which Valentine's mother who had come to stay with us developed influenza, Valentine fell downstairs, the Pekinese was sick and the kitten and I ran a fever? Fortunately, it was too ambitious. Fortunately, yours was, too.

I am going to make you feel dreadfully envious. By next week I shall be rolling and abounding in church services; for we are going to Italy. Valentine will roll and abound from motives of devotion; I, because I have found that the only way to avoid guiding sacristans is to go to a service and sit well at the back.

Warner to Maxwell, October 20, 1963:

We travelled from Florence to Rome in the same compartment with an elderly Canadian couple, in Europe for the first time. They were amiable— and I would have said, as unenlightened as blancmange. But the man, after staring at the rows and rows of vines, looping from tree to tree in heavy swags, exclaimed: All the trees are holding hands. Which shows what Italy does to people.

Maxwell to Warner, November 4, 1963:

The part I like best about travelling is shopping, though at home I almost never look in a shop window and hardly ever buy anything. It has to do with the other life, I think, the person I might be if I were someone else. The Pisans were so angry when we passed through that city in 1948—with reason; the American planes, on their return flight, used to lighten their load by dumping whatever they hadn't used on military targets on the Campo Santo and other treasures—that I couldn't think about much else, and failed to notice the curve of the Arno. We did climb the Leaning Tower, we always climb everything, and were scared to death. There is no railing, you remember, and as you get toward the top, the angle of the floor pitches you unpleasantly toward empty space. There were so many replicas, large and small, of the Tower that it took my appetite for them away, but I suppose if one had a single replica, quite small, at this distance, after all these years, it might be pleasant. I just don't know. We used to have an alabaster replica of the Taj Mahal when I was a child, and I adored it, but didn't have sense enough to grab it when the household disintegrated. I was only twelve, and not too sure that I would not be among the objects that were not to be sold.

Maxwell to Warner, after November 22, 1963:

We are all limp from our recent attack of history [the Kennedy assassination], so much so that there seems nothing worth saying. Also, there is no mantelpiece large enough to go put the national head on, for comfort. I believe it all stems from the hysterical way that American presidents are nominated and elected. After that, the president is everybody's doll, to be loved, to be left out in the rain, or used for target practice. For some reason, no one has pointed out that there were two women in that car who owe their being alive now largely to accident.

The Attorney-General and the President's wife went through day after day, hand in hand, at one another's side, like two children, and his face was always swollen and stained with the tears that she did not allow herself to shed. Nothing was private, including the cardinal's last finishing chew as he disposed of the sanctified wafer.

Warner to Maxwell, December 1963:

I had hoped to send you another story by this time, one of my MORAL pieces; but there is a hinge that won't stay in—if you have ever had to fix a hinge you will know how maddeningly the frame half of it prefers to come away with the door.

I still wake up remembering that Kennedy is dead. It will show you how this country took it when I tell you that instead of turning up our noses with our usual Tory prejudice against any new man, everybody is anxious to find good in his successor, and to forget that he is a Texan.

Warner to Maxwell, December 15, 1963:

My waking moments are confused with cats and foxes. There is a pair of amatory foxes who serenade us every night; and as love always makes people hungry, we daren't let either of the cats out after dark. Quiddity is too young to defend himself, and Kit too stout. So from sundown onwards they both rage up and down the house exclaiming 'Liberty! Liberty!', and trying by every means in their power to wear down my resistance till the moment when I shall open the door and say, 'Get out, both of you!' It is very mortifying for them that so far they have not succeeded. During the day, when they could go out in safety, nothing will induce them to leave the kitchen hearthrug.

What very odd letters you get in the office of *The New Yorker*.

Maxwell to Warner, January 15, 1964:

I don't suppose I could persuade you to write a novel about Horace Walpole's nephew who used to drive four stags harnessed to a phaeton until he happened one day to meet a pack of hounds, and was devoted to a housemaid? You know the nephew I mean? And sold his grandfather's collection of paintings, to Catherine the Great, that are now in the Hermitage? And would say anything (and do nothing) to please anybody? I encountered his life in the *Country Life* annual, and long to have him undergo reincarnation at your hands. But then I also long for you to write more stories, and the two are mutually exclusive, or all but. I think I will instead settle for whatever you do do.

Maxwell to Warner, February 3, 1964:

I hope it is true that in the matter of your stories I am just a little unique, but in the matter of "Johnnie Brewer" I suspect we are all a little unique.

I will begin with myself. I took this sentence for the clue to the story: "England also contained castles, cathedrals, an unknown number of the oldest yew trees in England, Devil's Dykes, Devil's Beef tubs, Stonehenge, and his grandmother." Your lists are never haphazard, and I took this story to be a distant cousin to *Lolly Willowes*, or a grandnephew. As I read it, the hero, who comes from a new and fairly raw civilization and is therefore naturally attracted to everything that is old in the country of his mother's birth, is, in spite of or perhaps because of an almost American ingenuousness, given a taste of what lies at the heart of a civilization or a person who has reached a very great age—not evil as it is commonly thought of in the contemporary world but a much older, livelier, and more hair-rising thing altogether—something (as the Puritans used to say) abominable. All this against the background of the most ravishing descriptions of the English countryside that have ever been, or ever will be, written—something else that is only possible in a place of great age.

Number 2: Mr. [Robert] Henderson took it to be a story about a young Australian who went to visit his English grandmother and while he was there, in the middle of the night, he had an experience so horrifying that Mr. Henderson doesn't expect ever to forget it.

Number 3: Mr. Shawn read it as the story of two old ladies who are competing with each other for the boy's affection, both wanting to mother him, and jealous of each other's attentions to him, but thinks that the scene in the middle of the night needs to be toned down a bit.

Though I am conveying this suggestion to you (and you must of course feel perfectly free to act on it, if it appeals to you) my heart isn't in it. I think he read the story too hurriedly and doesn't understand what it is really about. It is successful as it stands—though horrifying (and meant to be)— and would not be successful if you toned down (that is to say did away with the conscious sexual intention) the scene in the middle of the night, because that *is* the story.

But it is not a story that can be printed in *The New Yorker*.
I will hold the manuscript until I hear from you.

P.S. I neglected to say that if we are all three wrong, or if I am wrong, it is most important that you set us straight.

Warner to Maxwell, February 7, 1964:

Now about 'Johnnie Brewer'—No. Now about the soup for lunch. Johnnie B. must wait.

You were the nearest right, because you saw the old women were part of the landscape; Mr Shawn was on a right line, for their competition and jealousy is what unlocks their sexual excitement. But I have misled you all, because none of you have seen that both of them are withering with boredom in their ravishing surroundings, and that why they talked about the hard winter was that it was something positive to talk about, the only interesting thing that had happened for years. I thought (but wrongly) that the quotation from Virgil, far from haphazard, and needing a careful grafting in to the story, would be pointer enough to why they seized on the novelty, the gobbet, or fresh young Johnnie. And another thing I now wonder if I established enough is Johnnie's blithe and heartless egotism. Did you feel, when he drove on into Wales, that any scar, any dint, would remain on him? It didn't. He drove all day, and spent the night at St David's with never a thought of the night at Bodkins because in the morning he would see the cathedral properly by daylight.

So I think a little later on I would like the story back, to see if I can readjust the values. At the moment, obviously the scene in the middle of the night is far too assertive; toning it down and toning up the boredom of *ergo tua rura manebunt* ["Thy lands are yet thine own," Virgil] might fix it. I should like to fix it; because lately I have got into a bad way of always having a reflective or analytic character somewhere about, a sort of Stockmar who exists in order to save me the trouble of making statements that can stand without being annotated. True, I am cunning enough to make my Stockmars rush to wrong conclusions—but a wrong conclusion is only a signpost to the right one. No! Down with Uncles! *

* Christian Friedrich, Baron von Stockmar (1787–1863), physician and adviser to King Leopold of Belgium, continued as unofficial adviser to Leopold's niece, later Queen Victoria, and helped bring about her marriage to Albert, Leopold's nephew.

Maxwell to Warner, February 19, 1964:

Edith Oliver [theatre critic and book-review editor of *The New Yorker*] has presented me with an inscribed copy of *The Venetian Glass Nephew*, which is a wind blowing straight out of my youth. On the flyleaf, or rather on the saffron colored endpaper, it says "Marian Dodd from Elinor Wylie with good memories of the pleasantest of bookshops Northampton, 1925." Oh the coolness of it. The very tips of her fingers. But all the same, her ghost appeared in Peterborough [New Hampshire], when I was at the MacDowell Colony one summer in my twenties, and no mistake about it. And when she was in her late teens, she and Emmy's Uncle Reinhold tried to fall in love. Unfortunately, he was all elbows (to the end of his life) and so the letters, which he read aloud to us, when we were spending the weekend with him in Princeton, were mostly reproachful. Started to read. Because he didn't read more than two or three out of a small boxfull when his wife snickered at something and he put the cover on the box and on my hopes. After his death I inquired about them, and his wife said she had gone through a truck-load of papers (he wrote books on economics) and the letters from Elinor Wylie were not among them. So he destroyed them...But what do I find between the copyright page and the table of contents? "To William, with my love." Never mind that it was a different William; there's not that much difference between one William and another. I consider it addressed to

> your devoted,
> William

Warner to Maxwell, March 5, 1964:

To William, with my love—and no equivocation as to what William.

Her [Elinor Wylie's] ghost appeared in Peterborough, her flesh appeared in London. I don't suppose there would have been much difference to the eye. She was made of dew and silver and the filigree of autumn-worn leaves. She was as much in earnest as a child, and as instantaneously. We met at some party or other, and with no more ado she began to talk about water, its quality and behaviour, and about Shelley's assignations with it, in his life, in his poetry, in his death. As you know, she believed she was his reincarnation. Maybe she was right. He never stayed long in any one place.

Maxwell to Warner, March 30, 1964:

I am now, thank God, in a position to make up for my neglect. To begin
with, I cannot tell you what a grief to me it is that Mr. L[obrano] is not
alive to read the new Mr. Edom story ["The Three Cats"].* That adorable
woman, with her hair tangled in the chandelier. I was utterly her slave,
proving what I knew already, that I now take my position among the
elderly, and save my patience for those moments when I am dealing with
the young.

Reading it, I was reminded of a set of figures I fell in love with, that
were quite beyond my means and not for sale. They were the Chinese signs
of the zodiac, in porcelain, *wearing hip boots*, and about 8 inches high, as I
remember. They were in the drawing room of Mrs. Robert Lovat, whose
husband was, as I remember, Secretary of the Navy, or of Defense, or
something, during the War, under Roosevelt. But at the time I saw them,
he was a New York banker, and I was taken there by John Mosher, in my
green twenties, because he thought I should improve myself socially. Since
I did not share this ambition with him, it came to nothing, naturally. Mrs.
Lovat was very kind, the room was full of people having cocktails, and
when asked to stay for dinner afterwards, I refused. She followed me out
into the hall when I left, to say goodby and to tell me how much she liked
They Came Like Swallows—that it was like "Disorder and Early Sorrow."
And this I couldn't forgive, so I never saw her again. I couldn't forgive the
comparison because I thought so well of my talent as a young man that I
didn't think it was complimentary to have it compared to something that
was infinitely better. It could only mean that she didn't know how good
"Disorder and Early Sorrow" was, she therefore couldn't know how good
my book was either. From the vantage point of twenty-five years, give or
take a year, I can only smile at my ferocity. The principle still holds, don't
you think? I looked, for a little while, for Chinese signs of the zodiac, and
occasionally saw them, always inferior and uninteresting. And then realized that I didn't have those hip-booted ones, I didn't want any. What do
you suppose has happened to them?

* The urbane Mr. Edom, proprietor of the Abbey Antique Galleries in St. John Street, London, first appeared in "A Flying Start" (1962), and would figure in a total of nine short stories
before Warner reluctantly set aside the character in 1968.

Warner to Maxwell, April 2, 1964:

Longing for those Chinese signs of the zodiac in hip boots detours me—and curiosity. I take it they were signs of the Chinese zodiac, and more susceptible to booting than ours, so insatiably quadrupsical most of them. Scorpio, for instance. I would not like to boot a scorpion, belling a cat would be child's-play to it. Or were they two-legged figures supporting the signs?

Anyway, I am thankful you saw them; and saw no more of Mrs Lovat. In the matter of casting her off for principle's sake, you, and the principle, were surely right. I suffered too, in my beginnings. I was compared to Jane Austen.

Maxwell to Warner, April 8, 1964:

Having finished the trial editing of "Johnnie Brewer," and also having ascertained that it is acceptable to the magazine, I now wish to report the presence of qualms, which you are free to disregard. In order to head off the sexual implications I have had to cut more severely than you will probably like, but that isn't what is bothering me, because you can put back the things that you think are a serious loss, and in all probability they will stay put back. What is bothering me is that the edited version is an entertaining perfectly publishable story, but Version #1 sticks in my mind, and I keep thinking what if you should read the edited version five or ten years from now and think *Oh, I've been had! The original version was the better one.* The original version in fact enlarged my idea of what nice, well-bred, intelligent, but very bored old ladies are capable of, even if I misunderstood it, which I did. It is not a pleasant story, but it made an impression on every person who read it. There is nothing to prevent your publishing one version in *The New Yorker* and another in an English volume and in a volume of short stories. I just want to put you on your guard, and then whatever you decide I will not worry about, since it will have been your decision.

And the signs of the Chinese zodiac are not the same figures as our signs, but all animals—a bull, a rabbit, a goat, I think, and so on. *All wearing hip boots.* It is a momentary relief to have passed some of the gnawing covetousness along to you. Did you by any chance ever find yourself face to face with Lady Ottoline Morrell? I have just started her memoirs, and lost my heart to the 5th Duke (the tunnel building one) of Portland. I may lose it all over again to her, since she is a sociable introvert, like me, and life is not easy for such but it is bound to be interesting, and at present she is driving her team of Shetland ponies in, I think, Windsor Forest, and has nobody to play with, and nobody has promised her that it is all right, because D. H. Lawrence and Virginia Woolf and Lytton Strachey are all in her horoscope. And God knows who else.

Warner to Maxwell, April 25, 1964:

I have come back with a disengaged mind, and read 'Johnnie Brewer' in its third state. And to my great relief—for it would have distressed me a great deal to think of all the trouble you have taken going for nothing—I have decided that it will Do. And that your qualms don't apply.

There is a slate reef near Hartland Point that has wrecked a number of ships because for the most part it lies under water. But at low tide it emerges, and is a pretty sight with the spray dashing over it. At intervals however it looks out with its black face from beneath all that white lace, and grins murder. I am delighted to find that the black slate structure of 'Johnnie Brewer' is as durable, and that any reader who takes it for 'an entertaining perfectly publishable story' won't know slate from putty. He won't have such quite plain indications, that's all.

It is very sad about 'A Jump Ahead'. But I don't feel it as much as I might because I am hatching another story. I had better break it to you, this one is about incest (Electra not Jocasta) ["A Love Match"]. It is to be very quiet and prosaic, with no shadow of calamity; in other words, with no shadow of morality.

It is too late for me to tell you anything to the purpose about Ottoline. But for your own satisfaction I will say that when she went to visit Theodore Powys at East Chaldon, the village swallowed with one joyful venerating gulp. It was middleclass gullets she stuck in.

Maxwell to Warner, April 29, 1964:

It is still not too late to tell me about Ottoline. I have been so pressed, with work and with a rash of social engagements, which I am usually clever enough to avoid, that the review is so far only a mass of notes. The person who is most delightful about her is Stephen Spender, in his autobiography. Especially, those attempts to set her conversation to, so to speak, words.

Warner to Maxwell, May 14, 1964:

There is a possibility that I may write T. H. White's biography.* Several of his friends want me to. His literary agent doesn't, having a personal pet in view. The complications are indescribable. T.H.W. left no literary executor, his estate executors are the Alderney Bank, who naturally rely on the agent. There are also a great many difficulties of copyright, and very likely the whole project may bog down.

The Sylvia-party went to amass some awe-compelling statements that may work on the Alderney bank and quell the agent. My First Reading Agreement with the *N. Y.* is regarded as such. Can this be extended into a possibility that if I do the book the *N. Y.* might like to have some of it as a Profile before book publication? I don't suggest you should or would; but apparently if it can be insinuated that you *might* this would be a valuable addition to the awe-compelling statements.

I have never had to deck myself in splendour before. It is very difficult— but as the Sylvia-party is being so loving and zealous, I must do what I can to help.

I never thought to become a Helen of Troy in my old age.

* T. H. White (1906–1964) was the author of some twenty books, including the Arthurian fantasy *The Once and Future King* (1958), the basis for the Lerner and Loewe musical *Camelot*. From 1947 until his death he lived on Alderney, one of the English Channel Islands, three miles square and ten miles off the coast of France.

Warner to Maxwell, May 30, 1964:

Here is my long quiet story about incest ["A Love Match"]. Keeping up such quietude makes me feel as if I had been dragged through a hurricane backward.

Warner to Maxwell, June 9, 1964:

I spent the weekend on the Island of Alderney which is populated by gannets and people who knew T. H. White, all of whom talked to me, many of them at once. I sought in vain for some one who would speak ill of him. They are all shockingly *de mortuis*. I suppose I shall have to go again later, when they will have had time to remember their less charitable feelings—though I wouldn't alter Mrs Herival, his charwoman, who referred to his bouts of drunkenness as his spasms. In fact, I believe Mrs H. may be the closest to the mark. He was subject to his vices, but *not* vicious.

I shall be in the infuriating quandary of knowing essential elements in the story which it will be impossible to state.

You will gather that I almost certainly shall be doing this book. There are still a few quarrels raging, but they are peripheral. But forbode not any severing of our loves. I shall still want to write short stories. In fact, I shall need to, to restore myself with some tractable fiction after warring with truth.

Warner to Maxwell, June 19, 1964:

As far as I knew anything by the time I'd finished it ["A Love Match"], it seemed to me in a rather good manner, and that I had cleared the hurdles with style; but I really knew very little, so I too have been holding my breath till you gave your opinion.

Incest is a wonderfully rich theme; or rather, it is a wonderfully enriching light, stretching a whole series of unexpected shadows from familiar objects.

6 [that is, the sixth story accepted that year by *The New Yorker*] adds to the pleasure even more than usual, for it means that I shall be in the happy state of helping to get a small boy on the way to a decent education. His mother has no money, his odious father won't stir a finger towards earning any, and our county education system will only allow grants to children who are clever at passing examinations, or mentally deficient (much the same thing, in many cases). He is neither of these. Valentine has been pulling every avenue and leaving no string unturned, whole convents of nuns have been praying for it—if Mr Shawn only knew, he has probably been worked on by whole convents of nuns.

Warner to Maxwell, June 1964:

When Edward was called Ned, my nose gave a twitch. By the time I came to changing and also not changing, I didn't even have to surmise.

Here was a story by William ["The Value of Money"], with every promise of being a very fine one. And it is. My word, it's a beauty; it moves with the pace a river does, not from impetus but from volume. If you are as one half as pleased with it as I am—but of course you must be pleased with it. One can't do a thing as good as that and not be aware of it. I felt about it as I do about Chardin—the same composure and gentle seriousness, and the power of knowing and conveying all the fine relationships within the composition, and awareness existing among these people with their separate secret lives—except for Dr McBride whose awareness is of the past and the dead. Oh William, it is a beautiful story. I am so glad you've written it.

My room is full of the smell of roses and new cut hay and of elder blossom; and coiled up in all this like the snake in Eden, is the smell of long wet winters in Ireland; Tim White's diaries, written twenty years ago and more, but still exuding a smell of damp and melancholy and a very faint smell of paraffin. I see I shall be leading two lives at once, rather as I did when I was translating *Contre Sainte-Beuve*. It is half-past ten, but somewhere just within earshot a haycutter is still traversing a meadow. The light scythes ahead and the bales of hay fall one by one into the following darkness. I have watched it, so I know. It is a far more fatalistic process than any daylight cutting, the grass and the flowers in the grass have a vividness, an intensity of life as the light seizes on them.

Warner to Maxwell, August 8, 1964:

White has fastened on me. I get up at 6.30 and work until 8.30, drinking black coffee and from time to time eating a little more bread & honey; and it is delightful. Not a bell, not a bore, not a telephone; and a sense of virtue that keeps me in a good temper all day. There is about five hundred weight of him disposed about the house. It is like trying to write the biography of a large and animated octopus—if octopuses are those things that writhe and thrash in every direction at once. I am getting involved in the queerest correspondences. There is a correspondence still *in petto* with a gentleman 'in the Persian Gulf' as Siegfried Sassoon expresses it, whose address has to be got from a nun in a convent in Worcestershire. And beside me is a letter from the man who stage-managed *Camelot*; who addresses me as Dear Lady, and is a Pet. I hope that the Voice of Duty will call me to go to Ireland before long, I always like a pretext to go to Ireland. Fortunately,

Camelot is coming to London, to see me. But in spite of the five hundred-
weight, there are the most agonising gaps and deficits. White determinedly
left a quantity of his notebooks and files in a coalshed in bleakest Yorkshire;
and the celebrated winter of '47 melted through the roof. Along the lost
was a long run of letters from a man called L. J. Potts, who taught him at
Cambridge. Potts is dead; the few of his letters to White that have survived
show that he was one of the best English letter-writers. Potts, I discovered
from one of these, knew, loved, had been taught by my father. I am inconsolable. I would give—well, I would give a great deal—to have known
Potts. It is a comfort that I know you.

Warner to Maxwell, September 15, 1964:

I worked and worked on White—and fiction kept on boiling up in me—
and then I started dreaming with the utmost vividness passages in his
diaries and letters which were exactly what I needed, but weren't in fact
there—and then I had a nice little subsidence and put my feet up and read
bulb catalogues and *New Yorkers*. Now I shall go peacefully back to White
again. He was a tragic and exasperating character, and as busy as a Jackdaw.

Warner to Maxwell, October 25, 1964:

O William, I could weep that I haven't written that story you dreamed
you were reading.
And that Keats didn't write that sonnet. But to be honest, it is the story
I grieve over most acutely.
You wrote so sympathetically (by which of course I mean praisingly)
about 'Between Two Wars' ["A Love Match"] that I must tell you that the
sentence, *loving each other criminally and sincerely*, lived for days on the
kitchen note-pad, flaked with reminders about icing sugar and chimney-
sweepers. It was the first thing in the story that came to the surface and I
caught it and pinned it.

Maxwell to Warner, November 18, 1964:

Our city address is still One Gracie Square, New York 28, N.Y. But a
more poignant question you could not have asked. The landlord, who is a

species of Sicilian bandit, though actually of Middle European origin, is forcing, at the point of a gun—that is to say, having to move—the tenants to buy the building at much more than it is worth, and turn it into a cooperative which will for three years be managed by him. He has thought of everything. On Mondays, Tuesdays, Wednesdays, Thursdays, Fridays, and Saturdays, and Sunday morning and Sunday evenings, my head is firmly in command and says "No one shall hold me up at the point of a gun." On Sunday afternoon, I feel the most awful clutch in the left side, and say to the imaginary participant in this scene, "Take everything, but leave me the view and the dining room where I can practice the piano in peace, and those cherry double doors." Treat me as someone so very ill that one does not ask, and when it is all over, I will tell you what happened.

Last Sunday morning at eleven forty-five I astonished my music teacher. It can't possibly happen again for another six months. But I began to play the third movement of a Kuhnau sonata and it *went*. I felt the angels protecting me from all the pitfalls, which I had investigated so thoroughly, in any case, that they were like old friends. I tell you this, not from lack of modesty, but from the certainty that you will rejoice with me and for me, and know that today the angels are not there, and the thumping is better kept behind closed doors.

Speaking of artists and the Inland Revenue, et al. I have a theory that artists shouldn't try to be clever about money (which they are quite able to do, being the cleverest people on earth) because it takes one's entire time; they should, instead, be clever about *making* it. As you, for instance, are. You write something, three or four words, on a grocery pad, and in due time back comes a check; a by-product, it is true, but money, nevertheless. If that isn't clever, I don't know what cleverness is. All the rest, the actual imagining and thinking and writing down, you would have done anyway, just to clear your head of whatever it happened to be full of. Right?

Warner to Maxwell, December 2, 1964:

I don't know if Brian Friel comes under your sway. If he does, please tell him how pleased I am to find him in the *N.Y.* (I spotted him some years ago when his English publisher asked me for an opinion on his book of short stories. There's such a lot of air moving through his sentences.)

Maxwell to Warner, December 27, 1964:

I have given my heart often and not always wisely, but this is the first
time that I have ever given it to a spoon.* But this spoon clearly was meant
for me. It is so affecting, those two not quite corners at the base of the
bowl, like the shoulders of a thin boy, and the apex worn on one side from
being scraped on plates that were broken as far back surely as the reign of
George II. I have a knowledgeable friend who can place it when he comes
back from the Virgin Islands. Or I just may take up hallmark reading
myself, to find out. *C. B.* is Charles Blakeston, I know. Don't ask me how.
He was the eighth of eleven children, and was very vain of the shape of his
calves, but truthful and kind and married for love and lived in a house that
suited him to a T, and it never crossed his mind that he would ever have to
leave it, and he didn't.

* Warner's gift intertwined Christmas and fiction. This same spoon plays a memorable part
in "The Three Cats."

Warner to Maxwell, January 6, 1965:

I wish you could see the two cats, drowsing side by side in a Victorian
nursing-chair, their paws, their ears, their tails complementally adjusted,
their blue eyes blinking open on a single thought of when I shall remember it's their supper-time. They might have been composed by Bach for
two flutes.

Warner to Maxwell, February 7, 1965:

My stepfather was one of my father's dearest pupils and possibly the stupi-
dest. He was nearer in age to me than to my mother, and when he came to
ask me for her hand I was perfectly delighted. His relations were not
delighted, and their side of the aisle at the wedding gave the impression that
they were gathered for a funeral, since his mothers and cousins and aunts
all wore black. Mr Saunter in *Lolly Willowes* has a certain likeness to him. He
died of angina, in his forties. I have never forgotten his large hardworking
dead hands folded on the shroud—like dirty lilies. He was one of the most
entirely good people I have ever known, and I was very fond of him.

Maxwell to Warner, June 1965:

My music teacher had a coronary, leaving me stuck fast in the Mozart C major sonata. It looked as if he might be being music instead of making it, as your dear friend Vaughan Williams said, but like all frail people he is riddled with the life force, or perhaps I mean raddled, and one day turned a corner, and will be home if not this week then probably next. I notice he doesn't speak of music at all, because there is some question of when he can play again ("if ever," his wife says, which is nonsense. Lock the piano and he would stop breathing.), so I don't tell him about my difficulties with fingering. And Mozart is sustaining, though I cannot do it. I would rather be not able to do Mozart than any composer I can think of. *

* Maxwell's teacher was Jean Dansereau, "a French Canadian virtuoso. The one time I played in such a way as to satisfy him he said sweetly, 'Why, Bill, I don't know you!' And I fell off the piano stool." His wife, Muriel Tannehill, mentioned in an earlier letter, was a lyric soprano, a protégée of Reynaldo Hahn.

Warner to Maxwell, July 22, 1965:

I hope you will have a very happy holiday in the chauffeur's cottage. What fun you will have with his books. When Valentine & I had our grand house in Norfolk, with a servant, we used to count the hours till her half-days & evenings out when we would rush into the kitchen and read her novels and magazines: not quite up to the level of Mrs Henry Wood (she was too young for that) but such a grateful change from Dostoevski.

Maxwell to Warner, July 26, 1965:

I was so angry at the election of Eisenhower in 1952 that I went to a party up the road and simulated drunkenness in order to behave badly. The hostess was a Democrat who had voted for that old goat, and that was what I couldn't bear. I used gross language, I believe I brought the children to the head of the stairs to listen, and I was treated with such forbearance that I eventually shut up, because, after all, when your heart is broken you might as well. His [Adlai Stevenson's] was too, clearly. He was never the same man again. Shortly after the election I went to Illinois, to see an elderly aunt, who was amazed (living in Bloomington, Illinois, Stevenson's

home town) at my enthusiasm. Bloomington is Republican, like most of
Central Illinois. I went to the library and looked up the back issues of the
Bloomington *Pantagraph*, and found that it had summarized his speeches,
instead of printing them. Oddly, when his will was probated, it turned out
that he had inherited one quarter of the stock of that newspaper. But they
still didn't print those glorious speeches. The political life of the United
States really doesn't bear thinking about, and I have stopped doing it.

P.S. Gladys Huntington was so angry that she put a formal curse on him,
pages and pages. None of it ever came true. The age of formal cursing is
over. So, thank God, is the Age of Eisenhower.

Warner to Maxwell, July 29, 1965:

   Oh, how I wish I had been at the party up the road where you simulated
drunkenness in order to behave badly. It is a very strategic idea—so much
better than just getting drunk when you would have had less control over
your behaviour and might have been quite inoffensive.

Warner to Maxwell, August 30, 1965:

   Do you know that the mss. of *Lolly Willowes* is in an exhibition at the
New York Public Library (Berg Collection)? I didn't, but a friend sent me a
copy of the catalogue. You ought to go and gaze on it in order to see what
a beautiful handwriting I had in those days and what a flowing pen. Begin-
ner's luck. If I had not written anything more I would think writing fiction
uncommonly easy.
   You really have the firm of William Whiteley (a merchant prince mur-
dered in his princely store by his bastard) to thank for *Lolly Willowes* and all
the rest of my books. I was in the stationery department buying sealing-
wax when I saw some blocks of smooth, lined paper being sold very cheap.
When I got my purchase back & saw how nice and unpopulated the pages
looked the next step was to want to write on them. So I sat down & began
Lolly Willowes—knowing roughly how I should end it but without the
slightest notion of what I should do in between.
   If I had the means I would build a handsome temple to Fortuity.

Warner to Maxwell, September 12, 1965:

Wales was heavenly—though at first acquaintance Fishguard (did I tell you of Valentine's insistence that we should be charmed by Fishguard?) did not seem heavenly at all. We traversed it from end to end, disliking it more and more, as we sought for Mrs. Morgan's guest-house where we had booked for two nights. And when we found it all hope seemed at an end, and we sat outside in the car with nothing to prop our dejected thoughts except Valentine's high-minded view that we could not slink away and bilk Mrs. Morgan. So I nerved myself to ring her bell (brass); and she came to the door, pale and sliding and false-faced; and assured me that I was quite wrong, that I hadn't booked, that she knew nothing about us. And with some hasty expressions of regret and meek acceptance I fled from her door, and leaped into the car and we drove away from Fishguard on the wings of this miracle (no doubt—someone had wanted our room for a longer let).

It is wonderful to see a miracle worked expressly on one's behalf, like a soufflé rising for you alone.

Maxwell to Warner, September 14, 1965:

After I got back to the office with this catalogue, I realized that of course the friend who told you about seeing *Lolly Willowes* on the third floor of the New York Public Library sent you a catalogue. *But what if she didn't.* So here is another copy, for the cats to peruse. It is a glorious show. There you are with Dorian Gray's buttonhole of Parma violets and Mrs. Woolf's note to herself about the plan of *To the Lighthouse* and Thackeray's minute perpendicular utterly legible copperplate, and Ouida's baroque silk thread. Looking at your handwriting I had a kind of seizure, as I rearranged my memories of you. I was that minute looking at you at an age which predated our first meeting, at the beginning of the war, in this office. The writing was the same, but younger, that was all.

I have picked up your letter of August 30, and see that it is as I surmised, the friend did send the catalogue, so I won't, unless you would like another, which seems unlikely. At this point of my life, I only want one thing less, most of the time, not one thing more, and especially not a duplicate of something I already have. Though I parted reluctantly a few minutes ago with something that didn't belong to me. Brendan Gill's oldest daughter had been going through old letters that had belonged to her great uncle, and suddenly said impatiently, "Oh why don't people write letters like this any more!" and handed it to her father, before she reached the end. He turned the page over to look at the signature and it was "H. James." From Washington, to a Mrs. Hill in London. And in a much more agile manner than I would have expected. It was during Oscar Wilde's visit, so it must have been before the period of stylistic inflation. Anyway, it was lovely, half-legible, full of corrections, sensible, written in a club waiting room, in obvious haste.

My brother-in-law, Emmy's brother, who is as beautiful as she is, has just arrived home from two weeks in England and informs me that the sun shone on him every day, so I know that it has also been shining on you, and done something, I hope, to clear away that discouragement. When we were married, we went immediately to my house in the country (where, though it is altered beyond recognition, we still live much of the time) and it was raining. We sat on either side of the fire, reading. For the last six months we had been struggling constantly to get to one another, or perhaps it would be more accurate to say that for six months I had been struggling to get to where she was and to persuade her that she was happy where I was, but at all events, she was persuaded, we had stood up in church and announced our intentions, and here we were and it was cold and raining and somehow not what it had been before or what we expected. That is to say, it had an aspect of all eternity. We were polite. But both secretly alarmed. And on the third day the sun came out and we both closed our books at the same moment and got up and went about doing things, in the kitchen, in the garden, and that was the end of all eternity, thank God.

Warner to Maxwell, September 20, 1965:

'Why don't people write letters like this any more?' They do, of course. You and I do. But somehow the old ones gather a patina, 'come together' like a soup on the second day. I am reading Constable's letters to his wife: they are so direct, so plumb in the middle of Mr & Mrs Constable, that it makes one's heart stand still.

Warner to Maxwell, November 10, 1965:

Goodness, dear William, where were you when all this [the Great New York City Blackout] happened? And did Mr Truax majestically open a closet and produce candles? Well, it has given Kate and Brookie something to tell their grandchildren (I take it they were safe home by then).

I longed to be there, to see the footlighting of the cars in the streets creeping up the shins of the black housefronts. Was there a rush of the emergency-minded to St. Patrick's to buy votive candles? Not that they would be much good, votive candles are designed to burn quickly away— but better than nothing. Well, I shall read all about it in *The New Yorker*— but meanwhile I am impatient and a little anxious to know how you got through the marvel of Science.

Maxwell to Warner, November 17, 1965:

The morning after the blackout, I felt the strongest urge to sit down and write you all about it and then I remembered how you had had years of such darkness in the war, and was ashamed of my own excitement. But since you have asked me, I will tell you that it was both strange and lovely. And not without fear, of course. If I had left the office when I intended to, I should have spent five hours standing up in a crowded subway train, somewhere between Times Square and 86th Street, and been rescued by firemen with flashlights. As it was, Mr. Greenstein came by with a question concerning something I should have done that had been left undone, and it took me a time to remember the details and offer the proper apologies and excuses, and so it was about five-twenty when I descended from the lower level of Grand Central to the still lower level of the subway platforms. Coming down the stairs, I saw at a glance that something was wrong. There were too many people on the platform, and this always means a delay in the trains. But my feet carried me on down the stairs, and I joined the other ruminants there, and then heard a voice speaking over the public address system, so low that it was like a thought in my mind, this beautiful sentence: "There is no power in all the subway." The only thing I can put beside it, for poetry, is something I once read in the *New York Times*: "All Thrace Is Lost." (In huge headlines, during the war.) We looked at one another, and then my native selfishness asserted itself, and I thought if all these people start to get on the Third Avenue bus there will be a lot of crowding and pushing, so I hop-footed it right up the stairs. (I was at the head of the platform, where it is less crowded as a rule. If I had been in the center, I could not possibly have left, because of the people pouring down the stairs. And when, five minutes later, the lights went out, people began to scream and push, and there were all the makings of panic. But some man lit his cigarette lighter and held it up, and this one small gleam reminded others that they had matches in their pockets, and so, instead of trampling one another to death they lighted themselves out into the open air.) On the second flight of stairs, with other selfish people in close pursuit, I met streams of innocent people coming down, and the ones going out shouted "No power," cheerfully, to the newcomers, who continued right on down, while they thought about this information. Out on the street, everything was normal, and I dogtrotted one long block to Third Avenue, decided which was the bus corner, and went and stood there, in a group of perhaps a dozen people. And suddenly it happened. It was rapid but not instantaneous. It was exactly like the closing of an eyelid. The darkness didn't merely come, it came down. From above. Perhaps the power failed first on the upper floors of the skyscrapers, but I can only guess, because as it happened I had such a massive surge of adrenalin in my knees (Emmy and the children uptown, and I in this canyon, unable to reach them or to take care of them, and *How could it be happening?*) At that point a lighted box came along—the Third Avenue bus, totally empty, and I began to crowd and push, to get on. When I had got my change and picked up my brief case from the floor, I looked around and saw that one of my colleagues was already sitting in the middle of the bus and was motioning for me to come and join him. We had parted less than ten minutes before. It was a youngish reporter named Burton Bernstein, the brother of the conductor, about whom the less said the better, musically speaking, and as we rode down in the elevator together, after a nod at each other, I had racked my brains in vain, for a conversational remark, and had decided that I would probably never have anything to say to him. You know how, as one gets older, one becomes suspicious of amiability with the young? Well, I sat down and we never stopped talking for the next forty minutes. I now consider him among my dear friends, though I haven't seen him since. He kept looking to see if the lights were on in Brooklyn and Queens and Jersey (they were on in Jersey but we couldn't see that far) and I kept seeing lights high up in apartment houses and being sure they were too bright for a candle. They were candles. I was and still am astonished as how exactly like a good deed in a naughty world the light of one candle shines. Meanwhile, at the street level, visions. The vision of a Horn and Hardart Automat lighted only by candles. The vision of a movie theatre marquee, wholly dark, but with human faces visible in the darkness. Not long ago Emmy and I went for a walk at dusk, having just arrived in the country, and to my surprise I saw that there is not simply twilight but a succession of them, each a little less light, and finally, when it is no longer twilight but night, even that is again a little less light. Total darkness is only indoors, in cellars and closets. As the bus moved uptown, slowly, we were of course aware that there were no stoplights at the intersections. It was like drifting downstream in a canoe. And lighted cars (for many of them had their interior lights on) kept sweeping past us. And where were we? 49th? 53rd? From time to time a voice would call out this information, learned from a quick glance, by the light of some car. The bus filled and emptied and filled again, over and over. Then there were policemen at intersections, with flashlights, but not at every intersection, guiding traffic. The visions continued. And so did the speculations, which got easier and less fearful with every moment that we were still unannihilated. Going down in the elevator today I fell into conversation with another reporter who had been talking to an English girl who said, No it wasn't at all like the Blitz. Then you knew what to expect (death and destruction) but this was eerie, and she was frightened. Less and less frightened, I arrived at 85th Street and Third Avenue, parted company with my companion, and stepped down into an atmosphere that was enchanted. Everywhere people were going about their business quietly in the dark. It was like another planet, where the sky, instead of being blue in the daytime, is black. I went into a corner bar, to get a pack of matches to light my way up eight flights of stairs, and found myself in a de la Tour. The bar was C-shaped, with the bartender inside the C, and in front of every man standing around it was a lighted candle, throwing the light up into his face from below, and a glass of beer. In all my life I have never seen a scene more beautiful. In daylight, the following day, I saw the same place but was unable to determine the elements out of which the magic had been arrived at. It was a plain uninteresting German bar, on a corner of Yorkville. From that corner to our building it is four long crosstown blocks. After the first, people began to thin out. Walking along beside a Puerto Rican messenger boy, I asked if he minded if I listened to his transistor radio. In Puerto Rico transistor radios are a status symbol. I was cordially invited, and so learned that it wasn't just New York City but the whole Eastern seaboard (learned erroneously; it was only the northeastern part of the United States and a little of Canada). In the next block I saw a tall young woman suddenly begin to run, and realized that she was possibly afraid of the dark doorways. In the block after that, I realized that the only other person nearby was somebody walking six paces behind me, and atavistic impulses of self-protection made me keep turning my head, and politeness kept me from turning it far enough to see how close the person was, or what he might be intending. In the final block I saw the moon rising over the river, bringing an end to the darkness. The super and the elevator man were in the lobby, and offered a flashlight, but I declined, having my matches, and started up the back stairs. To save my life I could not remember the floor I was on, but when I reached the fourth a kitchen door opened and a Negro cook with a lovely big plain face held a lighted candle out for me to see my way by, and told me what floor it was. On the floor above, a door opened again, and it was a little boy with a flashlight. And so on, until I reached the eighth, and there was Lily Mae, who is also black, and from Virginia, and the children. Ours and the two from next door, whom they knew only slightly until this evening, and now had become friends with. Six nights later I went to a meeting at school to hear a talk by Brookie's teacher, and saw her school notebook, the last page of which described my homecoming. The title of the essay was

My Current Event
The First Power Failure

It seems I walked in and shouted "There Are No Lights ALL Over The Whole Eastern Seaboard, from Canada to Miami, Florida." And that they then rushed into the next apartment and shouted "THERE ARE NO LIGHTS ALL OVER etc." Emmy was in the living room, and terribly happy to see me, and I made us a drink, and we had dinner, and then stood at the living room window. The radio had asked people to stay off the streets, and it seemed that it would be a good idea, in a city famous for its muggings. As you know, the crime rate went way down that night. The only explanation I have heard that makes any sense is Mary Cheever's. She said that possibly criminals are afraid of the dark. The river shone bright silver, like a poem by de la Mare, and the whole of Eighty-sixth Street was white with moonlight. The moon was huge, and lasted all evening. And looking down at the house across the street where twenty years ago, in the house of a friend, Emmy and I were eating wedding cake and drinking champagne, I saw a man and then another man pass along the sidewalk, under the trees, and thought is it a man or a werewolf? And all evening a police car with a revolving red and white searchlight on the roof went back and forth across the Hell's Gate Bridge and then suddenly it wasn't there any more. I put down papers for Daisy in the study, the way I used to do when she was a puppy and not allowed in the street because she hadn't had her first shots, and the fastidious creature didn't use them. We went to bed, the children having done their homework in costume, with the children next door, around our dining room table, by candlelight. The little boy had a mar-velous green velour hat on with a white plume, that I mistakenly (it was too small and rose on her forehead) encouraged Emmy to buy in Paris in 1948, and a wine-colored silk cloak that belonged to E's Aunt Betty, and looked like one of the heroes of "The Children of the New Forest." Kate was Elizabeth I, the other neighbor's child was, I think, Mary Queen of Scots, and Brookie must have been, though I don't remember, Helen Keller. Who else would she be? The next-door report was that the lights would come on at ten, and they didn't. When I woke at three, and saw that there were no festoons of lights on the Hell's Gate Bridge, only the two red, oil-fed I suppose, beacons at the top of the pylons, I began to worry, about food, water, everything. And when I worry I worry. At six-twenty I opened my eyes and saw the festoons of lights were lighted. And closed my eyes again, and through closed eyelids, five minutes later, saw the lights in our bedroom come on. The children were heartbroken.

Do not ever ask me how I felt about something without giving due thought to the length of the reply that you will have to cope with. I think this is the longest letter I have ever sent. I have written longer ones and not sent them, but instead put them in a book, where, years later someone I would just as soon not have had reading my letters has found them. This is, of course, the working of destiny, and not to be interfered with. Do you remember those letters in Elizabeth Bowen's novel [A World of Love] that decided it was time somebody came up to the attic and found them?

Maxwell to Warner, November 1965:

Everything [in "White in Ireland"] is engraved on my mind. The birds arrive. The letter comes too late. He leaves his desk just when he would cleave to it. I see the bed after he and the dog have spent the night in it. I smell the weather. I know the sound of his voice. Is it his writing or his feeling for animals that drew you to do it? I only know the book you sent me about the falcon and another story about climbing a mountain—a religious pilgrimage. I will have a go at *The Sword and the Stone* shortly. In general it seemed that the view you took of him was angelic—that is, not kind and compassionate, which is a Sunday school idea of what angels are like, but simply wholly knowing. Again and again and again the clear direct knowledge. And often terrible in its suggestion that there is no changing the way people are, or life. But that there is no use pretending that it is anything like satisfactory, either. I look forward now with immense curiosity to the beginning of the book, and what follows this section. And when I have finished, would you, as a favor to me, write another biography, about yourself this time?

How I loved it when he said "I must tell you one thing. If anyone shoots my dog, I shoot him." And there is a sentence about the dog that I cannot find this minute, which more accurately describes the emotional nature of that creature than anything I have ever read. But it is full of beautiful things. And a continual pleasure to read.

Warner to Maxwell, November 23, 1965:

I could not have spared a word of that letter [about the blackout]. Think! If you had not got launched in the full flood you might have left out the children dressing-up. They always know the thing to do in an emergency—and it is always right, and, being right, is always unexpected.

He [T. H. White] was interesting enough for a narrative but not important enough for a biography. I realised this first with alarm, then with delight, since it allowed me to use the narrator's devices of birds: references back and intimations forward. But at the same time I have enjoyed going back to the pursuits of my youth when I edited XVI cent. music and sat in committee debating whether to follow a manuscript which dotted a semibreve or a manuscript which didn't.

This scrupulosity gave me leave to force myself on his falconry friend, J. G. Mavrogordato, who lives in Wiltshire with two manservants, a goshawk, five falcons and two eagle owls. He didn't at all want to be visited on a fine afternoon when he might have been out on Salisbury Plain flying his peregrine. But he submitted—answered two questions, and then showed me round his birds. The manservant who had flown the peregrine came back while I was being shown round, getting out of the car with the bird on his wrist. A falcon is much more becoming to a man, even now, than an automobile.

But the strangest thing was the eagle owls. There was a fierce screeching while we were in the mews, coming from a shed next door. When he said he would show us an eagle owl too, and would we please stand back a little, and opened the door of a large shed, I expected to see the bird fly out. Not at all. It walked out, slowly, stumping, its feet spotted in beige feathers down to the talons, tall ears standing up on its head, enormous round fire-coloured eyes—and was exactly like a Court dwarf in Velázquez: Just about as tall, as erect, as burly, as intimidating. But the stare glowed like a furnace. He fed the furnace with a (dead) day-old chick.

Then we drove away, like Queens of Sheba; and he *was* so pleased to see the last of us.

25: xi:I kept this open in case there was a letter about White. I can't be praised too much (it is a taxing book to do and at intervals I despair) but *your* praises are more than much, they are a perfect fit, because you have seen what I was after.

No, it wasn't his writing nor his feeling for animals that drew me— though some of his writing I admire very much, and some I love. It was bowing to circumstances, plus the feeling of My God, why not?

He left no literary executor, no executors at all except the Bank of Alderney. After his death the B. of A., appalled at this mass of paper, applied to his literary agent, a good-hearted man, but his good-heartedness impelled him towards choosing as a biographer a no doubt most estimable client of his—but a second-rate writer. Cape, White's publisher, was appalled at the news. He applied to David Garnett, who said it should be me. So a charming stranger came down to lunch, and we sat on the lawn talking about White's diaries.* Diaries hooked me, as they would have hooked you; and I knew that White had always championed my books (we never met, but exchanged messages of esteem). So by the end of that visit I had said Yes.

I must admit that when the charming stranger came next time with *crates* of material I nearly said I must change my mind. But by then, I had been to Alderney, to White's persisting house, with the suitcases at the foot of the stairs as though he had just got back, and his uneasy suspicious ghost everywhere, and it was settled then. I was the cat in the hamper.

---

* David Garnett (1892–1981), author of *Lady Into Fox* and *Aspects of Love*, was a close friend of Warner's for nearly half a century. His portrait of her as a young woman can be found in *The Familiar Faces*; his correspondence with her was published in 1994. The "charming stranger" was Michael Howard, the chairman of Jonathan Cape, Ltd., White's publisher and acting literary executor.

Maxwell to Warner, before November 26, 1965:

Tomorrow afternoon we are off to Illinois for a family visit with my mother's sister, who was once so beautiful and romantic, and is now crippled with arthritis and gets around with a "walker." Who said "The beautiful and the innocent have no enemy but time"? Yeats? And my stepmother, who went into a nursing home shortly after my father's death, and never came out. But on the cheerful side there are a number of cousins I am extremely fond of, and the place of my childhood to look at once more, with our children. It is as flat as a table top, and most people are, for some reason, slightly larger than life size. The jokes go back almost to Grover Cleveland, and the one unforgivable sin is standoffishness, which, as it happens, is a failing that I do not have. Probably for the simple reason that I was partly brought up there. And of course the ghosts are everywhere, including my own collection. I turn a corner where I used to ride over the lawns on my bicycle delivering the evening paper, and nothing is changed. Or hardly anything. The changes all took place on the periphery of the town, out of consideration for my feelings.

Warner to Maxwell, November 26, 1965:

Whoever said 'The beautiful and the innocent have no enemy but time' was a Liar. Did he never go into a poulterer's shop and see the hares hanging head down with tin buckets on their noses for their blood to collect in?
Did he never go ANYWHERE?
Pshaw!

Warner to Maxwell, December 4, 1965:

Here is a little piece, snatched from the jaws of Christmas ["Churches Remembered"].
You will see that there are difficulties about complying with your request I should write my autobiography.
For one thing, I couldn't keep myself out of it.

Maxwell to Warner, December 7, 1965:

How compelling White is. Mysteriously compelling. I find myself, on the subway, carrying on a conversation with you about him, about the "narrative" vs. the biography. Assuming that the manuscript you sent me is the whole of the narrative, then I must tell you, as one of your earliest guinea pigs, that my curiosity is not entirely slaked by it. I am quite sure you are right about the only enemy of the innocent and the beautiful is time, because those rabbits were horribly convincing, but I wouldn't have said offhand that it was the importance of a person that determined whether he should be the subject of a biography but the matter of how interesting he was. And White is still very interesting to me. To begin with, he is clearly an original, and must, like other originals, have sprung from a soil well-flavored with oddity. But where? And from whom did he spring? And how did he become a writer? And did he never in his maturity love anybody but Brownie? And what happened to him after Ireland? I have the strongest sense of what he was like, but I could do with more of his company. As, for example, one was always happy to have more of the company of Laurie Lee's mother. You have brought him to life, in short, but the friendship is still in the early stages. If this is not the whole of 'White in Ireland' then you must simply disregard everything I have said as irrelevant.

Is an eagle owl the same as what the French call a *grand duc* and we, I think, call a great horned owl? And if so, do you know Colette's story (omitted, for some reason, from the English translation of *La Maison de Claudine*) about the children and the mysterious noise in the attic? I once translated it for Emmy, and it took me from eight in the morning to six at night, working like a Turk, because she was continually in the eighth or ninth meaning of the word. No problem if you know French, but alas I don't and never will.

Warner to Maxwell, December 10, 1965:

An eagle owl is *un grand duc* (there is a fine one in *Chantecler*).* No! I don't *know* the Colette *grand duc*. I must re-read *The Maison* more attentively. If you can translate Colette, no doubt you can also fly, sit on a bough & sing, dance on a cobweb, and dig the foundations of St Peter's.

---

* A satirical play by Edmond Rostand, author of *Cyrano de Bergerac*, in which all the characters are barnyard animals, mostly birds.

Maxwell to Warner, December 28, 1965:

Emmy and the children have had two days of furious skating on the Putnams' pond. I was spared this pleasure by having to come to the office. A pompous skater at best, I have to run into something or somebody in order to stop myself, and I could not help reflecting that with a wrist done up in plaster of Paris, Haydn and his binary trinary flourishes would be quite out of the question. Also I feel that when bookish people take up sports they are in something close to mortal danger, and shouldn't consider that it is the same for them as it is for other people to get on a horse, or put on roller skates, or pick up a tennis racquet. Now that I am safely middle-aged, it is easy. I smile at others' pleasure and pick up a book instead. But when I was young, it was sometimes a nightmare from which there seemed no way to wake. Baseball, for example. The ball seldom goes to right field, and if it does it is usually high and one is excused therefore if one drops it. But once in a high school gym class a boy who was also not happy with sports got there before me, I being detained to answer a question by the instructor. And when I looked around there was nothing open for me except shortstop, which is close in, and vital. What followed was, technically, forty-two errors, and the game came to an end because the players couldn't stand up any more, being too weak from laughter. I was stoical, but not amused, as the batted ball flew past me, between my legs, through my stiffened fingers. On the other hand, at a critical moment, I once caught a football that nobody expected me to and that I didn't expect to catch either. This was, rightly, considered pure accident, and no praise was showered upon me. No, once was enough. No more. Never again would I grow up, for anything in this world.

Warner to Maxwell, January 1, 1966:

We are both sympathetic to your views on violent games. When Valentine had been finished in Paris, the height of elegance with a skull on her dressing-table and everything fashion demanded of her, her parents went mad and decided she must have a course at a South Coast College of Domestic Science. There she was called on to play hockey. Since she did not know how to play hockey she was put to keep goal (I do not follow the reasoning). There she stood, detached as a heron, all scorn and misery, till she saw twenty-two beefy young women rushing towards her, brandishing hockey-sticks. She cast down her stick, and RAN for her life.

Don't ever think twice about asking me to amplify. I love amplifying. If I had lived when people illuminated MSS I should always have been looking for unoccupied capital O's and filling them up with the martyrdom of Saint Sebastian and a pig-killing. In less laudatory terms, I am a natural doodler and dawdler.

Maxwell to Warner, January 4, 1966:

The transit strike is very interesting, to fall back on Anglo-Saxon understatement. By which I mean that New Yorkers are only attractive in a crisis, at which moment they get a light in their eye and a spring in their step, the years fall away, they become physically charming and well-dressed and, instead of pushy, gallant. It is one of those changes that come from the gods, as when Odysseus is freshened up for the eyes of Penelope. Very curious. But perhaps having more to do with city-dwellers than the dwellers of any one city. It is equally true of Londoners, isn't it? Though I was once in the beginning of a Metro strike in Paris, caught in a mob with Emmy and a large square wicker basket, and no such change occurred. By good fortune we were able to extricate ourselves and walk home through the Tuileries gardens, but I don't remember it with any pleasure.

Warner to Maxwell, January 24, 1966:

I found a delightful accumulation of letters from you, going back to Dear Miss Warner and a day when you and Emmy first knew Kate's eyes would be grey. You write admirable letters, dear William. But as Mrs Venton the ironmongeress remarked of a piece of steak, 'I would defy the strongest dog in Europe to eat it', I would defy the patientest editor in Europe to range them; you never put the year-date; so if I had not known that Kate was born in wedlock I might quite easily have cast her into an appendix.

I do hope that when you are sitting in a Grand Jury Box making notes on a slate with a squeaky pencil you will remember that all this is taking place in 1966. In our law, at any rate, a whole case could be invalidated by a trifling error of that sort.

I shall worry about you, not that I want to. But I am convinced it is very dangerous to have anything to do with the law. I think you should carry a little bunch of sweet herbs to ward off jail-fever, and a foot-warmer in case there is a power-cut while you are considering your verdict, and some kind of sustaining meat lozenge for the same reason and a small foam rubber cushion. Two months, good God, with intermittent sessions hereafter. I hope at least that you have some of Wordsworth's sonnets at heart; since there will be no advertisements to read and translate and versify and set in canon and mentally embroider in cross stitch. You will have my prayers and I will write to you regularly.

My stepfather was called to sit on a Grand Jury one summer when I was staying at Little Zeal. And Norah and I cut sandwiches and knitted him mittens and saw him off with anxious hearts; and he was back in time for tea. I don't think our respective Grand Juries can be quite the same. But unless I can find a sofa with a knowledgeable gentleman on it, I shall have to remain in ignorance I suppose.

Thank you for the check. I overlooked it in my concern. You would do well to gargle.

Warner to Maxwell, January 31, 1966:

This is heavenly news. We shall see you and Emmy again, we shall meet Kate and Brookie. We shall all be overcome and tongue-tied for the first ten minutes, and after that it will be as if we had seen each other last week.

Wild roses that were half the ordinary size: Dear William, that story dived straight into my heart and will be there as long as I am ["The Woman Who Lived Beside a Running Stream"]. I am convinced you wrote it about me (I believe this is one of the Infallible Marks of creative imagination, that rainbow which gathers into its half-hoop all the colour and the weather of all one's life and says, Look! You.) It is perfection, dear William. I hang over it, as if it were a bird or a moth or a fritillary. Can you even remember how you wrote it? It gives not the slightest impression of having been written, any more than Mozart does. And I mean every word of this.

Warner to Maxwell, February 2, 1966:

In a vainglory of spring-cleaning (for in fact very little gets thrown away and the hoards are as confused as ever) I went through some old diaries and found this record of a dream.

'The choir were singing:

> *Venus, of her teeth disarming,*
> *Teach a newer way of charming.*

It was from one of Handel's oratorios. The oratorio was called Galahad.'

Isn't it sad that one never adequately meets one's dreaming self?

Warner to Maxwell, February 4, 1966:

What a day! First all those cheques, now a Derain, a Sickert, a Matthew Smith, a Stanley Spencer & an Edward Lear.*

The Sickert is the loveliest. It is the view from a dusky room with a French window on to a sunlit street. It is bathed in siesta and poetry. The Lear is one of his Asia Minor pencil & wash pieces. It is about two massive chimney-pot granaries, which are out of the book you gave me for Christmas—architecture without artists. The Derain is a small oil, three slender aristocratic jugs on the usual rumpled cloth; the whole canvas is orchestrated in a dark peacock blue. I long to take it out of its frame—it is framed as if it were a dangerous bulldog. The Matthew Smith is a deep summer landscape with a turbulent sky of chestnut-brown clouds. The Spencer is one of his imitation Michelangelo's: Some prophet or other in seaboots. It is a dishonest work, palpitating with religious sincerity. But there is lovely brushwork in some of the bits he just filled up.

Don't you wish I wrote art-criticism? Such infallibility.

* Warner had the paintings in her house for safe-keeping while their owners were away.

Maxwell to Warner, March 4, 1966:

This [John Updike's "The Mastery of Miss Warner," in *The New Republic*] would have come along to you in due time, but I thought I would give myself the pleasure of sending it to you. In the light of how many people have said that "A Love Match" is a masterpiece, I hold my breath, retroactively, for what might have happened. It was *The New Yorker's* first excursion into the subject, to the best of my knowledge. Mr. Updike has reason to know that if there is a variant reading, with a writer of your gifts, it is more than likely to be that both are the author's, and to have sprung from an impulse that was the author's, not ours, and so "editing" is not simply to be assumed. He continually rewrites his own stories after they have appeared in *The New Yorker*, and in fact *during*. What he was really concerned with— the nature of your endings—seems to me an imaginary concern. Once a story is nailed down, it is the author's privilege, and indeed duty, to tie the bow in whatever fashion suits his fancy. But in general the review struck me as most entertaining, and often discerning.

I am playing hookey if that is how you spell it for the second day in a row. I have decided that I am too good to survive in my present circumstances, and that a little continuous departure from strict good behavior is my only hope. By which I mean lying, balky behavior, duplicity, connivance, and in fact whatever can be carried off with an air of innocence.

Warner to Maxwell, March 12, 1966:

Thank you very much for sending me the Updike article. (I have the highest possible esteem for goats; the comparison—I mean, I think, simile —delighted me.) . . . Valentine snatched the tear-out from me and sent it to Chatto & Windus; but they will return it, and then I will write to thank him—and to explain my reasons for the different ending of the 'Swans': not only that *The New Yorker* wasn't easy with the first one, though that probably made *me* uneasy too, till I saw what was wrong with it, false sentiment, just the same false sentiment that the man had cherished about Ireland when he was young.

But it was your earlier letter that really made me realise I had accumulated a career: where you wrote of the large scrapbook with my name on it. That stopped me in my tracks. I was like the old woman who woke up under the haystack: 'Look-a-missy, look-a-missy, this is none of I.'

How pleased my father would be; and how disconcerted, after his citation of the text in Isaiah. You can look that up too, it is in 'The Young Sailor'. Part of his disconcertment would be—because, like me, he had that soi-disant modesty which really springs from inattention—to find his admonition had been attended to.

Endings: I believe it is partly a national trait: the English sentence dying away in a mumble and a wave of the hand. I was reading a collection of Pritchett's short stories yesterday, and was amused to find how often he did the same thing.

Hookey—yes. I spell it hookey. I am glad and thankful you have been playing it. I have been playing hookey, too: in my case, sneaking out into the garden and weeding for hours on end when I ought to be indoors writing White, writing letters, getting my skirts shortened, spring-cleaning the larder and keeping out of the cold north wind. I make a habit of coming indoors with a little handful of chervil, so that if I meet Valentine I can say disarmingly: I just tripped out for a few herbs for the soup. I doubt if it deceives her, but the little attention is placating.

Warner to Maxwell, August 1, 1966:

Tonight is a happy holiday from conscience. I discover I am so well advanced in poor White's decline and fall that I can take an evening out and write to say I hope you are all well home and over those first ghastly days

Sylvia Townsend Warner in 1954

Valentine Ackland and Sylvia in the mirror at Frankfort Manor, "that lovely house so much too large for us but never too large for our love"

Frome Vauchurch, in Maiden Newton, Dorset, as seen from the river

"As you see, I cannot work unless I have perfect order around me": Maxwell to Warner, February 24, 1970

Brookie and Kate

Emily and William Maxwell at Yorktown Heights in the mid-1950s

when everything is put away one can't remember where and 200,000 letters are cascading from every piece of furniture. This is the 200,001st. You
can read it with a calm mind, it needs no answer.

I am living in two tenses, and very agreeably. White's late diaries are so
agonisedly personal that he bequeathed them to his publisher with a proviso that they must remain in the publisher's hands. I needed to read them,
and with leisure, so we have made a solemn compromise. The diaries, in a
solid yellow tin trunk, c. 1890 I should say, are deposited in the Dorchester
Museum; and every other day or so I am let in to the Hardy room, where
they repose, unlock the trunk, and take relays of them to the library. It is a
charming library, very large, with very solid smooth tables and chairs, and
singularly unvisited. A few old gentlemen or old ladies come in to read
periodicals; a young woman is doing research on such a large book that she
spreads it on the floor. One day the curator had a conversation with an old
gentleman in a white raincoat about a portrait of Hardy which represented
him with a broken nose. It was debated as to whether or no Hardy had a
broken nose. I intervened in a godlike manner, & said Sir Sydney Cockerell
spoke of it as broken and that he could be trusted as a careful observer. We
all decided with pleasure that S. S. C. could not be wrong. The statue of
Hardy in the town of Kensington shows him with a straight nose (it is the
work that Augustus John called the statue of a frustrated market-gardener
(it has some borage round the feet)) and nobody likes it except visitors.

All this is quite delightful and makes me feel I am back in the North
Library of the B.M., with the added pleasure of being old enough to speak
with authority about eminent noses. I loved the Bodleian too, but nobody
could call it either calm or spacious.

I hope to keep this up for several weeks more, verifying my notes and so
forth. Indeed, I am pondering what other nice little bit of research I can go
on to. At the worst I could make a sociological survey of whether more
visitors read *The Guardian* on Mondays than on Tuesdays, their sexes, per-
tinacity, and so on. Categories always give birth to sub-categories, it is what
they are there for.

Maxwell to Warner, September 20, 1966:

Rooting in the attic, I came upon five or six letters and postcards from you
from the late thirties. We have been writing to each other for about thirty
years now.

I work away at K.570 [Mozart], struggling with the problems of coordination and totally forgetting what I am trying to coordinate. It is like trying
to make lace with heavy gloves on. And yesterday when I went for my lesson, my teacher uncharacteristically heaved a deep sigh as we sat down at
the piano. I was startled, and then told myself that the sigh was not over
me, though it could well have been, because he is too kind and affectionate, and never seems to expect more than nature can perform, and so must
be because his wife and sister-in-law had been picking at each other, making scenes about what happened sixty-five years ago and was unavoidable,
in any case, or it might be because he was giving a lesson right after mine,
without leaving him any time to play himself. Anyway, for finger exercises
and stretches he often gives me arpeggios and scales that turn out to be
lifted from Chopin, and this morning it was from one of the nocturnes,
and so beautiful when played in its proper context, that I expressed my
delight, which led him to go and get the book, and for the next hour he
played his way through it, saying constantly *I must not do this...I haven't the
strength for this...* and then playing it, or part of it, because it was so marvelous and so unlike anything done before. He is seventy-six, with a bad
heart, and his career was dogged by ill luck, as perhaps I have told you. He
was Mary Garden's accompanist for many years, and played for Jean de
Reszke's lessons, and at last, in the thirties, began to play with orchestras
and had his first solid success in Germany, just as Hitler was taking over. In
America the jinx took over, as before, and it is too painful to think about
even, but he wanted me all the rest of my life to remember that music is
more than coordination. We never did get around to K.570, at which the
child in me, unprepared, because it would have required a lifetime of prac-
ticing, not the ten or twelve hours I had been able to give to it, rejoiced,
while the man marvelled at what he was hearing. I do not think any living
pianist can touch him. On the other hand, he could not do it, his health
ruined, the jinx always in the wings, on a platform. It had to be where it
was, and for me. If you are lucky, you find yourself in the field where the
flower is growing. You don't buy tickets for it. Dear old, old friend, tired-
ness one gets over, but don't allow permanent melancholy in the house.

Maxwell to Warner, October 17, 1966:

This leads me around to the subject of a collie dog named Trixie, long
dead. Before I was married I was much in and out of a household near

Brewster, N.Y. A husband and wife and two small children, a boy and a girl, and the little boy wanted a dog. He talked of nothing else. And his mother thought a collie would be nice, and I looked up kennels in *Harper's Bazaar* and found one on the other side of Long Island, and drove there and bought a puppy, I should think about three months old, for $50, which is about a sixth of what it would cost now, and started back, in a café-au-lait Ford touring car, dating from the year 1936. This was just before America went into the war, because after we went into the war I couldn't have got the gasoline to drive to the far side of Long Island. The puppy whined and settled against my thigh, and from time to time moved in and out of my lap, and sometimes put its paws on my shoulders and looked searchingly into my face, and all the while I talked to it reassuringly—roughly a hundred miles of reassuring conversation, and arrived at the house in Brewster just at dusk. The little boy's mother came out of the house and carried the dog into the house in her folded arms, and the little boy didn't at first see it, because he was playing with a little dog of carved wood, but when he did he made only one simple gesture—he put the carved dog aside. Well, so far so good, but the dog grew faster than the little boy, who was afraid of him, and would have been much happier with a smaller breed, and I couldn't manage to forget that ride, and was ashamed that I should begrudge the child the dog, but I did love it, and as it happened, the dog loved me. Year after year, and even when he was stiff and old, he would come to me and begin to whine conversationally, as if asking did I remember that trip we took together when he left his mother and came here to lead his New Life. I don't know how I could have managed to take him away from that family, who loved him, but only moderately, or if it was impossible, but what I regret is that I didn't even try.

Warner to Maxwell, October 20, 1966:

This is the advantage of man-made things. They don't give their hearts as the collie puppy did. Poor William! It is a very sad story, too sad for me to say anything comforting about it.

DULL see WEEM ["A Brief Ownership"].

This is awful. I supposed all was now clear, that my additions and your inspired sentence about 'Dull—as I seemed to know as if I had actually been there' had established that my Dull owed no allegiance to the gazetteer's Dull, and was entirely my own invention; and my stay there a brief idyll with a seaside resort in Bohemia, a castle in Spain, a Dull that never was.

Sit down, William. Lay a wet handkerchief across your forehead. Clear your mind of fact. Read Gal. 4. Is it not plain and manifest that there is an actual Dull (in Perthshire, 70 miles from the sea, etc.)? And that in having negligently learned this from the Gazetteer I had to submit to geography and leave the Dull I had conjured up from a name on a page and supplied with that idealistic dumb gardener?

I don't know how to make this any clearer. I can't go on adding more explanatory postscript sentences like Mrs Finch writing about an arrival by train. *Je sois au bout de mon Latin*—at any rate for the moment.

Warner to Maxwell, November 29, 1966:

How dreadful that all your women have colds. Will they unitedly give the fragments that remain to you? Poor, poor Emmy! Nine people to dinner . . . if I were Emmy, I would *stay* in bed, and I would enforce the sense of it by eating quantities of raw garlic and parsley in sandwiches. The garlic does cure colds, the parsley is reputed to quell the stink of the garlic & doesn't. Did I ever tell you that in Delaware I went into a wayside drug store for a safety-pin or a sandwich or something—and that there, above a box of violet cachous, was a notice saying DIGNIFY YOUR BREATH? The war was a few days old, Valentine was developing influenza, I was full of sorrow and perplexity: but I saw that notice.

Warner to Maxwell, December 20, 1966:

I hear from *The New Yorker* that you are ill. I am so very sorry and so concerned. The shortest days are such a bad time to be ill in. And I know that you take influenza badly, so I think, of course, it must be influenza. And instantly I think of all the other things it might be, and all of them so disagreeable. I am like the rather terrible sergeant's wife we had to entertain during the war who appeared at every meal in a different blouse and said of her stay in Egypt that the Egyptians were so diseased: 'not *nice* diseases.'

This news which slid like a goblin out of my agreement cheque has taken all the sparkle out of the news I was going to tell you. Still, I will tell you. Dear William, I have finished White.

I incline to think it may be rather good. It is a great deal better than the Irish section you saw, for everything has been tightened up and pulled together since then.

It is strange to come out of this long *solitude à deux* and wander about in an empty mind.

Dear William, take care of yourself. Don't begin to act better till you feel better. Don't begin even then. First, convalesce. *Then* recover from convalescence.

Maxwell to Warner, December 28, 1966:

Trust you to pin the tail on the donkey! It was virus pneumonia. Not a terribly severe case, and I did enjoy the strange fauna and even stranger platitudes that the fever presented me with. I felt so like de Quincy, whom I have read so little of I cannot spell his name. But little elephants, the size of a Labrador retriever, with shining black *fur*! and bottles floating past the bed with messages in them!

Warner to Maxwell, December 31, 1966:

It's a pity you can't come to Painswick in Gloucestershire to recover your strength.

It was the kind of hotel which has a great many old ladies in it, and as a writer of short stories I was enthralled to discover how a single sentence can *place* a character—'Mrs. Walker has China tea'—or rouse one's deepest curiosity, as when one of the two Miss Grays (sisters but they don't often meet) said informingly to the other, pointing to an empty table with a paper napkin in a tumbler on it, 'That's Mrs. Washbourne.' Valentine said it was like living in one of my stories but worse.

Maxwell to Warner, January 13, 1967:

It was so kind of you to send me the posthumous V. Woolf. I would not have known it even existed. And wasn't it strange—like a sleight-of-hand—the way it turned up in the pages of *Mrs. Dalloway*. It seemed to me, in its innocent way, to have in it the same dreadful threat that hangs over every page of that novel—like the relation of "heat-lightning" to the real thing. Those cretonne animals are not to be trifled with. Horror is just beyond the margins of the next page. But how I wish someone had made a recording of her reading voice! How could the BBC not have done this?

Meanwhile, I have made a happy discovery. Someone pressed a copy of *A Pair of Blue Eyes* on me. It is the first novel of Hardy's I have read since I polished off *Jude the Obscure* in college thirty-five years ago. He is not the same and neither am I. But good God, I had no idea there was anything like it—like those descriptions and those simple extraordinary sentences, that *style*—anywhere. The rewards of growing older. One sees not only worse but better. Now where shall I go from here? *The Mayor of Casterbridge* or *Far From the Madding Crowd*? Just when I was coming to the end of Conrad and thought there was no one left in the world to read!

Warner to Maxwell, January 18, 1967:

Do you know Proust was enormously impressed by *A Pair of Blue Eyes* and drew several leaves from it? By the time this letter reaches you, you will have decided which Hardy novel to read next, so I will only say that it would be a pity not to know *Far From the Madding Crowd*. It was my first Hardy novel, as well as one of my first novels. I read it in one of those 'Railway' editions, now quite priceless among collectors (ours lost heaven knows how long ago), and I can still remember the physical excitement which shook me at his 'grand effects': a girl crossing a swamp, a thunderstorm at night, Sergeant Troy's sword exercise. And above all a night-piece of the morning constellations. I can't have been much over ten (I remember the room where I was reading it and it was our last year in that house). Then I had to be quite grown up before I could enjoy another Hardy. The innoculation had taken so thoroughly.

Both my publishers—my rightful Chatto & Windus & White's Cape agreed to share my favours—were delighted with the final copy of that book & since then have been making my life a misery by minutiae and careful queries, and have I this & have I that? I am like those children who spend their time crawling about under cotton-looms in Manchester factories, fastening loose ends. It is tedious in the extreme. It would be a pleasure to do it for somebody else's book—but not for one's own. It is like trying to get sand out of one's navel.

Warner to Maxwell, February 2, 1967:

I have written myself back into a good temper, but really I am in a very bad one. This is why. Last summer a lady called Professor C. D. wrote to me to congratulate me on my discerning views on Fuseli. She was writing a book on Fuseli, & would like more of my views. And then gave me chapter & verse for it, from *Lolly Willowes* where as you cannot possibly be expected to remember, a young man called Titus was going to write a book about Fuseli who was an unappreciated genius. So I wrote back saying that the views were what would come very naturally from a clever young man in the 1920s but were not necessarily mine.

This morning, my dear William, I had another letter from Professor C. D. to inform me that she is writing a book about me (she seems to finish her books with great rapidity). It will be in a series called Critiques of Modern Fiction, and the publishers are the Southern Illinois Press. And she has agreed with them without as much as a by your leave to me. I feel extremely incensed. And of course she wants to know this & know that and expects me to write her book for her. I wish I were wicked enough to fall in with Valentine's suggestion that I should tell her that in my youth I was England's most distinguished lady cricketer and now collect grasshoppers.

But why I am pouring out all my woes to you (and I'm sure you'll agree with me that this is a trifle arbitrary) is to put you on your guard. *She lives in New York City*; and I don't doubt that at any moment she will be snuffing round the *New Yorker* office. William, I implore you! Do not encourage her. Say that our relations are purely editorial (whatever that may mean, but it sounds cool, doesn't it?). I suppose you couldn't copyright me?

All these years I have lived unspoiled, never a biographer, barely a professional critic has laid a rude hand on me. I haven't yet composed myself enough to be able to write to her. When I do I shall suggest that she *reads my books*. If she reads them all perhaps she will become discouraged. Meanwhile I seriously entreat you to act as my literary executor and keep me to yourself.

Enough of this bold-faced slut.

Maxwell to Warner, February 1967:

Oh I do hope she calls me! In the first place I have had a certain amount of experience. Emmy and I used to see something of J. D. Salinger before he retired to a private corner of Vermont, and you have no idea the pleasure it gives me to say to aspiring young Ph.D. candidates "Mr. Salinger doesn't like his friends to discuss him *or* his work." But I think I shall discuss you with this Shakespearian clown. Or rather your work. I shall tell her that the novels are the work of a secret society, each being by a different hand, which is why they are so different from one another. And that there is an affiliated sub-secret society that is responsible for the stories. I shall hint, rather heavily, that I belong to the latter and am the author of *The Cat's Cradle–Book*. And that the greatest of all your books is unpublished, waiting in the British Museum—a four volume novel about Richard IV of England, the facts of whose reign were suppressed, in all the history books, by Cardinal Wolsey, for political reasons. Oh you don't think she will *neglect* to call me?

Warner to Maxwell, February 14, 1967:

I have at last plucked up my courage and written to Professor D.—taking a line of noble resignation (there was not much else I could take, was there?) but concluding waspishly that my books are totally unautobiographical. I have left a good margin of conjecture for you to fill up with your inspirations that I am a syndicate. It is a beautiful thought, it explains everything, it reconciles *The Death of Don Juan* with the *Tortoise*. PLEASE be the author of *The Cat's Cradle–Book*. It was an artful stroke to dissemble your self in the Introduction. That must have thrown a great many readers off the scent.

Warner to Maxwell, March 6, 1967:

Hardy: I would say, *The Woodlanders*, unless you have read it already; or *The Return of the Native*. The *T. Major* always strikes me as a poor attempt to regain *Far From the Madding Crowd*, though critics consider it a preliminary to *The Dynasts* (by the way, *The Dynasts* is very fine indeed, and very meaty and would do to take to the West Indies if you get there). *Desperate*

Remedies is technically enthralling, his dementia of cup and lip plots at its extremest; but one can only read it cold-heartedly, I think. *The Woodlanders* is lovely, it has a Samuel Palmer quality, a hazy glow. And it has one of his best-imagined women. Perhaps that is why his women are better than his men—that he imagined them with more feeling. And of course their skirts were a considerable help—I mean, he was freer to imagine their sexuality.

I wrote, eventually, to C. D.—a polite letter but it would have deterred a bear in rut. It did not deter her. She replied that of course she would respect my wish for privacy and invited herself to come and interview me when she is over this summer. She is probably more obtuse than vile. This merciful assumption makes me even more determined against her.

Warner to Maxwell, April 25, 1967:

White left me completely drained. No harm in that, provided I filled up again. But the question was, what had I filled up with? The real me or a soft drink? The question was sharpened by a letter I found when we got home asking me if I would become a Fellow of the Royal Society of Literature. I reasoned with myself that they had got to me alphabetically, but I couldn't help feeling it was an intimation, a kind word from the undertaker. Now my mind is at ease. It must have been alphabetical.

Maxwell to Warner, May 1, 1967:

All these years, through thick and thin, it has (sus)stained me (Oh, that Freud!) that somewhere in the State Department there is a document on me stamped "Prematurely Anti-Fascist": I contributed to a fund for medical supplies for the Spanish loyalists. The rest of the story is sad. Later I saw a report of what happened to the money contributed to the Spanish Republicans. The fund I had contributed to led the list, so far as money actually getting to the place it was intended for and not being syphoned off into "administration"; *ten percent had been used to buy medical supplies for those unfortunate soldiers.* Do you ever despair of the human race?

I haven't quite so much since I came home from the West Indies. On the other hand, I have been more absentminded. Yesterday morning we went on daylight savings time, and the day before people kept telling the children about it, which was just like dropping this information in a well. I rose and started to put the coffee on at what I thought was two hours before my music lesson and it turned out to be only one, and what is Sunday morning without grapefruit, poached eggs on English muffins, and three pieces of bacon and three cups of café au lait? All day long we were one hour behind. It was the day of the children's piano recital, and instead of being as heretofore the first parents there we were next to the last. Brookie played something by Kabalevsky and Kate "Für Elise" and allowing for parental complacency, I do think they were among the small few who had any business being at a piano. And, an hour later than usual, by daylight savings time, two by regular, we got into the car to drive to the city. I said "Where is Daisy's leash?" No leash. So I went back and got it, checked the front door to see if it could blow open, left my keys dangling, and off we drove to town. For years Emmy has carried a second set in her purse and, two weeks ago, the thought of dragging all this needless weight around prompted her to take them out. I wasn't worried because I know the super- intendent had another set. He was off drinking beer, and the keys on our hook were from before the lock was changed. It took two hours and a half, a great deal of telephoning locksmiths, and $36 to get us into our own home. Fortunately, Emmy had made sandwiches of dark bread and the meat from the pot au feu, and the next-door neighbor was home, so we sat and ate supper in her living room. The locksmith, when he came, was a boy built on the lines of a lead pencil, and as dirty as a chimney sweep, and he had, judging by the marks on his face, been in a fight the night before. The lock turned out to be pick-proof and had to be driven out with ham- mering, and I was glad it was his hands and not mine that held the chisel. "Does this happen often on Sundays?" I asked when he was finished. "All day long," he said. "Seven days a week. Is this the first time it has happened to you?" "Yes," I said. And then he said thoughtfully, "I don't suppose we would have met otherwise." Breaking my heart, though not for the first time. But so polite he was, under all that dirt.

Warner to Maxwell, May 5, 1967:

What a present to make me on the 1er Mai. 'Prematurely anti-Fas- cist.' . . . It soars above all other mortal distinctions. Oh, the inexhaustible solemn fatuity of the official mind. Stamped, too, not just endorsed. They had a stamp for it. Spanish Medical aid was /36 or /37. For at least four years you were a Communist Sympathiser, if not worse. Then, *aliter visum*, they saw it was just a youthful error: wrong, but rescindable. Prematurely anti-Fascist. Not in step with us, but we will overlook that. Thank God you told me. I might have died in the night and never known.

Maxwell to Warner, May 8, 1967:

The Royal Society of Literature has found a way to bring honor to itself, if you will allow us to say so. But I am pleased, all the same. Will you be formally inducted, in robes? Will it mean a typographical upheaval in *Who's Who* and such reference books? No doubt, no doubt. The trouble with honors is that they come so very long after they are deserved, in most cases. But do be careful because one public acknowledgement has a way of begetting another, and you may not want to be a commemorative postage stamp.

Maxwell to Warner, May 15, 1967:

I am nearly through with *The Woodlanders*, and mildly fretting at it, because the person I loved was Marty South who cut off her hair, and her father who thought the tree was going to fall on him, and I wanted the novel to be about her, and him. Also, will you please tell me how people in Hintock learned that Mrs. Charmond was seen with Mr. Fitzpiers in Baden, under compromising circumstances. What I love about *The Woodlanders* is the wood. When I am reading it, my pockets fill up with acorns, and I smell last year's leaves, and the light that comes from the reading lamp is filtered through treetops.

The apple trees were ready to open last weekend but couldn't, because it was too cold. Brookie and the little girl next door are making a house in the woods. It is adorable: it had walls (a twig nailed between two saplings), a garden, a welcome mat, a stone fireplace. They are out there all day, with all my best tools in a basket, and B comes in at dark glowing like a Vermeer. The lilies of the valley have doubled their patch over the winter. I am a wealthy man.

Warner to Maxwell, May 31, 1967:

Here is the Edom piece ["A Pair of Duelling Pistols"] (aren't you sorry that more is not known about the Miss MacMahons?)

The Ring. How can I explain about the Ring. Like heaven, it is a temper and not a place. Rings are gang-ups of dealers who are in agreement not to bid against each other at the auction. The first Ring bid goes unchallenged (or is only raised against an outsider's bid). After the lot has been bought cheap the Ring proceed to a knock-out among themselves. Each gets a proportion of the sum of the first bid, one gets the object and the profit he will make by selling it again. It is a conspiracy, and illegal. Almost all the big dealers belong to their appropriate ring. Not long ago there was a public inquiry into the system, designed to Scotch it. Dealer after dealer gave evidence and said how wicked it was, he'd never do such a thing—and went on doing it.

Valentine has several times been invited to join a Ring. The first time, in her innocence, she thought it was a kind intention, thanked them politely but explained she was in such a small way that she'd rather not.

It is a regular thing; I am sure it must obtain in USA sale rooms too; but I don't know what it is called there. Ask some wicked business man, dear William. (It doesn't only apply to antiques.)

Warner to Maxwell, June 12, 1967:

Here is the complete White book—raw and uncorrected but here it is. How odd it will feel to you to have all these galleys sans the obligation to write in their margins—I would have felt securer if there had been William's marginalia.

Valentine has a sampler which begins:

> *My loving parents, pray be pleased to see*
> *This little piece of work performed by me.*

But I admit, to me it seems more like the Bayeux tapestry. How I ever got to the end of it is only to be matched in marvel by how I ever had the audacity to set out on it.

Warner to Maxwell, July 13, 1967:

I was too cautious to say so before—it being such an uncommonly thick wood—but I have another story ["Bruno"] finished, and when I have brooded over it a little longer and trimmed it, I will send it to you.

As you may have noticed, I tend to make pets of my characters. This can be engaging, because readers feel a creative petfulness too. But it was becoming a habit, so in this last story I have been at the utmost pains to pet nobody. Impartiality requires space to remain unmoved in. So this is quite a long one too. About 6000 words.

It has been, still is, extremely & gloriously hot, and I am holding my breath because of Robert le Diable. He is the most many-petalled, sumptuously empurpled of all the old roses. His petals are tissue paper thin and he blooms in mid-July. If the weather holds, in three or four days time I shall have such an army of him and such a bower of scent as will pass all words. If the weather breaks, I shall have fifty or sixty decaying brownish knobs.

In another good rose year towards the end of the last century the wife of an Eton master took it into her head to send a formal invitation to the provost of Eton, to meet Lord Alfred Carrière, M. Loris Van Houtte, Commandant Beaurepaire, Baroness Rothschild, M. le Prince Camille de Rohan, *et al*. Not being much of a gardener, the Provost arrived in a frock-coat.

I have wished I could send an invitation to you. The big bush roses like alba Celeste have done so well that they were almost up to the Sissinghurst standard. One could look in at roses behind roses and up at roses above roses. Very good green peas, too—but their names do not stick in my memory, except Fillbasket.

Maxwell to Warner, July 15, 1967:

It [*T. H. White*] is the best biography I have ever read. I sometimes think I was intended to be the person who of the entire human race enjoys your work the most. This may or may not be true, how can one tell, but surely this selfless accomplishment belongs with the very finest things you have done, and is as clearly stamped with your mind and personality as any of the novels or stories. No one who was not a novelist could have done justice to the Neapolitan costermonger episode or to the blind / deaf woman's first visit, or used the passages from the journals in the way you have. But it is always White who holds the center of things, never you, who so easily could have. Those one sentence observations by which you let the curtain fall upon a scene or situation keep the whole book up to the concert pitch of the beginning. What they must have cost to write I can guess from your letters. What they seem like is the dispassionate, compassionate comment of the angels. The person White most reminds me of is T. E. Lawrence, who was also intended to be something un-Anglo-Saxon (a Hebraic prophet?). White was obviously a kind of saint, who for reasons that were not his fault had to contemplate his own identity when he would have been so much happier in the knowledge of God. Both men have a susceptibility to vulgar excess. But where, & perhaps because he meant to be, Lawrence is a mysterious figure, White is as clear as—White's *heart* is as clear as a child's. Or a glass of water. Because he was so hideously warped by his beginning one can never not care about him. But the tug of war between his talent and his impulse toward destruction (—"but physically and emotionally I can't keep thinking that destruction may prove a very satisfactory passion"—there he speaks for half the human race, including yours truly) keeps the book as taut as a fiddlestring, and with his increasing deterioration it rises to a climax as a novel would, and like a novel has a heart and center in a single passage, the journal entry for Nov. 6, 1957: "I tried in tears tonight to say the General Confession..." His death was not the "good" death he intended, but a real death, stark, alone, not "lonely," and horrifying. I can hardly believe I never saw his body lying half out of that bath. Or that I never saw him, or that (most of all) *you* never saw him. He is continually seen. I am glad there will be photographs but they are not at all necessary. Unbelievably sad though his life is, it would have been far more so without this comprehending book. Somehow, by making him understood, you have released him from the trap he was caught in. To that extent, it is like a Greek tragedy. And for other reasons as well. And it is just possible that the trap is the clue to everything—I mean, by his feeling for animals, he was one of *them*, and because he was one of *them*, you could do the book as you have done it. Anyway it is a masterpiece I shall be reading many times. And the second—so that I can make a report to Mr. Shawn—has already begun. It arrived the very day we were leaving for Oregon—wasn't that fortunate? As if the U.S. Post Office realized the importance of getting it to me on time. Kate says solemnly, "Daddy, I hope you are intending to write Sylvia and tell her how much you like that book." She doubts my good manners, pertly, but partly it is pleasure in the thought that it is your book I am so excited about.

Warner to Maxwell, July 22, 1967:

You say everything my heart wished you to say—and one thing which illuminates a motive I had in writing the book though I had not formulated it to myself: of course you are right. He was an animal, 'one of them'. I must have admitted this subconsciously, else why should I have felt such particular *consent* to the passage about trying on the gasmask? I can remember feeling that here, at any rate, was something I needn't reconsider.

One has a dozen motives, hasn't one? I did partly undertake it as a dare; seventy is rather an advanced age to begin an entirely different technique. Partly as a rescue operation; because his literary agent was doing all he could to persuade the trustees-executors to give the job to a very inferior flashy protégé of his and Michael Howard [his publisher] and John Verney & Harry Griffiths [his close friends] were frantic to avert this. Partly because I wanted to do something that would take a long time and involve some sort of research (a Bestiary, in fact). But from the day I went to Alderney I knew I was to do it because it was a human obligation. He had then been dead less than four months. His suitcases were at the foot of the stairs, as though he had just come back. The grander furniture had gone to the sale room, but the part of the house he mainly inhabited he still inhabited. His clothes were on hangers. His sewing-basket with an unfinished hawk-hood; his litter of fishing-flies, his books, his *awful* ornaments presented by his hoi polloi friends, his vulgar toys bought at the Cherbourg Fairs, his neat rows of books about flagellation—everything was there, defenceless as a corpse. And so was he; morose, suspicious, intensely watchful and determined to despair. I have never felt such an *imminent* haunt. I said I would like to stay on and poke in the books; and Pat & Michael Howard and kind Harry tactfully left me. I poked in the books— and immediately found an unposted letter to David Garnett & took charge of it. I sniffed at the coats, took one down, was almost felled by its weight and massiveness. I looked out of the windows at his views. I had been left so tactfully that no one had shown me where the light switches were. And when I left, it was dark and I had to grope my way in darkness down two flights of twisting stairs and out by a back door. It was all I could do, to lock that door, to lock up that haunt and go off swinging the iron key. I went back to the hotel and told Michael I expected I'd do the book.

If this were a ghost story I could tell you that when I was there, alone the next evening, it felt quite different. It didn't. It was unchanged. The only difference was in me. I felt more at home in it.

Even so, it was like feeling at home in hell when last summer I read through those diaries he bequeathed to Michael. Michael was tied by the bequest not to let them out of his keeping; but we compromised by a transfer to the keeping of the Dorchester Museum. They were lodged there, locked in a yellow tin trunk which in turn was locked in the Hardy Room. To the reverent delight of the Museum's janitor I used to have the Hardy Room unlocked, and unlock the yellow tin trunk, and carry off one volume at a time and sit reading it in the Museum's Library. I can't tell you how eldritch it was to sit in that calm Victorian saloon, with perhaps two or three local ladies gently gossiping in a corner or a regular visitor puffing at *The Times*, with White's raving, despairing soliloquy whispering on and on in my ear. It was that I ran into at 3 Connaught Square [White's address in St. Anne's, Alderney], and locked up in the empty house.

(Zed, to round off the story, was killed in a car accident two years ago.) [He was a young man White had loved.]

Maxwell to Warner, August 8, 1967:

"Bruno" isn't right for *The New Yorker*. It is beautifully written, but it has a curious quality: you give your sympathy to the characters, each in turn, and then withdraw it. As if in the end you had come to dislike them all impartially. Which is perhaps the case, and your intention. At all events, I don't think you ought to change anything; it clearly is what it is; that's what came. Now that you are delivered from White, will you do more? I know you won't hold this particular failure to like something against us, and besides there is much in the story that we did like. Will you do five or six more right away and one after another?

Your letter about the visit to Alderney went to Oregon and then to New York and then to Yorktown Heights before it caught up with me.* It is a story of course. Did you not think of it as that? I was enchanted. I have been reading *The Once and Future King* with great pleasure. The boy's being turned into a fish and an ant are particularly successful, and all those lovely scenes of medieval life. And the badger's story of creation. I am just at volume II. I can see how he must have bewitched his friends, and children.

The house in Wellfleet, where I left Emmy and the children last Monday, is charming. Imagine a house built in the shape of a lean-to, out of pieces of other houses. All the windows had a previous life. And I think most of the lumber. The wall of windows faces oak trees, a thin screen of them, in front of a large pond. It is small, and the man who built it had an eye. He also liked solitude. It is in a wood, two miles from the main road, and the sandy road you get to it by is full of tree roots and chuck holes and famous for people getting stuck in. My heart sank when we arrived, to be leaving them in such a difficult place. But then we went swimming in the pond, and found that we were only a five minute walk through the woods and over the dunes to the sea, and after that nothing, not even a day of rain, dampened our pleasure. It is really Maeve Brennan's house—she took it for the summer, and rented it to us for the month of August, with her four cats and elderly Labrador, all old friends. Pansy, Daisy, Rupert, Juno, and Bluebell.

* The Maxwells kept a "country house" on Baptist Church Road, Yorktown Heights, New York, for mre than fifty years.

Warner to Maxwell, August 22, 1967:

I read about the race riots [in Newark and Detroit], and was as sorry as if it had happened here. I daresay that before long it will be happening here. I sometimes think there are too many right-thinking people. If they were fewer they would be forced to assert themselves and so have their right-thinking attended to. Something seems to have eviscerated public opinion. I remember how the news of the Amritsar Bazaar raised an absolute wasps-nest roar of right-thinking people. The wrong-thinkers roared too.* Now here I am, at the other end of my life, saying I am sorry. I ought to be ashamed of myself. *Où sont les talons d'antan?*

* In the Amritsar massacre of 1919, British soldiers killed hundreds and wounded thousands of Indian nationalists.

Warner to Maxwell, September 14, 1967:

There is a sort of half-baked railway strike going on, and I may have to revise my boast to you about taking the car northwards [to Wales] by train. The sensible thing to do, of course, would be to go a lesser distance. But we both feel we want quantities of sea air and salt water, and on this island one has to go a long way to get these in their native prime condition—and Valentine is intolerant of anything other. Ships and waves and ceaseless motion And men rejoicing on the shore did nicely for Coleridge, but men rejoicing have no charm for her. So it must be Ultima Thule. How enchanting Coleridge is from the moment one gives up expecting to admire him! ON REVISITING THE SEA-SHORE AFTER LONG ABSENCE UNDER STRONG MEDICAL RECOMMENDATION NOT TO BATHE. Do you remember the third stanza of that, with its dazzling last line?* A friend of mine, much under his influence, once spoke of his birthplace as Mary St Ottery. When I hear good men who have never known a moment's emancipation in their lives saying how dreadful that the young smoke marihuana and take L.S.D. I think of Coleridge and say nothing.

Valentine has now come back from the garage. New brake-pads had to be fitted to the car. They grunt implacably, nothing Mr King can do will stop them grunting. She can and will not drive to Scotland, she can and will not drive to Dorchester even, in a car that disgraces her by grunting like a pigstye. So there we are! *Voyez le prochain numéro.*

* 'Fashion's pining sons and daughters, / That seek the crowd they seem to fly, / Trembling they approach thy waters; / And what cares Nature, if they die?'

Warner to Maxwell, October 31, 1967:

It is interesting how characters continue their lives in one's head. The Lizzie of 1962 [a character from the Edom story "A Flying Start," now returned in "Sopwith Hall"] is now five years the worse for living with Mr H[arington]. It was bound to happen. She was *en pâte tendre*, would chip here and there; little veins, called crazing, would run through her surface which in 1962 was tranquil. In another five years she will be much more comfortable and the fraudulence which stole the locket will have developed into a placid obstinate self-preservation and a motherly providingness. Her children will love her and strangers will say What a nice gentle creature she is—and must have been rather handsome when she was young. Yet I had not 'A Flying Start' to refer to, and had largely forgotten it. I am very pleased (I was sternly brought up NEVER to say this: one should say *much*) that you have taken this Edom. I thought its opening one of my best soufflés.

At the moment I have five different calamities all needing support and counsel from me: a hysterectomy with where-to-put-the-dog trouble, two nervous breakdowns, a runaway wife and a funeral which will inevitably be involved in the flood that now rises round us. The grave will be full of water, the coffin will bob on top unless some large stones are lashed on: but this must be left to the undertaker, I can foresee but not manage, beyond putting up a mourner or two and supplying sandwich fillings. And I hope I may have solved the dog. On the whole, the runaway wife is shaping best. She is a member of one of England's most stiff-necked high-minded and priggish families and the object of her middle-aged passion is a flimsy *mauvais sujet*. They are very happy, and I hope their incompatibilities will weld them together. This hope is sincerely felt by her injured husband. It is he who is getting my support and counsel and I have just assured him that he will soon feel very happy with the divorce he has served seven years for, like Jacob the Patriarch. But I *do* wish I could have her account too. Unfortunately we have little in common except a mutual knowledge of a story by Charlotte Yonge in which the hero is an albino curate with eyes like rubies: this is cordial, but not enough.

Warner to Maxwell, November 9, 1967:

That funeral got somewhat out of hand. The officiating cleric went berserk, sprang into the pulpit and PREACHED!

Warner to Maxwell, January 11, 1968:

I am very glad you were not burnt up in your car. I really am. I should be poorly off without you and as well as that I love you without the spur of self-interested motives. But some of the story is just as I would expect. Have you noticed that it is always harmless people like you & me, people who can't bear to inconvenience others or disturb or disquiet them who burst into flames in the midst of gas tanks and so forth?

Yes, it is very sad for us both that Mr Shawn doesn't like the Edom stories. He comes of a sombre race. For myself, I come of a savage & contradictious race and my only reaction to his statement that my other stories 'are wonderful' was to resolve that I will never write another. But I doubt if

I can substantiate this noble resolution since I am in the middle of one at this moment. It is very short and black as pitch and he will reject it.

But don't be distressed that you have had any part in encouraging me to write about the A. A. Galleries. All you have done has been to incite me to enjoying myself—the act of a friend.

Maxwell to Warner, January 17, 1968:

Mr. Shawn is such a fantastically gentle man that it really wouldn't do to entertain, for long, savage emotions toward anything he says or does. I think some of the humor, and drama, and excitement, of those stories depends upon a certain knowledge of and taste for aesthetic objects, which experience has not happened to throw his way. And that is all it amounts to. And speaking of attics, my long-lost, bitterly lamented grandfather's Morris chair, that went all through college with me and followed me to Harvard, has turned up in a house in Urbana, Illinois—the house of a friend, where I lived as a graduate student before I jumped the academic fence and came to NY. I cannot wait to place my bottom in it once more and open a book and continue where I left off thirty-one years ago. But imagine having a friend things are safe with!

Warner to Maxwell, January 22, 1968:

It is an *admirable* review, a wonderfully true portrait of Leonard [Woolf], a beautiful balance of the two. You have managed what I would have supposed impossible: you have conveyed the unique amalgam of Leonard's Jewish-Hellenic mind; the combination of the Rembrandt Rabbi, lined, careworn, old past calculation, impersonally truthful, with the dry serenity, grace, impersonal speculativeness of Socrates. As you say, rocks & trees. He is both.

And by leaving Virginia to speak for herself you have kept her in ghost-dimension: vivid and dead. I have read the review several times, & each time I read deeper and admire more.

Here are some fragments as a thank-offering.

1) Scene, the kitchen at Monks House. Troy, the Siamese, leaps on the dresser & begins to eat the cold mutton arrayed for lunch.

Sylvia, tactfully: I have never seen a Siamese muzzle so ebony black as Troy's.

Leonard: But Oh, his soul is white.

2) Leonard & Sylvia meeting at Juggs Corner (the Parsons's house) speaking simultaneously: How are you?

Sylvia: I am a lady. I must be answered first.

Leonard: I am almost a gentleman. I am very well.

3) Again at Juggs. Ian Parsons & another are talking about some project of filming *Lolly Willowes*. I feel pettish. Leonard sees this.

'Don't be foolish, Sylvia. You had the fun of writing it. You have no right to object if now it becomes profitable.'

4) A luncheon at Boulestin's, after which I have to go on to make a speech. I am in pains of stage fright, but trying to hide it.

Leonard: Do you like leopards?

Is it one of those triangular chairs, as used by the Ven. Bede? I am very glad you are re-united, however you fit into it.

Warner to Maxwell, February 5, 1968:

While I remember, I must tell you that one of the things which distracted my attention from 'Sopwith Hall' & 'Furnivall's Hoopoe' was that I spent some time neatly collecting all my unpublished & unfinished prose works (Legion) into a black japanned deed-box painted with imitation chinoiseries in gold & silver paint. And tied to the box is a tag label and on the tag label is For William Maxwell. No obligation; but there they are. I painted the box and I am very proud of it. It is one of my Emmy-works. Yours too, if you feel so inclined.

Warner to Maxwell, February 8, 1968:

But just now I only want real life, for I have been reading in the *Daily Telegraph* a short account of that horrible and fascinating story of the two parents in Arizona who drove their daughter with her dog into the desert (to larn her not to spend a night out) told her to dig a grave, gave her a pistol, told her to shoot her dog. So she shot herself. It is the periphery of this which fascinates me. Did they drive the dog home? If they have other children, what did those children do? And the man she spent the night with? In short, What did the neighbours say?

Maxwell to Warner, April 9, 1968:

I am so bemused (when I am not thunderstruck) by events that it takes me days to draw a logical conclusion. It [the assassination of Dr. Martin Luther King] is the Kennedy assassination all over again, with a difference. Just as heavy-hearted, but hardly anybody but me seems to be having trouble with his tear ducts, and everybody (everybody white, I mean) is so ashamed. For years now, Negroes have not been willing to meet my eyes on the street; they look at a point in space, I look at them. But since last Thursday night, Emmy noticed, they look at you, and not without sympathy. *They* are not in despair. I think they have at last what they have been wanting for a long time, a black Christ. We have LBJ and Bobbie Kennedy and Mr. Nixon and Rockefeller, who looks and acts more and more like a Golem, and the Vice President, who looks like Punchinello, and [Senator Eugene] McCarthy, whom I have several times given up completely, but just when that happens he does something so ingratiating. He went to Atlanta yesterday, no, the day before, and didn't charter a plane, or pose for the photographers, hardly anybody even knows it, I think, and went to see Mrs. King—he paid a call of condolence *and went home.* Anyway, except for McCarthy they won't do, and maybe he won't either. How I wish I had never read *The Decline and Fall of the Roman Empire.* Yes we do have somebody. We have the mayor of New York City [John V. Lindsay], who night after night, before, during, and after the rioting, which was much less here than almost anywhere, because of him, one can only suppose, walked the streets of Harlem and Bedford Stuyvesant, saying how sorry he was. We also have, it would seem, an unlimited supply of assassins. Like the poor, they are always with us, only they didn't always have telescopic sights on their rifles. The nice thing about this office is that when something happens that nobody can bear, nobody runs off at the mouth. They walk about politely with their eyelids lowered, lest they see something you'd rather they didn't. But I despair. I despair of my country. If there was a wilderness I would cry out in it, but that too we've disposed of. The lumber interests. We can't even pass, let alone enforce, legislation about guns. I despair.

Warner to the Maxwells, May 6, 1968:

It gave me such confidence to find that I could lunch with the Maxwells in [London] W.1. as the most natural thing in the world that I easily went in to suppose that Valentine could drive from East Sussex to West Dorset without calamity. And so she did, a return journey through a green landscape which had been grey when we came that way before. And is really none the worse for it, & mystically considerably the better.

You gave me such a happy & restorative day that I went back to Mayfield a changed being. No one is ever unkind to me—or if they intend it, I don't notice it; but as one grows old one becomes insatiable for kindness & the sense of being cushioned against misfortune which it brings. You came to London, my dear dears, just when I needed you.

Thank you & bless you.

Maxwell to Warner, after May 7, 1968:

The happiness went right on. We drove to Amberley with a young man I once rescued from Ellis Island and his wife and little girl, through the ravishing spring landscape, and that afternoon Emmy and I walked on the downs with Bobby Urquhart and a young Arab girl, the older sister of one of Kate's school friends, so small is the world, and they had so much to say to each other and that could only be said standing still, and Emmy liking a brisk walk, we soon left them behind in the cowslips, and a rain came on, and we arrived home cold and wet in time for tea. For tea and funny remarks by the fire. And dinner came along in God's good time, as it always does in that house, by which I mean about quarter of ten, and I went to bed at midnight, taking two sleeping pills to dispose of the record player, and Emmy came up at two and the young saw the dawn. And in the morning we walked again, on the wild brooks this time, and another ravishing drive and then more of London, two full marvelous days. You do know every picture in the National Gallery, I'm sure, and so there is no point in asking if you know the little Longhi with a title something like *Some Masked Persons at a Menagerie*? It is actually half a dozen masked women looking at a hippopotamus, and simply wonderful. The young man who played Algernon in *The Importance of Being Earnest* was so good that he made up for the fact that everybody else was not quite what they should be. Or at least not to be compared with the Gielgud–Pamela Brown–Margaret Rutherford or Edith Evans revival. But the lines were delivered so clearly that not one was lost, and it is still the most dazzling comedy ever written. Do you remember when Lady B says "He looks everything and is nothing," and the young man under discussion complacently preens himself? And of course no cucumbers in the market not even for ready money always breaks me up. We had exactly twice forty-four pounds of luggage, without the two pounds of postcards in my raincoat, or the fossil that was presented to Emmy in Amberley, which she did up in blue tissue paper so that it looked fragile and carried in her hand. A very polite young woman collecting statistics for the Board of Trade asked me if I would mind saying how much money I had spent and I said not at all and told her and she didn't turn a hair. Which is one, but only one, of the reasons I love England. It is almost impossible to imagine a circumstance in which somebody would turn a hair. Our whole visit had an Arabian Nights enchantment about it, but it wasn't delusion or quite illusion. All the things one has to ignore, work one's way around, or directly contend with in America seem to be absent in London. I felt among my own kind, which is more than I do at home. Neither of us wanted to leave, and it was, in fact, fortunate that we had so much to go home to, or we might be there yet.

It gave me so much pleasure to think of your homecoming, which must have been something like the one I had once when the army decided I was never meant to be a soldier, and I returned to a house in the country deep in snow, and turned on the lights, and found everything untouched (my friends had said they would come and do something about it, if necessary) and put *The Magic Flute* on the record player and drew a deep breath and realized that I could go on living my life. This afternoon we are off to the country, with the children and a friend for Brookie, and with any luck the lilacs waited for us. If they didn't, something else will be in bloom, so it isn't serious.

Love, and so much more that doesn't need to be said.

Warner to Maxwell, June 15, 1968:

I thought of you with particular compassion for being in Ireland at the time of the [Robert] Kennedy assassination. It is much worse—as I found in 1939—to be out of one's native land for calamities. Not that the Irish would have been unconcerned. But their concern would have had a different slant, so to speak, moved on a different current, and this must have enforced a sense of isolation.

Here the outstanding reaction was oddly political. Robert K.'s death was felt as an item in a tragedy of violence & destiny, almost as if it had occurred in a play by Webster or Tourneur, too extravagant a horror for real life.

Maxwell to Warner, July 8, 1968:

I thought of you, in the bath, in Ireland, because the water was indeed soft, and whenever I passed the Four Courts Hotel, and at odd times in between. We were all very happy there, and had extraordinary weather to show things off in their best light, but were happiest in the extreme southwest, when we cancelled our hotel reservations for a couple of days and threw ourselves on the devices of Fortune, who came up with a house—"the Canon's House on the rocks"—in a garden that was like the fingers of a hand, and when you peered through the flowering shrubs you saw the ocean churning fifty feet below. The house was on Smerwick harbor, at the extreme end of the Dingle peninsula, and the woman whose house it was, a Miss Siobhan Fitzgerald, was so queenly and spoke in such beautiful 19th century syntax. The canon had been an army chaplain during the first World War, and his pictures were still there, and so was his furniture—mahogany sideboards and Morris chairs of a kind never seen in America, and a particularly handsome cabinet of shallow drawers which I took to contain his sermons, but it was, as you would have known immediately, for his butterfly collection. Twenty years ago the canon died and left his house to his housekeeper, the queenly woman, and if you are ever moved to put the car on the ferry and pay a visit to the Dingle peninsula, I will draw you a map of how to find her. It is engraved on my heart.

I looked so hard at the Irish landscape and the people in it that I almost wore out my eyes, such as they are. How I love alert, observant faces. And that 100 foot herbaceous border in St. Stephen's Green. And the shopping in Dublin. And the insides of those 18th century houses—unrestored—were like a poem of a particularly hair-raising kind. I imagined living in Dublin, as an expatriate, though I don't suppose we ever will. Still, you can't tell. Life in America at this minute has the quality of being in a besieged city. And it could so easily take a turn for the worse. The long twilights were even more satisfactory than the bathwater. It was like having everything you had ever lost given back to you. You are used to this phenomenon, probably, but I simply couldn't get over it. Twilight, and then the half light that comes after that, and then the quarter light, and the eighth light, and then the almost darkness that is still somehow a kind of light, in which the shapes of things emerge in all their solidity, and people are doing very odd things—such as fishing at eleven thirty at night—and the supernatural is not at all implausible, suddenly, and the night birds so— I thought of you every time I heard a skylark, which was often, because you had taken us to hear them, on a day when they were silent. Emmy thinks she heard a nightingale in Parknasilla, when I was asleep. Why not?

Your friend, the Enamoured Traveller

Warner to Maxwell, July 13, 1968:

While I was doing these proofs Titus frisked in at the window saying that in all his life he had never seen me doing *that*: and what was it for? He came here in January, 8 weeks old, to be Valentine's kitten, with an anxious face and a voice from ear to ear: and already the cloud was hanging over the house, Valentine in this strange pain and I so worried. If it had not been for Pericles he would have had a sad babyhood. But Pericles, after one stern glare and a low growl, melted: and in twenty-four hours had adopted him, so he is really Pericles's kitten; romped with (with suitable pulling of punches), pillowed, guarded.

Pericles is terrified of aeroplanes. One morning when both cats were out with me, a lowflying naval bomber from Yeovilton came over. I saw Pericles give one leap, start for the house: then *stop*, William, and go back to Titus and shepherd him towards me. Course of time has made it less essential for P. to be so invariably noble & I am glad to say they now steal each others' meals on an equality. One should not enlarge on one's animals —but I thought you would like to know what a charming pair attend us. I will only add that Pericles is by Mozart and Titus by Purcell.

Maxwell to Warner, July 24, 1968:

How lovely, that story about Pericles and the airplane.

The inlet you enquired about is, by Yorktown Heights standards, quite large. I am sending you a map, so you can judge for yourself. Though the wind was not blowing when we were there, I was given to understand that it often did. The house is in a garden shaped like a human hand. I am not making this up. Each of the fingers has grass and flower beds and flowering shrubs, and if you peer through the shrubs you see the water, *a long way down*. Last St. Patrick's Day the vegetable garden went, and Miss Fitzgerald's voice fills with grief whenever she mentions this. You look over the garden walls and see water and the other side of Smerwick Harbour, and Brandon Mountain, usually with its head in the clouds. In certain kinds of weather I dare say you wouldn't see anything, including your hand in front of your face. The house is one story, a bungalow with a shallow porch, and shutters on hinges let down out of the porch ceiling and are bolted to the porch railing, because of the wind. Like the house, they are heavy and old. Red tin roof visible for miles. If you walk to the village of Smerwick, which is only a couple of fields away, and consists of six or seven houses and their outbuildings, and then up across a couple more fields, to the highest point, you find yourself looking down not on the harbor but the ocean. I thought this at the time, but on looking carefully at the map I think it must not be true. I think you find yourself looking straight out toward the mouth of the harbor, which is wide enough to look like the open sea. (Or maybe it *was* the sea.)

The view in all directions is enough to unhinge your mind.

The beds. Emmy and I were given a double bed, with the best Indian silk counterpane, and, naturally, a deep cavity in the middle. I stuffed two extra pillows under the mattress (all the time we were in Ireland I kept having to call hotels we had left that morning to tell the maids where to look for the missing pillows) and Emmy and I clung to the sides all night. Then we discovered that Brookie's three quarter bed had a lovely hard mattress, so we changed rooms with her, since she likes hammocks. I don't know what Kate's bed was like, but I will ask her. There were only three bedrooms, all rather small. The bathroom is almost large enough to give a party in. The furniture is, as perhaps I told you, mostly the Canon's, by the looks of it. Some old mahogany, some very interesting variations on the theme of the Morris chair. The pictures are half the Canon's (scenes of the battlefields, First World War) and half Miss F's (variations on the theme of the Sacred Heart). It is homelike, very plain, very clean. The food is very simple—homemade bread and butter, potatoes, fish from the sea, lamb from Ballyferriter, lettuce, and the worst stewed rhubarb I ever tasted. It taught me not to go around saying recklessly how much I liked stewed rhubarb. The tea can stand unsupported by the teapot, but you have been in Ireland. If you were thinking of taking any animals, I think it would be better to inquire. Personally, I would think it unsafe. The drop from the garden to the sea and the rocks below is something between thirty and fifty feet. Maybe more, and though not dangerous to a human being who wasn't given to sleepwalking, an animal with an ounce of curiosity would be in danger of his life. On one of the fingers there is a greenhouse full of geraniums. The garden I found very interesting. The villagers are cordial, judging by Miss F's niece and sister, and Maurisheen the postman, and the policeman, whose name I never learned. They didn't sound like Synge in English but probably do in Gaelic, which they speak among themselves. The prevailing tone, I thought, was rather George Eliot. Except Cerne Abbas, I never saw a place that worked such a powerful spell on the inner-most mind. But you know how little, actually, we have travelled, and you might know dozens of places that are the equal to it or much better. On the other hand, you just might agree with me.

As I remember, bed and breakfast at Miss F's was a guinea a person. The extra meals were not expensive. She said, back in June, that she has room in the latter part of August, but wouldn't long, probably. But if one went in September, wouldn't it be breezier and more oceanic? And by that time surely the Americans would have gone home. She has Americans from California and Dutch people from Holland and I don't know who else. Maybe you might do what I didn't quite dare to do, which is to ask to see the contents of the butterfly cabinet. The food is cooked on a turf burning stove, and the house smells of it. It took some persuasion to get her to take us in when we dropped down out of the blue, but it was one of those times when I meant not to fail. If she had said a final no, I would have thrown myself down on the grass.

Warner to Maxwell, July 29, 1968:

This is all grapevine and must not be mentioned; but I must tell you at once as it will please you. I heard this morning that 'A Love Match' will be awarded the Katherine Mansfield Menton prize for 1968. I look on this as a triumph for incest and sanity.

A house smelling of turf and geraniums in a sea-girt bower almost sends me straight off to Miss Fitzgerald, and the map you so kindly enclosed transports me, just to look at it. We shall certainly go there before long. But not I'm afraid just yet. Valentine isn't yet in a state to enjoy intense enjoyment. We shall begin with the more moderate excitements of Wales, and keep a cushion of hotel staff between us and the realities of wild life.

Home-made bread & butter, fish from the sea, lettuce and home stewed rhubarb...My dear William, there are blessings and suavities. Edward Ardizzone [the English illustrator of children's books] & I met at a wedding last week. With champagne glasses in our hands and our best clothes girded about our loins we stared at each other with ashen faces as we recalled what we had severally endured at Healion's Hotel, Belmullet. At the end of three days of tea, stale baker's bread, metallic bacon and hard-fried eggs at every unremitting meal, I went out and ate grass.

It was a wonderful wedding, high & low. It began with the March from *Figaro*, played by the bridegroom's band of personal friends on wind instruments. The operation was done by a bishop from Australia, wearing a light summer cape, and the Dean of Windsor, who had the Blessing smitten from his mouth by a resonant amen from the band which he hadn't expected. Susannah Wesley, the family donkey, tied up in blue satin bows, came on as a dessert for the village children to go rides on. The bridegroom and his bevy of best men were dressed by Carnaby Street. The bride looked like a swan in a morning mist. I wore my hat. Valentine enjoyed it all very much and looked like the Empress Theodora. We are both much the better for it. Oh yes, and a detail I mustn't forget. The long tables under the awning were trimmed with vases of peacock feathers, gently twiddling in the light breeze. (Sacred to Juno, patroness of marriage.)

Can you grow sweet-peas in your stony garden in Yorktown Heights? (You certainly could if you planted them in a mixture of peat and kept them watered.) By hook or by crook I must smuggle you a packet of Unwin's Old Scented Sweet-Peas. The flowers are small, in bright Hundreds & Thousands colours. The smell is ravishing and so strong that half a dozen blooms will scent a room. I am enjoying mine so passionately, so carnally, that I can't bear it that you & Emmy should not have the same pleasure.

Maxwell to Warner, August 7, 1968:

To think that somebody actually managed to be married to music from the *Marriage of Figaro*! Emmy tried it, twenty-three years ago, but the organist failed to get the message, and what we got was the Love Death from *Tristan*.

Kate's camp was in that mild rural country just west of Bar Harbor—Sargentville, Sedgwick, Blue Hill—do you know it? So beautifully under-populated. We stayed in a bed-and-board place run by a large woman who moved with the lightness of a dancer—a thing I always enjoy seeing. I held forth to Emmy on the Maine character, with her as a model, only to dis-cover that she had lived there four years and before that in New Jersey. But without the generalizing faculty, where would novelists be? And along with all the other deplorable trends that one sees in American life, including the need for assassination, there is a new one: the waiter plunks your dessert down among the dirty dishes, on an uncleared table. This is the end, so far as I am concerned.

Warner to Maxwell, October 17, 1968:

I have planted some well-grown trees—at least the National Trust will plant them for me—to repair an avenue. Each with a leg-guard. The thought delights & ennobles me—and leads me immediately to the stories told me by Owen Morshead. He was for many years Librarian at Windsor Castle and in course of this traced a missing volume from some series, got it back, put it on the shelf. And on the next—rare—occasion when George V visited his Library, drew attention to it. H.M., a tidy orderly man, was so pleased that he began to talk about the wickedness of people who borrow books, only to be equalled by the wickedness of those who lend them. 'Do you know,' he continued, warming to his subject, 'there are *some* people who keep books in their spare bedrooms?' But the relevant story is about Queen Mary. She and Owen were staying in some grand house or other. It had an avenue. Halfway down it she paused, leaning on her umbrella. 'All my life I have dreamed of planting an avenue. But I never had the chance.' And then one says, Happy as a Queen.

I have just finished *Last Exit*.* I am profoundly impressed by it. When I
cast about for something to compare it with, I think of Swift and after
Swift, Beethoven. Swift was a bare writer—music is a barer statement than
words, and states not only by notes but by ethos, by a rhythmical conviction. It drives on to its end. One takes this for granted in music because
progression is a law of musical being; but such progression isn't part of the
writer as he writes (poets do have it, though, more or less) unless a fury of
narration drives him. Fury of narration, I suppose, is what *Last Exit* has
And what a triumph of actual writing. Compare his exceedingly limited,
metallic and foreseeable vocabulary with the richness, freedom, license of
Joyce—I mean, in method of saying it; Joyce never at a loss for an expedient, this man never feeling an expedient is necessary. Lord, what a book! If
I could have my way, I would make it compulsory reading for Greats, like
Marx's *Capital*.

And another thing: his austerity. Not a moment's glorification of his
subject-matter, no concession to the writer's natural impulse to endear or
recommend or exculpate what he's writing about; or to breathe morality
over it.

If I go on, I shall rant. You may have noticed how very difficult to keep
one's discrimination when one has just been knocked flat.

I am glad you are better. But don't let yourself be hurried on the path to
being well. We had a dear old doctor here, one of the old lot; & whenever
one of his patients had a baby he always prescribed a bottle of neurophos-
phates for the husband. He never lost a mother, or a father. He was as lean
as Death and smiled (when he smiled) like a dragon. For a happy year—
during the last years of the war when there was such a shortage of people
to do anything that people did anything, regardless of custom or legality—
I worked as his dispenser. It gives one a most interesting insight into one's
acquaintances to make up their medicines, to know who has colchicum
and who does nicely with a regular placebo.

See what a long letter I have written you—as St Paul said to the Dalma-
tians. It is because you are an invalid and should be cossetted.

* *Last Exit to Brooklyn*, Hubert Selby Jr.'s novel of the dark underside of urban life, regarded
at the time as violent, graphic, pornographic.

Warner to Maxwell, October 20, 1968:

I was delighted to see 'The Green Torso' again. It arrived when I was in the middle of doing a variety of useful & necessary acts, and I dropped everything and gave my whole mind to it (Everything seems none the worse).

Galley 9. 'I pawed at his fly . . .' Oh dear, I hope there will be no missishness about this. I'm afraid I should take it very ill. You see, I have to convey the breakdown and destitution of those down-at-outs, *without expatiation* (which would have muddied the introduction of Marco). I did it in a sentence. I mean that sentence.

Maxwell to Warner, November 4, 1968:

There is no problem about that sentence [in "The Green Torso"]. I should have cleared it with Mr. Shawn in the first place and not have put you in the position where you had to speak forcibly, but I am happy to say that when you speak, forcibly or otherwise, around here people listen, and the sentence will be printed as it stands. In general *The New Yorker* tries to move with the times without trying, like *The New York Review of Books*, to drag the times along after it. It has only been a short while, a matter of less than ten years, since I argued in vain against the excision of this beautiful sentence [from a John Cheever story]: "With love in his heart and lust in his trousers, he moved across the lawn." But as you see I cannot therefore ever forget my editorial failure, though in all probability the author has.

Two galliardias and two California poppies were blooming in the country this weekend. I went out intending to cover the roses, but was the object of universal sociability, which went on until two o'clock Saturday night, and Emmy and I were hard put to it to plant six de Graaf lilies, what with the incessant neighborliness. The wire baskets are around the roses, and if only it rains cats and dogs, I will perhaps be able to fill them with buckwheat hulls and cover the mounds with earth and salt hay. If it is another heavenly weekend, I don't answer for the consequences. Your old friend may be talked to death. But one gets to the country and the unpolluted air and the smell of decaying leaves, leaf smoke, and (a mystery) pumpkin pie makes one simply lean against Emmy. Everywhere you look it is so clear, for once there are not too many leaves on the trees to see each one. And the sunsets and the stars coming out, and planting by the last daylight, the light that comes over the hill in an arc after the sun is already down, gilding everything with literary echoes of "L'Allegro" and "Il Penseroso." And at night, when we get into bed, and turn the light out and hear the unbelievable quiet. For some time New York has been an uninhabitable city. It isn't at all the place you remember. Hence this lyrical outburst.

Maxwell to Warner, December 3, 1968:

Yes right down the line on "Being a Lily." Who could possibly resist it? Not I. Not Mr. Henderson. Not Mr. Shawn.

You will be interested to hear that last night I attended an unriot. At the Young Men's Hebrew Association on Lexington Avenue. The Greek poet George Seferis reading his own poems, with a Princeton professor [Edmund Keeley] preceding him with the translations and Senator McCarthy introducing him, and showing the same regrettable tendency to talk about himself introspectively that he did in that lamentable campaign. Outside the building we had leaflets thrust in our hands. Greek politics. Inside people were admitted one at a time, under protest. The hall was filled, the poetry in translation very good and in the original very unintelligible. Mr. Seferis is shaped like a musical top and wore a red tie and a red handkerchief in his coat pocket. When the question period came he proved to be impermeable, partly because of an insecurity with the English language that reminded me of my insecurity with French, and partly because he really was that way. A dark, terribly handsome young man rose in the back of the audience and said "I would like to ask... Mr. Seferis how he can live under tyranny." The word tyranny had to be delivered by hand by Senator McCarthy to the poet, who then replied sensibly that one lives under many burdens. The dark young man had an accomplice, middle aged, further front, who rose five minutes later and repeated the question. Very alarming, but not so alarming that one was surprised when the question period came to an end so much sooner than usual. The eminent figures stood up, the bearded young rushed toward the stage with programs to be autographed, and as the poet was advancing toward them with a smile of gratification, the velvet curtain descended abruptly, severing all connection. I waited to see if he would

crawl under it but he didn't. And the morning *Times* had to be content with
the students rioting in Ocean Hill–Brownsville. On the other hand, the electric toaster gave up during breakfast and a light bulb exploded in my study
right beside the laundress leaving pieces of glass on my unfinished opus
about my father's family. There is a strike at Con Edison, and I think what is
happening is that unmeasured quantities of electricity are beginning to leak
through. Also the telephones are behaving *very* strangely.

Warner to Maxwell, December 7, 1968:

Yesterday was my birthday—a day when I resume my cat nature & eat
on woodcock cooked bloody—so it was most appropriate that your letter
with the news of 'Being a Lily', & the velvet curtains descending and the
light bulb exploding right beside the laundress should arrive then.

But why, said Valentine, was the laundress there to be spattered with
glass? I expected she comes in once a week to work the washing-machine.
And why, Valentine persisted, should the washing-machine be in William's
study? I fell back rather weakly on the hypothesis that your study is a pas-
sage-room (have you not observed, I said sternly, that the moment one
begins to study in *any* room it becomes everybody's gangway?) For all that,
I would rather like to know why there was a laundress in your study
(unless USA has borrowed the term from Clifford's Inn, London: see
Samuel Butler). Had you asked her professional advice on some detail of
the book you haven't yet finished (*please* finish it. It will be the kind of book
I adore) about your father's family?

I hope she isn't a poltergeist—like our evacuee who festered at a touch.
Very often they don't indulge in these dangerous sports out of malice; it
just flows from them, like the electricity which you surmise is leaking from
Con Edison. Pray be careful. This is such a dangerous time of year with all
this goodwill about & everybody in such a temper because of Christmas
shopping. As I remarked long ago to the ambient air in Whiteleys Ltd.

> The time draws near the birth of Christ
> When everything is overpriced.

Such a pity that Marx wasn't alive & there to hear this probing economic
statement. All my own, too. I hadn't read him then.

Warner to Maxwell, December 14, 1968:

Unless the customs have been there before you, if you look between the spine and the spine's cover of *The Corner That Held Them* you will find a packet of Mr Unwin's Old Fashioned Sweet-Pea seeds: also, no doubt, some spores of anthrax, broomrape, rabies & Communism.

Maxwell to Warner, December 18, 1968:

And, though I have trouble believing it, it seems so sly not to have left a message or sent an arresting policeman or anything, the customs men— who else?—did abstract those seeds from your Christmas box. But to replace the beautiful wrapping paper and string— as if nothing had happened! Extraordinary!

Warner to Maxwell, February 6, 1969:

Another thing which made me badly wish for you was the big Constable canvas in the Burlington House exhibition. In the middle distance is Waterloo Bridge, being opened, with some puffs of cannon-smoke; and the river is alive with boats and barges decked with pennons and trappings, and as it is a choppy day the surface of the water is sending off darts of light. It raised me from the dead just to look at it. It is though Constable had taken a long steady appraising stare at Canaletto and then charged straight through him. And that is not all. The owner of this glory is anonymous in the catalogue. There he sits, somewhere in the Midlands, I daresay, keeping his treasure to himself. *Un vrai Milord.* I wonder what else he has.

Maxwell to Warner, February 1969:

In between mailing you checks, I think and talk about you; we all do. Emmy this morning, Kate yesterday. How do I think Valentine is; as if my nearsightedness had reached a point where I could see across the ocean. I think Valentine is brave and good—what I have always thought. Some years back, when we were at the beach, the house across the road in the country caught on fire, and the two people who lived in it were wakened by their dog, who perished. So did they, almost. When we got back they were both in the hospital, and we used to go to Mt. Kisco to see them every day for weeks, and what I remember was David's eye, the only part of a large man that was visible through the bandages. And so lacklustre. I will never forget the day I made the eye smile, with a feeble joke of some kind. Your letter reminded me of it. What I hope with all my heart is that Valentine is tearing around in a little car, going sixty between hedges, and swearing under her breath at traffic policemen.

Warner to Maxwell, February 28, 1969:

I still feel extremely resentful about those sweet-peas. If I thought the leather bottoms would grow them in their own gardens I would not be quite so incensed. But I can't find it in my heart to be so broad-hoped about them.

Warner to Maxwell, April 4, 1969:

Next week, if all falls out in a concatenation accordingly, I am going off for a weekend myself. Repose, very fine cookery, listening to music. My host has a mission in life: he finds neglected church organs and restores them. Then he plays Buxtehude and Frescobaldi, his neat feet dancing among the pedals, while Ruth & I wander the empty churches—which this time should still keep a smell of their Easter daffodils & primroses. Ruth is invaluable to him, she has such flawless absolute pitch, that he has only to say, Ruth. B flat, and she obliges. So he doesn't need his tuning-fork. If one were to include one-tenth of the remarkable people one knows, in one's fiction, no one would accept it. Real life remains one's private menagerie.

Maxwell to Warner, April 16, 1969:

Just when I was running back and forth on the high wire with little cat steps, balancing the card table, the umbrella, the dinner plate, the pitcher of wine, and the red rubber ball, and thinking this is something to be doing all at once, I got a summons for jury duty. I have served briefly on a case involving a heroin pusher, which stopped abruptly when the pusher in question settled for a lesser charge. The only dramatic moment was when the clerk of the court said "Will the defendant rise," and I started to get up out of my chair.

Warner to Maxwell, June 14, 1969:

It will be a light to my path to have another book by William to look forward to. But yours means a great deal more to me. Do, do prolong the creative convalescence as far as you can. Keep your feet up. Have a cup of cold soup at 11 A.M. and champagne at 6 P.M. When people other than the loved talk to you, look at them dreamily and say 'Um. Well, perhaps. But not this week.' Have you stretched yet? That particular emancipating stretch of a reasoned being.

Warner to Maxwell, August 8, 1969:

I have a story finished. It is very long and VERY moral. One of my worst. I conceived it in a fury against those social improvers who encourage childless couples to adopt a child as a expedient for begetting one of their own. Is there an American term for those china eggs which are placed in nests to encourage hens to lay? We say nest-egg; but that is ambiguous and suggests savings-banks.

This should have been a sublime summer, roses and raspberries and syringa and hay a parting present to my old age. But it hasn't been. Valentine has been increasingly unwell, increasingly depressed; her shoulder is only slightly better and the rest of her is worse. Now she has been put on a hormone pill, which will contain (it is said) any further developments. In fact, it is a sort of suspended sentence. My renowned levity, given me in compensation by the Gods, is beginning to grow very weak in the joints and tattered round the edges.

Warner to Maxwell, October 9, 1969:

I opened that *New Yorker* with the alarming cover at random and began to read at random. And I was so sure it was you that I went back to the beginning and read on, enjoying William, till I came to the name at the end and didn't even feel clever at expecting to find it ["The Gardens of Mont-Saint-Michel"].

The *climate* of your writing, dear William, is unmistakeable. It is the climate which wild flowers thrive in; benign to primroses and wild hyacinths; and wild roses don't lose their delicate pink in it. It is the climate of a sea-coast, gentle even in a south-westerly gale when ships are being wrecked only a mile away.

*Maxwell to Warner, October 15, 1969:**

I am enclosing a really splendid piece of oratory, by Brendan Gill, to be delivered right about now over station W.B.A.I. The streets are very quiet, the all-important ball game is just finishing, and whether the mobs that are supposed to materialize around four or four thirty do is the thing that is worrying me. If they don't, I think I will cover my face with my toga like Julius Caesar. The young are collecting signatures on street corners, and wearing buttons, but it is so far not like the student processions of May 1968 in Paris, and nothing short of that will affect that pinhead in the White House. Emmy and Brookie and a friend are meeting me in the music shop downstairs at four and going two blocks south to the park behind the library, for a mass meeting there, and then we are going to walk five blocks north to my club for supper, where Kate is to join us if there is no grownup who has agreed to take her in charge and deliver her home (she hopes not to have to live through such an historic occasion in the bosom of her family, and who can blame her. Did Patrick Henry say Give me Liberty or Give me Death to his mother (though he may well have been thinking of her when he said it)?) Anyway, from there we are walking north to join a candlelight procession moving south from 83rd and Lexington to Rockefeller Center. I would wait and tell you what happened instead of what is supposed to except that I am taking a plane to Illinois to see my mother's sister, in the hope of getting some information for my book. She is the last member of that generation alive, and in her eighties, and Will she remember is the question. I like terribly being in the climate of the sea-coast, because it is there that I am truly happy. The years fall away, I am full of energy, feel seventeen years old, and sing. Oh you have as usual put your finger on the essence of the matter.

---

* Vietnam Moratorium Day, the most widespread public protest against government policy in the United States.

Warner to Maxwell, October 19, 1969:

Please may I keep Brendan Gill, at any rate for the time? I want to show it to a spirited Quaker we know, and if possible get it read in meeting. It is magnificent.

I loved your letter, with its sense of controlled preliminary movement. I felt as if I were there too, taking part in that mysterious *family* gathering of the like minded. You did not know when you wrote what a very powerful and impressive affair it was going to be. And I suppose knew about the support from the army in Vietnam. That, if anything can, should make Nixon think—not twice, not again. Just think.

The black arm-bands in the field was front page news here. Having lived under a censorship, I can't be sure whether it was so fully reported on your side of the Atlantic; so here is a photograph which was in the centre of Thursday's *Times* front page. But of course you see *The Times*: still, I send it as a token of fellow-feeling.

I hope you get what you want in Illinois. Even if you don't, you'll surely get something. Ghosts rise like Djinns from family teapots.

Maxwell to Warner, October 20, 1969:

Oh it was something I will never forget. When Emmy and Edith [Iglauer] Hamburger and Brookie arrived in the music shop, Emmy had a dark red coat on, and Brookie a scarlet maxicoat. She is 4' 11" trying to be 5' and I was grateful. Red is easier to keep track of in crowds. We ended up behind the speakers, facing a row of amplifiers, and could hear perfectly what the backs of the heads said. But Brookie couldn't see, so I hoisted her up on the pedestal of a statue already crowded with demonstrators. The speeches were excellent, even McCarthy, who was so disappointing a speaker during his campaign. The "forty thousand people" in Bryant Park may well have been a hundred thousand or more. You know how newspapers go on. It was a sea of people, sometimes strange looking as to clothes and hairdo, but so nice.

And of course Kate turned up at the club without her friend. They had got parted in the crowd leaving the park. By a policeman, who wouldn't let Kate's friend go, and in seconds Kate couldn't even see her. But what with telephoning and walking up and down 45th Street and saying Sister Anne, do you see my Brothers coming, she was found, in time to eat a good dinner and proceed up Fifth Avenue to St. Patrick's. At which point my party showed a tendency to come apart. I had to run after the children yelling and scolding and yanking at the maxicoat. We ended up in West 49th, in sight of the cathedral steps, holding our lighted candles. All of Fifth Avenue was *paved* with people, sitting peacefully on the pavement holding candles and singing. Sometimes we sat and sometimes, when the view was obstructed, stood. I made the girls put their long hair inside their coats, because of the candles at their backs. My raincoat still has wax tears on it, which I can't bear to have removed. At one point silence began to emanate from somewhere, on whose instructions I don't know, and it grew and grew and spread all through that crowd. I can't tell you how marvelous it was to hear thousands of people being silent, with their arms aloft in the V symbol, and their faces lighted by candles. And such beautiful faces. Mostly young, but not all. Some rough boys said sweetly to Kate, Where can we buy candles? and snap went three candles. If they had said where can we get food or clothes or our hearts' desire, it would have been the same I felt. It was like Woodstock without the drugs. Or the mud. But at one point some people in front of us started to leave and some people behind us were trying to get closer, and I saw why Emmy doesn't care for crowds. She and Edith were swept away, and I just barely managed to keep the children together and entice them into a less crowded spot.

Later that night there were candlelight processions here, there, and everywhere. At ten minutes after one, Emmy and I were wakened out of a sound sleep and went to the window and saw a parade coming down 86th Street, which is very wide, and coming fast. By the time I had got the children out of their beds it was under our window. Students, mostly men, but girls too, carrying candles and torches and singing and in such a good humor, but also coming so fast, and with such purpose and *force*. I never saw anybody march that way before. It was revolutionary, though it ended up peacefully in front of the mayor's house, two blocks north of us. I cannot tell you how moving it was. It made me feel that that's what the streets are for.

Warner to Maxwell, November 4, 1969:

It was a magnificent letter. I felt proud to have it and proud to pass it on with Brendan Gill's speech and your letter before, to our Quaker friends.

By now it will have been read by a great many sympathetic violent pacifists.

Beyond all, I am grateful to you, for it revived Valentine to the excitement of reality. It set fire to her, perhaps the last thing to do so. For she is dying, dear William—slowly, irrevocably. Every day is a sad step downhill. There was a sudden worsening about a fortnight ago, when the disease clamped down on her. It will be a matter of weeks yet, and the worst is still to come.

Our doctor says she will do better here, with me, and the river, and her books and belongings and the familiar noises of the house, than she would be in any sort of nursing home. He is an obstinate unillusioned man but I trust his obstinacy to be merciful. What there is to be done I share with our dear Sybil and an alternating hireling, hospital-trained but retired into a married woman. People are being kind. The postman *creeps* into the house & sets down parcels as if they were of spun-glass instead of his old hurried emphasis.

Except when I am with her, I feel like a ghost, a ghost in a house that is known but unfamiliar. I rehearse the unimaginable *pas seule* I shall enact later on.

It is strange how one's mind *refuses* to believe that this thing happens to everyone—death and loss, and watching them approach.

Warner to Maxwell, November 11, 1969:

Valentine died on Sunday morning. She was deeply under morphia. I was with her to the last and laid her out, helped by our kind Sibyl who had shared the nursing. No stranger's hand touched her fastidious reserve.

This evening her coffin was carried out of the house and put in a forget-me-not blue van—which would have surprised her. I heard her spirit laughing beside me.

I am passionately thankful that she is out and away, and that in a fashion we are back where we were, able to love freely and uncompromised by anxiety and doubtful hopes and miseries of frustration. One thinks one has foreseen every detail of heart-break. I hadn't. I had not allowed for the anguished compassion and shock of hearing her viola voice changed to a pretty, childish treble, the voice of a sick child.

Death transfigured her. In a matter of minutes I saw the beauty of her young days reassert itself on her blurred careworn face. It was like something in music, the re-establishment of the original key, the return of the theme.

Don't think I am unhappy and alone, dear William. I am not. I am in a new country and she is the compass I travel by.

Warner to Maxwell, November 26, 1969:

A matter of business. Many years ago when *The New Yorker* pensions plan started, and contained the clause that one could name some one else to get it, I named Valentine: since it seemed then that I would almost certainly die before her— Please, can the pension now revert to me?

For though I hope in time to write again, I can't foresee when, or how. It might be something totally other. (I think being a pensioner and a contributor were to be compatible.)

You can deduce from all these grand words that I am being a conscientious executor.

One lovely thing has happened. Within minutes of Valentine's death I saw her original beauty, her young beauty, flood back into her face. I rang up an artist friend of mine [Joy Finzi] and asked if she could possibly come to make a drawing. She came early on Monday (having been oddly convinced all the week before that she had a Monday engagement though for the life of her she could not remember what it was); and all that day she sat perched on a high chair by Valentine's bed and at intervals called me up to consort.

The drawing is finished & here—a pale pencil drawing, almost like a silver-point. The house has a centre again. It assures me that she lived, and that I shall die.

She left you, as well as a folder of S. T. W. and her set of my books, her small table-clock. It chimes hours & half-hours with a pretty treble voice. It must wait to be professionally packed. And a small brooch apiece to Kate and Brookie. 'My two dearest' she says of them: both were given to her by me, love-tokens. These are so small that if you had a flying friend coming to or going from this country, they could be conveyed without adding an ounce to his luggage. Otherwise, they can travel with the clock.

No, I am not alone. She is more living, more real, than I am myself. She pervades my days. But I can't talk to her, tell her of this thought, that bird which flew by; I cannot consult her, nor ask her to put a new flint into my lighter. These *trivia* stab my heart. And I can no longer serve her. That is most annihilating of all.

Warner to Maxwell, December 16, 1969:

With a heart as normal as a stone I went to spend this last weekend with friends in Berkshire because they wanted to change my air. Their telephone rang. It was a telephone on which Valentine had often rung me. With an idiot intensity I thought, She will never telephone me again. And for a moment the whole of my grief was comprised in that deprivation. There is no armour against irrationality.

Warner to Maxwell, January 26, 1970:

Valentine always knew what people would like. It was a sixth or a seventh or an eighth sense of hers. And today the clock was collected by the professional packers. It has a pretty treble voice. She saw it many years ago and wanted it (she too was addicted to clocks) but felt she should practise self-control. So I made some excuse or other, a sudden remembrance of ham maybe, and *ran* to the store with my heart in my mouth in case someone else had bought it; and brought it away concealed in a muff. It was as long ago as muffs. So it has a pretty story too.

Warner to Maxwell, February 9, 1970:

This is the season of snowdrops and gipsies. Snowdrops are part of Dorset churchyards & the gipsies on their rounds come to pick them, and sell them in little bunches supported by an ivy leaf. This morning the old mother gipsy with a low-pitched voice like my grandmother's came to the door. 'And how's your lovely daughter?' she asked. 'Dead,' said I. I wished Valentine could have seen that rigid Roman face, set in its defensive expression, turn pale, hollow itself, sink into woe. And there was an epit ome of tribal misfortune, tribal pride, in her comment. 'She never scorned we people.'

The Welfare State, with everybody so genteel and secure (and apprehensive), has weighed heavily on gipsies. Only a few down-at-heels aristocrats, like ourselves, respect them and are pleased to see them. Birds of a moulting feather, we recognise each other. My celebrated black felt hat, *Paris-tient-toujours*, bought there in 1937 & worn till 1944, a vow, like the Infanta Isabel's shift, finally went away with a gipsy; and when Valentine saw it on her head, later on, she said it looked *completely* at home there, no difference in its ethos at all.

Warner to Maxwell, February 13, 1970:

Lead you down the garden path? I wouldn't lead you; but did I never tell you the story of how, when I was young and gay, I sat for a whole hot afternoon in a small tent telling fortunes for 2/6 for some worthy purpose, I can't remember what; and gave my clients a great deal of advice what to do; as for instance to buy three and three-quarter yards of green ribbon at the nearest draper's and then leave the shop walking backwards; and how, twelve months later, a strange woman arrived on my London doorstep, saying thank God she had traced me at last, everything I had told her had come true and would I please, please tell her some more?

Maxwell to Warner, February 24, 1970:

And himself as— as you see, I cannot work unless I have perfect order around me.* I was just having the last run through my book when a friend, noticing that I had written that a 19th century revivalist named Barton Warren Stone had an engaging personality (a thing I had picked up second-hand, from a dull book, so I couldn't amplify), asked what was so engaging about it. We happened to have as a house guest at the time a Harvard professor whom I first knew when he was a little boy of ten, and so I still call him Holmsie, though he is six feet tall and very Calvinistic. I complained to him of the difficulty of finding religious books in so secular a place as New York, and he went back to Cambridge and found the autobiography of B. W. Stone in the library of Harvard College, and sent me a card all nicely filled in, whereby I could borrow it through the New York Public Library. But when I went there, the office that does the borrowing said, Have you tried the Union Theological Seminary and the Episcopal Seminary on 9th Avenue? The first didn't have it, the second did, and it is unfortunately marvelous. It will take at least a couple of months to use it properly without throwing the proportions of the whole book off. What I would like is to run the whole thing—it's only about a hundred and seventy pages—as an appendix. Imagine a backwoods clergyman in pioneer days who writes like the younger brother of the author of *Tristram Shandy*. I am perhaps exaggerating some but not a great deal. He is on a journey and is put up for the night by some pious Baptists. When he has put his horse away, he goes in, and finds the mother and daughter spinning in the parlor, and the old man talking to another old man about a discovery that has just been made, that a house made of logs sawed in the moon of February will never have any bedbugs. "I interrupted my silence (I am quoting from memory) to ask if a similar discovery had been made about fleas. The answer was in the negative..." An angelic man, who couldn't open his mouth without saying something remarkable, which mostly people didn't have the sense to put down. And driven half mad, like poor Cowper, by sermons on hellfire and damnation. The book hasn't been reprinted in God knows how many decades, and was never widely read, I think, except as fuel to heap on the flames of religious partisanship.

* See photograph on page 3 of the insert.

Maxwell to Warner, March 9, 1970:

The box of books arrived on Thursday, the clock I picked up at the post office on 85th Street this morning. I took all my copies down from the shelf and put Valentine's in their place. I had everything but the small book containing two stories, which I thought I did have, and must have perhaps in the country, where my copies now reside. These are yours, I said to Brookie, and Valentine's set is for Kate. So that the inscriptions on the flyleaf are now safe in the hands of someone who loved her deeply. Many of the English editions I had never seen before, and God willing I think I shall read my way through them, to see what the words look like on different pages. The clock was marvelously packed, in a muff of excelsior. I fastened the key on the handle before I came to work, and said to Emmy that we would start it up this evening. It is exquisite. I also feel that you have sent me a part of the house and that when it is started up we will hear, in its ticking, late afternoons and grey mornings and a thousand odd moments in Frome Vauchurch. Our lives as we get older—and not just through this —draw closer and closer. I wish you were going to Sicily with us. I feel that the Sicilians would love you and they may not love me, but perhaps Emmy and the children will—will what? I don't know what. I feel no confidence about Sicilians. They have been mistreated too long, by too many different mistreaters. In 1948, which is that last time we were in Italy, Emmy and I were everywhere mistaken for brother and sister, travelling incestuously, and universally smiled on.

Maxwell to Warner, March 1970:

When I got home with the greatest delicacy I approached the clock, wound it a little, and waited—no, first I set it and was ravished by the little chime, then I wound it and nothing happened. And while I was looking for a lever that could be released and start things, the second hand began to move: it moved twice round the dial, just long enough for me to fall in love with the clock, and stopped. And would not, having captured my heart, do another thing. I went to the phone and called an opera singer who has a clock somewhat like it, which belonged to her Aunt Clara, and therefore it is always referred to as Aunt Clara's Clock, and she said to clasp it to me lovingly as if it were a child and then bend forward so that the child's head touched the floor. I did, and nothing happened. She used to take her clocks to a Swiss firm that was most dependable, but they sold out to a Pole who was not, she said, but if I would bring it to the country we would go together to a man in Croton who is very confident... If there is one thing that fills me with misgivings, it is a clock in the hands of a man who is very confident. So bright and early the next morning I put it in my briefcase and went to Tiffany's, thinking that any number of elegant women, friends of Edith Wharton, must have gone there with just such beautiful mechanisms; and was given a card with the address of a firm on 3rd Avenue that Tiffany's felt to be most reliable. By now quite late to work, I went back the way I had come, found the shop, saw at a glance that there was not a timepiece in the place that didn't antedate the sinking of the *Titanic*, and put Valentine's clock on the counter and the man said "How charming!" Then he turned it sideways once and said "I will get in touch with you in a couple of days." It is a long time to be separated from something you have just fallen in love with, but at least I have the key, in my left hand coat pocket.

The Attorney General of the United States is asking for permission to take prints of the soles of the feet and specimens of the handwriting of people who might have criminal tendencies. I could have known that we were due for a revival of phrenology. We have had everything else. Pity this unfortunate country.

Maxwell to Warner, March 1970:

When you say I feel pretty sure I shall never write another novel, I feel like what Thomas a Buile said in a pub [in the poem by James Stephens]. I know that everything you wrote was directed toward Valentine, and that she was your climate, but please don't forget that I am here. If you stop writing you will hurt my feelings terribly.

P.S. While I think of it—have you ever noticed that if a waiter has any philosophy in him it will come out during the serving of the salad course? The waiter in the dining room of the Hotel Jolly in Syracuse was in his late twenties, and very nimble, with the smile of a satyr. And when the busboy asked him how many of us were having insalata mista, he answered cheerfully "Tutti animali."

Warner to Maxwell, April 13, 1970:

I have begun to write again—No, not a story, not a novel, and nothing for now. An archive. I found that Valentine had kept quantities of my letters, as I had kept quantities of hers. Reading through them, and putting them into sequence, I realised that it is a notable correspondence and the sort of thing that should be put away in a tin box for posterity. So now I am entirely absorbed in writing the narrative links and explanations and so forth. I am mid-way in the prologue. It is far the best thing I have ever written—and an engrossing agony. I am terrified that I should die before I have finished this. A month ago, it was the only thing I had the least inclination for.

And you, dear William, must be the tin box, since it will count as my Literary REMAINS—absurd phrase. It can't be let out till there is a safe margin for every one to be dead in.

I must go and talk to Mr Palmer. The foundations of the house are giving way, and he is repairing them, aided by such a very very old man that there is really nothing of him between his sharp chin and his large gothic feet—just a faint continuity.

Warner to Maxwell, July 12, 1970:

And you have nearly finished your book [*Ancestors*] and think that *here and there* it may please me. If we are to go by your other books, it will wholly please me and some of it will please me very much. I hope it is already pleasing you, that you are enjoying that delicious stage of titivation, life-saving last ideas for an adverb; and writing them down on calendars, cheques, bills, manifestoes and smooth wall-surfaces.

I am not quite as infertile as you think. The Valentine–Sylvia letters needed annotating. I adore annotations; and in places, a linking narrative. It is interesting to write without the least thought of publication, and intending only equity and accuracy.

Maxwell to Warner, July 1970:

A check. I think of you working over those letters, annotating and re-experiencing. A very old friend of mine [Garetta Busey], who was the first to introduce me to your books, prose and verse, is getting ready not to cause anybody any trouble when she dies, and was sorting and returning to the writer letters she had saved. Including mine. They come in batches. Last night's batch had an account of a visit Mr. [Robert] Henderson (who was my college roommate) and his first wife made, in the middle of winter, to a Wisconsin farm that was my second home and real family. With one of the girls of the family we had been off somewhere dancing, and drunk a good deal of 3.2 beer, and he and I were both as drunk as Chinese poets, and rode home in the rumble seat together, and the girls sat in front. And at one point I said (I have my own word for it, though I don't remember any of it) I said to him, during that 18 mile drive, "Some day we'll be dead." And he said, "Too bad for the world when we are." And I said, "No, too bad for us." I was twenty-three at the time.

Warner to Maxwell, August 2, 1970:

PLEASE, dear William, will you write at once to the very old friend who was the first to introduce you to my books; and give her my love, and my gratitude for doing so, and, so doing, inaugurating a friendship which

means so very much to me. For I like to think—pray do not disabuse me—
that it was because you liked my books that you appropriated me as your
charge with *The New Yorker*.

Suppose I had been in the hands of some eminently worthy and
painstaking person called Halibut? What we both would have missed.

How is that book you are so discreet about? When shall I read the first
page?

I am lost to the world in those letters. Annotations have always been my
besetting delight. Some of them, I find, need to be extended into snatches
of narrative. David Garnett said to me long ago 'What you write best
about is love.'

Warner to Maxwell, October 9, 1970:

I have often thought how bleak and inattentive to your kindness I must
have seemed that first time we met when I came to the *N.Y.* office; but I
was in tatters and extremity from watching Valentine in a frightful combat
with a New England vampire. I still don't know how either of us got away
with our reason. The vampire is alive and thriving to this day, so I hear.

Ich bin der Welt abhanden gekommen ["I am lost to the world"]. It is very
kind of you to want me to come to America [to address the American
Academy of Arts and Letters]. Later on perhaps I may; but if you know
that song of Mahler's you will understand that I am best here. I am about
halfway through the letters. I find that they need rather more than annotating (which is a pure human pleasure), and so I am writing bits of linking
narrative. They can't—yet, at any rate—be published, but I am sure they
should be preserved. I am confirmed in this by seeing their effect on the
young woman [Susanna Pinncy] who puts in a Sunday morning whenever
she can, typing them. She is a reserved cat, but every now and then she
comments, and her comments are so close to the truth that obviously the
letters themselves must be absorbingly true.

Warner to Maxwell, October 29, 1970:

It makes me very happy to think of you reading our letters, sharing
them with me. And happy to think that Valentine will become more real to

you, more living. You endeared yourself to her by being such a good friend to me. Now she will endear herself to you.

Warner to Maxwell, November 5, 1970:

'In all her ten thousand years, Tiphaine had never been known to rise in the air.'

What is that out of? A story ["The One and the Other"] I am writing to hurl myself through a hard week by pretending I am some one quite different.*

It is probably waste of ingenuity: the week would go on by its own momentum anyhow.

It is so cold that the cats say we must go to bed immediately.

---

* This was the first of Warner's twenty stories of fairy-life, improvisations that so delighted Maxwell. Most were collected in *Kingdoms of Elfin* (1977). This story, published in *The New Yorker* as "Something Entirely Different," lived up to its title.

Maxwell to Warner, November 1970:

The last cluster of letters set me to thinking how there are two fears and most people have one or the other and maybe they are the same fear: that they are afraid to call their soul their own, or that they are afraid it will be seen. The effect of Valentine's letters is of the soul unsheathed, in utter and final fearlessness. I have never read anything like them. Such style, and without a moment's thought to it. I will never again read the word happiness without thinking of them. And in the supplemental narrative—what I started to say is that all my life I have been confidently watching you outdo yourself, and you have again, but by so far—the night ride, and the simple summation of all the aspects to her love, simply exceeds, as prose, anything you have ever written. It is as if you were possessed.

Warner to Maxwell, November 20, 1970:

Yes, you told me about the 21st January. Before then you will get a long short story ["The One and the Other"] that even *The New Yorker* won't be able to enlarge itself enough to take. A pity, because it is a queer good story. The only other person who could have written anything like it is you; but it is much bonier, there is practically no flesh on it at all, and no breath of human kindness. But it seems to me that the bones live.

Does Emmy know the coloured page of mushrooms in the *Petit Larousse*? Mushrooming is rapture. For one thing, they are so extremely beautiful; for another, they are such a caress to gather. Does she know the blithe Mussorgsky song of the girl gathering mushrooms to poison her mother-in-law?

Dear William, I have an idea that you sometimes worry about how I get on. Apart from being an Elle—those Scandinavian she-goblins who are only façades, no inside to them, no behind, I contrive to manage rather well. The cats remind me to eat (this morning they unitedly assured me that by far the best way to cook a daube is to deposit it in a cat) and put me to sleep very cleverly; and the village is touchingly kind, the butcher boy is as fostering as a father, the woman from the winestores calls me Dear, when the kitchen cooker went wrong Mr Palmer the builder rushed here on a Sunday to put it right: everybody who remembers Valentine commemorates her by kindness to me: except the people at the Post Office, who are new and do not remember Valentine, and would be disagreeable even if they did. They are remnants of Empire; they came back from Kenya, and Kenya is well rid of them. They are convinced that every one who goes into the post office intends to insult and murder them—which is hard on simple old women who go there to collect the old age pension or post a knitted comforter to a son in Newcastle upon Tyne.

And, crucial and central, after all those years of being looked after by Valentine, I have been got into such good ways that I go on looking after myself as her deputy.

At least a hundred more letters have turned up—in a tin marked bisco tini di Novara, in Valentine's workshop in among a rabble of tins and boxes in which she kept things that might turn out to be useful—such as keys, corks, knobs, flex, beads, candle-ends, fishing lines, Christmas-tree candle-holders . . . They are all by me, which is alas! But they fill up a whole stretch between 1934 and 1938, so the dialogue is restored, and they may be counted among things which might turn out to be useful. And there will be more blissful annotation.

Warner to Maxwell, December 22, 1970:

And all this time I have been thinking how painful you would find it to write and say that Mr Shawn couldn't and wouldn't. I can echo his comment and say 'Remarkable.'

I am truly very much pleased. I admire the story ["The One and the Other"] myself, and feel justified by it: justified, I mean, in supposing that *something entirely different* is still possible for me, that I can still pull an unexpected ace out of my sleeve.

Maxwell to Warner, January 1971:

Your presents to us made a separate Christmas inside Christmas. I was in the greatest need of the sea-weed emulsion. It doesn't say specifically what it is for, and I took it to be for writers who rewrite their book [*Ancestors*] in galley, which is what I have been doing. All Christmas day I opened presents and admired other people's presents and in between, sitting at a card table in the living room, I sneaked in a correction. At the end of the day I went and took a sea bath and was most wonderfully restored. If only you had sent a bathing machine with it, but it would never have got through customs. I was put in the mind of bathing machines by a book Emmy gave me, of pictures by Boudin. I regret very much that I was born too late for them.

The galleys were supposed to be handed in on the Monday before Christmas, and failing that, on the Monday after New Year's. I think this time I will make it. Today I had a communication from the son of one of my mother's cousins, in answer to a letter I sent him in September, and for a moment I despaired. But fortunately, it is impossible to make head or tail out of the document, or even make out whose account it is, though the details are often fascinating. All the people mentioned have the same names, generation after generation, in parallel families, and no dates to distinguish them. At one point I thought I was going to end up with the Mormons in Missouri, but it turned out to be friends of ancestors, not the ancestors themselves who "went off to Missouri and had a big time in the wild new country." The narrator of this really extraordinary rigmarole stops at one point to observe "I do not think that there is anyone that could tell things any straighter than I can," and then goes on to say "John S. had four brothers: himself, Thomas, Harry, and James, James was drowned in Grassy Creek in 1843." And once in a while, it doesn't matter: Such as "We were landing in a boat at Chamber's Landing, with cord wood one time, and Adam and John (possibly my great-grandfather's brothers, though I wouldn't bet money on it) were there with a team, helping to land, I really do not know whether it was wood and I was there helping them or not. I think it belonged to my grandfather, and at dinner time we fed the horses and rested. Adam and I got to skuffling, and Adam was a whither bugger. I had the best of Adam—got him under—and had a hold on him that he could not break. I never did see anybody make the horrid exertion that he did. I always thought that Adam hurt himself by trying to extricate himself and get the better of me. I do not know that he ever married at all. Adam was never well after that, he went into quick consumption, and that fall, began to complain and went to Texas and back again with my father..."

So real, and so correct for the period, and no way on earth of knowing who was who.

Warner to Maxwell, January 18, 1971:

And so here it is, the last of the Edoms ["The Listening Woman"]. I am sorry to part with him. He was so much a part of living with Valentine, and made her laugh when laughs were not so easy-come-by as they had been, and encouraged a great deal of consultation—or rather, a great deal of enquiring and depending. Every serious expert ought to have an attendant smatterer—like Nature's neat arrangements of incompatible animals who supplement each other. And the Edoms one and all represent my stages in smattering.

Warner to Maxwell, February 14, 1971:

My other publisher (Michael Howard of Cape) was here last week. He told me that a publisher's office with no letters to come in or send out [because of a postal-strike] is a lotus-bed. He has never known people so sweet-tempered, so amiable & relaxed, with all their better qualities ripening like peaches on a south wall. I am in much the same blessed emotion myself. I sleep as long as I and the cats please—no need to set the alarm in order to open the door for the post-man. At intervals the telephone rings and a kind voice from Yorkshire or Wales or the Lizard asks me if I am still alive, or I am a kind voice myself and ask after a cat in Kent. I listen to a great deal of music. I have had some delightful letters from Horace Walpole, who is visiting country houses.

Warner to Maxwell, February 28, 1971:

I was so glad, dear William, that you persevered when I was only a voice which didn't hear you. Once I heard you, it was as though you were in the room; and I had no sense of astonished beginning, imminent ending—just a sense of talking to you again and of being loved and understood.

And perhaps this makes me seem even more ungrateful that I don't think of coming over in May. But I am tied to the letters, to her poems and mss—*to her*. Here, I am still in her ambiance. I spend most of my time in a strange straying conversation with her, not so much haunted as possessed. Even at the cost of days when I am nothing but a machine which feels the cold, I can't interrupt this conversation. And though I made various attempts at staying with people who were everything that is kind to me it didn't really work—it was a jolt into a life I had forgotten. Here I live and continually remember more, see with her eyes, consult her, depend on her. She knew—for we discussed it before her death—that I should live on here, by myself—and she approved.

She herself was convinced she would survive. 'I will never leave you,' she said in a letter of farewell. In the light of this it would seem childish and materialistic of me to cling to this house. But as I am both childish & materialistic I half-believe that when I leave it, I leave her. And leave myself.

Maxwell to Warner, March 19, 1971:

I do not think you ungrateful for not coming over in May. I would not for anything in this world have you turn away from your present conversation with Valentine. It would be like wanting you to turn aside from your destiny. Coming to America would have served other people's purposes brilliantly, but not your own. And of course I wanted to see you.

You didn't begin to call me William (I must go searching for the letter, in order to know how long ago), I began to call you Sylvia, by mistake. That is, in a moment of absentmindedness you signed a letter with your first name only, and with some uncertainty, because my admiration made me shy and we had been writing to one another for such a long while as Miss Warner and Mr. Maxwell, I did it. I said "Dear Sylvia," and threw you into a distressed confusion. You wrote back that you weren't sure that you *could* address me by my first name, and I wrote back that it was perfectly easy to revert to our ordinary practice. I *think* I wrote this. And you wrote back that—what did you write? I forget. All I remember is that we didn't revert. We went on from there. But of course under the name of Mr. Maxwell I had loved you with all my heart, from the moment you walked into my office, so it wasn't all that important how we addressed each other.

My book is now out of my hands, and what I mostly regret is that I won't again have a chance to write this kind of book. It is a distillation of memory and family history in which you don't have to bother with anything except the point of the thing. And it gave me a chance to relive a part of my life that mattered emotionally very much. I don't feel that I am about to die, but say that I were called out of the room, so to speak, it is all right; I have rescued the things that mattered to me.

Warner to Maxwell, March 26, 1971:

Dear William-for-we-don't-know-how-long.

Today I shall post you two more porridge-coloured envelopes, which will take you as far as 1938.

You are a departing stage away from your book, & I am a stage nearer reading it. And I long to—but at the same time I deplore your condition. However one glosses it over with assumptions of relief, however much water one washes one's hands with, it is miserable work, isn't it, to go away from a book? I still remember the darting anguish with which I wrote the Envoy to *Mr F.'s Maggot*—a most inartistic proceeding.

I hope your cold is better and the kettle put by—though I have nothing against kettles. I remember many happy days with them in my childhood, with my father coming with story-books & champagne. Champagne for everything above the waist, brandy for anything below it, was the medicinal way; and I am still a credit to his theory.

Warner to Maxwell, March 31, 1971:

I don't know about symbolism. Officially, I can't bear it, either; but I suspect that I am a symbolist born and dipped (as the chemist at Harrow who was a churchwarden was denounced 'a Baptist born and dipped' by a fellow-churchwarden.) For certainly, I have an objective mind, and don't believe it would work without being a pincushion for associations, and associations are double-entendres. Perhaps it would be safer to say that I can't bear other peoples' symbolism; that I would like to think of myself as a plain practical Defoe: but when I look at my writing I have to admit this is merely wistful thinking.

And could I dislike the symbolism of others as briskly as I do if I were not a pot calling a kettle black?

Here I must leave off, or presently I shall be implying that you may be a symbolist, dear William.

Warner to Maxwell, April 9, 1971:

Nancy Hale was quite right.* My father died when I was twenty-two, and I was mutilated. He was fifty-one, and we were making plans of what we would do together when he retired. It was as though I had been crippled and at the same moment realized that I must make my journey alone. My mother exclaimed, Now you are all I've got left—a cry of angry desolation. What on earth did she want in a daughter that I didn't have, you ask. A son. For the first seven years of my life I interested her heart; and I was an amusing engaging child and she enjoyed her efficiency in rearing me. But nothing compensated for my sex and later on it turned into doing her duty by me, and doing one's duty by inevitably hardens the heart against. And later still, she was jealous, and I could do nothing right. Valentine said that what she felt about me was an inverted possessiveness.

The person to be sorry for was my stepfather. He was much younger than she, gentle, affectionate, rather dunderheaded, inexhaustibly kind. She scorned him in her heart, and had no kindness for him, and no respect for him, and he wasn't so dunderheaded that he didn't know it. I put some of him into Mr Saunter in *Lolly Willowes*—but as I knew him first when he still had all his ribs about him.

Ice cream is the best thing in the world for an injured tongue—though Valentine made one of her fallacies of hope when she thought it would act as a frozen cosmetic. We were driving to visit the Machens, and it was a very hot day, and so long ago that the car was an open car; and our faces were scorched and unbecoming, so she bought two ice-cream cones and we rubbed our burning brows with them. Soothing at the time, but ten minutes later we were glazed like eclairs and it stuck. Only the very happy are so very silly, so paradisally silly; and perhaps it takes genius to be so divorced from the rational.

* "The American novelist and short-story writer," Maxwell explained in 1982, " whose father also died when she was twenty-two. Thirty years later, staying in our house in the country, she walked past an open door and saw me with my older daughter on my lap, brushing her hair, and remarked dubiously, 'I suppose it's all right, but don't ever die.' "

Warner to Maxwell, April 30, 1971:

I went down to Chaldon about three weeks ago to spend a weekend with my cousin Janet [Machen], who rents part of the Chydyok house— Llewelyn & Alyse [Powys]'s half—on the downs near the sea.

On our way down to Chydyok we stopped for me to plant some more snowdrops round Valentine's grave: there are some already but one can never have enough snowdrops. It was a brilliant afternoon, with a wind from the sea, whirling cloud-shadows across the very green churchyard grass; and the rookery was in full shout, with parent rooks flustering overhead feeding their newly hatched young. I planted the snowdrops, absorbed in industry, then, feeling I would like a rest, I looked round for somewhere to sit on. There, all ready to be sat on, was the stone slab, rather well-cut, with everything of names and dates on it, and Valentine's choice of *non omnis moriar*—everything except the date of my death.

And as I sat down on it, William, I felt the most amazing *righteous* joy; as if I were doing just what I should, par excellence what I should; and that here was my indisputable right place. It was the first time since her death that I have felt the slightly rowdy emotion of joy.

Warner to Maxwell, May 21, 1971:

And I have a message for you from V. S. Pritchett, whom I met last Sunday: it is, that he wishes you were *his* editor, & can scarcely refrain from tearing me in pieces with envy that you are mine. I made no effort not to look smug. It would have been dishonest not to look smug.

Warner to Maxwell, June 9, 1971:

I thought only Turgeniev gave me the dreamlike & contented feeling of reading something by Turgeniev—but I wasn't far into *Ancestors* before you were doing it too. Thank God I haven't finished it yet. I am like the man walking through the twilight meadows in Strauss's song: *Ich gehe nicht schnell, Ich eile nicht* ["I do not walk quickly, I do not hurry"]. I intend never to finish it. I may come to the last page, but it is not a book I shall finish. I shall go back to it, and hear you and your ancestors conversing about family connections, who married who, who died of what; and sometimes it will be to a background of Katydids, & sometimes the wind will howl down the chimney and the conversation will turn to wolves; & snow drifts will melt into droughts and God's providence will always be a mystery and righteousness like plain sewing.

Oh, it is an *entrancing* book! I read it with the accepting intimacy of a child half-asleep listening to that linked spilling of family stories, one incident, one character, calling out another. And you have done it so beautifully, dear William, so delicately and so firmly, like unreeling the silk from a cocoon. And heaven threw you that inestimable jewel of the Christian church, and you wore it with no more emphasis than on a daisy in your buttonhole. If a moth had written a book...

Meanwhile, I suppose you have committed a classic and for years & years to come students reading American history will be told to read Maxwell.

Well, your ancestors should be pleased with you, and pleased that you have fostered Kate & Brookie to carry on the strain.

The book was here when I got home from Aldeburgh, where a fierce north-east wind ripped the sea into white horses and bowled spindrift along the public beach, and where Peter Pears & Ben Britten were so kind & welcoming to me that I did not once feel I was an anachronism, and where one of the pleasures was being driven by Ben and watching his pianist's hands on the steering-wheel.

Warner to Maxwell, June 27, 1971:

While I was ill, I read Nathaniel Hawthorne's *English Notebooks*—interminable and soothingly irrelevant, and just what I wanted. When I came to 'all ruined abbies are much the same' I felt an obligation to share the pleasure. Have the *English Notebooks* ever been appreciated in *The New Yorker*? Shall I think about this? He suffered most expressively under the climate and thin bread and butter. The *Oxford Companion to Eng. Lit.* says he was 'much occupied by the mystery of sin' but it doesn't seem to have been much trouble to him in this country—a great improvement. So much so, that I had to consult the *Oxford Companion* to make sure he really was the same Nathaniel.

Warner to Maxwell, July 20, 1971:

'That American woman' [Elizabeth Wade White, Warner's rival for Valentine's affections] wasn't incompetent (as you suppose); and as she was pure Connecticut, I don't think you need recognise her as a countrywoman. She was the worst kind of Connecticut, moneyed and pedigreed, and had never been crossed in her life. She was determined not to be crossed, and this took the form of a mercantile caution, an insistence on being certain of Valentine as a possession—as an investment, so to speak. She could neither risk nor trust. So she could never love in the present; she was always stipulating, nursing a contract; and as a result, resenting, grudging, and feeling ill-used. A grudge is a safe investment, and she managed her grudges competently and was never at a loss for something to reproach Valentine with (one of her reproaches was that I spent that September in Yeovil).

I must write two narrative links for /39 and /40 but I can't settle to them yet. It obliges me to remember so much misery; and that I was the cause of it; for it was I who brought her into the story; she was a soi-disant friend of mine, from a much earlier meeting in the States.

I shirk it, as I now shirk facing any aspect of sorrow. Which is why, dear William, I still have said nothing about Chapter 17 of *Ancestors*. And really can say nothing now. That is the climax of the book, the best writing in the book, best led up to and best departed from, is nothing to do with it; at any rate, nothing to do with what you felt as you wrote, what I felt as I read. Oh, the poor child; and the arid grief of childhood and adolescence! The parching grief, the untimely frost on the young leaf! Survival is inexorable. I'm sure one has no hand in it.

Maxwell to Warner, September 1971:

I have been reading a book that an elderly friend sent to me, called *A Hundred Years in the Highlands*. It is by a man named Osgood MacKenzie and was published in the twenties, and the beginning enchanted me, but then he got down to the real subject of the book, which is the slaughter of birds, and I pick it up and put it down with increasing disgust. As he tells how many of one species after another he killed, he mournfully concludes that there are now none of them to shoot at, without making the final step in the chain of logic that would lead him to understand who is responsible for this. From the time he was eight years old, nothing on four legs, nothing with wings, was safe in any place where he was.

When I was about nine years old, my older brother took me rabbit hunting with him. I was simply there to watch, and did, and when he scared up a beastie and took aim and missed, and the rabbit escaped across the snow, I was delighted and he was so mortified that he never took me again. How much I have to be thankful for, including the fact that I have had the privilege of writing to you all these years.

Warner to Maxwell, September 27, 1971:

I never had anything so orderly as a religious period. What religious feeling I have is totally anarchic, could be aroused by Stonehenge or an old kettle in a ditch, but never by a system. I have no more control of it or comprehension of it than I have of my vagaries in the supernatural. Another example of this turned up the other day. We knew a sad old *mauvais sujet*, a man damned in a good wife; and one day during his lifetime I happened to be in a conservatory opening on his study. The study was empty; but he was there, sitting at his writing-table with his hands clenched on his bowed head and a pistol on the table. Mark my words, I said to Valentine. But nothing came of it. I had misfired. He has been dead ten years or more. Last week I happened to say to his niece, 'I could never make out why

Uncle Beresford died in his bed,' and told her what I had seen. She turned slightly green and asked if I knew about Mr Huxtable. Which I didn't. But Mr Huxtable was the previous tenant and he killed himself. My misfire was a right and a left, I got both gentlemen, *feu* Huxtable haunting the bowed head about the pistol.

The letters from 63 [Warner's number] onward are so sad and my memory of the last years still so raw that I had to take myself off and hide in plain hard work and useful futilities. I am perfectly well, but made of damp sawdust. If I were in an hour-glass, *I would stick.*

Maxwell to Warner, October 5, 1971:

The letters are now all numbered correctly. I have been re-reading Valentine's later poems in the light of the letters, and been very moved, as Kate is, without knowing what is in the letters. The little clock has become such a central object in our lives that I wonder how we managed without it, and I never hear it or see it without thinking of where it came from. I escape whenever possible into *Middlemarch*, which by good fortune I had never read before. I thought I didn't like George Eliot.

The only way I know to dry out the dampness of sawdust is by writing. It is the only cure, for the likes of you and me, for it doesn't matter what evil under the sun, including those that are incurable.

Warner to Maxwell, October 10, 1971:

Thank you for telling me about the little clock and that it is in its right place. She had a very pure aim, a straight eye.

Next to the clock on her desk and almost as often consulted was the Nonesuch edition of Montaigne which I gave her when we lived at Frankfort Manor (Florio and all that, much scuffed and all its back pages annotated; we used our grandeurs). I would like to know it had rejoined its neighbour of so many years. May I send it to you? It would please her; she had a great affection for you, you know—not only because you fostered me, but you yourself. 'You must say Yes,' as she wrote to me in one of the early letters.

Warner to Maxwell, October 25, 1971:

But it isn't good news that you have *already* had that chest cold of yours. It leaves too much time for you to have another.

In the same spirit of loving interference with which I recommended raspberry leaf tea (my first interest in darling Kate) I beg you to use *goose-grease*. England would have been depopulated long ago if our ancestors had not rubbed in goose grease back & front when winter nights enlarged. If you can't get it in N.Y.C. tell us and I will send you a little pot (It doesn't smell).

Warner to Maxwell, November 11, 1971:

I do what I can for myself—I am a very poor vice-Valentine—I go early to bed & read *Pride & Prejudice*. Because I know it so well, I read it, so to speak, peripherally. I realise that as time went on Wickham began to have a fellow-ly feeling towards his father-in-law. But also, as I heard the wind out-crying the owls, that there were advantages about Mrs Bennet which Jane Austen was too young to appreciate. She saw to it that there were good fires kept going, and no lack of rich soups, whereas Charlotte's housekeeping grew bleaker & bleaker till poor Mr Collins lost all his sleekness & eventually was henpecked.

Warner to Maxwell, November 19, 1971:

I came home after posting the last envelope—as though I had just committed a serene suicide; with an inexhaustible choice of times & places where I might haunt. I have kept, pretty consistently, the vow against remorse and against regret (it would be blasphemous ingratitude to admit regret into the span of so much happiness); but I must take your word for it about the letters of the last decade. I can't reconcile myself to that slow, grinding accumulation of ill-health, calamity, and self-exile. (It is strange that only after she knew she had cancer did she allow herself to *trust* our love again). I feel a childish indignation, a child's outcry of 'It isn't fair.'

But she keeps her word. She does not leave me. And remembering that deep folk-belief that the dead are at the mercy of the surviving—(Do you know that Breton story of the mother who saw her dead child shivering in a pool of dirty water, and cried out, and the child answered, Your tears, Mother?)—I try to match her.

What to do with them? Keep them for the present where they will be warm. Then, I suppose, deposit them with some humane place of learning —by humane, I mean somewhere which is not lost body & soul to science. I thought of Yale, because it already has letters of mine in its George Plank deposit. But in a way I would prefer some smaller institution, perhaps some woman's University. And with a time-bar of twenty-five years, which should see everyone involved safe dead.

But now Soo Pinney, typing an autobiography, which Valentine wrote at white-heat in the summer of /49 for me to take to Yeovil [*For Sylvia: An Honest Account*], insists it should be published, that it is too cogent to her generation (she is 28) not to be given to them. And that raised the question whether a selection of the letters should not be made (edited by you, dear William—as I would like—or by Kate, in whom I feel great trust, as a fore-runner) to coincide with my death. Considerations in a threatened world, dear William. I thank my stars that you are my literary executor; perhaps more fervently than you do!

Warner to Maxwell, January 9, 1972:

Your bedroom fireplace should have had a fire in it. When family pews meant anything, they had fireplaces in them, and the eldest son of the family poked them up before the sermon. At that date you never saw a gentleman on his knees. He remained seated & prayed into his hat. My poor father couldn't, because if he went to church it was to the school chapel, dressed as such; and for some deep mystical reason you can't pray into a mortar-board.

One of the Winters' Nights Entertainments of old age is recalling customs that were commonplace in one's youth: they start up like wyverns and Demon Kings.

If I don't immediately respond to that copy of 'Love', it will be because I'm in Denmark. Paul [Nordoff] & Clive [Robbins] are there, working on impaired children, and their hired house sounded so agreeable & they invited me so feelingly that I said *Done!* The truth is, I was growing rather alarmed by the way I was acceding to routine; compliance with it felt increasingly like madness. 'Now I hang up the teacup on the 3rd hook. Now I put the blue plate in the rack.'

I wish you knew Reynolds Stone. He has a soft voice like bees in a lime-tree, and I have never heard him exclaim or known him talk for nothing; and he will fight like a tiger to save a tree, a badger, an old printing-press.

He had a wonderful commission last year. A very rich old man in the North with acres of woodland, asked him up to take portraits—no, not of the family—of particular trees. And all day Reynolds sat in the woods looking like an old tramp and in the evening dined with the very rich man on oysters and saddle of mutton.

But did I send you a copy of *Boxwood*? His engravings & the poems I wrote to go with them because the publisher had asked him to supply suitable quotations & I found him in despair in a morass of anthologies.

He works at one end of a large long room, walled with books, corniced with stuffed birds in glass cases. He works at a massive table, matted with every variety of confusion & untidiness, graving minutely on a small block. The other end of the room is a turmoil of wife, children, distinguished visitors, people dropping in—Janet's roaring lion-house, for she is a bishop's daughter & has lion-hunting in her blood. And there sits Reynolds not merely immune, but liking it. He likes to work amid a number of conversations he needn't attend to, he likes to feel people within touching distance of his glass case.

Warner to Maxwell, February 7, 1972:

Thank you for your loving machinations (I am sure it was your machinations, though you did not entwine your signature with Mr Copland's and Mr Barzun's).*

I am really extremely pleased and set-up and cockahoop, and was on the brink of telling the butcher about it, since he happened to be the first foot to my honours; but he was busy tieing up a round of beef for Mrs Lamasys.

How DID you do it?

No doubt you know the form of the letter. I particularly esteemed that reference to 'the American Ambassador or some other properly designated person.' I like to see Ambassadors kept in their station.

---

* The American Academy of Arts and Letters, and its parent body, the American Institute of Arts and Letters, of which Maxwell was president, had elected Warner an honorary member.

Warner to Maxwell, February 16, 1972:

I am glad the books have arrived, glad for many reasons; that they are where I want them to be; that you have something from Frankfort Manor, that lovely house so much too large for us but never too large for our love; and that they prompted you to write one of the most *harmonious* letters I have ever received.

When the power-cut is cut (one comes to think of it like that) I will go upstairs to Valentine's room and hunt through her hoard of photographs for one of the house, and you can keep it in Montaigne or in *The Cat's Cradle–Book*. It will fit either of them. The things I can't give you is the smell of the house: wood-smoke, stored apples & pears, roses & reed-thatch, and the noise of the trees.

Warner to Maxwell, March 13, 1972:

Psychological intuition in biographers is a prevalent social custom just now, and there is too much of it. One of the reasons why *Ancestors* is so engrossing is the fact that you took Ps. Int. by the throat & strangled him with one hand while you did the same deed to eloquence with the other. An infant Hercules.

Warner to Maxwell, April 9, 1972:

Mozart: when I read your letter I realised that not only have I loved him since the first notes of him I heard, but that I have never ceased to love him differently. There is always some new aspect, some new illumination, some undiscovered facet. Paul, one of my hosts at Vaerlose, and I began to talk about the *Flute* at dinner & at midnight we were still talking about the *Flute*; Paul averring that the Queen of the Night is the moon. An interesting reading.

They were both so kind and cosseting to me, stalking in with my break-fast tray as tall as Victorian footmen. Impossible to learn a word of Danish except off shop-fronts. Every one speaks English. To hear Danish spoken I had to go to the village (Lutheran) church where I *sat* through the Creed in a blue-painted pew. Being reasonably conversant with the Creed and so comfortably placed to give my mind to it, I understood it very nicely. The sun shone, the larks sang, and the ice was melting, lying on the water like lily-pads. I admired the dexterity of some mallards on a canal who alternately swam & skated.

Warner to Maxwell, April 17, 1972:

Well, I went to the U.S. Embassy and stood smirking while Mr Annenberg read my citation and presented me with a vast portfolio & a small button. I liked him very much—such a cosy man.

What is the correct formula for being an honorary member of the A.A.A.L.? And is it those four initials only, or 'tother four, or the lot? I ask because I was told long ago that if one supports a worthy cause or writes injuriously to the Press, it doubles one's efficacy to have letters after one's name: that people in desperate need have even put Fellow of the Royal Zoological Society after their names. Not that I ever despised those multitudinous Fellows: they got one in on a Sunday, or after dark, when the Kinkajou woke up and sucked raw eggs.

One of the emotions of old age is amazement that one was alive so long ago. I suppose that is why so many people write autobiographies. They are trying to convince themselves that they really were.

Warner to Maxwell, April 22, 1972:

You aren't the only one to mislay. Objects have got so bold about it in this house that they mislay themselves in front of my eyes and remain in front of my eyes, mislaid. I put it down to pollution.

For some time I have been admiring a large black and white cat, a solid shapely cat with one eye in a black surround so he looks piratical, who promenades in the field across the river. I must have looked at him too warmly, for now he comes into the garden. He does not harm, he makes no offensive, but he *sits at* the rightful inhabitants; and they enlarge their tails and hackle up their backs; from embarrassment, I think. Not a paw is raised; but the effect is un-restful. It reminds me of a Peace Committee I attended in Brussels in 1938, when the only smooth tail was Krishna Menon's, who annoyed everybody so exhaustively that he went about filled to the brim with the milk of human kindness, the embodiment of suavity and tolerance; and handsome as the Destroying Angel. No. I think it was 1937.

Narrative Seven is finished: it was neck and neck which of us would finish the other. In the end I had to throw away three earlier versions and do it on a sterner plan. It is strange to think that during that summer when I was feeling as hollow as a hemlock stalk you were there all the time; and that when I came to the *N.Y.* office I was so accomplished in dissimulation that you thought I was the person who wrote so airily and securely. There was a Thurber drawing on the wall. I hope it is still there.

Please tell Maeve Brennan how much I admire 'The Springs of Affection'. I could hardly endure to read it but was too spell-bound not to; though at intervals I had to come to the surface and howl.

Warner to Maxwell, May 4, 1972:

Is *Munby* published in U.S.A. yet?* It certainly will be, and *The N. Y.* will certainly want to review it. If you have not fixed a reviewer yet, may it be me?

If you haven't yet read *Munby*: he was born in 1828, gentry, an intellectual in an onlooking way, with a profound interest in working women, the dirtier and the more Amazonian the better: no philanthropy, very little sentiment: a *drang*.

He loved and finally married a maid-of-all-work. The book is made of his diaries, with a few scraps of her own reminiscences—which are the best of all. Mayhew, Samuel Butler, an aura of Tennyson, and for queerness, and arbitrary tragedy, it could be a novel by Hardy—but convincing, which novels by Hardy seldom are.

---

* *Munby, Man of Two Worlds*, by Derek Hudson. Warner's review, "Close Distinctions," was never published.

Warner to Maxwell, May 30, 1972:

Here, meanwhile, and much nearer my heart, is a photograph of Frankfort Manor, and of Valentine and myself when we lived there: Valentine taking it in a mirror, and me adjuring her to hold her head up. And here is a poem she wrote there. She certainly had you prophetically in mind when she wrote it, for that is exactly, Dear Mr Maxwell, what you have become since, Dear William. She was convinced that she would outlive dying; and if she was right (she constantly surprised me by being right) she must think of you with profound trust and gratitude.

Here is a fragment of classical marble. The day after the Duke of Windsor's death, friends called to condole. They were met in the doorway with the message: 'The Duchess is sorry she cannot see you now. She is with the Duke.'

Valentine's poems: the selection is killing me. The choice, the page layout, the sequence (a million times more demanding than the sequence of tonalities in a music programme); and their increasing melancholy, which rends my heart.

Maxwell to Warner, June 1972:

The two photographs I have placed in Montaigne, for safe-keeping, since it is that and the clock I would seize if the apartment caught on fire and they are within easy snatching distance of one another.

Frankfort Manor is all that I imagined it. I feel I have pruned the vines, which I like to think are a climbing yellow rose. It is a house that is endlessly indulgent with one's imagination. And the two of you, in the Vermeer-like light, giving off emanations of happiness. And the poem: It is very strange. Where another person might, I think ask something as serious as that of someone, perhaps the wrong person, even, she depended on the faculty of recognition. I felt this when we were all there together. I felt deeply accepted. I felt she felt my affection for you was sturdy enough and would do. And it is. She was, as you say, right. And there is no doubt whatever in my mind that she has outlived dying.

Speaking of which, do not, for my sake, and for hers, let the selection of the poems, and the arrangement, undo you. It is of so serious an order that it will simply come to you, the way it came to me that I must marry Emmy. It will fall into place, you will see.

I have stopped to look at Narrative 4 and the Introduction to *The Cat's Cradle–Book* to see if those are yellow rose vines all along the front of Frankfort Manor, and you don't say, so I can have any kind of rose I want, wouldn't you say? The Dutch gable I hadn't remembered, and was struck by it in the snapshot. But more struck by the happiness—that people stand in a certain way when they are transubstantiated with love.

Nancy Hale sent me, from England, a book—*Recollections of Virginia Woolf by Her Contemporaries* [ed. Joan Russell Noble]. It is quite monotonous; they all had virtually the same thing to say, but I recommend that you get it from the London Library for two reasons: you will find yourself on page 174, and there are 9 pages written by the Woolfs' cook [Louie Mayer] that put the whole of Bloomsbury to shame, they are so much more perceptive and so much better written. 154–163. The account of the morning of her committing suicide is enough to stop your heart. It's all there: The terror that followed the discovery that she wasn't anywhere, and the searching, and the false hopes, and the recognition finally that there was nothing more that anybody could do. It is extraordinary.

Warner to Maxwell, June 14, 1972:

Yes, you were deeply accepted. She had no reservations about you—and she was prone to reservations, and suffered from that most powerful kind of jealousy which is neither rational nor revengeful: pure as prussic acid. You were not only accepted on my account, you know. You were absolutely accepted, and at the deepest level of respect and affinity.

Now what am I to do? Marchette [Chute] has importuned that the Letters should be published now—as an example of love, she said, when such examples are badly needed; and that it is base & *fainéant* of me to skulk to the shelter of a receptacle. I put her off (base and *fainéant*) but on her last evening she set her teeth in me, tossed aside all my practical objections— and I found myself saying that perhaps a privately printed edition which I could pay for. And there we left it, except by then I had both of them at me, both trampling on perhapses; and it was their last evening and almost their last morning.

But I have a sting in my tail. I am too old for negotiations. They must undertake that.

Now I must break off and listen to Stokowski. He is ninety, & has repeated the programme he conducted sixty years ago. What a lot of times he has been round the Cape; and the wine with a rounder bouquet for each voyage (he is now teaching the audience how to polish its applause by

bringing it into an orderly diminuendo). I have never heard a finer adjustment of tempi (Brahms no. I); scarcely a hairsbreadth between the second
& third movement and yet the change establishes a change of mood in the
first bar. And that *Respice finem!* as though the whole symphony were one
sweep of the bow.

And now he has let his orchestra have a releasing rampage through
Tchaikovsky's *Grand Russian Circus*.

I wish you could have listened, in this room smelling of turkscap lilies.

Warner to Maxwell, July 10, 1972:

Your letter came this morning. I was still thinking about it, and washing
my hair, when the telephone rang. My cousin Rachel, to tell me she had
long suspected she was under a curse, and had now been assured by an
expert that she was—and it was a curse of long standing, extending
through generations, and did I think it had come in from the Highland side
of the family. She was perfectly convinced, and, like all the demented, perfectly convincing. Reason would have been heartless. On the principle of
Feed a Fever, I supplied more instances of hereditary doom and recommended trying an exorcist. After her, my hair still dank about me, came the
parson, to ask how I was keeping and could I let him have a large kettle for
the Youth Club's canteen. I couldn't, but consoled him with strawberries.
The next telephone call was to ask me if I could adopt two frogs—a nature
conservationist, and frogs are a dying race because of farming poisons.
Again I had to refuse, three cats made this garden unsuitable for frog con-
servation. All this before mid-day. This island is inflexibly lunatic. I hope
this will make you gratefully resigned to a calm prospect of being rained
on in Mass.

What I was thinking about while I washed my hair was your suggestion
of using Valentine's piece of autobiography as an introduction to her
poems. I wish we could. But several people—and that detestable sister—are
still alive; and as her name must accompany the poems, there would be no
possibility of avoiding identification.

Valentine had no illusions, but equally, no rancour. She never attempted to
stem mine; and after that family morass of Christian hypocrisy, I daresay it
was a solace to her.

I have thought of offering it to Alcoholics Anonymous as a document. A great many of their clients are intellectuals, the writing would help to fortify them. She wrote it in a storm of intention, when she thought we would be separated. I remember the torrent of her typewriter going overhead. I doubt if there is a revised line in it; certainly not an untrue one. She felt life so passionately that truth was her only means of expression. She was as single-minded as her falcon. I would be ashamed to read her praises of me if I did not know their entire honesty.

I fumble on without her.

Except when I see something she would have enjoyed. Last week I was staying in a house where I watched foxes by moonlight, and saw them with her eyes.

Maxwell to Warner, July 24, 1972:

Both your letters reached me. I think when I have a moment I must go back through the VA–STW letters in search of your Cousin Rachel. How anyone, no matter how demented, could enjoy your affection and think they were under a curse baffles me. On the other hand, I hope she doesn't resort to an exorcist because I like her so much the way she is. And on the third hand, supposing one had three, would Valentine's sister sue the publisher or you for libel? In America it wouldn't be possible but I know English libel law is different. In any case I am sure you are not concerned about sparing her feelings, which don't bear thinking about. It is too good for Alcoholics Anonymous. I mean, it is too remarkable a piece of writing to be put to any non-literary use. If you decide to publish the letters it could be as an appendix to that. Or—if only books were as free and easy— inserted right at the moment she wrote it. That strikes me as the best of all. Like "The Death of Father Zossima" or that long tale—"The Man on the Hill" or some such title—stuck into the middle of *Tom Jones*. Or "Tom Outland's Story," inserted into the middle of *The Professor's House*, that most prophetic of all American novels.

Speaking of foxes by moonlight, last night we all went to a neighbor's house to see some movies he had taken in China in 1939 or thereabouts, marvelous they were, and they walked home with us and on our front lawn, we stood looking at the full moon through binoculars. I saw nothing I couldn't see without them, but it was three times as large, which was

agreeable. We are having a heat wave, and there was a pleasant feeling of
being in the vicinity of a blast furnace. The bats flying around when we left
home were invisible or gone to bed, but there were fireflies. And
mosquitoes. And a general reluctance to separate. The softness of a summer night.

Only one rainy day in Wellfleet, and a lovely vacation. I got through a
volume and a half of *Clarissa*. I do not wonder at the fate that befell her,
but neither can I stop reading it.

Warner to Maxwell, September 4, 1972:

And by now you will have finished *Clarissa*.

I shall die happier knowing you in the arms of Richardson. Short stout
arms with rolling-pin wrists & pudgy hands; but once in them, one is in a
corner-seat for the rest of the journey.

Women wept all over Europe, do you know, for Clarissa—and longed all
over Europe, no doubt, for Lovelace. I don't think many women longed for
Sir Charles Grandison; being at heart rakes and the Pursuit of the Irre-
proachable without surprises; but Harriet is a Pet, and he develops her brilliantly, and personally I think it a better book than *Pamela*. But why do I tell
you all this? For, infallibly, you will go on and read them and decide for
yourself.

The first thing I ever wrote by way of journalism in U.S.A., when I went
as Guest Critic to the *Herald Tribune* in 1929, before you were born, my
dear, was a piece about Richardson. They allowed me to pick whatever
new book I chose, & there was a new book, dullish, about Richardson, so I
chose that and ceased to feel I was far from my home. That was the time
when Ben Huebsch [her American publisher] met my boat & asked me
what I most wanted to see & I replied 'Brooklyn Bridge & cinnamon toast.'

Warner to Maxwell, September 25, 1972:

Dear Mr Norton.

Do you remember, long ago, I used to pretend to be Mrs Gaskell to you
and tell you what Valentine was doing at that moment, & where the cats
were sitting and how many daffodils were out already. They were delightful letters to write. Suppose I try again.

I finished the volume of selections for Valentine's poetry—almost entirely to my dissatisfaction. By the end I began to feel an accumulated guilt that I was not doing it rightly, and almost a terror & unwillingness to be doing it at all. The next hurdle will be the proofs; but those I can turn to a calmer colder heart who won't have Constance's speech ringing in its ears all the time.

Then, shaking like a frustrated steam-engine, I cast about for something to do, & spent a devoted three days turning out her work-shop from head to foot. It had not been touched since before her death & had been chaotic then. Some of the details of the chaos, such as a small mouth-organ & the locket trimmed with ermine I wore as a child, were reviving—like finding mushrooms in a city churchyard.

All this time I was picking & cursing strawberries. I had an enormous crop, & my principles are of a niggardly kind that can't let food go to waste. But I got one pure pleasure out of this. I was picking & cursing and searching who I could give the next lot to when I saw a paddle rise above the garden wall. And looking down, there were two boys in a canoe. So without explanation, I commanded them to keep about, & hurried (to Valentine's workroom) for the shrimping net, and filled it with strawberries and lowered it down to them. They were silent and acceptant; & it was all very Tennysonian, & I realised that when they are old men they will remember those strawberries.

Since then I have sat too long in the garden in an east wind & caught an interminable cold. But the Lord had mercy on me and sent me a totally unhoped-for cleaning woman. And she is a Cockney born & calls Pericles Socks. She cleans very well, too.

Maxwell to Warner, October 3, 1972:

All I can say about the book of Valentine's poems is that if, for any reason, unpublished work of mine had to be left in somebody's hands, I would much prefer that that person were you. It is inconceivable to me that she wouldn't feel the same way.

As I sat here wondering what date you were visiting critic of the *Herald Tribune* it occurred to me to broaden the sphere of wondering to include the question of why you have never collected your reviews and essays into a book. Then I could sit down and, with a good light over my left shoulder, read it. So will you please do that? Otherwise I am obliged to go to the New York Public Library and dig that piece on Richardson out, and whatever else accompanied it. I may anyway. But surely the book is a good idea?

Last Sunday afternoon I was asked to say something at a gathering in honor of my publisher [Alfred A. Knopf], who lives in Purchase. The occasion was also in Purchase (N.Y.), at Manhattanville College, a Catholic institution of higher learning that somehow detached itself from the Church and is now simply a college. The location was superb, and the gardens right out of *Country Life*, the buildings all new but one, and that one was a castle, built in 1882, of grey stone, with a keep, etc., on the crowning hill of the estate. It had been built by the grandfather of Ogden Reid, whose wife you must have known when you were writing for the *Herald Tribune*, since he owned it and she largely helped him run it. While I was waiting around I fell into conversation with a middle aged young man who was presenting the publisher with a map of Purchase at the time of his birth (1892) and since his name was Whitlaw Reid was moved to ask if he had lived in the castle. He had been born in it, he said, but never lived there, though he often came to have lunch with his grandmother. The smallest room I saw was forty by eighty feet, and the ceilings were at least twenty, and no doubt there was a footman behind every chair. But when he came to speak a marvelous thing happened. Winding the whole thing up he said *"Plus ça change"* and stopped and looked nonplussed, and then he looked into the air a minute and then he consulted his notes and then lifting his head to the microphones he said triumphantly, *"plus c'est la même chose."*

Thank you for the Tennysonian incident of the two boys in the canoe. I shall remember it myself when I am an old man, which will be much sooner than they will.

Warner to Maxwell, October 9, 1972:

I am so astonished at having written anything at all that I can't judge this ["Four Figures in a Room. A Distant Figure"], except to know that it is what I meant, that you will understand it, that Mr Shawn may need you to

explain it. If he wants to know why the little boy was there for no apparent
reason, he was the child of Fanny's husband who left her for a very young
girl who died in childbed; and Fanny snatched him as a kind of self-vindi-
cation. But either I write a story from the angle of Miss Belton, or make
this one lopsided with explanations of the superfluous.

He was there, in fact, because I wanted him, and because I am a realist
and constantly facing the unexplained.

You need not go to the New York Public Library where you &
Marchette would become public nuisances by conversing. I shall post you a
book of cuttings where Valentine told me to stick reviews and so forth. You
will find "Richardson" there. Irita Van Doren was the person who dealt
with me. Mrs Ogden Reid was in a royal suite somewhere overhead. I like
rooms forty by eighty myself, and on the rare occasions when I have had a
footman behind my chair I have found it congenial, but far beyond all else,
I like a grand staircase.

There is nothing in the book I shall post you that I want preserved—
except possibly *The Countess Montgomery*—but thinking over what you once
said about a collected volume of my more polished nonsense in the dark
backwards of *The New Yorker*, I began to consider a posthumous collection.
If it happened to sell well—and extraordinary things happen to the dead—
it couldn't be raked in for Death Duties, and would bring in a small extra to
my Cousin Janet & my dear typist Soo, who under my will will share this
house. For instance, it might pay for mending the roof or painting its face.
I don't like to leave it unendowed. Janet says she will sell teas on the lawn to
my American admirers, but she is sanguine.

> *And my spirit underground*
> *Will smile to think of the Inland Revenue*
> *diddled for once.*

What do you think?

As a result of Lord Longford's earnest antics & my own sobering
influenza I was driven to meditate on why I don't love Milton; which I can't
reconcile with my devotion to *Comus* & Lycidas and Al. and Pen. Pornography. Eve is bad enough, the way he shoves her compliance under one's
nose: but he is much worse about her cookery, her fruits & jellies. And

then I saw in a blaze of light that St Agnes Eve is sensual & pure because he wants what he describes, whereas Milton describes what he didn't desire; and that pornography is exploiting what leaves one cold.

However, I shall not write to Lord Longford. And I shall love *Comus* with a tranquil mind. And venerate the temperate Dryden more than ever. Oh! how I wish he'd walk into the room. We should get on so well together. 'The lady of the spotted muff.'—I still shake with the rapture of first reading that.

Maxwell to Warner, October 1972:

I think the story is marvelous, and in sending it on to Mr. Shawn I didn't raise any questions of whose child the little boy is. If he asks me I can tell him, but it would never have occurred to me to wonder who any child under a piano was, since it was bound to be my double, in any case.

In going through old letter files in the attic (E. B. White has been collecting his, for a volume) I came upon a cache of letters to Mr. Maxwell dating from 1948 into 1952. I don't in general like to read my own letters, but sometimes when they are descriptions of happiness I do. It is assuming a lot to assume that you feel likewise, but anyway I am, and hence the enclosure. And there is another, handwritten letter that I thought you might enjoy part of [sent from Great Eye Folly, October 28, 1950]:

"I am doing what I always say people shouldn't do—writing on my knee by a fire. Just outside the window—perhaps twenty yards away and two yards down—the North Sea is working itself into a fine gale and the Siamese kitten is sitting beside me in an 18th century child's armchair which I found in the lumber-room of this strange house.

"This place is *heaven*. It is like nothing but Shelley's Villa Magni—except that it has salt marshes behind it instead of chestnut wooded mountains. We got here yesterday. There is no tenant so far as the Dorset house, but thank God we wasted no time waiting about for one. There is such a shindy going on outside that one can't tell what is wind and what is breakers—and when the kitten stirs I hear the little bell on his collar."

I am flying to Illinois for my stepmother's funeral. She never tried to take my mother's place in my heart and I would not have appreciated it if she had, but she was a very good stepmother, and, considering the differences in our natures, this can't always have been easy. She was eighty-three and had hardening of the arteries, and for thirteen or fourteen years after my father died she was under sedation, and in tears. Then at the beginning of this year she got better, and was able to enjoy life again. I am meeting my two brothers, who live in California, at the Chicago airport, and taking another plane to Springfield airport, where we will be met by relatives and driven north to Lincoln. I don't know how I will manage to sit quietly and listen to people praising Nixon for ending the war in Vietnam, but if I don't keep my mouth shut, my older brother and I will get into the kind of argument that is not pleasant at funerals. If he drives me too far I will tell the story of the man who met the Duke of Wellington in the street and said "Mr. Smith, I believe?"*

Thank you for your letter. There was no part of it that didn't enchant me. And I see that I must go now and read Dryden. I don't think I have read a word of him but the "Ode to St. Cecilia's Day," and if you were to offer a suggestion about where to begin, I would be most indebted.

I look forward to the arrival of Valentine's scrapbook. I look forward to it intensely. I envisage two posthumous books, for the farther further diddling of that swollen party you referred to. And meanwhile, when I get back from Illinois, I will look into the matter of the uncollected New Yorker pieces. The list is being made up now.

And thank you for the clarification about pornography. You have simplified my life, and God knows it could stand simplifying.

* The response attributed to Wellington was "If you believe that, you will believe anything."

Warner to Maxwell, October 19, 1972:

Witchcraft again. Or why should my letters from Great Eye Folly come to your hand when I am sending Donald Gillespie [from an unpublished story] there to die as he wished to die?

I bless the witchcraft. I had forgotten the assertion of the little bell on the kitten's collar. He was very young, very slender—& indomitable. He used to sit at the edge of the waves, staring them out of countenance, taut with excitement and perfectly composed. And when he'd done with that, he used to walk off to the shed where the fisherman kept their crab-pots & fall asleep in that heavenly, that paradisal smell.

Three years later, after the tidal wave, we went back to see what had happened to the house. The hinder part, which faced inland, was still standing. We could scramble up the stairs. We pulled open the door of the room, Valentine's sitting, above where I wrote those letters. It was strange to look down into the blue summer sea, basking & undulating there.

The people in the village—those of them who were left—spoke of the inundation as 'the great surge'.

Did you quarrel at the funeral? I rather wish you had, for I'm sure that when you quarrel you do, you quarrel like a tarantula. Nothing can make a funeral satisfactory: the person one wants to meet at it is underground.

Which Dryden to begin with? I suppose 'The Hind & the Panther'; but 'Annus Mirabilis' is glorious when it comes to land and deals with the fall of London. And if neither bites, try *MacFlecknoe*: you will find him very congenial in these pre-election months. Even from here we can see through Nixon—which won't prevent a great many worthy tolerators being glad when he gets in.

I am glad you like that queer story—which is a far cry from the careful carpetting of the last one, isn't it? I oscillate like the flame of a dying candle.

Maxwell to Warner, October 1972:

I am very pleased that *The Flint Anchor* is going into paperback but I think if I were asked I should say that it ought to do this under its own name, and that it is not part of the business of paperback publishers to decide what title will in their imagination (for what else is it) sell well.* You might consider kicking them in the shins. It is a very vulnerable part of the masculine anatomy. (I started to write American instead of masculine, for some mysterious reason. Sunday morning, as Emmy wound up a conversation with our nearest and dearest neighbor in the country, Mrs. D said "Kill Bill for me—I mean kiss Bill for me." Nothing mysterious here at all.)

I had no sooner received the new life of Virginia Woolf [by Quentin Bell] into my hands, last Monday, and agreed to write a review of it, remarking to the editor, "I'll drop everything and do it," for I sometimes take months, than I had a telephone call from my older brother and found myself on my way to Illinois to a funeral. My stepmother, who was 84, and had been ill a long time. She was a Catholic, and the strangest of the many strange things that happened to me was that, during the funeral mass, the relative who was sitting next to me, my stepmother's sister-in-law, whispered "We take communion now, we go out this way"—indicating the left side of the pew. Unable to believe my ears, I said "What?" and she repeated the same words, and when she got up I got up and stood in front of the altar and had a wafer put on my tongue. Which has been the tongue of an atheist since 1923. Such is the force of a polite upbringing. And if she did not mean me to do that, what did she mean me to do?

The night I arrived, going up the walk to the front porch of the funeral home, as it is euphemistically called in the United States, though I don't know that "parlor" is much of an improvement, I was stopped by a series of old acquaintances, and in the third cluster of them was a very bent old woman with an exquisite profile, who when they told her who I was, exclaimed "Billy!" (my childhood name in that town) and kissed the tips of my fingers. I knew her only slightly when I was growing up and I can only conclude that, in the razor's edge between living and dying herself, she has come to regard everything and everybody as beautiful and miraculous. As indeed they are.

It went on like that the whole forty-eight hours I was in Illinois. With my stepmother's death, my father's three sons inherited his two farms. As I explained to Emmy, it is like what happens when you double the recipe.

After a while I became aware of that fact that nobody had mentioned Nixon or McGovern or the Vietnam War. I came home without having heard a single reference to the election or the national disgrace.

* The book was reprinted by the Popular Library as *The Barnards of Loseby*.

Warner to Maxwell, November 6, 1972:

An enormous cheque (thank you very much) followed by an enormous envelope with my unbooked bits from 1936–72.

I looked at the earlier ones with veneration, thinking that they had been read & accepted by Mr Ross. It makes me historical. The fire extinguisher in 'Maternal Devotion' raised his high-minded curiosity about machinery —there were several marginal enquiries in the first proof—and 'A View of Exmoor' was changed from its original title of 'A View of Dartmoor' because he had asked the first six people he met that morning what they associated with Dartmoor & they all said, a prison.

I suppose he liked my tone of voice. I can't account for it otherwise, for there are a good many in the envelope he should not have accepted.

I have been combining hostess-ship with muscular rheumatism. All my own fault, I acceded to the one and brought on 'tother by over-gardening. Today the astonishment of being out of pain almost persuades me that I am dead. But alive I am, and the painters are in the house, few things could be more convincingly mortal than that.

Or more reposeful. All they need is cups of tea at statutory intervals. And at 5 P.M. they go away, so I don't have to sit up till midnight entertainingly conversing.

Warner to Maxwell, November 27, 1972:

Your stepmother's sister-in-law is in mortal sin. I hope you don't mind. She imperiled you, too, but in a lesser degree as you didn't know what she was up to; and the bent old woman who kissed your finger-tips has restored you to innocence & a state of grace, so I won't worry about you.

Warner to Maxwell, December 19, 1972:

Did I tell you the romantic result of my N.Y. story 'The Listening Woman'? A parcel with quantities of silver bows & tissue paper, sent with a sender's name perfectly unknown to me came not long ago. I undid the bows. Out of the tissue paper came the tip of an ear which I instantly recognised though I hadn't seen it during this century. The unknown sender had noticed in the lament for lost objects of one's childhood the printed calico cat with pink paws. The pattern of such cats has survived in USA; the establishment where he works keeps a basketful of them & people come from furthest Brooklyn to buy them. So—as you see. He is identically the same cat, with a mild serious expression—not a whisker of art or fancy about it.

Warner to Maxwell, December 1972:

The wine-strainer, dear William, is for the author of *Ancestors*. It belonged to my Scotch grandmother, Flora Moir, whose given name was transmitted to her through two successive godmothers, the elder of whom was the god-daughter of Flora Macdonald.

Her father, George Moir (2) was a friend of Thomas Carlyle, who recorded him as 'a small clear man' (clear in the sense of enlightened). Henry Cockburn said he could have got anywhere if it had not been for his Aberdeenshire accent (George Moir (1) was a wine-merchant in Aberdeen). As it was, he was professor of Rhetoric in the University of Edinburgh, and Sheriff of Ross-shire (Scottish Bar). He called back his translation of *Wallenstein* from the printers when he heard that Coleridge was translating it.

Maxwell to Warner, December 1972:

I did part of my growing up on a farm in Wisconsin. Motherless children master the art of acquiring second, and third, and fourth families. The farm had been in this particular family since pioneer days, and the family had been comfortably well off until the Depression, when a bank in Milwaukee adroitly substituted its own worthless municipal bonds for Mrs. Green's perfectly good government bonds, after which the resemblance to *The Cherry Orchard* was considerable. They had a very rich relation, living in South Bend, Indiana, who used to send them what were blithely referred to as poor boxes, and which Mrs. Green and her daughters always opened with excitement, expecting (though experience had taught them exactly what to expect) a kneeling mat for gardening, a piece of silver in which the line of beauty lay superimposed exactly on the line of utility, a sachet, a book of wood engravings, a part of the ocean, an onyx ring, or God knows what. Something to delight their hearts is what they were foolishly expecting. What they got, on one occasion, was twelve dozen heavy black silk stockings that had been used and not washed afterwards.

Will you enlighten me as to the uses of a wine-strainer? Something tells me that it is not used merely in decanting. Is it for an earlier stage, and do you also use a cloth with it? So easy to imagine, all those godmothers. And by the time I have arrived at the first my own genes are already back in the Scotland they came from. Did you know Flora Moir, and did you like her? And did she know Mrs. Carlyle, as a child? And did Coleridge ever finish his translation of *Wallenstein*, or was he interrupted by a return visit from the man from Porlock? I think of all this, and all of them, and of you when I hold the wine strainer in my hand, admiring the noble simplicity of the design. So clearly before the Age of Fuss.

I am reading *Kidnapped* for the first time, and groan every time somebody addresses a remark to me because it is such a long way from the Highlands.

Warner to Maxwell, January 10, 1973:

Indeed I knew Flora Moir. I loved her next to my father, and she loved me next to him. And her father loved her beyond all others. I can't say for his father, the wine-merchant in Aberdeen. Ask your Scotch genes. The wine merchant may have fixed his heart on a pretty daughter, but fixed it would have been: there is a bull's-eye gravity about the way these people love. The wine-merchant's father had been sent down to the port to meet two girl cousins from the Orkneys. One of them came off the packet so deadly sea-sick she could hardly speak or stand. It was done in a flash. No, my Flora didn't know Mrs Carlyle. The Carlyles were away to Ecclefechan before she was out of leading strings. But I daresay the wine-strainer did.

Wine-strainers were more functional then. A lot got into the bottles beside the juice of the grape: lees, pips, an odd wasp or two, native soil. By my time, it was useful if a bit of the cork got in—so tedious to fish out of your glass with a spoon. As for the translation of *Wallenstein*, it was probably just one of Coleridge's projects.*

I hope your mothering Mrs Green was philosophic enough to wash the twelve dozen (!?) pairs of heavy silk stockings and restore them to society (she could have plaited a splendidly morose hat out of them). During the later half of the war when there was nothing between the tatters of better days and contemporary wear-me-downs a local clergyman came into the W.V.S. [Women's Volunteer Service] holding with abhorrence a parcel of choirboys' surplices which bats had shitted on. 'You might find a use for them as cleaning rags.' The desecrated surplices were linen; and as my fellow-workers didn't feel an urgent need for cleaning rags, I took them home, had them professionally washed, cut out the best bits and made a fine pair of drawers for Valentine, round the legs of which, in acknowledg-

ment of their church's dedication, I embroidered *Loué soit S. Nicolas.* I
found them, light as cobwebs, after her death, put away in tissue paper.

* Coleridge's translation of *Wallenstein*, a verse tragedy in three parts by Friedrich Schiller,
was published in 1800.

Warner to Maxwell, March 31, 1973:

Today has been a glorious event: I have walked downstairs with both
feet. At the beginning of the week I tripped on the topmost stair (I have no
idea how or why) and cascaded down them on my back, reflecting during
an interminable interval on the inconvenience of broken pelvises, cooking
from a wheel chair and the fill-ups in *The Times* about old solitary women
found dead after months of no one having noticed their absence (the last
seemed far the best). At the bottom of the stairs there was a pause for reality, and I made some discreet experiments and found I still had an unbroken neck and an uncracked pelvis—but two, as I thought, ruined feet. So I
got back on my horse in the traditional way, and groaned along to the
kitchen and gave myself an arnica and some left-over black coffee, and
three hours later I had rung up the local taxi and kept my appointment
with the woman who washes my hair. I had braked with them all the way
down the stairs and put too much determination into it, and they were
confounded and driven backward like those people in the psalms; and that
was all there was to it; except shock. The cats' shock was far worse than
mine. So, you see ... born to be hanged. I defy you to find where the crack
is in this story ["The Five Black Swans"] between writing with both feet
and with one.

For all that, I had some wistful thoughts about how much pleasanter life
would be if I lived on the yonder side of your wall. For one thing, I could
rub you with goose-grease. Have you exhausted it, has it ceased to charm?

Valentine thought well of *The Good Soldier.* I couldn't keep up with it—
partly because I knew I ought to. I hate books that excite my sense of duty.
I think his ideas of noblesse oblige came from some inflamed genes of his
German ancestry, didn't they? I saw him once when I was in New York in
1929. He had a red face, unanimously red; and was stout and upright.

Maxwell to Warner, April 1973:

I don't know which is more shocking, the fall or the vision of physical incapacity. Yes, I do know. The fall was worse, while it lasted. But a vision of that kind is undoable, and undoing—I thought of Elinor Wylie. And then I thought, thankfully, of what bones you must have, what good solid bones. And then I thought, if such a thing happened, I would just go and get her and bring her home. There would be queuing up outside of all the people who love you, and you would have to fight us off with a stick.

The fairy story is on its way to Mr. Henderson and Mr. Shawn, but I don't feel obliged to withhold my opinion until after they have read it, since nothing they could say would make me feel that it was less than marvelous. It is, of course, why you slipped on the stairs. You cannot write like that and not be a danger to oneself, the mind being not in the body. I sometimes think that the greatest kindness anyone can do me is to remind me of what it felt like when I was head over heels in love. Which this does.

Warner to Maxwell, April 14, 1973:

Dear—Mr—Maxwell—Dearest—William

I am so pleased you like the second Elfhame story so much—and the bit I particularly like myself. I was smug as a cat when I wrote the passage about Tiphaine's first flight.

Now I am snuffling round the thought of a third story—about Brocéliande this time. To write it as I wish I would have to be the Duc de Saint-Simon. (Did you know, by the way—I only came on it by accident—that he was no more than the second duke? A very mediocre height from which to look down on royal bastards.)

The swallows have come. Valentine would have seen them days ago, she loved them so passionately that she compelled them; but I saw them this morning and even she could not have seen them more poetically; for I saw their shadows flick over the gangway outside my kitchen window. One year, a cold April like this one, we went to France without having seen a single swallow, and feeling outcast & deprived. Our first stop in a small town in Normandy, we went out for a walk before dinner & came to a small lake—an *étang*, neither pond nor lake, on the outskirts of the town with a public footpath round it, and the water lead-coloured. And suddenly

through the dusk came a flock of swallows, and they stooped down and
played above the water, swooping and twirling—for flies but for pleasure
too. There was such *impulse* in it. The cold still air, the grey sky, the leaden
water: and suddenly this living net of flight cast over it.

It is the most natural act to write to you about swallows. It was the first
of your books you sent me. And I had scarcely finished reading it when it
was borrowed, and never returned: stolen, in plain English. Have you a
copy you could send me? Sent as a loan, it would be returned. I keep that
commandment, at any rate. And have you read *More Joy in Heaven*, an early
book of short stories, long out of print? (by me). If you would like to, I will
send you my copy, on the same terms. They were written at Frankfort
Manor, in my large room enlarged by two mirrors, with its casement windows looking out on a lawn and on a wall of trees. There was not a window in the house that did not look out on trees. And it was such a house to
sleep in. But you know exactly what it was like, for you have the Montaigne
which I gave her there, and inscribed '*Que sais-je? Que je t'aime*'; and which
exactly resembles it.

I never told you how much I liked the V. Woolf article which cost you so
much, and which you dedicated to Louie [Mayer, the Woolfs' cook]. She
shone out, didn't she? She called her eyes her own, the essential thing. As
for Virginia and her Bloomsbury, one is forced to remember that she was
lineally descended from the Clapham Sect.

Warner to Maxwell, April 27, 1973:

The Clapham Sect. It was Sydney Smith who called them so. They were
Evangelical—one might say High Evangelical, pious but not damp. They
did a great deal to abolish the Slave Trade as well as drinking their tea without sugar which they also did. They were educated, wealthy, a high proportion of bankers among them, they lived in large houses with gardens,
vineries, libraries, round Clapham Common which was then breezy and
rural. They examined their consciences, and adjoining consciences, they
lived plainly but not poorly, they thought highly of each other, saw no
harm in going to the theatre, intermarried, talked to each other, wrote letters of advice and discrimination to each other, took a deep interest in each
other... Let Saints on Earth in Concert sing... Do you see what I'm getting

at? Virginia [Woolf]'s grandfather was one of them. The Bloomsbury Sect
was even more so, for there was no one as irreverent as Sydney Smith to
stick a pin into the bubble. And both sects did a great deal of good:
Clapham scuppered the Slave Trade, Bloomsbury scuppered the Royal
Academy. (Both, of course, still exist. But never mind, there's nothing like
so much money in them.)

You see, I just happened to be born disliking sects.

Thank you very much for *They Came Like Swallows*. As I began to read it,
I found I knew more and more of the characters as they walked out of
Ancestors. I remember the close of the story from when I first read it, and
admired your control of it. I am unsure whether I can read it again, now
that I know you, and better what it must have been like being tossed about
among relations. I see that tossed about expression almost every day in *The
Times*: those children from Vietnam.

I will send you *More Joy* next week. I'm afraid they won't be much pleasure to you; they are an unlicked lot—though I enjoy 'Blood Royal' because
I loved inventing Isambard.

'The Black Swans.' ? 'A Dying Queen.' ? I was better at titles in 1935.

Maxwell to Warner, May 1973:

Neither my mother nor, so far as I know, any member of my family ever
drank tea with sugar (I wouldn't dream of it), and so, reading your letter, I
find myself drawn to the Clapham Sect, but I do alas see what you are getting at. How I wish you would rewrite the *Encyclopaedia Britannica*—just
for me. I know it is a project of some scope but it wouldn't require twenty
volumes but just one fat one. After which I, just from reading it, would
shed light on everything, wherever I walked.

Warner to Maxwell, May 4, 1973:

I am feeling hangdog and apprehensive because next week I shall have a
man from Belfast [Robin Perry] staying here. He is a man who hates noise;
sensitive, not unduly opinionated—for an Irishman, a natural solitary; and
since the beginning of this wretched rumpus, has been in the middle of it,
for he works on the *Belfast Telegraph*. He has a cantankerous mouth and

that cantankerous Ulster accent; and since most things in Ireland except explosives still belong to the 18th century, I suppose one might call him a Whig. I felt so sorry for his large sensitive ears that I asked him to come here for a rest if he ever got a holiday. He's got it, and he is coming. I can't think how to behave. If I ask about Belfast, it will throw him back into what he comes to get away from; if I don't, he will think me unsympathetic, and, in my English way, not giving a thought to Ireland: if I just listen I shall begin to dislike him for his Ulster accent. And more than that: I have a superstitious feeling that all the tedium & violence and terror will come here with him and infect the house as though seven devils were loose in it.

But he is fond of cats. I must leave hospitality to the cats. Pericles always knows unhappiness, and turns himself inside out for a poultice to comfort it.

Warner to Maxwell, May 13, 1973:

No! You did not tell me that you were going to Ireland on the 22nd. Brute beast, William! If I had known earlier I would have tried with all my power to persuade you to come here. Or I would have put on my hat & come to Ireland to see you. All I can do now is to sulk & forgive you.

As a token of forgiveness I will mail you *More Joy in Heaven*. As it will arrive after you have set out for Ireland, I will address it to you at *The New Yorker*. It is my only copy, by now it is *the* only copy, and I don't want the poor thing to be drowned in the post. I should have sent it earlier, but some one else was reading it. I feel like the Cumaean Sibyl with this belated interest in my works.

Maxwell to Warner, May 15, 1973:

I don't know which of the three [Elfhame stories] I love the most. And it ["The Revolt at Brocéliande"] *is* like Saint Simon. I hang over the page, and each thing that happens drives the previous thing out of my mind, I am so affected by what I am reading. And so I go back and reread and reread. Yeats said, "Only that which does not teach, which does not cry out, which does not persuade, which does not condescend, which does not explain, is irresistible." These stories are all those things. With the element of enchantment. And of absolute authority. Please don't stop here.

Maxwell to Warner, June 6, 1973:

The house we were staying in looked out on Dalkey Bay, and islands, and a near lighthouse and a far lighthouse and Howth and the coast of Wales (they said; I never saw it), and Dalkey Bay is not much more than a channel between the shore and the islands, which were, of course tempting, being inhabited by goats and seagulls, and with a roofless 12th century chapel, a Martello tower, and a ruined gun emplacement from somewhere in the middle of the reign of Queen Victoria. I mean sooner or later I had to get there, and was told not to try to row out to them because the current was very fast. In the end the gardener took us out in a rowboat with an outboard motor, and Emmy and I walked all over the island, knee deep in wet Queen Anne's lace. I climbed up into the Martello tower and the gun emplacement, and she, not liking heights, wandered off and found a seagull's nest with three eggs in it. I would tell you what they looked like if I weren't absolutely sure that you already know. The goats stared at us, the view in all directions was sublime. In my next life if I don't succeed in being a story by Chekhov called "Gooseberries" I shall be an island.

Warner to Maxwell, June 22, 1973:

You won't be surprised to hear that I am doing another. It begins with the werewolves at Brocéliande (they were too good to be slighted), it ends at the court of Blockula in north-east Sweden. I cannot understand the process of mind which writes these stories. It's certainly not imagination. Imagination doesn't come into it; I may throw in a little invention from time to time, over the mechanics, though more comes by logical deduction. For the rest, I sit and wait for it to accumulate. The closest analogy I can think of—an inelegant one—is a Boil.

Maxwell to Warner, July 21, 1973:

The little house in the woods where I have been going to write after breakfast turned out to have a hole in the roof directly over my table. Such a disorderly, Hogarthish sight, a pile of damp unanswered letters and unfinished manuscript. But also, not so cheerful, two big spots on the binding of *More Joy in Heaven*. Being rain, it seems to have left no trace, but I am

ashamed. I should never have risked taking the book to the beach with me.
And wouldn't have, except that I couldn't be parted from it.

As for what is between the covers, if you had ever shown the slightest
tendency to that sort of thing, I would wonder if you were having me on.
To make such small claims for what is surely one of your best collections.
"A Village Death" is a masterpiece, but I loved them all—the little boy who
was sitting on the toilet and looked like the sadfaced monkey door-
knocker, the postman and that wonderful girl who waited for him under
the wild cherry tree at the crossroads, the youngest daughter of the third
Earl Stanhope (I could give a whole lecture on the short story from that
one), the row kicked up by "The Thought of Thought" (inevitably I
remembered how people used to go on about The Meaning of Meaning),
the old woman who stood on the kitchen chair to pick the last rose of summer ["The Nosegay"], and the woman who was such a bad housekeeper
and died in a fire, prophesying ["Celia"]. Wonderful, they are, and so fresh
in the effortless beauty of the writing. Also, something I think I would be
aware of even if I hadn't known that they were written during the period
when you were living at Frankfort Manor. They are formal and ironic but
they are also unguarded and unafraid, and all this makes for a special kind
of sadness. They are terribly sad in a way that suggests an equivalent happiness somewhere nearby.

In answer to your questions: I did both art and letters at *The New Yorker*
for four years. After I had been there three months I was given a story to
edit, and since I didn't know what editing was, I took out the things I didn't
approve of and made it the way I would have written it. That isn't, of
course, editing, but it passed for it, and Edmund Wilson gave me a lecture
on the editorial fallacy, which he said was to change things for the sake of
changing them, and that was helpful, and next I was put to work on galleys. Mr. Ross had, on an average, sixty to a hundred queries on every story.
Most of them were infuriating or demented or just plain uneducated
("Ariel, who he?") but four or five were inspired, and it was my job to spare
the editors' feelings by sorting the wheat from the chaff, adding the proof-
reader's queries, and the checker's, etc. [Wolcott] Gibbs had the fastest
mind I have ever encountered (though by no means the deepest) and it was
never possible for me to finish asking a question before I realized he had
already got the answer. He resigned to review plays, and Mrs. White

resigned because her husband wanted to live in Maine, and the first thing I knew I was up to my neck in *The New Yorker*. It was Louise Bogan who pulled me back to writing again, by precept and example, and exposing me to *Das Lied von der Erde* and the poems of Rilke and one thing and another, and at her urging I began to write stories, and one of them she said should be longer, and it turned out to be *The Folded Leaf*, which I sent to her through the mail, chapter by chapter and version after version, until it was done, and then she presented me with the title for it. By this time I had resigned from my full-time job, and spent a summer in Santa Fe, and come back to a tiny apartment in Greenwich Village, and been enticed into part-time editorial work by Mr. Lobrano, who was lonely.

Maxwell to Warner, August 2, 1973:

I could inform you that there are no poisonous boleti on the Cape. We found them everywhere, and ate them with rapture. Emmy at the last minute decided not to bring the mushroom books and so we dared not eat the other kinds, but kept picking them and looking at the undersides to see if they had gills or spores. Later we would come upon them, and I was struck with the fact that a mushroom lying with its stem in the air looks either abandoned or as if it had committed suicide. Emmy was equally struck with the fact that in their old age mushrooms turn into snow-white, or an angry greenish-yellow, powder puffs. As if one stage more and they would turn into a fairy. There was also a spider in the woods that on certain mornings spins lace handkerchiefs. All over the ground, about six inches square they are, and pure cambric. Seeing them, on our way to swim in the pond, we thought of you—that is to say, of Brocéliande.

Maxwell to Warner, August 2, 1973:

An awful lot of fuss on these galleys ["Visitors to a Castle"]. I think I would have been firmer about screening them if staying up half the night listening to the Watergate hearings hadn't sapped my strength. It is like trying to make yourself go to bed while reading *Madame Bovary* for the first time. And in any case, when will we ever again have a chance to *watch* such villains explaining away their really matchless villainy. And butter still wouldn't melt in their mouths. The whole scale of words from compunction through remorse is inoperative, as Mr. Ziegler would say.

Warner to Maxwell, August 6, 1973:

'Muse, sing of Rats.' We can turn to mushrooms. I am enchanted with the notion that mushrooms are on the brink of turning into fairies. It has been a good mushroom year here too, though all this science applied to fields has lessened their area. It has been especially good for puffballs. A class distinction: every farm labourer knows they are poisonous & tramples on them. Intellectuals slice them and cook them in butter and batten on them.

Maxwell to Warner, August 1973:

We got home from Maine on the 16th, my birthday, and found *The Nature of the Moment* [Warner's collection of Valentine's poems]. It arrowed in at just the right moment. I opened it to page 52 and was stunned. Who was the poet who was blinded and had his tongue cut out and his hands severed? I cannot read any of the poems without thinking of the letters. Each is a dimension of the other. You have put the poems together in a way that reminds me of the way the low juniper and blueberry and wild rose and God knows what all else grows on that uninhabited island off the coast of Isle au Haut. Into a carpet, is what I mean. Not a single leaf is crowded, but when you look down you are dazzled by the perfection of the adjustment. One after another the poems come to life for me, very much like the dearest child, the weakling, hardest to wean and rear.

Perhaps if I read the poems that are being published in *The New Yorker* just now more conscientiously I would enjoy them, but I tend not to, and I have just begun to see why. They seem as often to be concerned with unconscious rather than conscious feelings, and unconscious feelings can only be expressed, it would appear, by a display of virtuosity in arranging objects and disconnected glimpses of experience. Valentine's poems can only be approached through one's own experience, I was about to say, when I realized that the converse—that they can only be approached through *her* experience—was equally true. Which must mean that they can be understood and felt either way. But not by a distracted reader. Today every poem I turn to moves and amazes me.

Maxwell to Warner, August 1973:

The chains that bind me to your work are made of clover and the details on the galleys are never a burden but a delight, akin to turning the pages for a musician you love. Let us have no more talk of feeling ashamed and of burdens. The galleys of "Visitors to a Castle" arrived home safely and with no problems attached to them.

Because of the way that the Brocéliande stories come to you and because of the authority that they possess, as of actual first-hand knowledge, I am uneasy about making any kind of editorial suggestions—I am uneasy about it under the best of circumstances; in an ideal world there would be no editors—lest you be led off course. And in "The Ambassador" ["The Mortal Milk"] you have departed in two rather important ways (probably without even knowing you were doing it) from the previous Brocéliande stories: (1) it is not an entirely independent story but depends on the reader's having read "The Revolt"; and (2) it lacks a pedestal.

A majority of our readers, I am sure, would not dream of passing over a story by you, if they opened the magazine and saw it. In all the thirty-some years I have been working here, *The New Yorker* has always been edited on the modest assumption that, being a weekly, it is bound to be read in a hit or miss fashion. To the best of my knowledge, this is true. And that one cannot count on the reader's having read anything, though a good many read everything. It is wearisome for the writer to begin each time as if this story were the first and only story in what is actually a series of them, but I am afraid it is necessary. If you were writing a book of stories, with no thought of publication in this magazine you could say, "It was his Cousin Beliard, who had backed him through the Ib and Rollo affair and now came to remind him etc." Ib and Rollo are no part of the present story—that is to say they are completely missing from it—and so would you, could you invent some other reason for Melior's displeasure with Aquilon? And re-invent Melior and Aquilon?

In each of the other stories there has been a formal introduction in which you established the geography and social climate of Brocéliande or

Llwyn Onn and then proceeded to throw dust—fairy dust—in the reader's
eyes. In "Something Entirely Different" by having what the reader assumes
to be an ordinary footman and nurse (not that footmen are all that ordinary in the year 1973) suddenly take to their wings with a stolen baby, and
also by the blandness by which you explain how the blood of fetchings is
replaced by a distillation of the same weight of dew, soot, and aconite. In
"The Revolt" by invoking Wace and his incompetent investigation, and following this with the story within a story of the turfcutter's son who was
sent out to fetch some wood and saw two fat men dressed in scarlet sitting
under a live oak, holding each other's hands and weeping. And in all the
stories by a number of technical devices, such as starting from outside
fairyland ("Mortals cannot see fairies...") and also from a great distance, as
if you were Gibbon surveying the history of Rome ("Brocéliande was the
foremost elfin court in all Western Europe...") and then moving in closer
and closer, and by a certain precise attention to geography ("Tiphaine's
kingdom lay on the Scottish border not far from...") and by social detail—
the court amusements, the rituals of the state occasions, and so on. All that
is pretty much missing from "The Ambassador," with the result (for me,
and for the other editors too) that Aquilon and his entourage kept slipping
into mortality. I felt I was reading about people of a different period—the
period, say, of Queen Christina—and only now and then did they seem like
fairies.

I do understand that one cannot grow a boil on demand any more than
one can cure it in the twinkling of an eye, but do think about the possibility of a formal introduction here as elsewhere. It occurred to me that one
way to begin the story would be with the description of a hunting scene:
first, what mortals heard or thought they heard, and then what was actually happening, Melior and Aquilon hunting by moonlight, with the pack
of werewolves baying and the stag crashing through the forest. Are werewolves also invisible? like fairies? Anyway, it would give you a chance to
establish Aquilon and Melior as characters without reference to the story
of Ib and Rollo, and also to convey the characteristic beauty and chill of
Elfhame. Over the years your sleeves have proved so capacious I have no
hesitation in asking you to produce a bravura hunting scene from them,
but on the other hand you may have something even better that would set
the fairy kingdom alongside but also outside the mortal world.

Warner to Maxwell, August 25, 1973:

Here you are ["Beliard"], dear William. God help us!

Warner to Maxwell, August 30, 1973:

You are perfectly right—your letter is catnip to me. As soon as I have got rid of this rather too affable week of hospitalities, I will get to work on your queries.

I shall make it clearer that Aquilon is not an exemplary Elfin, because he sucked a mortal nurse. Any mixture of mortal and fairy is explosive. Think of the Angevins. Indeed, my first intention was to call the story 'The Mortal Milk'; but I thought this might be going too far.

The trouble with all these stories is that I am too conversant with my milieu. One of the troubles: the other is that in 'Something Entirely Different' I was too categorical about Elfin longevity. And I have been my catching my foot in that ever since.

Maxwell to Warner, September 4, 1973:

My dear, just go on writing like that and He won't need to help you. I finished it ["Beliard"] five minutes ago and my hair is still standing on end.

Warner to Maxwell, September 7, 1973:

Your letter came this morning. It made me so pleased that it has been read several times: more than pleased; elated.

And since you liked 'Beliard' so much, I am brave enough to tell you that I shall presently be off on another. This time, a Teutonic kingdom, called Wirre Gedanken. But I don't stay long in it, as the story is about five high-minded fairies who leave Wirre Gedanken in order to lead better lives & meditate. Their names are Ludo, Moor, Tinkel, Banian & Nimmerlein. Their intentions are hampered because of currency: fairy gold, as you know, is dead leaves by the morrow. They are forced to run up bills with country shopkeepers, pay, and move elsewhere.

I found Wirre Gedanken in a cook-book. It is a sort of fried bun. It seemed to me it would be sinful waste to find such a name & do nothing with it. It means, according to the cook-book, Troubled Thoughts.

I have still to invent the catastrophe, a catastrophe for five persons. But if I don't fuss about it, I expect it will come.

Warner to Maxwell, September 23, 1973:

I wish you had done that doctoral thesis on fairy tales when you were at Harvard. I'm sure it would have been delightful. I know it would have been valuable. As far as I know, there isn't such a book, even now. Damn the fool who deterred you—and deprived me. If you or I were in charge of young persons with a thesis to write, we would not be such oafs.

What *did* you write?

There are a great many questions . . .

How did you go to Harvard?—a scholarship, an exhibition, pressure from some discerning patron? Or just because you wanted to? What did you specialise in?

Do you know, I don't believe I could write at all if it were not I had you for a reader. I might toy with ideas, but I wouldn't write them down.

Maxwell to Warner, September 1973:

Speaking of dreams, did I or did I not tell you that I. A. Richards said, long ago, in a lecture at Harvard, that he woke up with his face bathed in tears because he had dreamed these lines, so beautiful and so moving to him:

Halt thou thy steed
And let it feed
On more than meets the eye.

Maxwell to Warner, October 1, 1973:

I don't remember ever being made so happy by anything, by any statement, as by your saying that you might not write at all if you did not have me for a reader. It is a fact that I read what you write most passionately— Oh what am I trying to say. As a child I had a tree. It was in the side yard.

An elm. And large even when adults looked at it, but very large in my eyes. I sat in the roots. A squirrel had a nest high in the branches. I didn't own it except in love. And how the woman next door knew this I have no idea but she always referred to it as "Billy's tree," and when my mother died and my father sold the place, she bought a certain number of feet of the yard, including the tree, which she would point out to me when I came to see her as a grown man. Tree, yard, house, and in a sense she herself are all lying under a brick apartment house and safe from it, while I draw breath. If you were to stop writing, to toy with ideas and not bother to put them down, I cannot tell you what a deprivation it would be to me. So that this will not happen, Valentine and I work together.

Because I wasn't allowed to write the thesis I wanted to, I didn't write any. I jumped the track, became a writer and editor. One small aspect of anything is never going to be right for me.

Warner to Maxwell, October 3, 1973:

Your letter about *The Nature of the Moment* came very kindly. And I did not answer it, could not answer it. When Valentine died, all the words fell off like leaves after a frost. I think of her constantly, I talk to her in my mind. I can scarcely talk about her—never as my heart would like to. And your letter came at a cruel season; when we knew our last summer was ending and grieved so desperately & behaved so decorously; and she with such determined courage tried this nostrum and that on the chance it might rescue where the second operation had only spread the infection. Sometimes it seems to me a lifetime ago, and sometimes it seems to be now.

One of the saddest things was the thought of her poetry, the death of a hope which had been so brilliant, which she had held for so many years and through so many disappointments. You know all about that from the letters.

It took me a long time before I could nerve myself to another disappointment, and write to Chatto & Windus about the selection. Publishers are prisoners of their metier. But C. & W. are better than most and I was given an allotted number of pages. It was the most taxing thing I have ever had to do. I went on doing it in my sleep, waking in a panic because in a dream there had been a poem I had lost. And by the light of day—so many I had to reject because there was no room for them. Who for the boat, who to let drown?

Warner to Maxwell, October 8, 1973:

Never mislay a pleasure. I might die in the night, so I will write to William now.

I bless the woman who saved your tree.

> *Casting the Bodies' Vest aside*
> *My soul into the boughs does glide:*
> *There like a bird it sits & sings*
> *Then whets, & combs its silver wings,*
> *And, full prepared for longer flight,*
> *Waves in its plumes the various Light.*

The last line is exactly what starlings do.

This evening at dusk Mr Cleall, spouse of my dear Mrs Cleall, came to saw off the dead boughs from Nestor. When we first came here Nestor was such an old apple-tree his lower boughs leant on crutches. He was—is—a pippin, variety unknown, and bore quantities and quantities of very small brown-skinned apples that lasted on into February and tasted rather like medlars. But last winter was too mild for him. The sap never properly ran down, it got clogged & when the spring came it couldn't properly run up either. A tree gangrene. But he has three full standing boughs, he will live I hope. All our cats in their kittenhood began climbing on him, he was their Nursery Slope.

Mr Cleall sawed him very well and respectfully, and then we spent some time at the gate, saying how much we liked Mrs Cleall. 'Not that we don't have a set-to from time to time,' said he; boast of a satisfied husband.

How very right of you to shake off Harvard. You got the essential, the lyric horse feeding on here & now. That was what you went there for.

Maxwell to Warner, October 16, 1973:

I am mailing you an old story of mine ["A Final Report"] about the woman who saved my tree. I did seven or eight variations of it, and when I did the last one I found, accidentally, an earlier one that was better, that was, in fact, the best I could do, but I was so tired when I finished it that I put it in a drawer and forgot about it and went on trying to write the story. I await "The Blameless Triangle." Turkey in Europe—Good God how marvelous.

Who wrote "Casting the bodies' vest aside / My soul into the boughs doth glide"? Is it you? Is it Valentine? Is it Herbert?

When I was a little boy I had a natural aptitude for metaphysics. That is, when I asked what happened when there was no chimney for Santa Claus to come down and was told that in that case he came down the radiator, I had no difficulty believing this. In the same way, I believe that Valentine is from time to time in my vicinity, while never leaving yours.

I had settled down to a cup of tea that was just right for drinking and was three-quarters of the way down the first page of "The Blameless Triangle" [the story of Wirre Gedanken] when there was a bomb scare. The article in question was believed (possibly) to be on the twenty-first floor, in the office of a sports publishing outfit—handball magazines, something—and the twentieth floor was evacuated. I stood in the corridor of the building, by the street doors, reading on, and finished it at my desk, only by that time the tea was lukewarm. I don't know what Mr. Shawn will say about the buggering but I expect to be amused for the next forty-eight hours by the recurring thought of it. I love the story and I trust to God he does also.

Warner to Maxwell, October 19, 1973:

Dear me about the buggery [in "The Blameless Triangle"]. Surely, whatever Mr Shawn has to say about it he must have said many times already? I can't believe (I'd like to) that I in my extreme respectable old age am the first person to pose the problem. If I am, may I have a commemorative plaque in your office, please?

The poet who cast the bodies' vest aside was Andrew Marvell ["The Garden"]. And on Monday I will mail you his poems: even if you have a copy already, it may not be a small one like this, a packable copy.

Do you remember how, long ago, I wrote to you in a rapture of expectation about how we were going to stay at Bozanko Cottage in Cornwall? We meant to stay for a couple of months, so we took the silver candlesticks & the wooden spoons and a great many books, and Valentine gave me this copy of A. M., and a lot of painters' materials because I wanted a change of mind from writing. And it was everything we hoped, with trees on hills behind us, and an estuary in front of us—only cold. But that was because it had not been lived in recently, & anyhow, the weather was colder than one expects in Cornwall. It stayed colder, we were feeding the birds; but we pulled firewood out of the woods, went for drives, were happy—it was like our first house, Miss Green's Cottage at Chaldon. And then on the fourth morning there was no water. Our landlords, the National Trust, sent a man to thaw the pipes. It was the main which was frozen. It ran through the hill under the trees, the ground was like iron, it was not possible to thaw it. And before the end of a week we raked out the sitting-room fire, & packed the candlesticks, and said goodbye to a fond illusion, and drove away to a hotel in Falmouth. Where Valentine put a much better face on it than I could. But perhaps it was worse for me. Yes, it was worse: Bozanko had been her idea, and her present to me. I raged to see her thwarted.

So the book (I have another Marvell) will come to you with love from us both. I think it very likely she is in your vicinity. She liked you very much, she esteemed you, she relied on you and relied on your affection for me. In fact, I suppose you were the only person she completely relied on: she was extremely sparing in her reliances.

When I had *The New Yorker* of March 1963 [with "A Final Report"] I was in no state to read it. She was in the Brompton Heart Hospital, being kept alive with ratsbane.

It is like the armature of *Ancestors*: the arrangements of wire and cotton-reels & selected solids that sculptors make before they begin to put on the flesh of a bust. I used to see them in Dobson's studio, & on one occasion contributed a hair-pin to Mr Asquith. I know her exactly. And with fellow-feeling. I could so easily be her. It must be exactly true, for when I finished the first reading of it I was left with the sense of But is that all? which one has after a truth. (The deficiency being, of course, in one's own truthfulness.)

It is also like a Picasso, the indubitable woman with her hat trimmed with a knife & fork, for instance. I don't wonder you wrote so many revisions, for it seems completely, flawlessly spontaneous.

Maxwell to Warner, October 25, 1973:

It is rather as I feared: Mr. Shawn loves the new story ["The Blameless Triangle"] up to the buggering and at that he sticks—not on grounds of impropriety but because of the joke, the play upon the double meaning of the word fairy, which may not even have been in your mind but which will, he says, inescapably be in the reader's, and which is, especially in the theater, shopworn. He doesn't at all want to let go of the story, and thinks it has some of your finest writing in it, especially the final paragraph, which he admired beyond words. I asked him if his objection extended to the Provincial Governor and the boy on his knee and the Armenian acrobats and he said Heavens no. Just that one joke. Are you willing or able to consider the possibility of a different turn of events in Turkey in Asia at this point? I love the story so much I don't know how I will stand the waiting for your answer.

I have started *Wilhelm Meister*.

Warner to Maxwell, October 27, 1973:

All can be well, provided Mr Shawn will let me keep the conversation on pp. 13, 14. (I cannot, cannot abandon Moor exemplifying the Law of Diminishing Returns, not Ludo on the language of love.)

But after the conveyance and foot warmers on p. 15, they will meet with a disappointment. The Provincial Governor wants a westernised audience for his poetical works. They are mystical (Sufi) and amatory, and he reads & re-reads, and if it weren't for the food & the comfort & the sables, they could hardly bear it. But they do.

Meanwhile there is constant shouting in the streets, & Mustaffah still will think of tearing out their wings. *But no joke.*

The joke never occurred to me. Fairies never had much vogue here & had faded into limbo on a bed of pansies. But I am sure Mr Shawn is right. No one hates jokes more than I do, I am most grateful to him for saving me from this one.

Maxwell to Warner, November 1973:

What I love about *Wilhelm Meister* is what I loved about *Werther* and *Elective Affinities*—that what seems like historical reconstruction is really just ordinary social detail to Goethe. Scenes, pictures, costumes, that remind me of paintings were to him simply the way things were. The beginning drags—perhaps because I am reading it in the evening before bedtime, and

I am not fond of Goethe's sermonizing, but I do like the people. I am at the place where he finds (Oh most unlikely device!) in the scarf that he tore from Marianne's neck the note from her elderly protector—in short not very far along. *Faust* and the novels are the only works I haven't read in German, way back in my youth. *Dichtung und Warheit* was what I loved, though I also liked the plays. The eighteenth century love of generalities I find rather tedious unless they are Gibbon's generalities, in which case I have to lie down on the floor so I can laugh more comfortably. But I wouldn't dream of not finding out what happens to Wilhelm. Also, the fact that I am reading a book you love makes me tend to love it also. At the moment, I should confess I am playing multiple chess: i.e. Horace Walpole's letters to William Cole, and a Simenon, and Nigel Nicolson's book about his father and mother, and a book on Samuel Butler.

I hope you liked the installment of "The Perils of Pauline" in which the tapes that were there two weeks before were suddenly non-existent. One hopes that he [President Nixon] is safely tied to the railroad tracks and that the engineer will fail to see him in time. Why is it that legislators behave so much like hens in a barnyard? What, at this point, have they got to lose? If it were a work of Literature I would be betting on Reynard the Fox, but Nixon is a split personality, one half of which is Queer, not so dear, Mrs. Goose. I will be glad when it is all over and we have not—but is it safe even to frame the sentence? Sometimes to imagine something is to bring it on. Oh yes, and the letters of Jane Austen, so different from the letters of HW. Would they have got on, do you think? Perhaps. The attraction of opposites.

Maxwell to Warner, November 7, 1973:

I forgot to say that your asking, about the story I sent you ("A Final Report"), that you had finished with it and then asked, "Isn't there something more?" was not because the story was the truth but one of your acts of—*prescience* isn't the right word. *Oversight* would be, if it didn't mean something else. *Extra sight.* Reading your letters, I asked myself, "If there were something more, what would it be?" and memory promptly produced the answer. I don't know whether I thought of it while I was writing the story, and rejected it for non-literary reasons, or perhaps had simply forgotten she was the subject of scandal. Her husband's business partner was burned to death in a fire, and they took him into their house on 9th Street, to live with them. In a short while the tongues were wagging. Her husband stayed in Chicago a great deal of the time, and I (by then, I guess, in my twenties) found it simply unimaginable that two people with *grey hair* could be in love with each other, or making love, or both, and so resolutely turned my mind away from it. Grey hair and a pince nez. Who knows, who knows. Things didn't have to be true to be said by the gossips of that small town. Would it have made the story better if I had put it in? I mean, would it have made it into a more solid whole? I don't know how many years Mr. Wilson lived there. A good long time. The scandal didn't deter anybody. But it may have been the real reason that she never went out of the house. Do you like Jung's idea of a Heaven where the angels are intensely curious about the arrivals from earth, and the more ordinary the life the more curious they are about it? I thought of this because it seemed to me that such facts as the one I have been speculating about must be written in the stars, that the Milky Way is a very long novel about small town people everywhere, not just those I remember from my childhood.

Warner to Maxwell, November 9, 1973:

I think Horace Walpole & Jane Austen would get on very well, provided she did not laugh at William Cole. *She* had no amour-propre whatever, he could have laughed at all she held dear without upsetting her. She was of all women, the most libertine.

Warner to Maxwell, November 12, 1973:

Yes, it was that [in "A Final Report"]. I don't think you could have put it in, unless you had completely altered the *intention* of your story; but, it certainly was that. And the neighbours didn't condemn, oh no! they mitigated, and referred to them as 'the poor old things'. Of all small-minded sins against the Holy Ghost, this debasing of pity is the vilest. And it is common as dirt—only dirt is too dear a comparison.

I have found the solution for President Pauline Nixon. Instead of a tape not existing, and so on, make one plain old statement. President Nixon did not exist. This would clear all scores.

Maxwell to Warner, December 1973:

I am looking forward to Kohoutek. It used to trouble me when I was a child that I had just missed Halley's Comet. Glenway Wescott remembers it as looking like a whiskbroom. He was wakened in the night and taken outdoors to see it, and remembered it, as I once woke Kate and Brookie and carried them outdoors onto the terrace at Martha's Vineyard to see a spectacular display of the Northern Lights. Only when morning came they didn't remember it.

Warner to Maxwell, December 10, 1973:

I don't think you need grieve over Halley's Comet. At least, I myself found it disappointing. It was too neat. I had formed my ideal comet on a pious mezzotint of the Last Judgement (in a Norfolk lodging house) where there were several, large and untamed. It hung (the mezzotint) above a black horsehair sofa and I can still remember how the horsehair rasped my knees & added to the ferocity of the Last Judgement.

Maxwell to Warner, December 13, 1973:

This letter is to be read with a skeptical mind. I don't at all know that what I am saying is right. But it is what I think, and the other editors are in agreement. The trouble with "Snipe" [a precursor to "The Climate of Exile"] is not in the story, which is powerful and compelling, but in the outer framework.

You and William Blake are the only two people who can make me believe, without reservation, and with my adult mind, in fairies. Forgive me if you know by heart this passage from Yeats' essay: " 'Did you ever see a fairy's funeral?' said Blake to a lady who sat next to him at some gathering at Hayley's or elsewhere. 'Never, sir,' was the answer. 'I have,' he replied; 'but not before last night. I was writing alone in my garden; there was great stillness among the branches and flowers, and more than common sweetness in the air; I heard a low and pleasant sound, and I knew not whence it came. At last I saw the broad leaf of a flower move, and underneath I saw a procession of creatures of the size and color of green and grey grasshoppers, bearing a body laid out on a roseleaf, which they buried with songs and disappeared.' " The fact that you and he do not entirely agree doesn't interfere with my believing either of you. The builders of Hadrian's Wall being exasperated by the continuous scornful tee-heeing of fairies is just as compelling as Blake's account of the funeral in his garden. It is compelling because it is stated with and on (your own) authority. But when you say, "It would be strange if William Shakespeare never encountered a fairy. He was born on the outskirts of the Kingdom of Arden and must often have played truant there when he was a child," my faith, which most of the time you have absolutely, whether you are writing about fairies or mortals or objects in an antique shop, falters. You are not telling a fact but offering a hypothetical fancy. The fancy is interesting, just as Virginia Woolf's fancy of Orlando living several hundred years and changing his sex while he was Ambassador to Constantinople is interesting. But I never have been able to believe that with my whole heart; I think she is making up a story about V. Sackville West; nor do I quite believe in Sir Sagamore and his revels. It isn't that he or they strain credulity, but that they seem literary in origin and not of a piece with other items of supernatural information that you from time to time pull out of your pocket. He is not real to me the way the astrologer is real, and Snipe doesn't have the depth of character that Aquilon and Beliard have. What happens to him is real, but his reactions are those of any well-intentioned mortal who becomes tangled in a situation he doesn't understand. I miss the mixture of the enchanted and the cruel or chillingly inhuman in all this part of the story. Oberon's reflections move me, but Oberon himself one has more or less to take on faith. Is he or isn't he Shakespeare's Oberon? He could be a character in an opera.

What's to be done? Is it that the revels are too generalized? Is it that you once more are writing about matters you know so well that you forget to impart elements of them? Is it possible with a piece of writing this finished to begin again and construct a different framework? I don't know. If you are satisfied with it, I wouldn't force myself to make changes that your heart is not in. Better to use it in the book as it stands and send us another story. If you see what you might have done, an alternative approach that will make this story more like the previous ones, then put it aside until you have finished the one you are now working on and then have a go at it. We are not at all happy at letting one of these stories escape publication in *The*

4

New Yorker, but neither do we want to bully you or tell you how to write them. You will know best what to do.

Maxwell to Warner, December 17, 1973:

Brookie and [her boyfriend] Larry went to a magic show where a magician carried in the upper half of a dummy and sat it down at a table, and then he carried in the lower half and attached it to the upper half, and then there was some hocus pocus and the dummy stood up and walked over to the magician and gently lifted his head off and the magician fell over dead and was carried off the stage. Well something like that is my present condition. I noticed that "Beliard" was scheduled for January, and I happened to be looking in your scrapbook about something I was writing you about, and realized that "The Mortal Milk," otherwise known as "The Ambassador from Brocéliande," hadn't run yet—the magazine is never as real to me as manuscripts and galleys—so I told the scheduling committee not to run "Beliard" until they had run "The Mortal Milk," and just now Mr. Henderson appeared in my door to tell me that the reason "The Mortal Milk" hadn't been run was that it was still in Working Proof. I *think* I must have sent it to you, for your approval of the preliminary editing, but then what happened? Did you never get it? Did I never send it to you? Did you send it back to me but I never got it? *Where* are those galleys of "The Mortal Milk"? The magician's dummy has them.

I woke up this morning worrying about you, as a result of several articles in the *Times* (NY) about the emergency in Britain. You must promise me that if things get too difficult in Maiden Newton you will rush back to Wales, where, I feel, nothing can penetrate the charmed circle of that house. John Updike, speaking of his own difficulties with stories, says "I guess I'll have to resign myself to reading (with boundless admiration) Sylvia Townsend Warner, who gets better and better as she approaches one hundred years of age."

There was a horsehair sofa in my childhood, too. It was at the head of the stairs, where I often sat it my nightgown when I wanted the comfort of the sound of voices from down below. I believe the prickles would have penetrated any garment known to man. Where is it now? Does the magician's dummy have it too?

Warner to Maxwell, December 28, 1973:

The New Yorker has penetrated our penal system. Robin Wordsworth, who is a J.P. and an ex officio prison visitor, conveys my copies into Dorchester Jail, discreetly and implacably. You have many readers there, one a fanatic admirer. You have given him a purpose in life—to get the next number, and another breath of air. I don't know what he's in for.

'Snipe'. I don't see, so far, how I can fix it. I wanted to make Arden an English court, as Elfhame is a Scots one, & Brocéliande French. The ancient British revels, the casual social structure between Elfins & mortals, Oberon's private life as a hermetic, were to enforce this. I seem to have been too successful. But with six bullseyes in a row I have nothing to complain of. 1973 remains an annus mirabilis.

All this trouble would be saved if we lived near enough to hand things over the fence. I often wish we did. I chose to live on alone (I did not think it would be for so long) and I don't unchoose it; but it starves out a great deal of spontaneity...as I wrote these words there was a knock on the door & I rose with a curse on my lips. However, it was here to return a book & went away. Dreams are as dated as mushrooms, & I have no one to whom I can tell my dreams.

Maxwell to Warner, December 1973:

The *two* sets of galleys, in their envelope, were on my table under a pile of I'd rather not say what. Imagine a pile of feathers, a few pots and pans, some old clothes, a diary, a broken viola d'amore.

Warner to Maxwell, January 10, 1974:

My current story is called 'Winged Creatures' and begins—'When after many years of blameless widowhood devoted to ornithology Lady Fidès gave birth to a son no one held it against her.' It was a changeling and a new Kingdom: Bourrasque in the Massif Central. I know how it will end, but not how or when I shall end it. Then I shall break off, and attend to the garden which has been laid flat by the gales, and the house which is uncontrollably in need of spring-cleaning. I can't ignore its yells & tatters any longer.

How are you getting on with *Wilhelm Meister?* I am too polite to ask, Where did you stick?

The final proof of 'The Mortal Milk' was posted yesterday—soi-disant final; but we are the pawns of fate. And heaven knows when you will get it, for H. M.'s post-office only works half a day now. Her M. is now throwing another child out of the royal sledge to placate the populace. I think she is being rather precipitate. She hasn't an indefinite supply.

Now do not be uneasy about me any longer—though it pleases me that you should be.

Maxwell to Warner, January 22, 1974:

I hope all is well with "Winged Creatures," for if it is, then I shall soon be putting my feet in a drawer and leaning back in my chair and beginning to read. When I start to read one of your stories for the first time, I go deaf, dumb and blind (to everything not on the page) at the thought of pleasure in store for me.

I am not getting on with *Wilhelm Meister.* I stopped it to read three other books, two of which I didn't finish. Tonight I will look to see what I stuck at. My problem is that if I skipread or even hurry rapidly through pages that do not much interest me, I have insomnia. Isn't that odd? It must waken the dormant editorial mind, which I do my best to leave at the office.

Oh how I detest Inland Revenue! Without it, I should have made you quite comfortable financially by this time. I mean to the point where Valentine wouldn't worry. I know you don't. My love,

Warner to Maxwell, January 25, 1974:

How lovely for you to have an intellectual for a daughter. My father enjoyed his, once he'd brought himself to believe in it.

'Winged Creatures' is finished, & Soo will type the rest of it tomorrow, and you won't have to wait long to put your feet in a drawer. This is an unknown pursuit to me. Is it an ancient Harvard custom?—training poor scholars for draughty attics. How far up the bureau is the drawer? Do you keep anything in it? You always know the secrets of my heart, so I need not tell you anything about 'Winged Creatures', except that it is long, though I tried my best to shorten it; and that remembering your stricture that Aquilon was too human, I have made the fairy character in this a figure kept at a distance by being observed by a changeling of mortal dullness.

It would be fun to write one's biography from the view point of some devoted flat-footed friend. Robinson Crusoe by Man Friday.

She [Valentine] would have been very pleased about my riches. Indeed, she unconditionally was, and if she could have left me in her will she would certainly have left me to you.

Maxwell to Warner, February 1974:

If you have ever written anything more beautiful I can't think what it is.

Maxwell to Warner, February 6, 1974:

I guess I should begin with the drawer. It is on the left hand side of my desk, the bottom drawer of three, and when it is pulled out about a foot it is a very good height for a footstool, since the chair tips back. In it, covered with footprints, is a copy of "The Writer as Illusionist, A Speech Delivered at Smith College, March 4, 1955, by William Maxwell Price Fifty Cents." I only pull that drawer out when I am reading a story by you. The others I read with my feet on the carpet or my legs wrapped around each other. When I was eight, nine, and ten, I read lying on my back in dark corners, holding the book in the air, while people went through the room saying "You'll ruin your eyes." The Oz books, and the Hollow Tree books. The warning was part of the pleasure.

This story ["Winged Creatures"]: It isn't a matter of which is the greater triumph, Grive or Gobelet, they are both triumphs and all one triumph. And if my complaining that Aquilon was too human had anything to do with the two halves that Grive and Gobelet present, I am very happy. Halfway through, half out of my mind with pleasure, I suddenly grew anxious about how it would end and then realized that if ever a writer knew how to end a story it was you. But of course I didn't foresee the marvel that was coming. I really do think maybe it is the best thing you have ever written.

All this is my opinion, you understand; nobody else has seen it, and if they disagree with me I shall remove the drawer I put my feet in and throw it at them, pamphlet and all.

I have been to see Mr. [Milton] Greenstein about your tax problem. It is solvable, I am happy to say. It doesn't matter to us in the least if you don't cash the check until after the British financial year has closed. It is true however, that *The New Yorker* is obliged to list the earnings of all foreign writers with the Internal Revenue Service, which theoretically informs for eign governments of the amount earned by their citizens. So it is possible that Inland Revenue might write you about this uncashed check. I strongly recommend, even so, that you do not cash the check if it lifts you into a larger bracket but instead write me the date of the end of the British tax year and I will then write you a most apologetic letter, dated a few days after that, explaining how the check got attached to some material in a folder that by accident I just pulled from my file, my head is covered with ashes etc. and in short you didn't *receive* the check when you should have. Meanwhile the bookkeeping department has been informed not to make out any more checks to you until I tell them it is all right.

P.S. It is not only that, like your father, I have an intellectual daughter, but that she is psychic as well. A week ago today, Wednesday, she dreamt that a child was killed and there were people standing round grieving over it. Friday night when we got to the country we learned that, on Thursday, Linda Sternau's child fell off a slide and landed on her head, and died. The repairman came to fix the ailing refrigerator as Emmy and I were walking out of the house to go to the funeral. He was the tenth repair man and the head of a whole division of them, but we went on. The funeral was in the Baptist Church, which is circa 1840 and plain and small, with a small country graveyard outside dating back to before the Revolution. The minister was not as offensive as some, but I could hardly contain my impatience with him or keep from shedding tears. But when he finished saying that you know who was the resurrection and the life, he announced that the mother was going to say something. There at the foot of the pulpit the small coffin covered with a patchwork quilt of about the same age as the church. The child's mother is perhaps twenty-two, blonde. Both grandparents are handsome and so is she: German refugees from the thirties. She had hardly opened her mouth when I forgot how to breathe, and raised the commotion people do who are trying not to choke to death while simultaneously not raise a commotion. All my handkerchieves were in town, but knowing myself I had taken a square of white percale from the rag bag, and some kleenex. I gave the percale to Emmy and did with the kleenex, which might as well have been dipped in water. She—the girl stood there, talking quietly about the baby, with her mother and father and brother standing beside her, and having so little courage myself I find it impossible not to weep over it when I see it in other people. It was not a day for being spared. The snow was coming down exactly the way it did the day of my mother's funeral, and as we stood uphill from the open grave, I hid behind the backs of taller people, so the family wouldn't see me shedding those tears. The child's father had gone off somewhere about a year after it was born and never come back, and the grandfather, an extremely handsome man of about forty-five had moved in and taken his place. All last summer we saw them together in the swimming pool: the passion of a man of forty-five for a child of three. And there he was, standing by the grave while the child's mother and grandmother stepped forward and dropped a rose into the hole and the snow turned his hair grey in front of my eyes. A year from now, six months from now we will go swimming in their pool, and he will smile and be polite as only a German refugee from the thirties can be, and it will be as if the child had never existed. But he will never be a young man again. I saw it happen, in the falling snow.

Warner to Maxwell, February 9, 1974:

Your fourteen word letter came yesterday. I have never known a little candle shed its beams more restoratively. I was in a state of not knowing which way up I was, or what I thought about 'Winged Creatures', because as I suspected it was above my usual I suspected I was quite mistaken. You returned me to my right mind. Yes, I agree with you. I crossed Niagara on that slack rope without losing my balance, crossing my feet, waving my arms, sneezing or falling headlong. And it was an uncommonly slack rope; card-castles were nothing in comparison. Thank you, very dear William, you were a swift angel to write so immediately.

And this morning came your letter; and you could not have wept more at that funeral than I did reading your account of it. One of the things many German refugees feel deeply about is that they can't lie in their native soil.

I know of several instances when they have taken a handful of it, or had it sent after them. Not only Germans; but perhaps particularly them. And now, when he comes to be buried in that country graveyard the soil will have been natived for him by the child who lies there. Oh, poor people! And the girl's only child. A first child is always to some extent an only child, but this child irreparably so. They must be very good people, very upright and truthful to themselves. I am glad you & they have each other as neighbours.

Maxwell to Warner, February 11, 1974:

I didn't have to throw that drawer at anybody. What Mr. Shawn said, not for the first time, was "Where all this ["Winged Creatures"] is coming from is inexplicable." And "That ending will be remembered." John Updike dreamed some paragraphs that you had written, and woke, and saw that he could use them, and fell asleep, and woke and they were gone.

Warner to Maxwell, February 21, 1974:

Between ourselves, I don't find it inexplicable where all this is coming from. I fell back on Peter Pears's recent letter to *The Times*. They have a braggart Know-all called Bernard Levin and he wrote an ineffable muddle about the glories of past singers, especially a tenor called Julius Patzak, now dead. And said that never again would he hear such a performance of Mahler's *Das Lied von der Erde* as he heard far ago in Edinburgh, with Walter conducting, with Ferrier the mezzo-contralto, with the incomparable lamented Palzac the tenor. And Peter had a modest inch at the bottom of a column, saying that he too remembered that performance, but the tenor was not the incomparable Palzac, whom he lamented quite as much as Bernard Levin could. 'It was me.'

(Incidentally, idiom above grammar, what would this have been if it had read 'It was I'?)

Please give my sympathy to John Updike. I know those paragraphs. They happen to me. The best always get away.

Another cockney glory from my dear Mrs Cleall. Apropos of hungry children—go & lick the steam off the cook-shop window. It is like having elevenses with Shakespeare.

Maxwell to Warner, March 25, 1974:

I read it ["The Climate of Exile"] once last week, with my feet in the drawer, and again today, with them firmly on the carpet. And was nevertheless moved, as before. And thought, as before, of you and Valentine, which was perhaps the furthest thing in the world from your mind when you wrote it. As you said, how could *The New Yorker* run a sequel to a story it had not run? But that matter disposed of, my private pleasure was very deep, even deeper on the second reading. The first time I was struck by Sir Bodach's apotheosis, the second time it only seemed perfectly natural and what I dwelled over was the countryside, the climate of the North, that you always manage to write about so feelingly. And the climate of exile. It is a very beautiful story. I once knew a man who, when he was a little boy, went to the public library and asked for a sad story. This one would have done nicely, except that you have to be somewhat along in years to appreciate it. As with Snipe I, I have kept a xerox copy for myself, so that I can reread it whenever the desire comes over me. And I think you are right not to tamper with Snipe I in order to make this one possible because in the book they will both fall into what can only be seen as their proper order. Thank you for letting me have it.

Warner to Maxwell, April 9, 1974:

While I was having influenza one of my dying thoughts was that I must remember to write to you about that cheque when I was feeling stronger. You remember? That cheque for $3500 or so which you were going to overlook till after April 5th. That day is safely past, & if you please, will you send me that letter saying how sorry you are that it got mislaid on your desk.

Maxwell to Warner, April 21, 1974:

I cannot believe that I could be as disorderly as it turns out I have been: The check for "The Blameless Triangle," by some mischance, got put in the folder where I keep your galleys until they are ready to run in the magazine, instead of being mailed to you. And the date is *January* 21! Dear God, how awful. What will you think of me? Would you like a different editor? I am deeply ashamed.

In a house across the road lives my piano teacher, who is 84, and his wife, who was an opera singer, and who is 81, and her sister, who is 87, and was William Gillette's leading lady in a great many totally forgotten plays. Easter reminded me that when she was a very small child she took the flowers off her Easter hat and put them in water, and announced to her mother "If you don't they will wivver." Her mind is awash with old music hall jokes, such as "Take off your pants, you must be tired." She also threatens to take the carving knife to her brother-in-law. That's what life does to little girls who don't want the flowers on their Easter hat to wither.

Maxwell to Warner, June 18, 1974:

All is well with "The Power of Cookery." It was the flight that did it, much though I admired the cooking and the cook: that remarkable description of Queen Aigle unfolding her wings and the flight and her touching behavior afterward. This far along in the series—it is true of any *New Yorker* series—it more and more becomes a matter of walking over Niagara Falls blindfolded on a tightrope pushing a wheelbarrow, because you cannot help writing in the confident knowledge of the chilling quality and the utterly strange and the supernatural that you have established in the earlier stories and counting on this to maintain you in what you write now, and the stories have to be judged as if there were no previous ones, since there is never any certainty that any given reader has read them. So once more you have to establish your profound right to the material. But what a book it will make!

Warner to Maxwell, July 3, 1974:

I don't know whether 'Elphenor & Weasel' (as the present story is called) will be finished in time to catch you before you go to Wellfleet; so I won't risk not telling you before then that your story in *The New Yorker* ["Over by the River"] is like a Bonnard. And that I love it, just as I love Bonnard. You have the same elastic way of treating perspective; and placing colour; and portraying children in their exact height.

Warner to Maxwell, August 13, 1974:

I wait to learn what you think of Byron. When I was asked what I thought, etc. I replied I liked him because there was no nonsense about him. I surmise that Lady Melbourne felt the same. Happy woman—to crown a long career of contented vice with a chaste rapscallionity with Byron. Long, long ago, in my London days, I thought, sitting alone one evening, If Byron came in, there would be nothing here to keep him. And then my eye fell on 'tother William, dog William. And I knew a black chow with a blue lining to its mouth would rivet him.

Maxwell to Warner, August 30, 1974:

Valentine's work again: I did not intend to return to the office after I left Wednesday afternoon, and some trivial errand took me there after I had been to the bank on Thursday morning, and there was your envelope ["Castor and Pollux"] lying on my desk. No matter what my colleagues say, and I assume they will say yes, *I* know what you have done.

Maxwell to Warner, September 3, 1974:

If I have seemed absentminded in the last six or eight weeks it is because I have been absent. I have been with Lord Byron. His letters, Shelley's letters, Peacock's *Memoirs of Shelley*, Lady Blessington's unreliable *Conversations*, [Iris Origo's] *The Last Attachment*, and so on. All this in order to write a mere book review. But the pleasure of his company has been so great. (It is not true that the dog would have kept him; you would have, unassisted by any canine charms.) And the pleasure of reading about the people he associated with—for example Dr. Aglietti, his doctor in Venice. You know about him? If you don't, it will give me exquisite pleasure to send you a paragraph by Iris Origo, who, in general, strikes me as a rather cold fish. I mean I don't enjoy reading books about Byron by people who aren't in love with him, and so far she seems not to be. The book I am reviewing— *Accounts Rendered*—is by such a person, and I think you must know her since she is the curator of the Museum of Costume in Bath: Doris Langley Moore. In any case it is an absorbing book. I look around, in the twentieth century, and think what am I doing here, and how will I get back *there*.

Warner to Maxwell, September 6, 1974:

I am often absent there myself.

'The body is embarked' ... do you remember my poem about Allegra in *Time Importuned?** When I first knew the tomb under the tree with the spiked iron railing round it I supposed that the poet had climbed the railing in order to lie on the stone slab of that altar tomb. So I must have been a small child when I first knew Byron. For a long time he was the only poet I knew as a poet *outside a book*. On the way up to the churchyard one passed the wall-tablet saying 'Near this spot Anthony Ashley Cooper witnessed with shame & indignation the pauper's funeral.' (The pauper's body was in an occasional coffin used for conveying bodies from the workhouse. The coffin was on a litter carried by two men who were drunk. They dropped the litter, the coffin fell off, the pauper's body fell out, & the schoolboy Anthony Ashley went on and become Lord Shaftesbury.) You can't be *so* isolated from the early 19th cent. when you know me. And the view Byron looked on was the view, not much changed, from my nursery window.

He must have been irresistible; even the people who disliked him could not tear their attention from him. Above all women I envy Lady Melbourne. Think of having that young leopard rolling in one's boudoir, extending & retracting its shining young claws, offering its white stomach to be tickled, trusting one with its wildness. Have you noticed how everyone who comes into contact with Byron is made real by it? Caroline Lamb's idiot son, Mrs Mule [his fire-lighter], his menagerie, those Gambas. And the real hatefulness he bestows on those he hated.

I suppose it was because he was so completely truthful.

A. L. Rowse had an article the other day, saying we have not paid enough attention to his Cornish ancestry. Even allowing for Rowse's own Cornish ancestry, there may be something in it: a less trammelled, self-conscious variety of Celt than those island Gordons.

I can't go on wearing out your eyes, talking about Byron. If you were here, I would talk about him all night and about the century which

contained us both; and about his astonishing memory and wealth of information and wide reading; and about; and about . . .

* Byron's six-year-old daughter died of a fever while attending a convent school in Italy.
Warner's poem about her, "Allegra," carries the following epigraph, drawn from a Byron let-
ter of May 26, 1822: "'The body is embarked . . . I wish it to be buried in Harrow Church.
There is a spot in the churchyard, near the footpath, on the brow of the hill looking towards
Windsor, and a tomb under a large tree . . . where I used to sit for hours when I was a boy."

Maxwell to Warner, October 1, 1974:

The invading mortals took possession of the story ["Narrative of Events
Preceding the Death of Queen Ermine"] as well as of the Kingdom of
Deuce, with the result that the necessary miracle doesn't take place, the
fairies are not fairies, and the reader is never quite driven back upon Astonishment. As I write the words I think how ungrateful of me. There is the
further consideration that, at this stage of any series, each story must
somehow outdo all the others. And the consideration beyond that is that
you have nearly finished a book, in which those stories that are not right for
The New Yorker will nevertheless have their rightful place. It is a book that I
long to hold in my hands. Also those other two that you have up your
sleeve. Is there any reason for holding back on them?

It is my secret theory that writers are modest creatures who are waiting to
be asked. And in the right circumstances, that is to say, properly appreciated, could tell more stories than Sheherezade, without half trying. As I
was reading about the young man who hanged himself from a young
aspen and was cut down by Jessamy, I felt a stir of recognition. And then, to
my disappointment, he died. And without my recognizing who it was.
How stupid of me. In a curious way, this story is related to *The Flint Anchor.*
Both fill the heart with dread.

Warner to Maxwell, October 4, 1974:

I don't see how it [Maxwell's review of *Accounts Rendered*] could be bettered,
and I shall be everlastingly grateful to you for establishing Catherine Byron
in her own right. Byron would share my gratitude: she held up the witches'

mirror to him of what he might be when he was old: fat—so in fury & horror he lived on soda-water & biscuits; the prey of insolvency & magnanimity; burdened with Black Dogs and a bludgeoning tongue; and her solitary defeated death a product of his. And neither of them with a vulgar ha'penny's worth of dissimulation. How could they not be at loggerheads?

How I dislike writing on these penurious Blues; but they are said to be quicker, and I don't want to waste a moment, possible because when I write to you I always want to write at once...

Warner to Maxwell, October 12, 1974:

I am sorry you thought the Deuce story too mortalised. It seemed to me that Sir Haggard's mental processes could only be those of an Elfin, especially when he said that poisoning the child trespasser would inevitably encourage their over-populated parents to send more of them.

But as you say, it will go into the book—though you must not look to get it just yet. When *The Innocent & the Guilty* came out after Valentine's death I felt so bleakly desolate that I resolved not to undertake that agony again. Your theory about writers is correct; that they are modest creatures waiting to be liked. I would do a great deal to please you, dear William. But I don't think I can face another book. Anyhow, as I say to my profane admirers, I want to go on writing instead.

Warner to Maxwell, November 22, 1974:

I remind myself of my grandfather, who used to say: I shall write to the man & say: Dear Sir. And after he died they found his desk full of stacks of writing-paper, dated, and beginning in his flowing hand—Dear Sir— and nothing more.

Maxwell to Warner, January 10, 1975:

As I read about the C.I.A.'s opening 10,000 people's mail (steam? a teakettle in the Department of Justice?) I thought with complacency of how all those years I was expressing my opinion about Mr. Nixon et al, sometimes in letters to *Russia*. As I write that sentence I was reminded of a collateral relative of Emmy's, who lived in Old Lyme, Conn., in the late 19th century, and was heard to say, "Why I am talking out loud in church... Why I am *still* talking out loud in church..." And went on in this vein as they led her up the aisle.

Warner to Maxwell, January 14, 1975:

Ever since the Dept. of Fidgets renamed the English Counties we have been so rearranged, divided up, added bits to, codified, that our Maker wouldn't know us. Churches are shot into new dioceses and given whole new Bishops to fall out with; men in Yorkshire grind their sturdy teeth because they are now in Humberside—Humber being mud to the Ridings; total abstainers in Dorchester dislike being classified as D.T. 1. (I am a second-class drinker); Frome Vauchurch has been lowered, etc.

And I am in the last lap of another story ["The Occupation"]. Elfhame, this time. A party of high-minded Elfins secede from it in order to do a Walden; and devastate a manse without lifting a finger to accomplish it. It reminds me of Swift, she said modestly.

If the C.I.A. is opening our letters, I will remark helpfully that steaming is now thought tedious and old-fashioned. The doggy way to do it is to use a dissolvent. Pass the brush over the top of the envelope, take out the letter, photograph it, replace it, pass a brush of solvent over the top of the envelope and leave to cool. DO NOT CONFUSE THE BRUSHES.

You see how gay you have made me?

Maxwell to Warner, January 20, 1975:

And speaking of which, does the phrase "In youth is pleasure" identify itself to you? Mavis Gallant wants to use it for an epigraph, and thinks it might be Yeats but can't find it. It has perhaps suffered a sea-change the way "God marks the sparrow in his flight" became, when I was in college, "God is as the sparrow falls" and my English teacher tried in vain to get it straight in my head. God *is* as the sparrow falls, is my final word on the subject.

Warner to Maxwell, January 24, 1975:

Mavis Gallant was some centuries out. 'In youth is pleasure' is from a small lyric by Robert Wever c. 1550. It is in the Original [Oxford] Book, either the old or the new one, between Wyatt & Sackville. The first line, if she uses the index, is 'In a harbour green, asleep where I lay'.

Warner to Maxwell, March 6, 1975:

Your spring-cleaning must be rather impeded by the young man you have let into your office; unless you use him as a dumb-waiter and load him with papers you can't bring yourself to decide about. Even that would only be a pro tem stance, for you would have to unload him sooner or later; he isn't a nice quiet boy called Pending.

All this is made easier for me by living in a house too large for me. Things I can't decide about I carry into another room. So I can then give my whole mind to virtuous acts I have never committed before. This year my virtuous act was to collect those little heeltaps of soap and simmer them into a chromatic wash-ball. I doubt if I shall find a use for it, but it is nice to have done it once in my lifetime.

Does the appearance of 'one of those two young men' you mentioned —but they are new to me—'being groomed to fill the shoes of departing editors' portend that you are departing?* I wish you a happy departure, a blissful retirement—another book? But woe to Sylvia!

Meanwhile I remember to tell you that from April 1st to April 10th I shall be away, and there will be no one here to forward letters, so if there is any proof or problems they should come before or after these dates.

---

* One young man, the writer Daniel Menaker, became Warner's editor after Maxwell retired; the other, Charles McGrath, became editor of *The New York Times Book Review*.

Maxwell to Warner, March 12, 1975:

I thought I had told you. About two years back, *The New Yorker* decided on a policy of compulsory retirement at the age of 65 (though not, thank God, for writers) and, so that it wouldn't come as a shock, set January 1,

1976, as the beginning date. Actually, I shall be 67. It took some getting used to. For nearly forty years I have shaved with pleasure in the thought that I was about to come to this job. I was twenty-eight when I first came to work here, and about thirty when interesting work came my way in abundance, and if I had had to wait for Wolcott Gibbs or Katharine White to leave the magazine of their own accord, in their late seventies, I would not have had anything like so pleasant a life, and now, surely, after forty years, it is time some other young man had a go at it. The one I am training this minute [Daniel Menaker] has a particular susceptibility to your stories (otherwise I am afraid I would have found some reason not to be training him) and I do not think it will really be woe to Sylvia, and I am certainly not departing from you, only from 25 W. 43rd Street. I will try to write more, and have fewer reasons to say that I have left undone things I should have done. I shall write *long* letters to you. But I see that I have, unwittingly, hurt your feelings. If I hadn't, you would have told me where you are going to be from the first to the 10th of April. The journeys I have taken with you, the houses we have shared, over the years have immensely enriched my stay-at-home life.

Warner to Maxwell, March 17, 1975:

You sent a shot through my heart, but you did not wound my feelings so that I refrained from telling you where I shall be from the 1st to 10th April. I shall be in Sussex, in the house where I watched foxes on the lawn (I surely told you about the foxes by moonlight—and how the vixen sat on the table tossing down chicken-bones to her dog-fox?)

And after that I spend a night with Peggy Ashcroft to see her in *Happy Days*, up to her neck in the ground.

'Now there is nothing left but Volumnia,' she said to me. But Winnie has intervened since.

Katharine White wrote the letter of acceptance which began my career with *The New Yorker*. Very soon after that I was writing to Dear Mr Maxwell. When did we first agree on being on Christian terms? We were very formal & well-bred for a long while.

You are very artful in reconciling me to the young man in your office. I hope he will live to be as dear to some future story-teller as you have

been to me. In the meantime, I hope you will school him in reading my
handwriting.

Maxwell to Warner, March 19, 1975:

If, as I think, the time difference between New York and Dorset is five
hours, will you say to yourself between 9 and 10 in the morning, William is
lying awake now, waiting for it to be morning, I will think that you are
thinking this and perhaps break this boring habit. Or perhaps I may merely
think, at about four-twenty-two A.M., Sylvia is having a cup of coffee, that
will be enough. It is the solitude that is so objectionable.

Maxwell to Warner, April 8, 1975:

I went confidently to the desk drawer in my study where I keep your letters, expecting to quote to you from a letter that turned out not to be there.
For twelve or thirteen years, from 1940 until March 12, 1953 (it seems impossible, but it is so), we wrote to Miss Warner and Mr. Maxwell, and then in a
moment of absentmindedness you signed your letter of March 12, 1953,
"Sylvia," putting me in a quandary. Was it an accident or a Move? I felt that
(loving you as I did) I could not not respond. So I addressed you as "Dear
Sylvia" and threw you into confusion, loving (as you did) Mr. Maxwell, and
not wanting to part company with him. All of which you wrote me, in the
letter I can't find. And I offered to give Mr. Maxwell back to you and let
William retire from the field. But you are too—were too sensible to agree
to that, and in no time at all the embarrassment, never very great, had
passed. But what happened to the letter? It is in the house, perhaps, somewhere.* Or it may by accident have got into the general file, and been
carted off to the basement of this building, where the heat of the furnace
tends to make stored paper disintegrate. But I do like, looking back over
my shoulder, our prolonged familiarity with one another. Another Age.
  I have been reading the letters of J. R. Ackerley, whom I met once and
liked. They are more readable than most people's collected letters and now
and then rise to something remarkable, such as a description of Mr. Forster
in his extreme age, walking along the street in Cambridge, and making
way, out of his extreme habitual consideration for others, for pedestrians
who were, in fact, not there. It is as beautifully recorded as some of the

anbody I love being cold must stem from my childhood, from the big old

scenes in Cowper's letters, such as, for example, the time his dog brought him a water lily.

It should be full spring in Oregon, and is, instead, late winter. I made Emmy take her fur coat but alas was not there to see that she wore it, and she has been half frozen, with the dampness. I think my feeling about anybody I love being cold must stem from my childhood, from the big old house we lived in that was subject to drafts and required not only that the furnace be kept going but also wood fires burning, and it has all somehow got mixed up in my mind with love.

* In the letters that we possess, Maxwell first addressed Warner as "Sylvia" on December 7, 1951, telling her of Harold Ross's death, and her January 18, 1952, response survives. But the participant's truth trumps the archivist's.

Warner to Maxwell, April 14, 1975:

The day your letter arrived, I had just written, 'The Master of Ceremonies had been Lady Moorit's lover for many years. She trusted him as one trusts one's own pillow' ["The Late Sir Glamie"]. This is not a full statement of our long relationship, but true as far as it goes. We laid a good foundation with our prolonged formality.

Warner to Maxwell, April 22, 1975:

How are you feeling at 4 A.M.? At 9 A.M. I feel very affectionate, yet slightly abashed, for affection and compassion may not warrant, may not justify, my stealing up on you at so private an hour. If I could really steal up on you, I should be almost entirely practical, and offer you something to eat. A bit of plain bitter chocolate can be extremely sleep-making. The Tisanes, lime-blossom, camomile, peppermint, drunk when one gets in to bed sometimes do the trick. The only cleric I really respected—and he was a saddened agnostic with an odiously cheerful christian family—once pointed out to me that when Elijah sat despairing in the desert and told God he was no man, God immediately sent ravens with bread and meat. Will you think of me as a raven? Another useful proceeding—it almost always works with me—is the equivalent of a little plain sewing: some boring sort of memory with conscientious small stitches. To remember every detail of a street, a house, a garden; *once well known*: What tree it was that rustled over what wall; where the breaks in the sidewalk came, where the post-office was—or the garden shed with the bunch of bags hanging on what accustomed nail. If one can remember things, without emotion, conscientiously & in their order, one can *bore oneself to sleep*.

Maxwell to Warner, April 23, 1975:

I have read "The Late Sir Glamie" twice, when it came and when it returned from Mr. Shawn, and I have to report that, alas, it isn't right for *The New Yorker*, and that it is full of things that gave me acute pleasure. It is the problem with series—but the farther along in the series a story is, the stronger it must be, to overcome the reader's sense—the magazine reader's, so different from the book reader's—that there has already been enough of that particular thing, whatever it is. The same stories read continuously in a book produce an entirely different effect. In any case, the story is not a failure, it is just—compared with the longer and more substantial ones, on the light side, thistledown. But only as a story. There is nothing insubstantial about the writing. The set piece on spring housecleaning is of the utmost bravura, and I shall never look at a violet leaf without thinking of the Master of Ceremonies' ability, which unfortunately I lack—he must have been a distant kin to Colette—to smell things in the dark. Not to speak of the red geranium smell of the red fox, which left me stunned with pleasure. Also, there are times, and this is one of them, when my sense of the infallibility of our decisions deserts me.

I agree with you that the Vietnam Comment piece in the April 14 issue was remarkable; as a footnote to it, Anna Hamburger [wife of the writer Philip Hamburger] told me that 30 Vietnamese orphans arrived without the social workers who had been assigned to them (whose places had been taken by more important people) and had eaten their paper wrist bands, so that there was no way on earth of ever knowing who they were or what their destination was.

Warner to Maxwell, April 30, 1975:

O William, you (*vous*, not *tu*) have knocked me flat. I sent off Sir Glamie with gay confidence that he was what would do nicely: no mortals, no psychology, decently short, for a change; and an entirely new problem. Well—more was lost at Mohacz. And the garden has benefitted, for I had to spend two days weeding, weeding, weeding, to calm my mind.

I rose from my knees with the Christian conviction that you (*vous*) were wrong but that I would overlook it.

Did I tell you of the American admirer who fought his way to Peggy Ashcroft's dressing-room after *Happy Days*, and stripped off his cravat and begged her to accept it as a token of his admiration? as a votive offering, in fact, like the cravats gipsies join at Ste Sara at Les Saintes Maries.

Warner to Maxwell, May 16, 1975:

Oatmeal coloured envelopes: What do you think? Some library? George Plank left my letters to him at Yale, along with a great many letters from other people. But there ought to be some kind of muzzle put on them until Elizabeth Wade White dies, I suppose. And she will live forever, as Janet my cousin reports. Is there some woman's college where they could fit in? Anyway, not Texas, bloated with Bloomsbury. But for the moment, I would prefer to think of them under your wing. You could read them when you are retired.

I have seen the establishment of a ghost. She haunts a strip of the river bank, which is called Polly's Walk. Polly in fact was called Edith. She was an unobtrusive English eccentric, short, tidy, with a silver-headed cane, smoked, kept hens, kept herself to herself. She gardened for flowers & shrubs, and lived on cigarettes and eggs; and lived in a couple of wooden huts on the river bank. At intervals when the river flooded we used to wade through the floods with cordial gin and offers to get her away: which she always refused. She died in the winter of 1951: during a flood, but of heart failure because we were in Norfolk and could not visit her with gin. Now her garden is a narrow strip of wilderness, and she walks there and is Polly.

I have considerable hopes of being a ghost here myself, with troops of cats attending me. Ghosts, have you noticed, spring up like mushrooms in damp riverine surroundings.

I am reading Claire Tomalin's life of Mary Wollstonecraft. She is an alley-cat, with bites in her ears and an indomitable determination to make her mark on other cats. And then married Godwin and left never a mark on him. How could any woman marry Godwin? Do you know his letter to Mary (2), on the heels of Shelley dead? It is a conclusive proof that when Dickens invented Chadband he was not exaggerating, he was drawing it mild.

Warner to Maxwell, May 28, 1975:

Nothing could please me better than the New York Public Library. For one thing, Marchette [Chute] is a resident; for another, I love New York, have loved it from my first arrival; for yet another I believe that I already have a small footing there, for was it not they—it? ('The Oxford University Press in its wisdom has decided')—who bought the holograph of *Lolly Willowes*, and you saw it and my calligraphy of then delighted your eyes, wearied by deciphering my remarks in margins?

Please go ahead. Please be triumphant.

Restrictions: a five years *stop* from the date of reception by the Berg Collection; and meanwhile access by anyone wanting to write about, quote from, the letter-writers.

I remember posting the last oatmeal coloured envelope and walking home from the post-office feeling that I had posted my guts and that you would look after them; but I do not remember if I also sent you Valentine's autobiography about her years of being an obsessive drinker, and suddenly and inexplicably being set free in a total leap of desperation. It should be with the letters. She inclined to thinking it was an act of God. I myself attribute it to man's unconquerable mind.

Maxwell to Warner, June 18, 1975:

I have sent my first message, through Glenway Wescott, to the curator of the Berg Collection of the New York Public Library. She is away at the moment, it seems, and I will be away shortly myself, but I told him about what came in the oatmeal envelopes—how many letters, poems, pages of prose narrative, etc., it consisted of. He asked (being in the midst of disposing of his own papers) if you wanted to sell them and I said I thought not, but this does not of course tie your hands. If you present them to the Library, with the right to publish them retained by your estate, which is I believe usual, would you be able to claim a deduction, based on an appraisal of their value, from Inland Revenue? It is also possible that they will ask for some sort of arrangement whereby the original letters and other copy all come eventually to them. I will let you know how things proceed. When I was seventeen years old I was taken to see Mrs. Fiske in *The Rivals* and almost died of amusement when Mrs. Malaprop said "Lead the way and I'll precede you." I didn't know anything could be that funny.

P.S. Speaking of which, years ago I left a standing order at Heywood Hill for the Oxford Press new translation of Chekhov, and the volumes have been coming at intervals, and not long ago they were 35 shillings, and the latest was eight pounds fifty, at which point I began to worry about you, in a way that I hadn't since the end of the Second World War. I mean your material considerations, food, money. Is everything all right? Are you managing?

Warner to Maxwell, June 25, 1975:

Speaking of which, and the new Tchekov costing £8.50, please, don't worry about me. I manage very well. I've always had a penchant for thrift, it appeases a latent sadism in my nature: I like to get the better of difficulties. I have a handsome balance at the bank, and Antonia.* When I had a slight grippe in the midst of 'Foxcastle' & rang up to say I wasn't well enough to enjoy the show of Tudor Portraits at Montacute, she arrived with oranges, lemons, honey, orange conserve, eggs from their esteemed hens, and a mourning card, so that I instantly recovered.

Now in a moment you will be at Wellfleet—*and writing*. O William, how that rejoices me. You write so well, and this perhaps will extend over into your retirement. My ghost will sit outside your door, making such faces at intending visitors, & making such hints of the horrors within that they shall be scared away, spreading the news. 'You know those poor Maxwells.'

* Gräfin Antonia von und zu Trauttmansdorff, a young Englishwoman living in the next village, Warner's devoted friend in her final years.

Warner to Maxwell, 1975:

Ancestors came back from a delighted borrower. I instantly opened it and was among the Baptists, enthralled. I hadn't forgotten how good it is, but I re-realised it. William, there can be no doubt but that the novella you are now in knots about will be on the same level. It is your total absence of condescension that makes you the proper person to write about these people and their events. And never a breath of the grinding of an axe.

Warner to Maxwell, October 21, 1975:

I don't thank you enough for writing so much of my stories for me. There they sit in *The New Yorker*, looking so polished and erudite. I read them, and see your hand, held out to save, in almost every paragraph. They should bear a footnote at the end: Kindness of Mr William Maxwell.

But I am signally grateful for the division of *labour* because it was an occasion (or you made it so) for talking, really talking; for asking how you were and being answered pat, for saying how I wished to see you once again, & being told that very likely I might, next spring.

I don't see why a new & somewhat pedestrian life of Shelley should interfere with your book or whatever about him. You are in love, that is the essential, and in interest. You wouldn't call him an ineffectual angel.

Did I ever tell you that when I was crossing the Serpentine late in a foggy London day I happened to look over the balustrade & saw a plump white hand rise from the water & grasp the air? I knew at once it was Harriet. The nearest I ever got to Shelley—but not so far, after all. It was almost certainly Shelley's child she drowned with. I have never seen a horoscope of Shelley, but I am sure most, if not all, his planets were in water.

I am re-reading what I must often have urged you to read: Pitcairn's *Criminal Trials of Scotland*. 16th century Scotch gives me the same rarefied excitement as eating shellfish; and as poignantly as it did in 1926 or so, when I suborned my uncle to get it from the London Library for me. It is full of Maxwells, by the way.

Warner to Maxwell, November 19, 1975:

Here is 'Foxcastle'.

I suppose these are the last proofs with William in the margins...a long, contented intercourse. Thank you, & thank you for all your care, & understanding, & patience—the holes you have got me out of, the rough places made plain, the exquisite trouble you have taken.

Maxwell to Warner, December 1975:

"Foxcastle" is in the current issue. In some ways it is my favorite of all of them. John Updike says isn't it time you made a book of them, and I explained that you couldn't, because there were more to come. Though I treasure what you said about my care, understanding, patience, etc. you must know perfectly well it was none of these things but merely love. Going all the way back to *Mr. Fortune's Maggot*.

Kate is in town for a few days, and we went to see the movie of *The Magic Flute*—the second time, for me—on a very rainy last night, while Emmy went to a play with friends that I didn't want—the play, that is, not the friends—to see. *The Magic Flute* has an especially fine balloon for the three little boys to ride around in, and the Queen of the Night arrives in what looks like a photographer's backdrop, circa 1912: A new moon that you can sit in. Papageno was larger than Pamino and without feathers, and everything seemed perfectly logical because it was so perfectly beautiful. Though a small voice did whisper to me, No brotherhoods, *please*, it was drowned out by those sonorous choruses.

I lay awake for hours thinking that when I got to the office I would have to write two very difficult letters of condolence, and at five-thirty got up and did it, to my surprise. The thought of death, the death of people I have loved, makes me angry, and the one time I expressed this anger in a letter of condolence, the friend, whose mother had died, looked at me in amazement. She had not died in a hospital but at home, with her loved ones around her, etc. etc. But she died, all the same. And she was a very fine woman, and left the world a poorer place. Do I imagine it or is it a fact that only the wicked and the soulless die peacefully in their sleep?

Warner to Maxwell, December 7, 1975:

I am very grateful to you for snatching me from the slobbering jaws of influenza [by prescribing doses of Vitamin C]. In the days of Valentine, influenza was bliss; a rapture of repose, as Byron said of death; *luxe, calme, et volupté*, with iced drinks, support, clean pillowcases every hour, her stern tenderness. So now I have every reason to avoid it.

I follow your order, because it is the only order in the house. My table is a welter of little bits of paper saying: Remember Mrs Hodges, 11, 11, post Tomkins, more string, bird-seed, order crumpets for Saturday, cats' sprats, rector's bottle. The little bits of paper are mislaid, & others, conjectural, are added to them. The kitchen is a riot of feeding friends, droppers-in, cats, and birds. In my dementia I do Christmas with my little hatchet. Yesterday I addressed a letter to Mrs Casserole.

My singing-teacher held a small class for Mozart students, and we studied *The Flute*. I and a third Boy and a third Lady. I wonder now that none of us died, for he was insistent on production, and we had to practise with a cherry in our mouths. *Secco recitativo* with a cherry—no stem—in the mouth is taxing. Nothing like a cherry, he said, for teaching a forward production.

When I look back on my youth, I see it glittering with maniacs.

How are you? Have you properly got over that operation? Will you keep the New York apartment, or fold yourself inside the garden fence of Baptist Church Road? What is the name of the unfortunate man whose fate it is to deal with me after you leave *The N. Y.*?

What is man's chief end?

Death, I would suppose, since we practise for it every night of our lives. I understand your resentment at the death of people you love. I feel even angrier at the death of those who are cut short; or their frustration; like Ben Britten who cannot write the flute part at the top of an orchestral score without having his arm lifted for him, or Solomon with his technique and interpretation imprisoned in his palsied arms; even more for the young who go down into the pit in battles of the Somme. *That* is intolerable. I was brought up to think it a sin to waste bread, and I have lived all my life in a world that wastes life. When you shall hear the sudden surly bell, don't, I beg you, be angry on my behalf. Remember all the nets that didn't catch me, all the lies that didn't trap me, all the tar-babies I didn't get stuck on.

Maxwell to Warner, December 24, 1975:

If you want to know the truth, I think it was Valentine who prompted me to tell you how to avoid colds and influenza. I am by now totally accustomed to feeling her impalpable nudging. But clean pillowcases every hour outdoes everything in my experience of valetudinarian ecstasy and is just like her. All my life I will remember with pleasure the three months I spent with Thomas Hardy and virus pneumonia. It must be a special temperament.

About that person who will become your editor when I leave—his name is Daniel Menaker. I had him in my office for four months last spring, and grew to love him dearly, and he grew to love working on your manuscripts and galleys with me. His father was a Russian radical, his mother is upper-class New England Presbyterian but enchanting, and he is like nobody I have ever known. As open as a child, and nobody's fool, both at the same time. I have taken particular care to leave you in what I believe are not only good but the very best possible hands.

Except that, of course, I am not leaving you but only *The New Yorker.* All it means is that I will have more time to write letters to you.

I promise not to be angry at your death but please don't be in any hurry for you will take a part of me with you and I won't ever again like the world I live in quite so much.

Warner to Maxwell, December 31, 1975:

The cats sleep in a garland on the Indian tree which is a hearthrug, and I am calm as they, and shall go unrestrictedly to bed when I feel inclined to. New Year's Eve was a terrible affair when Ruth (Valentine's mother) was staying here. By eleven we had all become rather quarrelsome and constrained. Between eleven & twelve we fixed our languishing minds on the New Year drinks—still so distant. At twelve precisely, Ruth rushed to the front door, jerked it open, & exclaimed into the quiet dark: 'Get out and begone to you, you horrible Old Year!' I suppose only a good woman could let loose such a vomit of grudges and furies—but it was curiously shocking.

After that I was able to go out & cool my prejudices on the doorstep before coming in as The First Foot (a dark woman is lucky). Between one and two (with luck) we should have stoked Ruth with sandwiches, put her to bed, tidied the disapproving house, prepared the early morning tea-tray and staggered, silent, to bed ourselves.

Family customs should not be kept up after they decompose.

Maxwell to Warner, January 19, 1976:

I was caught up in the details of my retirement, which meant going through all my files and desk drawers, while carrying on my usual work. Christmas came and I was still at it, and in the end I went off home with a taxi full of cartons. The pictures I carried home one at a time. And both of the young men I trained are now occupying my office, for the time being. Since they are the closest of friends, it is an agreeable arrangement for them, and gives me pleasure, for I love both of them. I also love being home and being able to go to the typewriter morning after morning in my bathrobe and slippers. Reminding myself of King Valoroso XXIV in "The Rose and the Ring."

This is the seventh morning in a row that I have sat down to work on a novella about some farm people in Illinois in the twenties [*So Long, See You Tomorrow*]. The fact that I seldom set foot on a farm in my childhood, though my father owned one, somewhat impedes me.

Would it suit you if we arrived in the late afternoon of Wednesday April 14 and spent that night and the following day and night with you and took off for London on Friday morning?

Warner to Maxwell, January 25, 1976:

Dear Valoroso.

It enchants me to think of you writing in your dishabille, morning after morning: your pleasure now, & mine later. And to know that now you have a chance to make sure of the important ideal & second thoughts which one gets up with but which are lost by mid-day.

But not, NOT, that you propose to come here halfway through a Wednesday & be gone on the Friday. It is a mingy amount of time in which to look at Emmy, to talk to you. Mingy, puny, inadequate, bobtailed, parsimonious—all that section in Roget. Think how you will regret it when I am dead. Can't you possibly extend it on one side or the other? I am quite as good as Winchester, even if Miss Austen is not buried in me, and I might well be as good as anything in Summer Place, even though Brendan Gill seems to have overlooked me in his plans for your pleasure. This, too, is 'a Victorian house offering bed & breakfast in agreeable surroundings'— many more daffodils, for one thing, and possibly moorhen chicks. No river flows down Summer Place. Not to mention me, I add modestly.

The discrepancies & inconsistencies between the earlier [Elfhame] stories and those which I wrote later are like nothing but the Gospels, or Taverner's *Missa Salve Intemerata* which bore four conscientious scholarly Tudor Church Music editors into regular nervous breakdowns once a week. There we sat round a table, saying But if; or with a gleam of hope, But why not? And the tugs on the river hooted, clearer & clearer, as the traffic quietened, till the Almoner's house in the Charterhouse (where we sat) became almost as hushed as when it was part of the real Charterhouse, in the clayey moorish fields. That was a haunted house, if you like.

Maxwell to Warner, March 5, 1976:

What little difficulty you have seeing across the Atlantic Ocean. The thing I am working on, story (short or long) does derive technically from *Ancestors*. But it is about a murder that took place in the country near town, when I was a schoolboy, and used to play with the murderer's son. I have been having hell's own time with it until yesterday when it occurred to me to lead some of the horse from around in back of the cart to the front, and back it into the shafts.

Warner to Maxwell, March 31, 1976:

I have forsworn all my austere intentions and gone back to them [the Elfin stories]. I have just finished the last one. Its beautiful title is 'The Duke of Orkney'—who does not appear in it, but influences the characters. It is an infinite relief to be pleased with my work again: gayly & unregenerately pleased. I finished it at 2 A.M. this morning, which shows the sincerity of my pleasure.

Now it is at the typist & I have urged her to let me have it back while you are here. It has a painting by Leonardo—and me—which I should like to exhibit. It is the first time I have painted a Leonardo.

This will be the first time you have stayed here.

Warner to Maxwell, April 19, 1976:

I solemnly assure you that I am still here: ridiculous formality! When I write again I will try to remember to be at the Hotel Sorrento, Kidderminster. But the address has at least the claim that it is an address you know from top to bottom; that you know the bedroom has a pink ceiling, that the stair-carpet is in tufts, cat-clawed, that you have walked all round it, and seen the first row of green peas in the kitchen-garden and the primroses along the drive; and if you are uncertain of its environs, you have only to consult Emmy.

I am dumb with superfluous eloquence when I try to tell you how grateful I am to you and her for catching that 9.30 train and coming here for such a whisk of a visit when it would have been so much more prudent & sensible to stay in London. I have never been more approving of recklessness, nor, since Valentine's death, sure of being loved.

Now you are back in New York City, and in a heat wave. It must have been painful walking into your apartment with a heat-wave shut up in it; and scattered around with worthy remnants, lists of what to take to Egypt and so forth. I hope you went out to an air-conditioned supper, and were welcomed by Kate & Brookie and your novella. Had it grown a great deal since you left it?

Maxwell to Warner, late April 1976:

Emmy was astonished by the accuracy of your description of our homecoming, and I thought of the mirror that that kind Beast gave Beauty so she could sit and watch the life of her family at home. Three of the plants in the living room had developed scale and had to be doused with soap and water, and the novella expanded its leaves as soon as I sat down to the typewriter and every moment away from it ever since has been like a tooth ache. For some reason I was intimidated by the characters before, and what they needed apparently was to have the study to themselves for a little while. The accumulation of second class mail was only slightly smaller than the pyramid of Giza. And your two letters brought an attack of homesickness for that house where for half of Thursday, Thursday night, and half of Friday, we were both of us so utterly happy. Though I have been married to Emmy for more than thirty years, I have never seen her behave quite that way before. Inside, outside, looking at the house from now one side of the river, now from the other, as if it were a beloved face that she wanted to make sure she would be able to call up in her mind correctly. And I keep remembering things that again remind me of the story of Beauty and the Beast. How is it that when I went upstairs after lunch on Thursday and got into that huge, maternal, marvelous bed, it was as warm as if five cats and three or four stoneware bottles full of hot water had been preparing it for me? There is not another house in the world that can compare with that house, for comfort, for style, for the treasures it contains, on the walls, on the bookshelves, for the view from every window, from the open front door, and for the way it invites conversation. When I think of the garden I think I must have dreamed it. In a curious way (the shaving brush may be the clue) we haven't left it. Have you found it necessary to walk around us as you go in and out of the study? Does it interfere with your work to have two ghosts sitting there?

I have also had a telephone conversation with Dan Menaker and found out that all is well with "Never Another Leonardo" ["The Duke of Orkney's Leonardo"]. And since I tell myself that I am the person you wrote them for anyway, will you go right on writing those fairy tales for me, whether *The New Yorker* takes them or not? I cannot begin to tell you how much they have added to my happiness. Those that I had to send back to you mysteriously have come back to me and are quite as vivid in my mind as those that ended up in galleys.

When I got to London and couldn't find my shaving brush, after being so thorough about not leaving anything, I exclaimed "That sly Dr. Freud!" Anyway, keep it in the box labeled Maxwelliana, as proof that I left meaning to come back at the earliest possible moment.

Warner to Maxwell, May 1, 1976:

When I went back to my room it was William & Emmy's bed I looked at. When I look out of a window, I look over your shoulders. When a door opens, Emmy walks in. I don't know which I value most: that I saw you again, that I saw Emmy for the first time. Before, she had been a lovely figure in a tapestry, now she is living and loved Emmy. She wrote me a lyrical letter, remembering everything, fingering the recollection of it. I have a majestic Plan that when next you come to England, not only will you stay for a proper length of time with me, but that for a while you will have the house to yourselves. It was made for a house *à deux*. Valentine's room pines for someone to sit working in it, to lie in the window reading.

You might do the proofs of your novella there. I will of course come back in time to read them.

When I heard that Mr. Shawn was disinclined to take more Elfins, I was momentarily peevish, and said to myself, *vieux singe ne plaît à personne.* Though the next moment I was considering a new one. But what really concerned was the state of Mr Menaker's feelings. Just when we had made such a good beginning, and all.

Maxwell to Warner, June 1976:

My novella is terribly uneven, reads one minute like a story and the next like a novel, which it isn't. I change, and change back, and go searching through mountains of paper for part of a sentence I rejected. In short, it proceeds like a novel, even if it is incapable of stretching to any great length. And I derive a certain strength, in moments of uncertainty, by asking myself what you would do with a passage.

We lost a close friend, a couple of weeks ago. A photographer named Charles Pratt, a big man with red hair who liked to take photographs of flowers no more than an inch high, as well as cliffs I wouldn't like to fall off of. So full of life, he was. And addicted to reading Proust. His wife asked me to speak at his funeral, and there I was behind a pulpit so tall I couldn't see anybody in the first rows. The minister and an auxiliary Bishop of Pennsylvania kept quoting from the Scriptures, in one of those improvements on the King James Version, and I felt as if we were engaged in a tug of war, since they were acting as if nothing mattered but Jesus and his (to me, anyway) anything but attractive Eternal Life, especially after the language has been tampered with, and what mattered to me was a man who didn't snap pictures, he stalked them, like an angel searching out innocence in order to watch over it. I find all clergymen unbearable. And I am sure I would find Jesus unbearable too, and God exactly like my father, who was unbearable, although not as bad as Samuel Butler's.

Emmy falls upon your letters with just the same pleasure and love that I do. It was really very clever of me to be sick so that you could find each other.

Warner to Maxwell, June 11, 1976:

I am not so sure you would find Jesus intolerable. You should have something in common with the narrator of the Parables, with all the moral inclinations of man so wryly and disconcertingly outraged. Those heated and burdened labourers in the vineyard with all their Trades Unionly principles made hay of, for instance. I have learned a great deal from Jesus, I assure you. And this last week, I have learned a great deal about him, from a reproduction of Chagall's window of the Crucifixion, whose Jesus is entirely a Jew, with a long narrow sardonic face. The remainder of the window is a subaqueous swirl of incomprehensible characters including a rider on a prancing red horse. And Jesus has everything totally under control. When I can bear to part with this, I will send it across to you: but probably after you all come home from Cape Tragabigzanda.

I will keep my views on God the Father to myself, only remarking that he repented him that he made man—a common fatherly custom.

Warner to Maxwell, June 23, 1976:

The Thistles ["The Thistles in Sweden"] came this morning.

It is a lovely manner, noiseless as a reflexion: as though a reflexion on the past transferred itself to the page, without any interruption of writing it. And the reflecting surface is a lake, unflowing, unflawed, like Shelley's lake reflecting the honey-bees in the ivy-bloom. This *statement* is far beyond narrative, which one learns how to manage. I don't see how you can have learned to write without noise or movement. I admire it far beyond envy.

Today I heard that one of these little jump-up firms which proliferate like fireweed in the ruins of publishing wants to re-issue *Mr Fortune's Maggot*. And this reminds me of my duty towards my literary executors. If there ever should be any question of reprints of *Lolly Willowes* & *Mr F.* they should be done from the original editions, *not* from that Viking reprint of them in one volume with Reynolds Stone's engravings.

This is my only rigid proviso. I can leave the rest to you & Soo with an easy mind. I know you will be as discriminating & rejecting as when you were my *N.Y.* editor. And I will try to clear things away; or mark them for destruction.

The people who were attached to me might, however, like a collected volume of my Letters. I love reading Letters myself, and I can imagine enjoying my own. Tell me what you think of this, & I will make a list of where some might be found: as, for instance, in the George Plank collection at Yale.

With my legs aching as much as they do, I am particularly anxious not to be a burden to you. Apart from my legs, I would detest being a burden when for so long I have had the pleasure of being a pleasure.

I hope you & Emmy are having a relaxing do-nothing-much holiday. HAVE YOU BEEN INOCULATED for Swine flu yet?

Maxwell to Warner, July 8, 1976:

American publishing is (compared to what it was in my youth) a shambles, but I trust that Viking will be happy to bring out a volume of your collected letters, and if they demur I will bring it out all by myself, said the little red hen. Now that I know you have no objection to it. Judging by the letters in my possession there must be enough for twenty volumes, and that is exactly what I would like there to be, though I am not sure I could manage it, quite. But to begin at the beginning, what exactly is there in the Plank collection at Yale? And who are the people that you have written most often and intimately to, over the years? I ask these questions remembering that my father-in-law is ninety and my mother-in-law only a little younger, and both of them lucid, and that you could easily outlive the little red hen.

What you wrote about my story ["The Thistles in Sweden"] made us both very happy. And where will I find Shelley's lake reflecting the honey bees in the ivy-bloom? As for learning how to manage narrative, the simple truth is, you have; I haven't still. I have got myself in such a mess with those country people. Totally different and unreconcilable tones, too many characters, invention and memory separating like oil and vinegar every time I turn my back on what I have written. I go on entirely out of optimism, hoping that when I get some sort of first draft I can then hold the whole thing off at arm's length and see what if anything will save it. In any case one cannot go on doing what one has already done, and nothing that I learn doing one thing ever seems to be of much help with another.

I am upset about your legs and I am quite sure that Valentine is too. I also grieve every time it rains, and it rains rather often, that the rain is not falling on your garden. But plants are tough and people are less so, and will you please carry less water, and carry what you do carry in smaller cans. If necessary go in the house and stay there. What we lose every winter by the cold we replace, in one way or another, and you can do the same with what you lose by the drought. You are what is irreplaceable. Come and live with us and let the whole place grow up in weeds.

Warner to Maxwell, July 13, 1976:

You will find Shelley's lake in *Prometheus Unbound*. It is a lyric, & begins 'On a poet's lip I slept.'

I am glad you approve of a collection of letters. I will make out a list of possibles, and meanwhile here is an early one, kept by my father:

S.T.W. to G.T.W. Aug. 1903 Strete. Devon. 'There are a lot of cats, a yellow & a grey one and a little tabby kitten and a tabby cat (I think it is the kitten's mother) and a thin stripy one that belongs to the grocer, and a white one with yellow and black spots, which belongs to Mrs Wallis, and I think there are more.

Your loving Sylvia.'
aet.9—and much the same preoccupations as now.

Your story. I know that trouble with too many characters. I went out of my mind with *The Flint Anchor*, trying to make them all grow older simultaneously; and I had to kill off two bishops in *The Corner*. It sometimes helps to be lifelike: to make their first appearance a name or a comment, and build them up later. Proust's device. I have never had to tackle *invention & memory*; but I would rely on invention of the two; memory is the vinegar of the pair, and you remember the Spanish recipe for salad dressing: a profligate with the oil, a miser with the vinegar, a counsellor with the salt & a madman to beat it all together.

No, one never learns: it would stultify learning. Robert Bridges, finishing a poem: 'Casting it forth, my child, I rise above thee'.

But if you leave it all to come together, like a stew, it will come together. And meanwhile, you are writing it, & in heaven.

Love to you and Emmy, and a happy return to your weeds. HAVE YOU BEEN INOCULATED for Swine flu? BOTH OF YOU?

Warner to Maxwell, August 7, 1976:

The last Elfin ["The Duke of Orkney's Leonardo"] is scheduled for Sept. 20th, so Mr Menaker tells me. If & when I send him anything more, I will remember to tell him you want to see it. I like him very much, and for that reason I shall try to have something for him later on.
Remember to be inoculated.

Warner to Maxwell, September 14, 1976:

I like to know where you are, how you are? I can do nothing about

either, but I like to know. And I want to know how the novella goes, and if
you have resisted a libertine impulse to add a character from Wyoming
[where they had been on vacation], a homesick cave-dweller. And have you
had that injection?

I recently had a letter from a representative of the University of Texas,
who remarked, somewhere halfway down a flowing page, 'I must indulge
your patience.' I thought this too fine to keep to myself, so I will address it
to you. *Have you had*, etc?

About those letters. The person I have written to 'most often and most
intimately' is you. The letters to George Plank are in the Yale University
Library, and the man who could lay his hand on them is called Norman
Pearson. I suppose it would be called the George Plank bequest. He left
them all his papers about twelve years ago.

Have you ever known a murderer? It appears that I have done so. He
was a particularly amiable, generous, sensitive man, and I was much
attached to him, and grieved when he killed himself. A good project of his
had folded up for lack of support, and I supposed he killed himself from
frustration. Now his widow has told me it was from remorse because,
many years back, he had killed his first wife. I wish I could think she lied or
fancied, but she told me sincerely, to unbosom herself. The longer one
lives, the more one has to pity. He was totally unsuited to be a murderer. I
am haunted by the thought of his long memory of a frightful, incompatible deed. So much so that, as you see, I too have to unbosom myself. One
has to be Sophocles to take this kind of thing calmly—if Sophocles did.

My love, my true and not easily gained love to you both.

Maxwell to Warner, September 22, 1976:

As for the novella, I have finally admitted to myself that it is that, and
not a short story, and therefore have rounded up all the short stories that I
think worth putting in a book, and when I have numbered the pages will
give them to my publisher sometime next week. There are exactly twelve.
I think *Kingdoms of Elfin* will be ready before mine, which I expect to call
Over by the River and Other Stories. And perhaps Brookie will do the jacket
design, since Ilonka Karasz is no longer well enough.*

When we were in Wellfleet I lay awake one night thinking about the novella, and suddenly everything began to fall into place. I saw with excitement just how it should be, and sentences poured into my mind all night, nothing in my whole life was irrelevant, and in the morning when I got up and got dressed I was exhausted, could remember nothing I had thought all night, was depressed, and felt I had been the victim of an illusion, and that I now knew what it was like to a manic depressive in a manic phase. And did not even try to write for the next three days. Writing has to be done on one's hands and knees, I told myself, and continued to plod along. But gradually it has been borne in on me that what I thought that night was correct after all, but just a little too excited to be manageable. I don't know how long it will turn out to be: something under two hundred pages, I think. Anyway, it doesn't belong with the stories. If I would draw a picture of it it would look like this:

Turned sideways it is a woman. The worry that most dogs me is that it involves repetition of things, parts of things, I have already written. Even the repetition of repetitions. With this large doubt yapping at my heels I proceed, day after day. So far nobody from Wyoming has occurred, not even as a figure of speech.

About those letters. I am so moved to learn that I am the person you have most often and most intimately written to. I had fancied you might be as prodigal as nature. The real treasure is, then, within ten feet of me this minute. If you have ever said, I can't remember, and therefore I ought to ask you now: Do you want me to do the collecting and selecting for the publisher? Or to do the collecting and let Soo do the selecting? It is a labor of love that I think I could manage properly if you want me to do it, and I would not be jealous if you prefer to have someone else do it instead.

One of the two main characters in my novella is the son of a murderer, but I don't think I have known any murderers, though I have long known that I am capable of being one. And did in fact attempt to kill my older brother when I was ten years old or thereabouts. If I had I don't think I would have suffered from remorse. With three thousand miles between us we have lived out the rest of our lives peaceably for the most part.

I opened *The New Yorker* and saw "The Duke of Orkney's Leonardo" was in it, and turned the pages until I read the words "But never another Leonardo" and was straightway where I wanted to be, in your study, with you and Emmy, in that house that we both remember with such delight. I have just now been rereading the story. It is a marvel, as you well know. When I read "As for the caul, by some mysterious negotiation it got to Glasgow. There it was bought by the captain of a whaler and subsequently lost at sea" I know that what I am reading is hallucinated and a fact. I give a nod of recognition to Sir Glamie, advancing on what turned out not to be a poacher. *That* story will be in the book, I told myself. Thank God for that. I read column after column with admiration, with love, with recognition of that fact that if my own sentences now and then have a shape it is largely owing to a rapt perusal of yours. Then I came to the hedge-trimming and was once more back in Lower Frome Vauchurch. After that I read on enslaved by the story-telling, remembered once when I was fourteen years old and fought a girl not to a finish but to a standstill. All the furniture was overturned and we were so weak we could not stand up. It was my birthday and she had endeavored to give me my "spats"—fourteen spankings, a tradition in that place and that time. She was in love with my older brother and I have always regretted that she did not marry him, but we were of exactly matched strength, and neither could win out over the other. Then the pigs went mad and the kitchen chimney was struck by lightning. And when the Purveyor, clutching his heart, fell dead I couldn't have cared less, for I had become a faery. If you hadn't said that the painting was a Leonardo I would have known anyway by the description, but then I would have had to go without the words "but never another Leonardo" which are so like a wreath of carved ivory roses delicately tinted and entwined in blue glass ribbons. At the end I was emotionally exhausted and so must you have been when you finished writing that story.

The telephone just rang. It was Brookie asking if a dagger in the time of Macbeth would be two parallel lines converging at the end to a point, or triangular. I all but said, and in my mind did say, "Ask Sylvia."

* The Hungarian-born artist Ilonka Karasz (1896–1981) was a prolific designer of *New Yorker* covers. She created the dust jackets for five of Maxwell's books and illustrated his children's story *The Heavenly Tenants*.

Warner to Maxwell, September 26, 1976:

What a relief that it has gone into the right slot & will be a novella. Now you can be easy about its dimensions & have everything handsome about you, and I shall know what Shade to invoke on your behalf. There is a great deal to be said for the 19th cent. habit of buying the larger shoes & letting the child's feet grow into them. And now that it is a novella you will find it much easier to discard what has grown into a tangle, and leave out the explanations. At least, I have found it so. I send it a godmother's love.

Letters. I should like you to do the collecting; but above all, the selecting. And please do not let my letters to you be elbowed out by letters to other people: modesty can impel one to fatal acts. Damn the other people. I am writing to you now, with half a dozen other letters put by.

A dagger in the time of Macbeth—with my love to Brookie—would be for use. That is to say, it would have a graspable cross-hilt and a short, rounded blade, tapered but not sword-like. When I say rounded, I mean it would be rather thicker at the spine than at the edges. The ballads, where daggers pierce so deep they cannot be withdrawn, may imply a dum-dum bullet quality, a necked and shouldered blade. But this is just one of my ideas.

Warner to Maxwell, October 8, 1976:

I came out of my sleep this morning saying: Damn good taste. Every writer is entitled to have his worst work published. What do you think? I wished I had some one to discuss it with (that is my only objection to a solitary life: no one but myself to argue with so I monotonously get the better of every argument).

Maxwell to Warner, November 2, 1976:

I have just come back from voting. Nixon's legacy, the Public Relations men, have so befuddled the country (not to mention the candidates) that the under-educated do not seem to be able to remember who did what, or even where their own interest lies. Our black cleaning woman said yesterday, "They're just alike," meaning Ford and Carter. When pressed, she admitted that they weren't. I think what she meant was that she didn't like either of them. Nor do I, much. Thank God I have a garden to cultivate.

I have bit off more than I can chew, at the moment. And we are both reading the memoirs of the Brothers Goncourt. Emmy with delight, and I with astonishment. For I would have said it was a book I knew well, but something has happened to me since I last read it. And everything seems a marvel, one marvel after another. Is the book of Elfin also being published in the spring? I often think, with mixed feelings, about the fact that you might have retranslated all of Proust. I pick him up, at random, from time to time, and within a few pages bog down in those malformed sentences. I will read the Painter *Life*. I am, right this moment, having hell's own time doing a short review of V. Woolf's letters. What I want to say, and all I want to say, really, is that compared with yours they are on the whole very poor reading.

Two weeks ago I went to Illinois to say goodby (though I didn't succeed in doing this) to a very old friend who was dying of cancer [Garetta Busey]. When I was in my middle twenties she levered me out of a teaching job at the University of Illinois, into what turned out to be my present life. It was the rock bottom of the depression and I was scared to death. I went on her courage. I would have made a terrible professor. I found her heavily sedated, and read Bahai prayers to her (I remember now that I once tried to send her to you, a great many years ago. It was she who introduced me to your writing, with *Opus 7*) which I had no reason to think she heard. The next morning somebody said to her in a loud voice that I was there and she spoke my name. Part of it. She died the following day, in her sleep. After I had gone back to New York.

Warner to Maxwell, November 6, 1976:

You & Emmy are dearer to me than a waggonload of relations; and if I were pressed for money you are the first people I should turn to. But be easy. Inflation doesn't worry me. I proceed majestically in buying the things I like: wine, fruit, warmth, clean sheets, and save by not buying things I don't like. The other day I heard a woman lamenting that she had paid 38*p*. for a swede (vegetable, not human), and thought how economically I live, never wanting to buy swedes. I also buy the services of a rowdy Yorkshireman who does my tax returns for me. The claims come in and I pay them; but the Yorkshireman has acted as a sort of lightning conductor, and averted the shock.

I wish I had met, at the least, written to your dead friend who fished you out of teaching. I would have liked to thank her for making me known to you. I am sure she did a thousand good acts, but this must have been among the best of them, and the most durable. Not one of those flash-in-the-pan mercies. I expect she knew you were there.

To reward you for doing that review [of Virginia Woolf's letters], I must tell you the story of the pious Bottle. Ottoline [Morrell] and her blood-niece had an aunt in Oxford who died; and sweeping in black they went to have a last look at her. By the death-bed was a Crucifixion in a Bottle (like ships, you know). According to the blood-niece, Ottoline picked it up and concealed it in her mourning cloakings. But not unobserved, for the blood-niece accused her of theft & sacrilege. Standing in a quiet Oxford street the two ladies vituperated in voices like sea-gulls, language like fishwives, and fought for possession of the dear object, till in the contest the Crucifixion in a Bottle fell on the ground and was broken to smithereens. So they left it, & parted in anger & went their different ways in their swirling black cloaks. The blood-niece related this to Valentine, and here it is for you— simple and frank. I have met both ladies: the niece I disliked; she was rabbitic. But there wasn't an atom of vice in Ottoline. God rest her soul—if he can contrive to.

Maxwell to Warner, November 12, 1976:

I so much don't envy *myself* the job of reviewing VW's letters that I haven't done it. One curious thing I noticed—that there are three people she shows off to, Strachey, Duncan Grant, and Vanessa, and usually it is by being harsh or cruel or unkind or unfeeling about somebody. As if it were a game they played. It must have made her uncomfortable though. What I think it comes down to, for the reviewer, is not to judge something written privately as if it were not private: it is too much like condemning people for what they think of doing but don't. And wouldn't. Anyway, privacy enters into it.

The pious bottle, fought over, couldn't in the nature of things not end up by being broken into smithereens. Offhand I would have said that it is a long way from Lady Ottoline to Grimm's Fairy Tales, but I see it isn't. And that the solution to the problem of inflation lies in not buying rutabagas. You should be Chancellor of the Exchequer.

Warner to Maxwell, November 24, 1976:

I am twice as delighted: to hear that you will dedicate your book of short stories [*Over by the River*] to me, that there is to be a book of your short stories. When will I see them? Soon, very soon, I hope. You were not here long enough I'm afraid, and anyhow on the wrong side of the bed, to see that I keep *The Old Man at the Railroad Crossing* in the most complying shelf of my bedside bookshelves. Emmy's loyal eye may have observed it.

Warner to Maxwell, December 23, 1976:

Your V.W. review came yesterday, & I read it with my morning black coffee, and sighed that Leonard could not read it. He withstood as long as he could this rush to exploit Virginia. The unpublished short stories he did after her death were only allowed out if they did her credit. But now no one who ever clashed a bucket in the outskirts of Bloomsbury is disallowed from joining in the hunt; they run about with gobbets of Virginia hanging from their chops. And like all exploiters and those onto a good thing, they are greasy with piety.

'Shelley, rare soul! I have his trousers here.'

Warner to Maxwell, January 22, 1977:

When you last wrote you were reading the letters of Anne Thackeray Ritchie. I hope you have fallen in love for life, and will make her a habit. It is as though a small bird came & settled on one's hand with no particular consciousness of doing it, but sure of being well-received. Do you know her *Blackstick Papers*? She knew all the notabilities, alighted on them—her father's hostess—remembered with an easy affection, had gazed with veneration on George Sand, listened to Joachim. She was the perfection of dilettante, because she took delight; and her easy transparent English has inherited her father's button-holing without making a special thing of it. Another reason why I love her is that she exasperated Leslie Stephen. Think of the knotted emotions in his bosom when the unpunctual, mislaying, imperturbable lady of his house made that scandalous marriage with a young man half her age. *O felix culpa!* But he was too high-minded to admit such a sentiment.

This has been a dark week for me. Paul Nordoff died on Monday—of cancer in a hospital in the Ruhr. He was a bi-lingual, so he didn't have to die in a foreign language; and the man in charge was a friend of his. I rang him up twice a week or so—strange loving & lively conversations over the Pit. At the news he was dead I was thankful for his sake: he had dreaded losing his patience & gaiety: but I was appalled by the realisation of the total discrepancy between the quick & the dead. I first met him in 1939; and we had a long rapscallionly friendship, music a serious concern, our mishaps and opinions laughed over. Greatest loss of all, that he loved Valentine and set many of her poems; and never deformed his memory of her. Sometimes I feel as lonely as Memnon—do you know that Schubert song?—Memnon is silent all night, only at the first ray of the sun can he sing.

Warner to Maxwell, January 30, 1977:

I have once witnessed religious emotion. It was at Orta—a village about the size of Maiden Newton—but being Italian with a piazza and everything handsome about it. Valentine and I were variously aggrieved by the local catholics, and we went to Orta for Easter. I shall never forget the lighting of the new fire: outside the church, in the teeth of a wind from the alps blowing across the lake. The acolyte with a cigarette lighter had to make several attempts, watched with breathless co-operation. Finally, it was lit, and carried into the church—all dark, full of silent people, every one clutching a candle. Candle after candle was lit from the first fire, every one bestowing his light on the next. The old toothless man with garlic breath who lit my candle had an expression of such fatherly loving-kindness that if I went to heaven and God was not that old man I should feel defrauded.

As you know, there is no music in Lent. At the beginning of the midnight mass there was a bellowing overhead like all the animals let out of the ark: from the choirmen in the gallery, their Italian voices unloosed, singing execrably & with all their hearts.

Maxwell to Warner, February 1, 1977:

Between my fifteenth and twenty-fifth year I had a passion for opera,
and used to stand night after night through the repertoire. Only *Lohengrin*
was too much for my ankles and I had to go lie down on the grass, at about
eleven o'clock. I even contemplated turning *La Bohème* into a novel; knowing that it sprang from one. But mine was going to be better. Or at least
different. In Kate's room the recordings of operas extend across one shelf
of her bookcase and three quarters of the way through the next. I have
trouble believing that I never heard the music to Paul Nordoff's opera
about Shelley [*The Sea Change*], since the libretto is one of my treasured
possessions. Emmy and I did hear him perform singlehandedly *Mr. Fortune's Maggot.* He played the orchestral score on the piano, and sang all the
parts. With brio. The other evening Rubinstein played two concertos on
TV and was interviewed after and before. Looking toward him with rather
a shade more admiration than was polite, the interviewer said, "Mr. Rubinstein, what do you feel, after you have spent a lifetime performing beautiful
music and have acquired a vast store of musical knowledge, what thoughts
cross your mind when you consider that all this will come to an end with
your death?" And Rubinstein answered "I hardly ever think about it. I don't
believe there is a life after death because I am afraid that if it turned out
there wasn't I would be disappointed. But there is something, 'soul,' for
want of a better word, and I think that when the body dies it must be stuck
helplessly, without a home. Once in London (I am only remembering this
as best I can) Emmy Destinn asked me how Chopin played, and I thought
it a very stupid question, but I sat down at the piano and played something
I had never played in concert, and it wasn't at all the way I would have
played it. And when I finished I was quite pale and so was she . . ."

An acquaintance [Tobias Schneebaum] just back from New Guinea,
where he was living in a native village until he had his visa revoked (no for-
eigners are wanted until after the Indonesian election), was describing the
recent earthquake. (Speaking of Mr. Fortune.) His bed was moved about
four feet but that was all. A man he knew, in another village, woke and saw
that all the villagers were leaving the village and going up the mountain, so
he went too, and for four days stayed with them, without food or water.
When he wanted to go down they prevented his doing it. Across a crack in
the ground they had placed a twig, and they all sat and watched the twig

because it showed when the crack widened or narrowed. When the widening and narrowing stopped they all went down the mountain. A pilot he knew said that, flying over the area of the worst devastation afterward, he didn't know where he was. The forest was upside down, and there were four lakes that hadn't been there before. My acquaintance had been to a number of villages where no outsider had ever been before. Dropped by a helicopter, he takes off his clothes and waits for the reception. I expect that he will some day be eaten, but so far he is met with love. He is, as you would imagine, immensely delicate and civilized. And without preconceptions. Viz: "The chief stood in front of me and waggled his penis in my face and I didn't know what he wanted of me so I waggled my penis and that seemed to be all that the occasion called for."

Those farmers I am writing about have pushed me into a corner, where I cannot make beautifully shaped sentences or any kind of construction. I worry for fear they do not have the breath of life in them. That it will never come off. That the awkward length would prevent its being published if it did come off. And so on. I know that some of it is bad. The question is whether any of it is good. And I can't find out the answer until I finish it and show it to somebody. It is all based on a memory that turned out to be impossible. The chronology of my adolescence proves that what I remember vividly never could have happened. I spoke to Marchette [Chute] about this and she screwed up her eyes and said, "It's a question of faith." She is years away from the end of her present opus, and so far as I could see, quite unworried about it.

I didn't know Lady Ritchie's husband was half her age. How charming, and how like her. I will see if the *Blackstick Papers* are in the same library where I found the letters.

It used to bother me that we lived on opposite sides of the Atlantic, but since last April I feel that you are no farther away than, say, Putnam County, which is roughly ten miles from the little house in the country.

Warner to Maxwell, February 7, 1977:

Those farmers of yours seem (to judge by your recital of labour-pangs) to be getting along very nicely, and to have the novella well in hand. Their indifference to the shape of sentences and varieties of construction is true to life: it is how they build barns and mend fences; if they have seized on a memory that has turned out to be impossible that, dear William, is how they have always made their legends. I daresay you find them disconcerting, but I am sure you can rely on them.

I have spent today with Peter Pears: that is to say, he came to lunch, and as he came in his sister's car where she had not attended to the battery, at five P.M. on a beautiful spring evening we were still walking about in the garden waiting for a mechanic to set him going.

We discussed the problem of going on living after one has been cut in half. He has found his solution in the harp. There can never be another accompanist like Ben [Britten, who died in 1976]; and pianist after pianist has played beautifully in his pianist's compartment, and nothing came of it; but Ossian Ellis the harpist & he get along very nicely, and Ravel's songs, especially 'Sainte', bloom on harpstrings. I suggested they might try Moore's Irish melodies. It was one of my good ideas. He looks so gaunt, so solitary, that except for his height and his speaking voice I think I could not have recognized him. As I have been having influenza I daresay he felt equally at a loss. But the soup (J. artichoke, *Palestine soup, a palpable misnomer*) re-established me as me.

Maxwell to Warner, February 11, 1977:

It [*Kingdoms of Elfin*] is in all the bookstores, and I took a copy when we went out to dinner on Wednesday night. The hostess exclaimed at the sight of your name and said, "Mr. Fortune," and to my surprise didn't know the title of a single book that you had published since. How distractable the common reader is.

Dan Menaker told me that he was calling you about the new story ["A Widow's Quilt"], which everyone liked very much, he said. And I lapsed into complacency at the thought of what I had managed to do, which is to say leave you in the hands of someone who loved your writing and would, if he had a chance, love you. I am delighted about the British reviews. I am helplessly possessive about that book. What in anyone else would seem like prestidigitation is simply a Defoe-like record of—I do not seem to have the strength to finish that sentence properly and feel so safe with you that I don't even need to try.

Maxwell to Warner, February 26, 1977:

If Mr. Pears shows a serious interest in Paul Nordoff's opera about Shelley, you must listen to me; a request I seldom make of you (I hope). I know that you subscribe to the principle that the librettist should at any point give way to the desires of the composer, but it is no better, no more absolutely true than any other principle. On principle I am skeptical of all principles. And if you will dispassionately consider the changes which I think he made, or you made at his request, you will see that they were mistaken and perhaps kept the opera from being performed. They were, in any case, fatal to the line of the story and the action of the opera. If, as I suspect, you do not even possess a copy of the libretto as you originally wrote it, I am fairly certain that I do have it and could easily have it copied for you, or copied for me and send you the original, which would be more polite. I have never not been troubled by it, from the moment I read it. You had it absolutely right, and even now I feel that the music could be rearranged in such a way that it would fit the libretto as you originally wrote it. In any case you might show it to him and see what he thinks.

Warner to Maxwell, February 28, 1977:

I have been listening to Brandenburg *no* 5, and at the close of that interminable cadenza I heard the harpsichordist breathe a sigh of relief. Rarely, rarely does the BBC allow a moment of real life to get into its well-behaved programmes. Brandenburg 5 will include that harpsichordist's sigh whenever I hear it again.

One reason why my memory decays is that I have three cats, all so loving and insistent that they play cat's-cradle with every train of thought They drove me distracted while I was having influenza, gazing at me with large eyes & saying: O Sylvia, you are so ill, you'll soon be dead. And who will feed us then? FEED US NOW!

I should like to hear more about your attic.

Maxwell to Warner, March 10, 1977:

You asked about the attic and what's up there. It is shaped like a cross, and in very few places high enough so that you can stand upright. I put on gardening pads and crawl around on my hands and knees. The attic stairs unfolds from a ceiling in the hall. At the head of the stairs, in the most convenient place, are all the things that Larry left and seems to want us to keep forever for him, even though he and Brookie do not see each other any more. To the left, cooking utensils and a china cupboard and curtains hanging in plastic bags, and then an extension lined on each side by the children's toys, ending up in my papers and some family heirlooms, and a bookcase full of Kate's books. On the right, by the stairs, letter files, and things that can be inserted in a low triangular space over the dining room. Rolled up things. Then a pile of *Country Life* that I cannot bring myself to throw away because somewhere in it is an issue that has an article about the drawings people used to make around the address on postcards or letters, at Christmas time, in Victorian days, that Emmy wants. Then the largest and longest arm of the attic, with baskets on the left, then books, in low bookcases, then a coffin-shaped box full of glass and china vases, then a couple of low dressers full of bedspreads and bed pads, etc., then the cradle that Emmy was rocked in, of white wicker, and that, in fact, her mother was rocked in before her. And our children also, of course. Then a trunk containing all the things Kate brought home from Bennington College after her first year, and that are kept intact in case she should decide to go back, which is not likely. On the other side more bookcases, a doll's house I made for Kate copied from a Swedish 18th century townhouse doll house I saw a picture of in a book. It is a wonder, even if I did make it, and was inhabited for years by the Mozart family. Then more chests, containing woollens, behind which are tossed the suitcases, and more bookcases containing children's books, all the favorite ones, and then a great mass of framed pictures that we cannot bear to throw away and have no place to hang, and the Christmas tree ornaments, and a rocking chair with a broken seat, etc. Everywhere, of course, there is etc. And though we are continually disposing of things, things go up the attic stairs more than they come down. Sometimes there are wasps, but we have agreed to live and let live. It is very hot in summer and very cold in winter. And if you could stand up straight it would be in perfect order, but after a short period of crawling around I get dizzy and make for the stairs. Most of the things we cannot bear to throw away we do not want, but they were given to us by someone we are fond of and if thrown away the person would I don't know what. Know it instinctively, or suffer some misfortune. Or something. I haven't even begun to tell you what is up there. For example, a beautiful 9 x 12 oriental rug that belongs to E's brother. A plated silver punchbowl, very ugly, that was presented to my Maxwell grandparents. Window shades. Extra rolls of wallpaper. A folding army cot. Pieces of sculpture by a young man who taught Brookie when she was twelve years old. Lots of books, which we weed out frequently, and the books that are given to the library are invariably the ones I go up to the attic looking for, later. Aren't all attics like this, more or less?

Warner to Maxwell, March 14, 1977:

Oh, your attic! I followed your every all-fours step, dizzied with rapture at the immensity and variety of what every normal family accumulates in the course of being a family. And torn with envy, for I have no attic, only a boxroom, where Valentine kept things we might need if the lower half of the house was flooded: a kettle, candles, a tin of gingerbread nuts, a chess set, a tin of Parkinson's Old Fashioned Humbugs, some special polish for leather bindings (occupation is soothing), half a bottle of brandy, etc. To which I added my muff and a few discarded hats. These were for floating on the face of the waters, like the hats the young ladies of the Church of England Seminary at Salisbury were compelled to wear, and threw into the river when the yearly course of religious knowledge ended: a provincial version of that regatta of chamberpots at Cambridge.

There were a great many things in your attic I coveted: the rolls of old wall-paper, for instance. One thing I firmly removed—the rocking chair, to have its seat mended.

I strongly advocate that you & Emmy come here in September. It is the loveliest month in our year: distant woods look dark-blue, figs are ripe, roses have their second bloom. It is what Donne praised in Lady Herbert's 'autumnal face.' Antonia, who has just come in with a case of tinned pilchards in tomato, says I must add that people are much nicer in September.

(The tinned pilchards, I must make clear, are bought for the cats from the cash & carry store. They wouldn't waste a sniff on fresh tomatoes, but tinned with pilchards they never tire of.)

How I wish I could see the town-house doll house where the Mozart family lived. I didn't know that you were a maker with your hands; but now I do know, I see how inevitably you would have a talent for small things that demand skill and patience; and that stay stuck. Whereabouts in the Zodiac were you born? Did I tell you that an Admiralty enquiry into deep sea divers found that 80% of them were born under The Fish?

Maxwell to Warner, March 23, 1977:

I was born on August 16, and am therefore a Leo. Mavis Gallant says that the most noticeable thing about Leos is their complacency.

The dolls' house was a collaboration. Emmy found the furniture and papered the walls to scale, etc. and is the true miniaturist in the family. She has cherished all these years a miniature spyglass one inch long, which I believe belonged to her grandmother, made of ivory. And when you look through it you see Cologne cathedral.

You remember the woman in Isak Dinesen's story who sailed the seas looking for the perfect blue? In somewhat the same way I search for an interesting fact for you that you do not already know. When I find one that looks likely (viz: in Grove last night that as a small child Mozart had an ear so delicate and susceptible that he fainted away at the sound of a trumpet) and then shake my head; a musical fact that you are not conversant with? most unlikely. And about Mozart, more unlikely still. But someday I shall astonish you, as you astonish me every time I get a letter from you.

Warner to Maxwell, March 31, 1977:

If God ever made a better fruit, he kept it for himself—some eminent person said about the nectarine, do you remember? If God ever made a worse day, he must have made it for the Deluge. It is bitterly cold, remorselessly wet, dark and ill-natured. The house is full of slamming doors & bemoaning cats. All the daffodils are lying flat in the mud, every green shoot is wishing it hadn't, every nice new bird's nest is a ruin and no one has a good word for the Budget—except me, because I like the man's eyebrows. I would not dare to mention a cheerful tiding except to you. But a cable yesterday was delighted to tell me that the paperback rights to *Kingdoms of Elfin* have been sold and I shall get $22,000 by that well-starred book. So ever since then I have been furtively smirking, and making lists of extravagances to roll in.

You will also be delighted to hear that my blood pressure is exemplary. I was so mortified by my legs—once the joy of nations—swelling into columns that I broke my boast of not seeing a doctor for over ten years and sent for Antonia's crony. He is like a goblin death's-head—he even wears a goblin's hat—and during a long conversation about Sydney Smith and other characters of that date, he explored me from top to toe and found nothing to take against. He says he can cure my poor legs, so when you come in September you won't have to avert your eyes or I lurk in trousers.

I don't think there is any likelihood that he [Peter Pears] will want to produce Paul Nordoff's opera—for one thing, the orchestral parts are God only knows where. If he did, he would have to invoke me. If he does, I will listen to you about the libretto, though I don't promise to comply; I am still musician enough to know that certain vowel sounds won't associate with the vocal effect the music should convey: try singing *milk* sostenuto on a high note.

What kept the opera from being performed was that Columbia, who had commissioned it (University of) reneged, in a fit of McCarthy-mindedness, because both Paul & I were badged with unsound political views—Shelley, too, for that matter—and unsuitable for support. They did, however, pay a moiety of the commission. I have a copy of the libretto. One never knows when one offends. A setting of my 'Country Thought from a Town' by Alan Bush distressed his high-mindedness by mentioning God, and he had to ask me to tone God down into nature, or something inoffensive like that. So I did. People with tender consciences have enough to suffer from without their scruples being trampled on. There should be scruple-pads, as with corns.

Maxwell to Warner, April 13, 1977:

Emmy's brother gave me a couple of Paul Robeson records and though I
thought I knew what his voice was like, I am stunned. Our Chaliapin
whom we drove from the country. His speaking voice is just as brilliant and
extraordinary. The window is open and the evening air is full of squealing
children's voices. In the absence of sea gulls it will have to do. I don't *think*
they are murdering each other.

Warner to Maxwell, April 19, 1977:

Paul Robeson—oh yes! That voice that went down like the roots of a
tree. And he was a magnificent actor. The best Othello—the only Othello:
he explained the whole story by his reaction to the mislaid handkerchief:
there was magic in that needlework, & his reaction to the loss was a
voodoo acknowledgement. His Desdemona, however—Peggy Ashcroft—
told me that almost every day she got letters saying that no nice white girl
should act with him.

Warner to Maxwell, May 4, 1977:

The most sumptuous mattress of moss, dry grass & feathers has been
made in my letter-box. I wished with all my heart I could lie down in it,
instead, I printed Birds Nesting, Please do not Disturb., fetched a hammer
& drawing pins, fastened it on the front door above the letter-box. I suppose if she lays her eggs tomorrow I shall be her landlady for the next 6
weeks, during which time the front door will be immobilised, everything
will have to go to the back door, & every bird-lover in the square mile will
call to ask me how the birds are getting on. A proud position (tits, of
course: only tits & robins prefer to bring up their children in Gothic
homes), but rather a taxing one. (As I write this I remember that I have not
bolted the back door of the letter-box: another last act before I go to bed.)

If you persist in your intention to do a book of S.T.W. Letters: Mrs R.
Ballinger, of 576, Fruit Hill Avenue, N. Providence, R.I., and Mrs O.
Warner, of Old Manor Cottage, Hastlemere, Surrey, hoard letters from

me. God knows why. You must either cut or select. It is not as if I were Fitzgerald.

By the way, what am I to do about your letters? I have mountains of them.

Warner to Maxwell, May 20, 1977:

This day a month Antonia will be driving me to Aldeburgh, where I am to sit cocked up in the limelight, listening to Peter Pears reading some of my poems; and trying not to look too pleased with them. Me trying, that is. He is reading the long dream poem about following the burial procession of the cross to its grave in the desert, crossing the Mediterranean on air and meeting a shooting star going off on its own errand. He wants some more of the later ones to go with it, & this led to sorting through a vast stack of them. One would think I had never done anything else but write poems. When I consider how my days are spent I am at a loss to know how it all got packed in, & I am still preserving an air of leisure; and reading the leaders in *The Times.* And drinking coffee all day, as befits the great-great granddaughter of a Mevrow, if that's how she spelled it—it seems odd. Her married name was Reijnette—if that's how it's spelled; and her husband founded a town in South Africa.

But it was a great-great uncle, though also on the distaff side, who displayed such self-control and aplomb. He was on his way back from India, sitting on deck with his slippered feet resting on the rail, when one of the slippers fell off and sank into the ocean. So he kicked off the other. Now that *would* be an inheritance worth having.

Meanwhile, I have you, dear William, all the more endeared by not being a relation.

Warner to Maxwell, May 21, 1977:

As for you, you are fathomless. You lived in Chicago for ten years. When? Why? To fall in love with Lake Michigan, obviously, but on what practical pretext? It must be unusual to fall in love with a large body of water, but I can imagine Russians doing it, and if I give my mind to it this night I may be certain of the political exile who did, & watched his principles sink quietly into it, with only two or three bubbles bursting on its sur-face as a farewell.

Maxwell to Warner, June 3, 1977:

In back of the house across the road once occupied by my music teacher, and now only by his widow, who was an opera singer, there is an old rose bush under which were buried, by me, the ashes of her mother, whom I loved, and which had sat on the floor of my clothes closet for six months. It is a story in itself. The opera singer has a sister, now in a nursing home, who thought that the opera singer wanted us to do this without consulting her. Whereas in fact she was discussing all this time, with another neighbor up the road, the various things that might be done with them. So one day I did it, and told her, and it was quite some time before she spoke to me. I am thinking at this moment of not speaking to her any more, because when we crossed the road last Saturday evening with our drinks, she said "Something has happened to Maudie's rose." I went out to look at it, and saw that a species of wild rose had cosily settled down right next to it and was affectionately choking it to death. So I said I will come over tomorrow and dig the wild rose up. And did. After which I saw that a solid carpet of pachysandra was doing an even more thorough job. And started to pull it up too, but by that time I was hot and tired. I had also dis-covered a third plant with intentions. One thin stem of poison ivy emerg-ing from right beside the old rose. So, since I had gloves on, I pulled on it, and it broke, so the problem remains to be dealt with.

Before I noticed it, I must have brushed against it with my forearm, because that night I was awakened by the knowledge that I had poison ivy. I put the cream that has always worked so splendidly on it, and it continued to get worse and worse. It is, perhaps, a new species, or perhaps it was put there by the fairies. Anyway, I went to the doctor yesterday, and he gave me a shot, and this and that, and today it is better, but I am still cross at the ex-opera singer, because she waited until I had dug the bush up to tell me that the yard boy (I thought he had left for good) was coming later that after-noon, and he could just as well have caught poison ivy instead.

About Chicago. My life has been one long succession of pieces of good fortune, you being one of them. When I was fifteen, my father had a chance to stop carrying a heavy suitcase full of insurance forms around the state of Illinois and sit at a desk, in downtown Chicago. And I found myself transported from an overcrowded school of five hundred to an even more overcrowded and absolutely wonderful high school of three thousand pupils. College was a comedown from it, the teaching was so splendid. A woman who was not even one of my teachers used to take me to the Symphony concerts and to the theater, and because of her I heard Lotte Lehmann sing the role of the Marschallin. Imagine having *Rosenkavalier* sprung on you, with no preparation, at the age of 17, in the year 1925 or '26. Anyway, the whole course of my life was altered for the better. (Though not, of course, by hearing *Rosenkavalier.*)

We lived in an apartment two blocks from Lake Michigan. My room was also used for company, and on the wall, next to a light switch, there was a framed motto, which you will find in a story in the book that you so kindly allowed me to dedicate to you.* It is called "The Value of Money," and covers briefly my life in Chicago.

* *Hello, guest, and Howdy-do. / This small room belongs to you. / And our house and all that's in it. / Make yourself at home each minute.*

Warner to Maxwell, June 9, 1977:

So, tilted toward the opera singer's sister, I will say briefly God damn and blast the bitch, May poison ivy hunt her down and coil round her like Nessus' shirt. My poor William, I am so sorry for you. I have some outside idea of what it can be like, for when we were in Connecticut I met a young man who was feeling the pains of hell, or serpent's teeth, of zonal herpes from an encounter with it; and blotched like a leper. And he was considered to be getting over his. It is very honest and natural of you to wish it had been the yard-boy. I with it had been the opera singer's sister. The more so, since I remember your dear music-teacher, who led you to Clementi.

Since then it has rained, *bis, bis,* and at night it freezes, & the wind blows from the north, and my white, dark-eyed poppies and my irises lie with their faces in the mud, and the hawthorn blossom that drenched the trees in goat's milk and made a procession of every hedge was blown away, and you could have floated ten Arks on the amount of paraffin needed to set off the loyal bonfires. A pity, for the Jubilee celebrations were well devised,

with torchlight processions and people flaunting in fancy dress and borrowed plumes, surplices in great demand, girt about with blue ribbons and
worn with pink top hats. It is usual to say 'The children enjoyed it'—but in
fact it was grownups, steeped in middle-age and fortitude, who enjoyed it,
fiddled, and burned.

Warner to Maxwell, July 13, 1977:

Your shaving-brush sits in my bathroom cabinet, and from time to time,
unobtrusively, catches my eye with a mute enquiry when it will see you
again. I tell it to be patient; that you are busy with a novel. *Il reviendra à
Pâques, ou à la Trinité*, I say. We would like, meanwhile, to know how the
novel is getting on, & you.

I think I told you I was going to Aldeburgh, as part of the Festival programme. It all passed off very painlessly. Peter Pears read a number of my
poems, ancient and modern, so beautifully, that I forgot to be constrained
and sat enjoying them.

The finest part of the programme was when he & 'tother tenor (who was
there to sing various settings of me) leaped back over six centuries & sang
two *a cappella* pieces by Machaut. You remember what I said about
Machaut in *The Corner That Held Them.*

Maxwell to Warner, July 20, 1977:

In Wellfleet those passionate farmers suddenly seized me by the throat
and wouldn't let go. What it amounts to is that I committed adultery with
my best, my only friend's wife, in the year 1920, when I was twelve years
old. I am glued to the typewriter, the scissors and paste pot, until suddenly
exhaustion comes over me and I get up and wander around waiting for it to
be next day, so I can go on writing. It was all written months ago, but there
was a great deal too much, and it lacked a controlling hand, and a sense for
what belonged in the wastebasket. I don't know whether it is good or bad.
And I don't care. I only know that it is.

Louise Bogan once said, "The innocent and the good have no enemy
but time." She could have added a writer with a head of steam up. I work
with one eye on the calendar. Last fall, for Brookie's sake, and for my own,

thinking how much longer would it be reasonable for me to be sitting on a horse, I arranged for us to return to that ranch in Wyoming. And from there we are going on to Portland for a week, to see how Emmy's father is getting on without her mother, and then it will be September. I try to pick up the telephone and call the travel agent and arrange for airplane tickets and hotel accommodations in London and Amsterdam and nothing happens. I think how much reason you have to reproach me for not keeping my promise. And I think if you have to limit the number of times you go up and downstairs when you are alone, what would happen to your blessed legs if you were expecting Emmy and me for three days. But it is not that, it is my farmers. I am afraid to turn my back on them for longer than three weeks. They might not be there when we came home. I ask your forgiveness, and refrain from making new promises lest I break them too, but it appears that we may be taking a house on a Greek island with Emmy's brother next August, by which time I expect to be finished with what now possesses me. And if not, we will very likely be making the same trip we thought of making this fall, in any case. And if your legs have not improved we might carry you off to that hotel in Dorchester, and toot around the neighborhood from there.

Power failures after a thunderstorm are not unheard of in Westchester County. We went to bed by candlelight and the next morning, as we were getting breakfast, the lights went on and the dish-washer started churning at the place in the cycle where it had left off. I went to my farmers and it was mid-afternoon before we learned about the night of looting in the city. I think no one has ever followed Voltaire's injunction at the end of *Candide* more faithfully than I, but he didn't say, as I remember, that one would at all times be permitted to cultivate one's garden. Those things horses used to wear, when I was a child: Blinders. What makes living in the latter part of the twentieth century possible. The portents are not encouraging, and warnings invariably go unheeded.

Warner to Maxwell, July 23, 1977:
'He has better fish to fry' I said to the shaving-brush. Better?—the best fish. I am so delighted that you are up to the neck in a Book; pledged to it, fastened to it, not able to leave it in case something happens to it. I am so

delighted with that that I have no room for a two-pennyworth of regret that you won't be here next month. It is a pity that you cannot be William in two places at once; it is a pity that I am not on the other side of your fence; but these are irrelevant nuisances, & we must take them as part of the universal plan and think no more of them. God, Mr Maxwell! suppose you had come here and lost a page; a pang in a farmer's bosom, a button off his waistcoat.

Warner to Maxwell, August 16, 1977:

Your stories [*Over by the River*] have the quality of Chardin's pictures. You know how I like Chardin; you can gauge how happy I am to have their dedication.

Some I know already, but it seemed to me they are improved with keeping. Perhaps you have polished them, perhaps it is I whose appreciation has improved with keeping. And it is a comfortable pleasure to hear more about the Maxwells whom I love so much & have known for so long—ever since that first small trickle of acquaintance in 1939's first sight.

Though it was before then that I relied on your judgement.

Warner to Maxwell, October 7, 1977:

I did not know the details of [Robert Louis] Stevenson's death. It must have been just what he would have approved of—that assumption of responsibility. Do you know that at the time when the Boycott household in Ireland were being boycotted he wanted to go and live with them? It was that same assumption of responsibility which made him take such pains to write well: he was responsible to his material. He was a version of the traditional Auld Alliance of Scotland & France, a mixture of presbyterian conscience & Flaubert's literaturism. You should find him easy to understand, with your roots in Caerlaverock Castle. For years it was my ambition that you should visit Caerlaverock —which I suppose means Larks' strong hold —and that I should meet you there.

My nose *se rétrousse* over those Thames & Hudson books [*R. L. Stevenson and His World*], but for all that I like them, because I am incarnately a tripper, a reader of house plaques. I like to see what the place was like; though it would often turn out to be more to the purpose to show what X & Y saw from their windows. When Valentine and I visited Grasmere, and saw William's garden hat and Dorothy's favourite teacup—gawdy—Valentine opened the oven door in their kitchen. *It grated.* And in a flash I was there, watching Dorothy put in another of those mutton pies, after which William was so often indisposed.

Warner to Maxwell, November 20, 1977:

I am particularly entranced by his [Albrecht Dürer's] views of cities: the harbour of Antwerp with that swinging curve from spire to masts entranced me; and I particularly enjoyed the page devoted to the perspective of a tiled floor with a dog, an irresistible dog, asleep on one corner of it.

I have never liked his *grandes machines,* but where he is led on by hand and eye I could look at him for hours on end. And what bliss to be secured from any risk of seeing those praying hands.

There ought to be some international body which can impose a stop, a copyright, on works of art, so that a generation here & there should be able to see them *for the first time,* and then not again, dog-eared with familiarity. A sculptor said to me, If only I could see an elephant for the first time! But this doesn't apply to music, where the element of performance intervenes. Not long ago I listened to the Leipzig Gewandhaus orchestra playing the *Pastoral Symphony* as if they had never played it before—considerably slower, for one thing, & oh! the bassoons for the merry clod-hoppers. There are times when it is almost unbearable that I cannot ring you up & say 'Listen.'

Another thing I have been enjoying is a translation of Goethe's *Roman Elegies* (text on the l.h. page, translation on the other, so I can skip from one to 'tother & pretend I read German). Have you read them? It is such a pleasure to read honest *erotica;* not a snigger, not a snivel. Just the creak of the bedstead, and the girl doodling the hour of their next meeting in the wine spilled on the tavern table.

Maxwell to Warner, December 14, 1977:

I saw and picked up a paperback of the memoirs of Proust's housekeeper, Céleste Albaret. Are they dependable, do you know? And not someone's fictitious ghost-writing? Even if they are, I would much prefer reading the memoirs of a domestic servant than of anybody else. Virginia Woolf's book is a case in point. I look forward so much to the Painter [a biography of Chateaubriand]. Having read a (as I perhaps wrote you) one-volume selection from the Chateaubriand Memoirs that raised more questions than you could shake a stick at.

The idiom reminds me of my Aunt Edith's conversation, which was always astonishing to me because of phrases like "crazy as Dick's hat-band," whose explanation seemed over the hill of Time, beyond recovering. And that reminds me of that fact that we are now living in the Age of Costume. The young man who drove me home in a taxi yesterday was playing Bach on the tape cassette on the front seat and wearing a straw boater. I thanked him for his music when I got out, and refrained from telling him that I once wore such hats myself, when young, and so did everybody else. It would only have spoiled his pleasure in his own uniqueness, and it is true that I didn't also have a beard.

Maxwell to Warner, late December 1977:

Just when I was resolved never to write one more word about Virginia Woolf along came a book by George Spater and Ian Parsons, whom you probably know, called *A Marriage of True Minds* and there is so much in it that is fresh and sensible that my conscience obliged me to do a note on it for *The New Yorker*. The thing I like best in it is something which didn't get into the note: "The children (LW and his brothers and sisters) found their pleasures largely in the household and the homes of their many relations, who possibly were not fully aware of the interest the Woolf children took in them: a favorite card game was played with photographs of their numberous aunts and uncles in which the ugliest took the trick."

Warner to Maxwell, January 6, 1978:

I can't say about Proust's servant. She was famous, & gave talks on the wireless, & the tears she broke into were undoubtedly true for they came at the very moment and made hay of her. But how is one to tell? I believed her then. I think I do now, but with less certainty. She was got hold of by journalists, she knew distant days, and far better than any one else did, but that does not make her report reliable.

The grass is as green as grass, the skies are high & fathomless. The birds are singing. This morning, the first aconite bloomed in the path. I do not feel as graceful as the landscape. My legs are ancient monuments, they ache and give way, and my cats look at me deploringly, and say privately to each other that I am a shadow of my old self, a shadow even of what I was before Christmas. Belatedly, old age has clawed me in its clutch. But I am almost as good as ever in bed, they say; and if there is a cold spell later on, there we shall be, and Antonia will bring her little porringer and nourish us.

But I shall not re-read Colette. I have looked forward to doing this, & find to my grief that I have outlived her. I shall re-read your letters. I have *millions* of them and they re-read very well. Though I wish you had *dated* them. But it is too late to begin, and only something like Watergate or Teapot Dome emerges with a look of period. When was Teapot Dome? 1885?

Anyway, we have enjoyed each other for a long time, dear William.

Warner to Maxwell, January 29, 1978:

Do not worry about my chest. Except that in the mornings I wake grunting like a train going up slope—a notorious long haul—it is as nimble as ever. I must confess that the rest of me is not so seemly. About a month ago I had a sudden collapse. Antonia kept me in bed for a while, & for a while it was debated whether or no I had had a very small stroke. It wasn't; merely old age had laid a rather sudden grasp on me, especially my legs. I can only walk very slowly, & cling to whatever is near for a support. I have a doctor, who is the image of death, & prescribes so many different pills that if I took them all I should be incapable of taking anything else. Unfortunately, he cannot prescribe better weather. You have had blizzards. We have had floods, & now for the last two days the wind has blown like an ancient curse. But do not worry about me. When the weather improves, so will I; and meanwhile the worst of my sufferings is the amount of care, solicitude, visiting that I provoke among my friends. I have almost forgotten what silence sounds like.

How lovely to hear the whole of the *Winterreise*. Long ago I heard it sung by Peter & Ben—at the original pitch, which makes the soloist sound much younger & his sentiments those of youth, genuinely self-pitying & rhodomontade. And I shall never forget how Ben made the crow's wings flop, how heavy, remorseless & pursuing they were. The cycle has become the prey of baritones, out for a melancholy constitutional. It has lost its vagrancy. If I could have my way, I would keep it in a box with a lid, & only allow it to be sung by young tenors, not vocalisers, either. I have never heard what type of voice Schubert had, have you?

Maxwell to Warner, February 6, 1978:

If I had my life to live over again, I would date my letters. For your sake. And following your example.

On Saturday morning there was a letter from you and the Painter, at last. And that afternoon, when I fished the mail out of the mailbox, there was another letter, dated January 6. All that was unfortunately denied me was to be able to sit and hold your hand. If it is truly old age that has its grasp on you, which I much doubt, then it will relax its grasp when spring comes. I do not like to think of you having to make your way about the house clinging to the furniture for support. And me not there to fetch and carry. How I envy Antonia her situation in relation to you. But whereas she is tact itself, I would weary you to death with attentions. One more friend fussing over you.

As for your not being able to re-read Colette, isn't it perhaps not a matter of literary judgment but simply of not being able to repeat an emotional experience. I was profoundly affected by Mitsou's letters to her young Captain, by Chéri's despair over losing Léa, and by the little brown bear in the miniature circus act in "Lola" and a great deal else. When I look these passages up, I see that I made them my own by making them something slightly different from what is on the page. And am troubled at not being able to read my version of things. But bowled over I was.

If you are interested in literary immortality (and if you are not, then I am interested for you) all this rushing back into print of one book after another is a clear enough sign. What is in your books is not to be found anywhere else. When I despair it is not because I think the time will come when people can't tell a good book from a bad one (though there are always signs of that) but that there won't be any readers, and sand will, in a manner of speaking, blow over the pages of *Pride and Prejudice* and *Du côté de chez Swann*.

Teapot Dome was a political scandal of the 1920s, during the administration of Warren G. Harding, a dishonest president with hardly one brain
to rub against another. His syntax was much more remarkable than Eisenhower's even.

Maxwell to Warner, February 8, 1978:

Will you be especially careful in your voyaging down the halls, the
downstairs hall especially, where, I seem to remember, there is not very
much to cling to? I remember so vividly descending the stairs with my
grandmother (who was, of course, younger than I am now). Taking no
chances we clung for dear life to the banister, reached the Castle of
Chillon, turned right and proceeded on down to the cuckoo clock, and
turned to congratulate each other when we had successfully made it. And
are the cats considerate about not passing unexpectedly between your legs?
If one could only garden in the house, I feel you would be flying around.
Since the flowers in the carpet do not bloom, and the tiles do not have to
be thinned, there is simply no incentive for movement.

The New Yorker continues to send me books related to V. Woolf. Now
it is Sir Leslie Stephen's *Mausoleum Book*, somewhat gutted by her biographer, like the others. Reading it I am struck with what difficulties the
Victorians managed to place in the way of their happiness and how high-
mindedly they then proceeded to surmount them. Also that Julia Jackson
Duckworth Stephen's daughters so little resembled her. The Zeitgeist, perhaps. But what a relief it is to return to Rilke.

Maxwell to Warner, February 14, 1978:

All in the world I ask (and it is too much, of course) is to be neglected by
my entire acquaintance so I can read *Chateaubriand* without being interrupted. I told you, I think, that I had been reading a one-volume condensed
translation of the memoirs? So it is like finding someone who can tell you
all about a person you know and are curious about but don't know very
well. Until now, my mind was full of questions, which Painter is continually answering. And it is so interesting to see, in C, the 19th Century beginning to take its recognizable shape. I feel he is half a person and half a

Stradivarius. Speaking of which, when we come to England in May will
you show me the six volumes you wrote in your twenties on Tudor church
music? Do you own them? I simply want to see it. Reading it would be
beyond my musical-intellectual capacity, I suspect. Though the detective in
me would whip out a magnifying glass and start looking for tell-tale traces
of what was to come. I rejoice in the thought of two more volumes of
Chateaubriand to come, and marvel at Painter's courage in taking on all
those people and places and turning points of European history. Not to
mention the eastern half of the United States. And part of my pleasure is
that I waited so long for it. When I was six years old my mother and father
went to Kentucky to visit relatives, and the whole time they were gone
there was no oxygen in the air. I survived, but only barely. And then they
came home, and I could breathe again, but their trunks were lost, and in it
a paintbook that my mother had got for me. Two more weeks of waiting
made me exactly ready to burst when she at last put it in my hands and
I rushed for my paintbox and started in. It is the same with the
Chateaubriand.

Do not write letters if you have to make yourself do it. I have just had a
wonderful letter from Antonia, addressed by you, in which everything is as
clear as if I had been walking around the house talking to you. So I don't
need to hear from you. *I am there.*

Warner to Maxwell, February 17, 1978:

For the last two days I have been snowed-up, except for valiant people
who come on foot: my sturdy Cockney Mrs Do., and enthusiasts for bird-
welfare, who arrive with little canisters of nuts. I too do my best to feed the
birds, and calculate how much longer I shall be able to feed the cats &
myself. The cats trust me implicitly, and repose on heaters. No, they do not
get between my feet, and they are very comfortable at night, sleeping
pressed against me.

It really *is* cold. I have not been so cold since I was ten years younger,
and moveable, and could go out with sultanas for the thrushes.

I wish you could come in, and make a fuss of me. It is one of the ironies
of old age—that one longs to be made a fuss of, when one has built up a

reputation that one doesn't care for fuss. I am grown very old, dear
William. I hobble about on two baddish legs, and cling to anything within
reach. And I have grown so small, I scarcely know myself. And so slow. But
really I should congratulate myself that my wits are still about me. When
my mother was my age, she was senile. And I am not that, and I can still
see to read, & hear to talk; and if the weather were not so biting & blight-
ing I might not feel so like a dead leaf... *de ça, de là, comme le vent n'emporte.*

I remember Warren Harding—whose G. I always took to be Gamaliel,
but this may have been prejudice. He had a very communicative mistress,
who wrote a book called *The President's Daughter*—the height of silliness
and verbosity. It was one of my pleasures for years; but in the end it was
borrowed by someone who liked it so much that he forgot to return. It is
an archival book. Do you know it?* Have you ever heard of the daughter?
By now, I suppose, she is a respected USA matron, & sits on a Ladies Committee and deplores the manners of the present day, and can look a tea-pot
in the face without a blush.

* Nan Britton had claimed that Harding had seduced her and was her child's unacknow-
ledged father.

Maxwell to Warner, February 22, 1978:

In the middle of the night I address myself to simple-minded questions
such as Is the Walker known in England? I shall now
attempt to draw you one. They are roughly the shape of
a Roman capital letter C. And the walker stands inside
and proceeds by taking a step and pushing or placing
the object, which is of some very light metal, ahead of
him before taking the next step. I am haunted by the
thought of you putting out your hand for a steadying
piece of furniture that isn't, as it happens, there. Alas I
don't think it will do anything for the pain in your legs.
Wings is what you really need. Why has it taken me so
long to think of it?

If Emmy's father, who is about to be ninety-two, stays
well, we shall be taking a plane for England on April 30. And if you are in
a mood for visitors, or for being carried off to some agreeable place for

something that I haven't had the wit to think of...in short, we have between now and April 30th to think about it. I promise not to have bronchitis.

Maxwell to Warner, February 26, 1978:

I have been saying "Are you warm enough?" to Emmy ever since we were married; to the children ever since they were born. It is a kind of mania, that nobody I love should be cold. In the country there is a pile of English *Country Life*s about four feet high, in the attic, and a corresponding pile in my study in town. I read myself to sleep with them, and the fact that they are ten or fifteen years old only adds to the pleasure. "Oil-fired central heating" I read, of a beautifully preserved family sixteenth century house on the edge of Long Crendon with distant views. House after house after house, some of them houses I would not care to live in and others I would be delighted to live in if there were twelve in help, and all of them with oil-fired central heating. And you are cold. In one of the dearest houses in the world. In my savings account (largely because my father left two farms to his three sons) there is a good deal more than enough to do the trick. It gives me no pleasure sitting there accumulating compound interest. I don't need it and won't, thanks to *The New Yorker*'s generosity. I know you are and always have been provident. I also know that the Inland Revenue took the money that would have put oil-fired central heating in your house. The only thing I don't know is if you dislike oil-fired central heating. If you don't dislike it, would you make me happier than you can possibly imagine by finding out what it would cost and letting me send you a check to cover it? Instead of lying awake thinking "Is Sylvia warm?" "Are the cats enough to warm the bed?" I would be sleeping like a baby and dreaming of I don't know what. Consul Smith, perhaps. I am utterly serious. Please consider the matter—I mean please consider the matter of making me happy and you warm. Consul Smith turned up in a television program on the possessions of the British Royal Family, and I must say they do have a good many, don't they. Clock after clock after clock, none of them up to the one Valentine fell in love with and you hid in your muff and that I hear ticking this moment. I wouldn't be watching the television if Emmy were here: she is just about now opening the door of her father's house in Portland, Oregon. She left at nine o'clock this morning to fly out to see him because he

has had a series of setbacks as he is approaching his ninety-second birthday.
He never exactly said but somehow I got the idea from watching his face
that to be in the same room with her was quite all he asked of life. So there
she is. And here am I, in an apartment so quiet that you could hear a pin
drop, if there were anyone to drop it.

I do hope with all my heart that the cold (which did get into the American papers) has passed on to other places. *London 52, rain,* the *Times* says. As
the Queen was showing people through Buckingham Palace I looked to
see if I could see their breath. I could not. Oil-fired central heating, I said to
myself. Though perhaps not in the time of poor maligned Geo III. But that
was Buckingham House, a much cosier place. Though perhaps cosy is too
strong a word. I think, with remorse, of how warm you had the study for
me when I arrived with Egyptian bronchitis. And how you had warmed
the bed as well. I was so happy in that upstairs room I would have been perfectly content never to leave it.

Warner to Maxwell, March 5, 1978:

If this house were cold I would have pranced to say Yes. But it is warm,
even when I am not expecting William with bronchitis, even when other
houses are cold. I have 3 storage heaters, electric fires full on, a coal-burn-
ing kitchen stove: people come in from the cold world and exclaim how
hot it is. Central heating by oil could not make it warmer; & I am afraid
of oil.

So thank you with all my heart, & *Nenni!* But I expect you and Emmi in
May. I wish I could be sure of expecting you here, but at the moment I am
not fit to be a hostess, I crawl about the house, inclining to fall over, and
even when firm on my feet, I crawl. I may be a better creature in May—
with a hot April I could almost be sure of it.

I have talked it over with Antonia, & she hopes you will spend a night at
Baglake, which is a memorably tall, plain, mid-Georgian stone house, and
she would drive you over here. But here in Maiden Newton, two steps
from here, is Rainbow Villa, a memorably plain-headed contemporary
'guest-house,' which has comfortable beds & good breakfasts, & you have
never been in a finer example of British bourgeoisie. You could come on
here, sit in the garden, read in the house, visit Toller Fratrum (unchanged),
be given lunch & supper by me.

336   THE ELEMENT OF LAVISHNESS

And for the remainder of your visit, it occurs to me that you have never been to the part of Scotland you were fetched from: I suppose Maxwells have been there for much longer than they have been away from it. Familiar Great-aunts & slightly removed Cousins would survey you as you approached your Castle of the larks—wasn't it called Caerlaverock Castle? ... Today I have sat in the sun without an attempt at bravery. It *shone*, & crocuses came into bloom all round, exploded into bloom.

I am sorry about Emmi's nonagerian father. I hope this will not interrupt all our plans.

But meet we will.

Maxwell to Warner, March 15, 1978:

I think that, considering one thing and another, including the width of the Atlantic Ocean, that this is one of those times when wiser heads should prevail. Meaning yours and Antonia's. And without argument, also. So I am writing to her to accept her invitation for the night, and would you make a reservation for the following night, that is to say May 9, at Rainbow Villa. The only part of the plan that troubles us is our being given lunch and supper by you, and there are possible alternatives: we could have that pleasant man who drives the Maiden Newton taxi carry us off somewhere for lunch or supper or both, if you are feeling up to this. Or we could bring with us on a train a hamper of surprises from Harrods, and you could tell Emmy where the can opener is kept and be waited on by us. We can discuss this from London; we will call you shortly after we arrive. At the mere thought of it, the intervening six and a half weeks shrinks in my mind to nothing. In effect, we will be talking to you day after tomorrow. After, let us hope, a hot April.

A trip to Scotland had occurred to me, but it seemed a mistake to try and crowd Edinburgh, not to mention all that is north of it, into a couple of days. So I thought while we are with you, you could tell us where to go and what to see and we would, another time, hire a little car and set off in the footsteps of Valentine and you, how long ago I am no longer certain. I only remember that I have a snapshot of you against the Scottish moors. I would much enjoy a visit to Caerlaverock Castle, but great-aunts and cousins-once-removed in that part of the world have I none. Or rather, none that I know about.

Emmy's father has completely recovered from a small stroke, pneumonia, and pleurisy, and is going to his office as usual. And it is spring in New York. It came all in one day. Suddenly the air smelled of violets, which, considering the filth that lay everywhere in the streets, is as miraculous as anything ever recorded about the Christian saints. It may snow tomorrow, but the snow will not last, if it does. I woke in the country and heard a cardinal singing.

Maxwell to Warner, March 23, 1978:

I have at last the answer to your question [of January 29]. I found it in last Sunday's *Times:* "He (Schubert) mastered the piano, was a good violinist and singer (until his voice broke); after that he had 'the voice of a composer,' which means no voice at all . . ."

Maxwell to Warner, April 1978:

I went for a walk along the River in the late afternoon and it was *hot.* I thought, with pleasure, this will melt the snow on the daffodils in Dorset. And wished I could send you the man who had brought his bird, in a big wire cage, out to enjoy the fresh air and the sunshine. It looked like a large rosy finch, and was probably a parakeet. And so many babies, playing in the sandpile and trying out their vocal chords. Old men whose heads had sunk into their collar bone, like birds on a cold day. Joggers. Lovers. The usual.

I was so happy to be able to talk to you. And to Antonia, whose account of how things are with you is so utterly reliable. As her account of everything else must be. What bliss for you to have her there.

Because of driving to Philadelphia on Friday, we didn't get to the country until Saturday noon. And a dinner party and a lecture by a sort of religion oriented anthropologist (I don't know how to describe him) named [Joseph] Campbell. I am past the age of being lectured at, but I didn't much mind it. And between whiles, picked up the fallen branches that the March wind had left in the front and back yard, and cleaned up the flower bed that has the tulips and peonies in it. Since we are leaving in less than three weeks, it seems hardly sensible to more than give things a lick and a promise. I gave the apple trees a dormant spray, just in the nick of time. And the wild honeysuckle a haircut, so it wouldn't start strangling the white pine trees on the edge of the swamp. All this with a cold wind blowing, but still there was one daffodil out, and a sprinkling of other spring flowers, in a sheltered place on the south side of the house, sacred to the white violets.

The trip to Philadelphia was to see a private collection of paintings, the Barnes Foundation, which is rather difficult to get permission to see, a hundred people two days a week being the limit, and fifty for half a day on Sunday. The pictures were gathered together by a man who had made a fortune in a nasal disinfectant called Argyrol. There must have been a hundred Renoirs, almost as many Cézannes and Matisses. Modiglianis, Klees, Toulouse-L and Degas, Seurat, virtually everybody from the middle of the last century on, and a sprinkling of other painters as well, including a Courbet that by rights should be hanging in your bedroom. A languorous young woman, who went nicely with a Corot portrait of a woman past her youth, whom life had not treated as kindly as her merit deserved. The collection was so good that I don't ever remember feeling, not even in the Jeu de Paume, if that is how you spell it and it probably isn't, so many first-rate pictures. From the very best period of the artist, and then, from the periphery of the work as a whole. We spent four hours there, and usually one hour does me in, I think because I am constantly saying no, that doesn't appeal to me, I like that, but not that...Here I liked almost everything. Though the pictures were hung in a manner calculated to drive you mad. In classical balance, higgledy piggledy, by the size of the picture frame, and sometimes as many as three in a vertical row. Canaletto three feet above eye level. Also over the doorways, where you couldn't read the plaque. A Clouet over one doorway, a Gauguin over another, and over a third a *Fouquet!* The big Seurat was hung near the ceiling of a three story hall. I would gladly have devoted the next ten years of my life to rehanging them, but fortunately nobody suggested this.

My father-in-law, who just passed his 92nd birthday, has always been a good letter writer, but his letters have recently taken on a kind of radiance, as if he had stopped taking any ordinary part in life, stopped worrying, I mean, about the outcome of things, and simply looked around him with delight at the way everything is. As his housekeeper was driving him home from his office they stopped and got oysters because he had remembered how good they are fried, and he was about to sit down and eat them after he sealed the letter, and you'd have thought choirs of angels were about to join him.

You know I am not religious, but I do have this talent for knowing what is in wrapped packages. If asked to testify in court I would have said that when Valentine drove Emmy and you and me to a high heath so that we could hear the skylarks, no skylarks were heard. But either there or somewhere, I have heard them. Their song coming out of a cloud. In a dazzling brightness that made me squint my eyes. Inside this particular package is just that: a skylark in a cloud, giving directions to another bird, and then suddenly there are two skylarks singing in a dazzling brightness brimming with joy. I think of them continually.

POSTSCRIPT

᪲ ᪲

We stayed with Sylvia on our way back from Egypt in 1976. She said at that time, "If you want to see me again come back next year." I didn't manage this but instead we came after two years. We went to London for no other reason but to see her. However I knew that she was very ill and was more astonished that reporters should have located me because of my being one of her executors than I was at the news of her death. We went to her funeral and stayed with Antonia von Trauttmansdorff, who was living with a descendant of William Wordsworth. The funeral was in a very small church and largely managed by Sylvia's ex-garden boy [Colin House]. The church was cold, the service was brief, and Sylvia's ashes were buried in the churchyard beside Valentine. During the outside service, Antonia astonished me by picking up what I thought was a large dead dog and tossing it over a stone wall. What it actually was was a fox, I think a vixen, that had died in the churchyard apparently of natural causes, and Antonia thought it inappropriate for it to lie on consecrated ground. The rationale of this escapes me. The reason I didn't feel more grief is that life had become a burden for her. As you have probably gathered from her last letters.

—WILLIAM MAXWELL, 1997

WHAT YOU CAN'T HANG ONTO

by William Maxwell

Once upon a time there was an old woman who lived in a house by a river. The lane from the village ended at an old stone bridge half hidden by willows, a few feet from her garden gate. The river flowed around both sides of the garden and the house and came together just beyond the coal shed. Houses beside a river are always damp and subject to floods. And since it was often just as cold inside as out, she seldom bothered to close the front door until she went to bed at night. The cats never had to be let in or out, and the fish peddler never had to knock. He just stood on the back steps and hollered, and the old woman came to the door, and he showed her what was in his basket. The cats' meat man did the same. The house always smelled of the outdoors, and the old woman dressed warmly and didn't mind if there was a wreath of fog above the mantelpiece in the parlor.

The river was a little too wide for a boy to leap across and after the spring rains the current was swift, but for the rest of the year it was hardly noticeable. When the old woman leaned out of her bedroom window to see what kind of a day it was, she saw young boys and old men fishing, for it was only a short walk from the village. Usually they were staring so intently at the surface of the water that they didn't know anybody was looking at them, but now and then one of them saw her and tipped his cap or waved.

The old woman was the last living member of both sides of her family, and inevitably the possessions of one branch after another ended up under her roof. Some of them, if you were at all knowledgeable, were enough to take your breath away. She was so accustomed to getting letters from solicitors informing her of modest bequests of money and furniture that it came as a surprise to her that there was no one left to leave her anything. There was hardly room in the house for another object if they had. Old furniture wherever you looked. Old prints, old drawings, old paintings on the walls. Old books that people had to advertise for, often in vain. Old china and silver.

As always when someone has valuable possessions, there were people who cast a covetous eye on the contents of that house by the river, and if they didn't know the old woman well, they said, "If you are ever of a mind to part with that settee in the upstairs hall..." Or that Boulle cabinet. Or writing desk. Or pencil sketch by Turner. Or battered first edition of *English Bards and Scotch Reviewers*. And if they thought they knew her well enough to come right out and say it—"If you haven't promised it to somebody, will you leave me that Crown Derby teapot in your will?" And if they knew her better still, they said, "That soup tureen—Minton, isn't it? Lovely!" and changed the subject.

The old woman was fond of her possessions but not as fond of them as she was of her cats, and people who live alone get strange ideas, of course, and she had come to feel that her death would not be any great loss to the world and if she lived past a certain age might be a merciful release to her. But in her mind's eye she saw the furniture standing around on the lawn and being knocked down by the auctioneer's mallet and the garden grown up in weeds. Maybe there is still some grandniece or nephew or cousin by marriage, she would think. There weren't any that she knew about and so she resigned herself to the inevitable and only now and then, when she was pruning the huge Belle de Crecy rose bush or on her hands and knees in the vegetable garden thinning carrots, she would straighten up for a moment and look around her and sigh at the thought that this place, which she was so attached to, would not survive her in any recognizable form.

In her thirties the old woman had published a book of poems which had been praised by Thomas Hardy, and the praise brought forth a letter of thanks from her, and this led to her being invited to Max Gate to tea, and to a further exchange of letters, and his letters to her she had naturally kept. A young American who was doing a critical study of *The Famous Tragedy of the Queen of Cornwall* came upon her letters in the Hardy papers and from them deduced that Hardy had discussed his feelings about the production of the play in a letter to her. So he wrote to the old woman and the upshot was an invitation to stay in the house by the river. In writing back, the American mentioned the fact that his wife would be travelling with him, and the invitation was amended to include her. When they stepped down from the train, in the railway station of a town that was three and a half miles from the village, a taxi was waiting and drove them through some of the most enchanting scenery in the whole of the south of England. "Look!" they kept exclaiming. "Oh just look!" As the old woman was greeting them the young man broke into a fit of coughing, which made the fishermen look up in irritation, for it was loud enough to frighten the fish. The old woman said, "I'm afraid there is not much that can be said in favor of the English climate."

The young man smiled wanly and said, "I have a slight temperature but I didn't want to miss seeing the letters and..."

While he was finishing his sentence the old woman was on her way upstairs, and before he quite realized what was happening to him he was in a big bed warmed by stone hot-water bottles, with a down comforter over him, in a bedroom full of things that had come down a long way through both sides of the old woman's family. He slept, and woke himself up coughing, and heard voices outside, and slept again.

His wife, thinking to keep out of the old woman's way while she was getting supper, went for a walk and came back in a state of rapture at what she had seen.

"The sign at the crossroads said TULER FRATRUM."

"There used to be a Roman settlement there," the old woman said, nodding.

"—and when the farmer called off his dogs it didn't sound as if he was speaking English."

"The Dorset dialect," the old woman said. "Reading it in Hardy is one thing and hearing it spoken is another."

They carried trays upstairs to the invalid and then sat talking over a fire, and at dusk they wandered out into the garden to look at the daffodils. It was quite apparent to the old woman that the young woman had lost her heart to the place, which was not surprising. What was surprising was that she didn't seem to covet anything. Perhaps in America they didn't care for old furniture, being a new country.

The old woman lay awake that night thinking, which she didn't commonly do.

On the third morning, the young man's fever broke and he insisted he was well enough to get dressed and come downstairs. He sat transcribing the letters of Thomas Hardy in a room heated by a small stove, while the two women talked in whispers so as not to disturb him. At lunchtime the old woman said, "If there is anything in this house that you would like me to leave you in my will, just tell me." And when, after consulting together, they mentioned a book of no great monetary value but hard to come by, she was disappointed. "Are you sure there isn't anything else?" she said, and the young woman said, smiling, "There isn't anything in the whole house that we don't love." At that moment a car horn sounded. The taxi was at the gate, and the Americans said goodby, and off they drove, promising to come back next year.

The old woman went up to London to consult the solicitor who, over the years, had informed her of so many bequests, and he made notes of what she said. "On the condition that they live in the house," the old woman said. "No. Strike that out. There are to be no conditions."

When the American couple stepped out of the same taxi, a year later, the fishermen hardly bothered to raise their heads. The Americans went all through the house without touching anything, and then sat down in the cold little parlor. "I feel her presence," the young woman said, and a cat jumped into her lap and settled down there. "Pity we can't afford to keep it," the young man said. "I feel we'd be very happy here. But we have no choice."

He meant that, given their financial circumstances, they had no choice but to sell the house and everything in it—the Crown Derby teapot and the letters of Horace Walpole in fifty-four volumes, the Regency mahogany writing desk and the Sheraton tallboy chest of drawers, the pencil sketch by Turner and the pair of gilt elbow chairs designed by Henry Holland. Everything disappeared into the storerooms of a London auction house and a FOR SALE sign was planted by the driveway.

When the Americans returned to England two years later they drove south and west from London, in a rented car, to the Hardy country and made a detour to see what had happened to their house.

There was a NO FISHING OR TRESPASSING sign at the bridge, and the front door of the house was shut, there were curtains in all the windows, and the garden was grown up in weeds.

As they sat in their car, the young woman said sadly, "I keep thinking that there was surely something we could have done," and the river said, *No, there was nothing. The collecting of beautiful objects has to end ultimately in their dispersal. The old woman would have found the curtains odious, as indeed they are, but fortunately she doesn't know. What you can't hang onto you must let go of—that is the principle on which I operate, on my way to the sea.*

INDEX

Brown, Pamela, 187
Browne, Sir Thomas, 20
Burns, Robert, 104
Busey, Garetta, 12–3, 29, 129, 212–3, 308, 309
Bush, Alan, 319
Butler, Samuel, 107–8, 117, 198, 231, 265, 300
Buxtehude, Dietrich, 200
Byron, Catherine, 280
Byron, George Gordon, lord, 278–81, 293

Campbell, Joseph, 337
Camus, Albert, 85–6
Canaletto, 199, 338
Caravaggio, Michelangelo Merisi da, 56
Carlyle, Thomas, 245, 246
Carter, Jimmy, 307–8
Cather, Willa, 235
Cézanne, Paul, 72, 338
Chagall, Marc, 300
Chaliapin, Feodor, 320
Chamberlain, Neville, 4, 5
Chantal, Baroness de, 67
Chardin, Jean-Baptiste-Siméon, 62, 142, 326
Chase, Sibyl, 205
Chateaubriand, François René de, 90, 328, 331–2
Cheever, John, 196
Cheever, Mary, 153
Chekhov, Anton, 245, 252, 290
Chopin, Frédéric, 166, 312
Chute, Joy, 233
Chute, Marchette, 233, 239, 289, 313
Cleall, Hilda, 261, 275
Clementi, Muzio, 323
Clouet, Jean, 338
Clough, Arthur Hugh, 119
Cockburn, Henry, 245
Cockerell, Sir Sydney, 165
Coke, Thomas William (Coke of Holkham), 29
Cole, William, 265, 266
Coleridge, Samuel Taylor, 182 and n., 245, 246, 247 n.
Colette, 159, 287, 329, 330
Collins, Wilkie, 94
Conrad, Joseph, 170

Constable, John, 149, 199
Cook, Eliza, 43
Cooper, Anthony Ashley, 279
Copland, Aaron, 228
Cornell, Katherine, 5
Corot, Jean-Baptiste Camille, 338
Courbet, Gustave, 338
Cowper, William, 209, 286

Dansereau, Jean, 17–8, 146 and n., 166, 277, 322, 323
Dante Alighieri, 5, 61, 86
Defoe, Daniel, 220, 272, 314
Degas, Edgar, 72, 338
De Gasperi, Alcide, 60
de la Mare, Walter, 153
De Quincey, Thomas, 169
Derain, André, 162–3
de Reszke, Jean, 125, 166
Destinn, Emmy, 312
Diamond, David, 43
Dickens, Charles, 94, 289
Dinesen, Isak, 318
Don Quixote (Cervantes), 96
Donne, John, 51, 317
Dostoevsky, Fyodor, 146, 235
Dryden, John, 128, 240, 241, 242
Dürer, Albrecht, 327

Égalité, Philippe (Louis Philippe Joseph, duc d'Orléans), 89–90
Eiloart, Nora (STW's mother), 161, 220
Eiloart, Ronald (STW's stepfather), 145, 161, 220
Eisenhower, Dwight D., 36, 37, 38, 39–40, 146–7
Eliot, George, 54, 192, 225
Eliot, T. S., 76, 128
Ellis, Ossian, 314
Ellmann, Richard, 85
Evans, Dame Edith, 187

Faber, Frederick William, 118
Ferrier, Kathleen, 275
Fielding, Henry, 60, 235
Finzi, Joy, 206

Rouault, Georges, 42
Rowse, A. L., 279
Rubinstein, Artur, 312
Rutherford, Margaret, 187

Sacheverell, Henry, 109
Sackville, Thomas, 283
Saint-Simon, Louis de Rouvroy, duc de, 248, 251
Salinger, J. D., 172
Sand, George, 310
Sassoon, Siegfried, 142
Schneebaum, Tobias, 312–3
Schubert, Franz, 117, 311, 329–30, 337
Schurz, Carl, 74, 75
Scott Moncrieff, C. K., 80, 81, 84, 85, 105
Scott Moncrieff, George and Joanna, 105
Seferis, George, 197–8
Segar, Elizabeth, 78
Selby, Hubert, Jr., 195 and n.
Seurat, Georges, 338
Sévigné, Marie de Rabutin-Chantal, marquise de, 50, 66–7, 90
Shakespeare, William, 59–60, 86, 94, 268, 306, 307, 320
Sharaku Toshusai, 93
Shaw, George Bernard, 35
Shawn, William, 27, 72, 134, 135, 141, 183, 184, 196, 197, 216, 238–9, 262, 263–4, 275, 287, 299
Shelley, Harriet Westbrook, 291
Shelley, Percy Bysshe, 26, 136, 240, 278, 289, 291, 301, 302, 310, 312, 315, 319
Sickert, Walter, 162–3
Smallwood, Norah, 105
Smith, Consul, 334
Smith, Joseph, 8
Smith, Matthew, 162–3
Smith, Sydney, 249, 250, 319
Solomon (concert pianist), 293
Sophocles, 304
Spater, George, 328
Spencer, Stanley, 162–3
Spender, Stephen, 140
Stephen, Julia, 331
Stephen, Sir Leslie, 331

Stephens, James, 211
Sternau, Linda, 273–4
Sterne, Laurence, 208
Stevenson, Adlai, 36, 37–40, 146–7
Stevenson, Robert Louis, 246, 326
Stockmar, Baron von, 135 n.
Stokowski, Leopold, 233–4
Stone, Barton Warren, 208–9
Stone, Janet, 228
Stone, Reynolds, 228, 301
Strachey, Lytton, 139, 309
Strauss, Richard, 222
Suetonius, 86
Swift, Jonathan, 195
Synge, John Millington, 192

Tacitus, 23, 86
Tannehill, Muriel, 125, 146 and n., 242, 277, 322
Taverner, John, 66, 296
Tchaikovsky, Peter Ilyich, 234
Tennyson, Alfred, 231, 237
Thackeray, William Makepeace, 54, 148, 295
Theresa of Ávila, Saint, 113
Thoreau, Henry David, 53
Thurber, James, 109, 231
Tomalin, Claire, 288
Toulouse-Lautrec, Henri de, 338
Tourneur, Cyril, 189
Trauttmansdorff, Grafin Antonia von and zu, 290 and n., 317, 319, 321, 329, 330, 332, 335, 336, 337, 341
Trollope, Anthony, 96, 115
Truax, R. Hawley, 108 and n., 150
Truman, Harry S., 37
Turgeniev, Ivan, 99, 222
Turner, J. M. W., 113
Uncle Tom's Cabin (Stowe), 92

Updike, John, 163, 164, 269, 275, 292
Urquhart, Bobby, 187
Urquhart, Sir Brian, 38, 109–10, 118

Van Doren, Carl, 43
Van Doren, Irita, 239
Van Gogh, Vincent, 72